Cities and
Adult Businesses

Cities and Adult Businesses

A Handbook for Regulatory Planning

Edited by ROGER L. KEMP

McFarland & Company, Inc., Publishers
Jefferson, North Carolina, and London

LIBRARY OF CONGRESS CATALOGUING-IN-PUBLICATION DATA

Cities and adult businesses : a handbook for
regulatory planning / edited by Roger L. Kemp
p.   cm.
Includes bibliographical references and index.

ISBN 978-0-7864-3807-5
softcover : 50# alkaline paper ∞

1. Zoning — Moral and ethical aspects — United States.
2. Sex oriented businesses — United States.   3. Zoning
law — United States.   4. City planning — United States.
I. Kemp, Roger L.
HT169.7.C58   2010   346.7304'5 — dc22   2009045536

British Library cataloguing data are available

Cover image ©2010 Shutterstock

Manufactured in the United States of America

*McFarland & Company, Inc., Publishers
Box 611, Jefferson, North Carolina 28640
www.mcfarlandpub.com*

To those public officials who must adopt
laws consistent with their community's values

Acknowledgments

Grateful acknowledgment is made to the following organizations and publishers for granting permission to reprint the materials contained in this volume.

Alexander Communications Group, Inc.
Business Licensing Officials Association
Congressional Quarterly, Inc.
Illinois Municipal League
International City/County Management Association
International Municipal Lawyers Association
League of Minnesota Cities
Municipal Association of South Carolina
National Conference of State Legislators
Penton Media, Inc.
State Bar of California
The Boston Globe
The Columbus Dispatch
The Daily News Publishing Co., Inc.
The University of North Carolina
University of Illinois
Urban Land Institute

Table of Contents

Preface

Each year, many millions of taxpayers' dollars are wasted in lawsuits over the regulation of adult businesses. In many cases, local public officials do not adopt suitable policies and procedures until an adult business either makes application to locate in a particular community, or has already moved in. Adopting laws, policies, and procedures after the fact, and trying to make them retroactive, leads to legal battles in courtrooms all over the United States. The purpose of this volume is to examine the best practices that are evolving in a dynamic and rapidly evolving field.

The various case studies contained in this volume are typically applied in a piecemeal and incremental fashion in cities and towns. For the most part, citizens, public officials and government employees are preoccupied with existing projects within their own communities. They do not have the time to find out what other neighboring cities and towns are doing in this area, let alone what other communities are doing throughout the nation. For this reason, the various case studies presented in this volume represent an important codification of knowledge in this field.

The present work assembles, for the first time, materials based on a search of national literature and makes this important and timely information available to citizens and the public throughout the United States. The goal of this volume is to help educate citizens, as well as their public officials, on how to use these new zoning, planning, licensing, and other regulatory practices to improve the economic conditions within their own communities. This information will also help hold down the number of lawsuits, saving taxpayers a considerable amount of money in the future.

For ease of reference, this volume is divided into three sections. The first section introduces the reader to the rapidly evolving field of how municipal governments regulate adult businesses, and the various practices that are now available to achieve community planning and land-use goals. The second section and, by design, the longest, includes numerous case studies, or best practices, on how cities and towns are taking the proper measures and safeguards when permitting adult businesses to locate in their community. The next section focuses on future trends in this new and constantly changing land-use discipline. Several appendices are also included to provide the reader with a greater understanding of this complex field. Based upon this brief background information, and the conceptual schema developed to assemble and present this material, the four primary sections of this volume are briefly explained below.

In Section I, the first four chapters introduce the reader to the multiple dimensions of the subject. The first chapter provides an overview of cities and adult businesses, and the evolving role of the state and federal governments in this relationship. The second chapter examines the practice of using land-use regulations to influence the location and operations of adult businesses. The last two chapters are legal in nature. Chapter three sets forth details about the First Amendment to the U.S. Constitution, and statues and court decisions that have influenced the regulatory practices of local governments. The last chapter in this section reviews, in detail, court decisions relating to adult businesses, and offers sound advice from representatives of the legal community on how public officials should regulate them.

The Best Practices

The cities, towns, and communities examined in this volume, including the states in which they are located, are listed below. These cities represent great diversity based on their population, politics, form of government, geographic location, and wealth. In total, dozens of cities are examined in many states throughout the United States. A brief description of the best practices examined in each of these communities is set forth. These case studies represent an important and significant effort to obtain a body of knowledge on the best practices available in this very dynamic and continually evolving field. This codification of knowledge forms the essence of this volume.

Cities: Albany, Beckley, Boston, Charleston, Columbia, Columbus, Conway, Detroit, Erie, Forest Park, Harrisburg, Hartford, Hastings, Lemont, Littleton, Los Angeles, Lyons, Memphis, Middleton, Minneapolis, Nashville, New York, North Andover, North Bend, Oakley, Orlando, Providence, Raleigh, Renton, San Antonio, Saratoga Springs, Seattle, Shoreline, Southeast, Staunton, Tampa, Thousand Oaks, Toledo, Urbana, Waco, Wichita

States: California, Colorado, Connecticut, Delaware, Florida, Georgia, Illinois, Kansas, New York, North Carolina, West Virginia, Massachusetts, Minnesota, Ohio, Pennsylvania, Rhode Island, South Carolina, Tennessee, Texas, Virginia, Washington

Selected Best Practices

The best practices used in the above 42 communities, which exist in 20 states, came from a number of different sources. Some of these state-of-the-art practices came from state officials, many had their origin with elected officials such as mayors and city council members, and yet other ideas came directly from citizens. Nonetheless, a knowledge of these best practices should facilitate change by all of these individuals in the future. The major best practices contained in this volume are highlighted below, and explained in greater detail in Section II.

- Adult entertainment business zone is rejected by the voters.
- Agreement between county and cities to control location of adult businesses.
- Banning the sale of beer at adult business establishments.
- Balance sought between citizens and adult businesses to protect the rights of each group.
- Business Improvement District (BID) formed and used to clean up downtown area.
- Business licenses and permits used to regulate adult businesses.
- City Council develops work plan to regulate adult uses in appropriate zones.
- Citizens demanding stricter regulations for adult businesses.
- Creation of special districts to regulate the location of adult businesses.
- Distance rule adopted to regulate the location of adult businesses in relationship to other land uses in the community.
- Enforcement of existing laws used by city officials to clean up downtown neighborhoods.
- Expenditure of public funds used to stimulate private investment to revitalize inner-city areas.
- Geographic Information Systems (GIS) used to locate, and regulate the location of, adult businesses in cities.

- Industrial zones are used to determine the future location of adult businesses.
- Legal guidelines for cities issued by the State concerning adult business regulation options.
- Moratorium approved on all adult businesses pending approval of new regulations.
- Newly incorporated city approves first adult business regulations.
- Objectionable programming prompts new forms of regulation of public access television stations.
- Ordinance approved to control acts of public indecency at adult businesses.
- Overlay district created to regulate the future locations of adult businesses.
- Planning Board asked by mayor to review and update the laws regulating adult businesses.
- Planning process involves citizens and reinvigorates downtown and its neighborhoods.
- Public investment to restore historic buildings in inner-city areas reverses decay in "old" downtown.
- Public officials working with business leaders to improve the downtown area.
- Proactive legislation adopted to regulate adult businesses before one actually exists in the community.
- Regulation options for adult businesses are given to municipal officials by their State government.
- Restrictions on multiple-use adult businesses are upheld by U.S. Supreme Court.
- Revisions to existing regulations for adult businesses are based on recent court decisions.
- State officials try to help cities, and their municipal officials, on how to regulate adult businesses.
- Taxpayers pay for lawyers to help their city defend its adult businesses regulations in the courts.
- Update zoning laws and conditions to regulate adult businesses based on recent court decisions.

- Voters do not change their form of government, which was lobbied for and favored by the adult business industry.
- Zoning laws are used to mitigate the negative secondary impact of adult businesses.
- Zoning law guidelines for local government officials are issued by the State concerning the regulation of adult business.
- Zoning laws are approved to eliminate adult businesses in the city's Central Business District (CBD).

The Future

Section III examines the future of the relationship between cities and adult businesses. The topics examined include city governments, adult businesses, available regulations, and the law. These laws change yearly as new court decisions are handed down that impact what is acceptable legislation to regulate these types of establishments. One chapter focuses on the use of zoning practices to regulate land uses and businesses, and another examines ten emerging national trends that will help in planning for and developing innovative downtowns in the future. The concluding chapter examines how the urban center of our downtowns represents the future of American cities.

Appendices

Many hours were spent researching valuable resources to compile this book. While articles have been written on this subject, this is the first edited reference work of its type on this topic that offers options for communities to consider and use to regulate adult businesses. To this end, several important resources are included as appendices in this volume. These resource materials include the following:

- *Periodical Bibliography*—A listing of major periodicals focusing on contemporary issues in communities, as well as functional disciplines related to the various issues and problems facing municipal governments today. The website for each publisher is listed to provide immediate access to these periodicals, as well as information on how to order them.

- *Regional Resource Directory*—A listing of all of the community governments included in Section II. Readers wishing to follow up on any of the best practices are provided immediate access to each government via their online website. In those communities with the council-manager form of government, it is suggested that citizens direct their inquiries and questions to the Office of the City Manager. In those cities with the strong-mayor form of government, it is recommended that all inquiries and questions be made directly to the Office of the Mayor.

- *State Municipal League Directory*—Most states have a professional municipal league, which serves as a valuable source of information about their city governments. State leagues typically have copies of municipal laws and policies, as well as model practices available for public officials to review in their state. The website for each state's municipal league is listed to provide access to these valuable sources of online information.

- *State Library Directory*—Every state has a central state library, and they typically contain copies of state laws, both proposed and adopted, in an online database. Many state libraries also have copies of the various laws adopted in those cities and towns within their jurisdiction. These libraries are an excellent resource. The website for each state library is listed to provide the reader with direct access to this information.

- *National Resource Directory*—This list includes all major national professional, membership, and research organizations serving public officials, as well as related professionals, and concerned citizens. Many of these organizations focus on various issues relating to cities, zoning, and land-use practices, as well as major issues and subjects related to these topics. The websites are identified for each organization and association listed.

- *U.S. Supreme Court Cases and Adult Businesses*—Various U.S. Supreme Court cases have had a direct impact on local government's ability to regulate adult businesses. Listed in this section are 25 such Supreme Court case decisions rendered since the early 1950s. For ease of reference, these cases are shown in four major categories relating to adult businesses (i.e., pornography and obscenity, adult bookstores, nude dancing, and the secondary-effects doctrine). The entire case can also be reviewed at the First Amendment Center website, which is listed in the *National Resource Directory*.

- *Secondary Effects Land-Use Studies of Adult Businesses in America*—Many municipal regulations of adult businesses are based on the so-called "secondary effects" doctrine, which is documented based on land-use studies. A listing of studies that have been undertaken in communities in the United States is provided, organized by state and city. The full studies can be viewed at the Community Defense Counsel website, which is listed in the *National Resource Directory*.

The editor would like to personally thank the twenty or so membership, research, not-for-profit organizations, and private publishers that granted permission to reprint the chapters contained in this volume. These organizations and companies are listed by name in the acknowledgments.

As more public officials and citizens became educated about and aware of the possible options available to them to regulate adult businesses, and representatives of adult businesses become aware of the public's expectations, this field will increase in importance during the coming years. It should always be remembered that public officials have a right to regulate adult businesses. Likewise, adult businesses have a right to locate in a community, subject to reasonable and legal regulations. In this regard, adult businesses cannot be prohibited, but they can be proactively regulated.

Lastly, and perhaps most importantly, this is an examination of important and timely public issues of concern to citizens and local government officials, but it is not meant to provide legal advice and is not a substitute for consulting with your municipal or county attorney. As always, when confronted with a legal issue or question, contact your local government attorney, since certain unique circumstances may exist locally that may alter any of the "best practices" examined within.

SECTION I: INTRODUCTION

CHAPTER 1

Cities and Adult Businesses

Kelly Anders *and* Jude Balsamo

Adult businesses — establishments that offer sexually oriented material and entertainment — have become increasingly popular during the past 30 years. Many of the activities offered — including exotic dancing, films and sexually explicit materials — are protected by the First Amendment. However, many states have attempted to impose restrictions through local land use regulations and licensing provisions. Some regulations have been challenged as violations of the First Amendment rights to free speech and free expression, but a recent Supreme Court ruling may help states strengthen adult business regulations, and in some instances, ban nude dancing altogether.

State Actions

Twelve states — Alabama, Alaska, Delaware, Georgia, Illinois, Maryland, Massachusetts, Missouri, Ohio, Tennessee, Texas and West Virginia — specifically require or authorize a locality to license adult entertainment establishments. Their statutes generally define the establishments governed, require application, and provide for suspension and revocation of a license.

Illinois, for example, authorizes townships to license certain adult entertainment businesses. Delaware has established one of the most comprehensive licensing laws among the states, including restricting locations, creating a Commission on Adult Entertainment Establishments, and detailing requirements for licenses, fees and duties of an owner or operator. Arizona, Delaware, Georgia, Illinois, Mississippi, New Jersey, New York and Tennessee have laws to restrict the hours of operation or location of adult entertainment establishments. In Arizona, for example, certain establishments must close between 1 and 8 A.M., Monday through Saturday, and between 1 A.M. and noon on Sunday. Arizona authorizes localities to enact alternative restrictions on hours of operation; however, those regulations must be at least as restrictive as the state's laws. Only Alabama and North Carolina have expressly authorized the prohibition of nude dancing.

Legislation. A variety of bills were considered in 2000 to regulate adult businesses. Florida, Georgia, Maryland, Mississippi, New York and West Virginia considered legislation restricting locations of adult establishments. Legislation passed in Mississippi and West Virginia.

New York and West Virginia considered legislation to prohibit nude dancing in certain

Originally published as "Adult Business Regulations," *NCSL Legislative Brief,* Vol. 9, No. 11, February 11, 2001, by the National Conference of State Legislatures, Denver, CO. Reprinted with permission of the publisher.

establishments licensed by alcohol beverage control. Rhode Island considered a bill that would place a four-year moratorium on adult entertainment licenses. California considered authorizing a county or city to regulate sexually oriented businesses, taking into account the potentially harmful secondary effects, such as higher crime rates and lower property values, on the surrounding community. Delaware passed a law last year that restricts the right of new adult entertainment establishments to operate in certain locations, and adds tax evasion as a reason to revoke an establishment's license.

Federal Actions

Tension between state and local regulations and protected speech has found its way to state and federal courts, and the U.S. Supreme Court. The Supreme Court first addressed adult use zoning restrictions in 1976 when Detroit's "Anti-Skid Row Ordinance" was upheld in Young vs. American Mini Theaters, Inc. Since then, a majority of municipalities around the country have adopted similar ordinances that control adult businesses in an effort to avoid the potentially dangerous secondary effects surrounding adult entertainment establishments.

The Court's decision this year in City of Erie vs. Pap's A.M. may have far-reaching effects for cities and states that want to outlaw nude dancing. In Erie, the Court upheld a local Pennsylvania ordinance that required erotic dancers to wear g-strings and pasties while performing. The Court determined that the ordinance was a content-neutral regulation of speech designed to deter the secondary effects of criminal activity associated with adult businesses and that requiring dancers to wear minimal attire was the least restrictive way to meet that goal. Some constitutional experts have expressed concern that upholding the ban on nude dancing will dilute the rights to free speech and free expression around the country.

SELECTED REFERENCES

Bergthold, Scott D. "City of Erie v. Pap's A.M. and the Future of Sexually Oriented Business Regulation." *Municipal Lawyer* 41, no. 5, September/October 2000.

McMillen, Steve. "Adult Uses and the First Amendment: Zoning and Non-Zoning Controls on the Use of Land for Adult Businesses." White Plains, N.Y.: Land Use Law Center, Pace University School of Law, Spring 1998.

SUGGESTED CONTACTS FOR MORE INFORMATION

First Amendment Center
Nashville, TN
Telephone: (615) 321-9588
Website: *http://www.freedomforum.org*

National Obscenity Law Center
New York, NY
Telephone: (212) 870-3232
Website: *http://www.moralityinmedia/nolc.org*

National Conference of State Legislatures
Denver, CO
Telephone: (303) 364-7700
Washington, DC
Telephone: (202) 624-5400
Website: *http://www.ncsl.org*

CHAPTER 2

Adult Businesses and Land-Use Regulations

Lydia R. Marola *and* Rebecca Lubin

Adult entertainment uses can range from bookstores and/or video stores carrying a significant number of sexually-oriented material, to modeling studios, massage parlors and strip clubs. In almost every community, negative reactions usually greet these uses. This is even more likely if the municipality believes that it was caught off-guard by the use. Negative reactions can focus on moral objections to the nature of the use, or to real and perceived impacts such a use might have on a community.

While it is sometimes difficult to obtain statistical information about the adult entertainment industry, information regarding trends can be found in local newspaper ads and by noting news items concerning the industry. It is also important to note any other state laws which cover adult entertainment uses. As noted in the Village of Scotia study, in New York State the Alcoholic Beverage Control (ABC) laws and regulations of the State Liquor Authority have partial clothing requirements in establishments holding liquor licenses. ABC laws also require certain distances from schools and churches. (Many adult establishments have circumvented such laws by not serving alcohol, thereby making

local land use regulations the only laws which impact where such businesses are located.)[1]

What exactly can a municipality do about adult entertainment uses? Can they be banned? Can they be limited to areas that are away from schools and residential neighborhoods?

This tech memo will help answer these questions and provide you and your community with information about the various planning tools available to municipalities dealing with adult entertainment uses. We will review municipal police power and the rights of municipalities to regulate land uses, and look at ways in which the First Amendment freedom of expression protection and landmark court cases have significantly impacted municipalities' rights to regulate adult uses. Finally, using models prepared by the Village of Scotia, we will discuss what municipalities should remember when drafting secondary impact studies and local regulations for adult uses.

Police Power: Municipal Rights to Regulate

There is no simple answer to the question of what a municipality can do when reg-

Originally published as *Adult Entertainment Technical Memorandum*, September 1999, addressed to the Mayor and Board of Village Trustees, and published by the Village of Scotia, NY.

ulating adult uses. At least part of the answer can be found in a community's right to regulate land uses as part of its municipal police power.

Municipal police power is the power to enact regulations affecting private actions in order to protect the public health, safety and general welfare. Zoning and other land use regulations are exercises of municipal police power. Although this power has moved beyond its original intention and now allows municipalities to enact regulations protecting such things as historic properties and natural areas, police power cannot be used indiscriminately by a municipality in order to target a particular use or property owner.

A community can regulate land uses for a legitimate public purpose, such as addressing development issues, the ignoring of which has a demonstrable impact on the value of land and the burden of delivering municipal services. These issues are largely defined in municipal and regional documents such as comprehensive plans.

Usually, if a municipality determines that it would be in the best interest of its health, safety and general welfare not to have adult uses, then, through zoning or a local law, such uses could be prohibited. If it were that simple, that would be the end of the story. However, while municipal police power justifies a municipality's right to pass laws prohibiting certain uses in the community, adult entertainment uses may be protected under the First Amendment freedom of speech and expression provision, and therefore, must be allowed within any and all municipalities.

How First Amendment Protections Impact Municipal Police Power

Both the United States Constitution, in the First Amendment, and the New York State Constitution, in Article 1 Section 8, provide for the protection of every citizen's right to the freedom of speech and expression. Many forms of adult entertainment, including printed materials, films and live entertainment, are protected by the First Amendment. Municipalities are, therefore, not permitted to enact local regulations that totally suppress the freedom of expression associated with these activities. It should be noted that constitutional protections do not cover activities or material deemed to be obscene, and these materials and activities may be banned by municipalities. However, many of the most common adult entertainment activities, such as adult book and video stores and nude dancing establishments, while sexually explicit, are not considered obscene, and are protected by the First Amendment.

Keeping this in mind, it is the *content* of the adult entertainment activity that is protected under federal and state constitutions. The police power of a local government that justifies zoning and other types of local land use regulations cannot be aimed at suppressing or limiting the *content* of the use. "When municipal regulations impinge on an adult business's freedom of expression, they lose the presumption of constitutionality that normally applies to zoning regulations, and the burden shifts to local government to justify its restrictions."[2] Although the constitutional protection of the freedom of expression means municipalities must allow for such uses within their boundaries, this does not mean that municipalities cannot regulate adult uses. What this means is that municipal regulations cannot focus on regulating adult uses because of what those uses contain, whether it be sexually explicit printed material, videos, or nude dancing. Municipalities are allowed to regulate adult uses in a manner that seeks to mitigate the potential secondary impacts (increase in crime, drug use, lowering of property values, etc.) often associated with adult entertainment uses.

Prior to adopting any type of adult entertainment regulations, a municipal government must demonstrate that it has conducted or relied upon planning studies illustrating the need to protect certain areas of the municipality from the negative secondary impacts associated with adult businesses. The extent to which local governments can limit adult entertainment uses has largely been shaped through court cases challenging municipal regulations.

Courts and Their Impact on Municipal Regulation of Adult Entertainment Uses

Since local governments are limited in the extent to which they can regulate adult entertainment uses, municipal regulation has largely been a case of trial and error. Many regulations never make it to actual litigation, but those that do can have a significant impact on the adult use regulations in other communities. A number of state and federal cases have addressed municipal power over adult entertainment uses. Following is an overview of four important cases.

City of Renton v Playtime Theaters

The City of Renton, Virginia, after conducting public hearings and research on the impacts of adult uses, enacted zoning regulations prohibiting an adult motion picture theater from locating within 1,000 feet of any residential zone, single or multi-family dwelling, church or park, and within one mile of any school. At the time the regulation was enacted, no adult entertainment uses existed in Renton. Legal action was brought after the regulation was in place when Playtime Theater, Inc. acquired two theaters with the intention of showing adult films.[3]

In *City of Renton v Playtime Theaters*, 475 US 41, 89 L Ed 2d 29, 106 S Ct 925 (1986), the United States Supreme Court laid out a four-part test used to determine when zoning regulations for adult businesses do not violate the First Amendment. In determining the constitutional validity, courts must consider whether:

1. The predominant purpose of zoning is to suppress the sexually explicit speech itself, or rather, to eliminate the "secondary effects" of adult uses;
2. The zoning regulation furthers a substantial governmental interest;
3. The zoning regulation is "narrowly tailored" to affect only those uses which produced the unwanted secondary effects; and
4. The zoning regulations leave open reasonable alternative locations for adult uses.[4]

The Court determined that the City of Renton regulations met this test and the regulations were upheld. An especially important point was made with regard to studies from municipalities outside of Renton that were relied upon when determining secondary impacts of adult entertainment uses. "The Court stated that the city did not have to produce its own studies ... but must reasonably believe (on the record) that the studies were relevant to its concerns."[5] This is significant since many municipalities, especially rural communities, have difficulty conducting studies of their own.

Town of Islip v Caviglia

In the case of the *Town of Islip v Caviglia*, 73 N.Y. 2d 544 (1989), the Court rejected the challenge brought by the owner of an adult bookstore, stating the Islip regulations successfully met the test set forth in Renton. The Town of Islip, New York, enacted regulations that concentrated adult uses within an area zoned industrial. In addition, the Town also terminated and amortized adult uses located in the downtown area, which had been targeted for a major revitalization effort.

The court decided that Islip met the Renton test, finding the regulations to be content neutral and aimed at combating the secondary impacts of adult uses to allow for future development in the business district. This was supported through studies conducted by professional planners that supported the conclusion that adult uses have harmful secondary effects and that a "dead zone" was created in areas with existing adult uses that hindered development in those areas.[6] In addition, the municipal government wanted to eliminate only those uses that were shown to produce unwanted secondary effects in order to allow for the redevelopment of those areas. Although Islip's regulations allowed adult uses only in an area zoned for industrial use, the court found that provided ample space for the development for such uses.[7]

Stringfellow's of New York, Ltd., v City of New York

Arguably the most important legal decision in recent memory involving adult uses is from the New York State Court of Appeals in 1998 in the case of *Stringfellow's of New York, Ltd., v City of New York*, when the court unanimously upheld the validity of the New York City zoning regulations governing the location of adult entertainment uses within the five boroughs.

In 1993, the New York City Division of City Planning conducted a study of the adult entertainment industry in that city. The study concluded that in areas where there was a concentration of adult uses, the presence of these businesses produced negative secondary impacts such as increased crime, decreased property values and reduced commercial activities.[8]

Following the study, the City amended its regulations, placing restrictions on both the location and size of adult entertainment businesses. These zoning amendments were intended to mitigate the secondary impacts by breaking the concentration of adult uses in certain areas by dispersing them. The City's zoning amendments limited those districts where adult uses are allowed to certain commercial and manufacturing areas. Adult businesses located within districts where such uses are not allowed are required to conform to the new zoning or terminate the business at that location within one year of the amendment's effective date. In addition, businesses located

within permitted districts are required to conform with certain distance and size requirements. Several adult businesses and their patrons brought actions challenging the validity of the City zoning amendments under Article 1, Section 8 of the New York State Constitution. This challenge was based on the claim that, because the amendment defines adult establishments as those allowing the exhibition of "specified anatomical areas" or "sexual activities," it is content-based and unlawfully suppresses expression.[9]

The New York State Court of Appeals developed a test for determining the validity of zoning regulations under Article 1, Section 8 of the New York State Constitution. The test includes:

1. The zoning regulation must be justified by concerns unrelated to speech,
2. It must be "no broader than necessary" to achieve its purpose, and
3. It must provide alternative locations for adult use businesses.

The Court ruled that the New York City zoning amendment met the test and is valid under the New York State Constitution.[10]

City of Erie et al. v Pap's A.M.

The most recent United States Supreme Court decision on adult entertainment uses was made in March 2000 in the case of *City of Erie et al. v Pap's A.M., tdba "Kandyland."* The case was brought by Pap's, an establishment featuring all nude dancing, against the City of Erie, Pennsylvania, which had enacted an ordinance making it an offense to knowingly or intentionally appear in public in a "state of nudity." To comply with the ordinance dancers, such as those performing at Kandyland, must wear, at a minimum, "pasties" and a "G-string." Pap's filed suit contending the ordinance violated its right to freedom of expression as protected by the First Amendment.

The Court evaluated the Erie ordinance

under the framework set forth in *United States v. O'Brien*, 391 U.S. 367, for content-neutral restrictions on symbolic speech. In its decision, the Court stated that, "Although being 'in a state of nudity' is not an inherently expressive condition, nude dancing of the type at issue here is expressive conduct that falls within the outer ambit of the First Amendment's protection.... What level of scrutiny applies is related to the suppression of expression." The Supreme Court upheld the Erie ordinance stating that it met all four factors set forth in *O'Brien*.

The facts in *O'Brien* are similar to those in the case of *Renton v. Playtime Theaters* and in *Stringfellow's*. In meeting the four factors the Court determined that first, "the ordinance is within Erie's constitutional power to enact because the city's efforts to protect public health and safety are clearly within its police powers. Second, the ordinance furthers the important government interests of regulating conduct through a public nudity ban and of combating the harmful secondary effects associated with nude dancing.... The ordinance also satisfies *O'Brien's* third factor, that the government interest is unrelated to the suppression of free expression.... The fourth *O'Brien* factor — that the restriction is not greater than is essential to the furtherance of the government interest — is satisfied as well."[11]

Clearly, to justify zoning regulations for adult businesses, municipalities must show that the regulations are not directed at the content of the use, but at the elimination of the negative secondary impacts resulting from that use. These are often demonstrated through secondary effects (or impacts) studies. Based on potential impacts identified in the study, a municipality can then recommend land use controls to regulate these types of uses. While secondary effects studies can take carious forms, there are certain elements that should be included in any study. The *Secondary Effects Study of Adult Entertainment Uses* from the Village of Scotia (funded by the New York Planning Federation, and released in September 1999), is used as a model for how communities prepare these studies and their format.[12]

Introduction: Motivation Behind Desire to Regulate

In its study, the Village of Scotia discusses the community's concerns over adult entertainment uses and why it is considering regulation of such entertainment. The Introduction discusses the Village's decision to enact a moratorium on adult entertainment uses while the study and local law were being prepared. Also discussed are some of the legal issues that allow municipalities to regulate adult entertainment uses and the purpose of the secondary study.

Moratoria

Before undertaking a secondary study, many municipalities choose to enact a moratorium. Often referred to as a "stop-gap" or "interim" regulation, moratoria are intended to preserve the status quo pending the adoption of other land use regulations. Municipal actions that might prompt the enactment of a moratorium include preparing a comprehensive plan, a proposal to establish a new use that is not adequately addressed by incurrent zoning, or a municipal desire to ensure that community facilities may be made capable of servicing anticipated development.[13]

Regardless of the reason behind a moratorium, courts have consistently required that these regulations be adopted in strict adherence to the procedures set forth in the enabling statutes for the enactment of or amendment to zoning regulation. "The rationale for this requirement is that a moratorium is a form of land use regulation, in that it temporarily prohibits one or more uses."[14] In addition, municipalities should pay particular attention to the following when enacting a moratorium for any reason:

Purpose/Intent— there needs to be a clear public purpose to the action that is articulated in the moratorium.

The Extent of Coverage— be clear and fair on what actions are covered under the moratorium, as well as at what point during the review/approval process an applicant may gain exception. For instance, are all applications requiring site plan approval subject to the moratorium? Does that mean final approval is needed prior to the effective date, or is submittal of a complete application by such a date okay? Must the project have completed the SEQR process? There are lots of options.

Period of Coverage— Courts have been consistently uncomfortable with long and broad moratoria. Six months or less is usually fine. Extensions of a year or more may be trouble, particularly if this affects significant proposals.

Show Action and Progress— Timing of any moratorium is critical. It should be designed as a safe period during which real work is progressing toward updating a plan and/or regulations in light of legitimate pressures or trends. If a moratorium is initiated too soon and shows no progress, it could become challengeable.

If the Moratorium Becomes Controversial— Don't poison community willingness to make changes by fighting over a moratorium. A moratorium should be relatively easy to initiate once there is agreement on the concept and terms. Remember, consistent with the SEQR amendments of 1996, moratoria are Type II actions under SEQR — greatly easing the process.

Review of Secondary Effects Studies

Since most suburban and rural communities currently faced with the issue of regulating adult entertainment uses have no direct experience with such businesses, they must rely on secondary studies conducted by other municipalities to help identify potential secondary impacts. (As discussed earlier, in the landmark case, *City of Renton v. Playtime Theaters*, the United States Supreme Court determined that municipalities do not have to produce their own studies, but must state how the studies chosen are relevant to their concerns regarding secondary impacts.) Often these studies have been conducted in large metropolitan areas, but, as shown in the Village of Scotia study, this doesn't necessarily mean that they are not applicable to more suburban or rural areas. Often studies done in large cities are conducted on the neighborhood level, where the study area is actually no larger than many rural community centers or villages. Also, the mix and proximity of commercial and residential uses is often comparable between city neighborhoods and less urban areas.

For their study, the Village of Scotia reviewed studies from Austin and El Paso, Texas; Newport News, Virginia; Garden Grove, California; Islip and the City of New Rochelle, New York; and Indianapolis, Indiana. Research methods used included a comparison of areas that contained adult uses with areas that did not (control areas), a survey of professionals and residents, and gathering statistical data. Secondary effects studies included crime rates, impacts on real estate, traffic, noise and general neighborhood appearance.

Based on the review of these studies, the Village of Scotia concluded that all supported the existence of a number of negative secondary effects of adult entertainment uses, such as an increase in crime rates, decline in property values, and a general deterioration, both in reality and perception, of the neighborhoods in which these uses are located. Scotia also found that the studies were relevant to the Village since the studies did not focus on the city as a whole, but on much smaller areas. In addition, the impacts of adult uses on the study area were found to be independent of the size of the municipality.[15]

The Village of Scotia findings that were especially applicable to them included:

1) The smaller the commercial district, the larger the impact because the "negative halo" will affect a larger proportion of the municipality's business than it would in a larger city;

2) Because of the small size of the commercial districts the probability of substantial impacts of sexually oriented businesses upon residential areas increases, and;

3) Smaller places are more likely to have fewer days and hours of commercial activity than larger cities. This increases the likelihood than an adult business will have a larger impact on the area in which it is situated during off-hours for other businesses.[16]

Regulation Recommendation and Local Law

The next step after establishing the potential secondary impacts which adult entertainment uses may have on a community is to identify how best to regulate these uses in order to minimize negative impacts on residents and businesses within the municipality. Before choosing a regulatory method, the Village of Scotia:

Reviewed current zoning: The Village identified which zoning districts would currently allow adult entertainment businesses to locate as a permitted use, citing some of the undefined permitted uses within the Village zoning that an adult entertainment establishment may argue are appropriate classifications for their use. These included, but were not limited to, retail stores and shops, restaurants, theaters, membership clubs, drinking establishments and personal services stores.

Identified land uses sensitive to potential negative impacts: The Village identified sensitive areas "as possessing characteristics that are essential to the Village's character, quality of life, and economic success."[17] These areas include residential neighborhoods, the central business district, places of worship, schools, childcare facilities, recreation areas, parks and playgrounds, and civic and cultural facilities.

Reviewed legal considerations and regulatory options: An overview of legal considerations and regulatory options was presented to outline major court decisions that impact local regulation of adult entertainment uses. Regulatory methods of licensing,[18] concentration (which concentrates adult uses within a specific zone), dispersion (which seeks to prevent the concentration of adult uses), and the hybrid method (which concentrates adult uses within a certain zone and additionally restricts adult uses from locating within a certain distance of identified sensitive areas) were presented as options available.[19]

Based on this analysis, the Village of Scotia decided to adopt a local law regulating adult entertainment uses for the purpose of mitigating the negative secondary impacts potentially caused by such uses. Adult entertainment uses are permitted only in industrial zones within the Village and further restricted from being within a minimum of 500 feet from identified sensitive areas. A minimum separation of 500 feet between adult uses is included, as are signage restrictions.[20]

Options for Municipalities without Zoning

Municipalities without zoning regulations still have options when it comes to regulating adult entertainment uses.

Site plan review can be used to help mitigate negative impacts on neighboring properties within a municipality. It is important to remember that site plan review is not zoning. Site plan review does not "permit" or "restrict" uses. The exercise of site plan review assumes land uses are allowed, subject to the elements of the site plan that may be reviewed as determined by the municipality. Using our example, a municipality may choose to require any adult entertainment establishment to be subject to site plan review.

Under site plan review the municipality may review elements of a site plan such as those defined by New York State statute including;

- Parking
- Means of Access
- Screening and landscaping
- Signs
- Architectural features
- Location/dimension of buildings
- Adjacent land uses and physical features meant to protect those uses
- Any additional elements the governing body may specify

Using this method, municipalities without zoning may control certain impacts on the community associated with the listed elements, but may not control the location of such a use within the community. It is important to remember that adult entertainment uses can be included in a municipal-wide site plan review local law that includes other land uses that the municipality wishes to make subject to site plan review.

Municipalities without zoning may also use their non-zoning police power to regulate the potentially negative aspects of secondary impacts. Based on secondary impacts identified by a municipality, local laws may be enacted which regulate the nuisance, such as noise. Again, it is important to remember that these types of local laws should be municipality-wide and cover all uses. Adult entertainment establishments should not be the only types of uses subject to such laws.

Conclusion

As was stated at the beginning, community reactions to adult entertainment uses are usually negative. Some could argue that by regulating adult entertainment uses, especially in municipalities where no such uses exist, attention is drawn to the topic and, by regulating these uses, that municipality is suddenly allowing them in the community. As is evidenced in this tech memo, this is not the case. Because of the First Amendment protections allowed many types of adult uses, municipal police power to prohibit these uses is limited. Thus, these uses, without municipal regulation, are essentially allowed in all municipalities, often in more locations prior to regulation than after.

As is clear from the information presented here, municipalities do have the power to limit and confine adult entertainment uses to the places in their communities that they identify. When faced with regulating adult entertainment uses, municipalities should remember the following:

Identify the issues — what causes concern? Adult entertainment uses are often controversial and the issue or issues a municipality is most concerned with should be clearly identified and stated, ideally first addressed in a municipal comprehensive plan. As with any issue, communities should specifically identify what causes concern.

Identify possible solutions/tools as municipal options—While municipal police power is limited in terms of prohibiting adult entertainment uses, municipalities do have control over where these uses can be located to mitigate possible negative secondary impacts.

Conduct Secondary Study—A secondary study is required before drafting any adult use regulations. While there is no required format for secondary studies, municipalities should include secondary impacts, current regulations/zoning, sensitive land uses and legal and regulatory options.

Draft and implement regulations—Based on the secondary study and municipal options for regulation, draft and implement regulations that best suit the character of your municipality and best address municipal concerns.

Always involve the public—Involving the public throughout the planning and regulatory process helps build a constituency regarding the issues of concern for the community. When dealing with a potentially controversial issue, involving the public can also help educate the community on all aspects of the issue.

NOTES

1. Marola, Lydia R., and Blick, Greg. *Secondary Effects of Adult Entertainment Uses*, 1999, pg. 4.

2. New York State Department of State Counsel's Office, Opinions of Counsel: Municipal Regulation of Adult Uses After the *Stringfellow's* Decision.

3. Weinig, Lynn E. "Regulating Adult Entertainment Uses," *Municipal Lawyer*, January/February 1994. Volume 8, Number 1, pg. 1.

4. New York State Department of State Counsel's Office, *loc. cit.*

5. Weinig, Lynn E., *loc. cit.*

6. *Ibid.*

7. *Ibid.*

8. NYS Department of State Counsel's Office, *loc. cit.*

9. *Ibid.*

10. United States Supreme Court Decision.

11. *Ibid.*

12. The Village of Scotia model was funded by the Rural New York Planning and Preservation Grant Program with support from the J.R. Kaplan Fund and The Andy Warhol Foundation for the Visual Arts. Other municipalities are encouraged to review it. Copies of the Secondary Effects Study are available from the New York Planning Federation.

13. Damsky, Sheldon W., Catalano, Joseph M., Coon, James A. *All You Ever Wanted to Know About Zoning...* 3rd Edition. New York Planning Federation, Albany, NY 1999, pg. 15–1.

14. *Ibid.*, pg. 15-3.

15. Marola, Lydia R., and Blick, Greg. *loc. cit.* pp. 4–8.

16. *Ibid.*, pp. 8–9.

17. *Ibid.*, p. 10.

18. *Ibid.*, p. 10.

19. *Ibid.*, pp. 14–16.

20. *Ibid.*, pp. 16–17.

CHAPTER 3

Adult Businesses and the First Amendment

James Monge

Cities often fail to recognize the need to regulate land uses, and are taken by surprise when an adult use establishment opens. This chapter explores adult uses and the First Amendment, manners in which cities can regulate adult uses, and statutes that impact adult uses.

Regulation of adult uses — such as adult cabarets (i.e. strip clubs), adult bookstores, and adult theaters — can present significant challenges for Minnesota cities. Adult uses have constitutional free speech protections that complicate efforts to regulate them. In addition, adult use owners have a substantial financial interest in opening and operating adult uses. As a result, attempts by cities to regulate adult uses are often met with costly legal challenges.

Cities often fail to recognize the need to regulate adult uses. The city may be taken by surprise when an adult use establishment opens shop and the appropriate measures may not be in place to properly regulate the adult use. This may leave the city scrambling to respond to an unsatisfactory situation. However, attempting to regulate an adult use after it has already moved in is problematic. The adult use may locate in an especially objec-

tionable part of the city and it will be more difficult to remove or regulate the adult use once it is established. In addition, the city is more likely to become involved in litigation if it tries to regulate an adult use that has already opened its doors. Therefore, having a regulatory scheme in place prior to the opening of an adult use in your city is the best way to insure the city can control its harmful effects.

Adult Uses and the First Amendment

The First Amendment protects freedom of speech and expression. Adult uses — including adult cabarets, adult book stores, and adult theaters — are entitled to First Amendment protection. Adult books, magazines, and movies contain First Amendment protected speech. The United States Supreme Court has also found that adult dancing involves "expressive conduct" falling "within the outer ambit of the First Amendment's protection."

Cities must be especially careful when regulating adult uses because these uses are protected by the First Amendment. A regulation that is enacted for the purpose of restrain-

Originally published as "Regulation of Adult Uses by Minnesota Cities," Risk Management Information Report, April 1, 2007, by the League of Minnesota Cities, St. Paul, MN. Reprinted with permission of the publisher.

ing speech on the basis of its content presumptively violates the First Amendment. Therefore, cities cannot prohibit adult uses because of their explicit nature. Such a regulation would be an unconstitutional prior restraint on the content of First Amendment protected speech. An adult use regulation that violates the First Amendment will be struck down, and the city will be left without a means of regulating the adult use.

However, not all regulation of adult uses is proscribed by the First Amendment. Municipal regulation of adult uses will be found constitutional if the city can show that the regulation: (1) is a content-neutral time, place, and manner regulation; (2) is designed to serve a substantial government interest; and (3) does not unreasonably limit alternative avenues of communication. A city ordinance regulating adult uses will be considered content-neutral if its purpose is not to regulate content of the protected speech, but instead to lessen the negative "secondary effects" attributable to adult uses. These secondary effects may include prostitution and other criminal activity, drug use, increased incidence of sexually transmitted disease, decreases in neighboring property values, and blight. Cities have a legitimate interest in regulating the secondary effects of adult uses.

Prior to enacting an ordinance that regulates adult uses, a city must engage in legislative fact-finding that establishes the negative secondary effects of adult uses. Cities may rely on studies conducted by other cities to establish the secondary effects of adult uses, as long as the evidence relied upon by the city is reasonably believed to be relevant to the problem addressed by the zoning ordinance. Cities may also compile their own city-specific data, such as police reports and crime statistics to justify their zoning regulations. Failure to conduct the requisite fact-finding may result in the ordinance being struck down.

What Can Cities Do to Regulate Adult Uses?

There are several ways cities can regulate adult uses without running afoul of the First Amendment. Cities can regulate adult uses through zoning ordinances, licensing ordinances, and prohibitions against public nudity.

Zoning

Cities may regulate adult uses through zoning ordinances. A zoning ordinance may regulate adult uses by dispersing them or concentrating them into a particular area. Some zoning ordinances do both. A zoning ordinance that concentrates adult uses into a particular zone allows for focused law enforcement and prevents the secondary effects of adult uses from spreading into other parts of the city. A zoning ordinance that disperses adult uses spreads them out, thereby minimizing the secondary effects of adult uses. An ordinance that disperses adult uses might require that adult uses be "750 feet from other sexually oriented businesses, single or multi-family dwellings, churches, schools, bars, and public parks." Whether a zoning ordinance disperses or concentrates adult uses, the zoning ordinance may not deny a reasonable opportunity to open and operate an adult use somewhere in the city because, under the First Amendment, the zoning ordinance must not unreasonably limit alternative avenues of communication.

A city's zoning ordinance may also include provisions for amortization of nonconforming adult uses. A nonconforming use is one that was lawful at the time of its inception, but no longer complies with the current zoning ordinance. Amortization provides a grace period during which the time and money spent on a nonconforming land use can be recouped prior to termination of the use. Amortization of adult uses is authorized by Minn. Stat. § 462.357 subd. 1e (b). The amortization period must be reasonable.

Moratoria

State law authorizes cities to enact interim land use ordinances. The interim ordinances may place a moratorium of limited duration on particular land uses for the purpose of conducting studies to support a zoning amendment. However, moratoria on adult uses raise serious First Amendment problems. Moratoria that prevent adult uses from opening anywhere in the city have been struck down because they unreasonably limit alternative avenues of communication. In addition, moratoria that prohibit adult uses have been held to be unconstitutional prior restraints on speech. A city considering enacting a moratorium on adult uses should be aware that the moratorium is particularly susceptible to legal challenge.

If after consulting the city attorney the city council determines it is necessary to enact a moratorium on adult uses, then the city should take a number of steps to make it more likely the moratorium will withstand a legal challenge. The moratorium ordinance: (1) should be as short in duration as possible, (2) include finding based upon review of secondary effects studies, (3) include precise definitions of the adult uses regulated by the moratorium, and (4) define a temporary location for adult uses to operate during the moratorium. Again the city is cautioned that even these steps may not be enough to save a moratorium from a First Amendment challenge.

Licensing

A licensing ordinance is a prior restraint on speech and bears a heavy presumption against validity. Nevertheless, cities may impose reasonable licensing requirements on adult uses to control their secondary effects.

Because adult businesses are protected by the First Amendment, licensing ordinances must contain narrow, objective, and definite standards that limit the discretion of the licensing authority. Protected speech may not be censored simply because the licensing authority disapproves of its content. The licensing ordinance must also set a reasonable and definite deadline for approval, and provide for prompt judicial review of the licensing authority's decision. A licensing ordinance that allows administrative delay to restrain speech will be found unconstitutional.

Licensing ordinances requiring that applicants disclose their name, age, and criminal history and providing for background checks on applicants have been upheld as substantially related to the legitimate government interest of guarding against the secondary effects of adult businesses.

Licensing ordinances disqualifying applicants who have been convicted of certain sex crimes have also been upheld. The ordinance should enumerate the disqualifying crimes and set a reasonable limit on the period of disqualification.

Licensing ordinances setting a minimum distance between dancers and patrons and preventing the exchange of money between dancers and patrons have been upheld as furthering the legitimate government interest of preventing crime.

Cities may impose license fees for the issuance of an adult use license. The amount of the fee must be reasonably related to the costs of administering the licensing ordinance.

Prohibition on Public Nudity

The United States Supreme Court has upheld city ordinances prohibiting public nudity and requiring exotic dancers to wear "pasties" and a "g-string" when performing. In addition, cities may prohibit the sale of liquor in establishments where totally nude dancing occurs. In both cases, the city should be able to show that the regulation was necessary to prevent the negative secondary effects of the prohibited conduct.

Minn. Stat. § 617.242

In 2006, the State Legislature adopted Minn. Stat. § 617.242. The statute is intended to help municipalities address the opening and operation of strip clubs. However, there are serious doubts about the statute's constitutionality. Therefore, cities are cautioned not to rely on Minn. Stat. § 617.242 to regulate strip clubs.

The statute regulates "adult entertainment establishments." Adult entertainment establishments are defined in the statute as "a business open only to adults and that presents live performances that are distinguished or characterized by an emphasis on the depiction of sexual conduct or nudity." The statute does not regulate other adult uses, such as adult book stores or adult theaters.

The statute requires an adult entertainment establishment to provide written notice to a municipality 60 days prior to applying for a permit to operate the establishment in the municipality. If the municipality has no permit requirement, the adult entertainment establishment must give written notice to the municipality 60 days prior to commencing operation of the adult entertainment establishment. Upon receipt of the notice, the officer receiving the notice on behalf of the municipality must acknowledge receipt of the notice by certified mail, return receipt requested, and notify the governing body of the notice. The governing body may conduct public hearings on the proposed operation of the adult entertainment establishment and must give written notice by ordinary mail of the hearings to the operator of the proposed adult entertainment establishment.

The statute prohibits persons convicted of certain sex crimes from operating or managing an adult entertainment establishment for three years after discharge of the sentence. The disqualifying sex crimes include: prostitution, criminal sexual conduct, solicitation of children, indecent exposure, distribution or exhibition of obscene materials and performances, and possession of pornographic work involving minors.

Under the statute, a municipality is not required to provide, by zoning or otherwise, for a location within the city for an adult entertainment establishment to operate if another adult entertainment establishment already exists within 50 miles of the municipal boundaries.

The statute also limits hours and days of operation of adult entertainment establishments. In cities that do not regulate hours of operation, adult entertainment establishments are prohibited from operating before 10:00 A.M. or after 10:00 P.M., Monday through Saturday, and may not be open for business on Sundays or legal holidays.

In addition, under the statute, an adult entertainment establishment may not operate in the same building as, or within 1,500 feet of, another adult entertainment establishment; within 500 feet of residential property; or within 2,800 feet of a elementary or secondary school, church, synagogue, mosque, or other places of worship.

The statute applies to all municipalities that have not enacted an ordinance or regulation governing adult entertainment establishments. However, a municipality may adopt an ordinance or regulation that is consistent with the statute, supersedes the statute, or is more restrictive than the statute. In addition, a municipality may adopt an ordinance or regulation that provides that the statute does not apply in the municipality. The statute also provides that if a municipality enacts an ordinance or regulation that only regulates a portion of the operation of an adult entertainment establishment, the statute applies to the remainder of the operation not regulated by the municipal ordinance or regulation, unless the ordinance or regulation provides otherwise.

One federal district court, ruling on a motion to enjoin the statute's application, has already held that several of the statute's provisions are likely unconstitutional. The court found that the statute's notice, distance, and hours of operation provisions likely violate the First Amendment. The court's decision was not a final judgment on the constitutionality of the statute, but it does raise serious doubts.

There are a number of reasons why cities should not rely on Minn. Stat. § 617.242 alone to regulate adult uses, including:

- First, and most importantly, there are serious questions about the constitutionality of the statute.
- Second, the statue only applies to "adult entertainment establishments"; however the city will likely want to regulate other types of adult uses like adult bookstores and adult theaters.
- Third, it is unclear how the statute applies to adult entertainment establishments in existence prior to its enactment.
- And fourth, the general provisions of the statute may not meet the unique needs of any particular city.

As a result, cities should not rely on the provisions of Minn. Stat. § 617.242 to regulate adult entertainment establishments. The better approach is to adopt the zoning and licensing regulations discussed in the previous section which have proven effective. Cities should also consider whether to opt out of the statute to avoid any unintended conflicts that may arise between the statute and local ordinances or regulations.

Conclusion

The best way to control the negative secondary effects of adult uses is to enact adult use regulations before an adult business opens up shop in the city. Cities have a number of effective tools at their disposal to regulate adult uses, including zoning ordinances, licensing ordinances, and prohibitions on public nudity. However, First Amendment protection complicates regulation of adult uses. A regulation that violates the First Amendment will be struck down. Therefore, it is imperative that the city work closely with the city attorney to craft adult use regulations that will withstand constitutional muster and protect the city's interests.

CHAPTER 4

Adult Businesses and Recent Legal Cases

Jeffrey Goldfarb

SCENARIO: You've just finished drafting the conflict of interest letter requested by the Mayor, you have revised the contract with the city's trash hauler, drafted the letter to the guy who refuses to remove from his front lawn the inoperable '73 Ford pick-up which is currently sitting on cinderblocks, and completed the various other tasks that were due by noon. You finally have time to catch up on that big stack of *Daily Journals* sitting in the corner of your office. You read with interest the Supreme Court's recent decision in *City of Erie v. Pap's A.M. TDBA "Kandyland"*[1] where the Court upheld Erie's enforcement of its general ban on total nudity against an adult oriented business that provided live nude entertainment. After reading the case you start to wonder whether your city's adult oriented business ordinance is up to date. You pull the good book (the city code) off your shelf and find that the adult ordinance, which was last updated at the beginning of Mr. Reagan's second term, only allows adult oriented businesses with the approval of a conditional use permit. This causes you to wonder, "is this a 'state of the art' ordinance?" Well, given the changes that have resulted from the numerous decisions on cities'

efforts to regulate adult oriented businesses, your city's ordinance is as much a "state of the art" ordinance as that '73 Ford pick-up truck resting on cinderblocks in the guy's front yard is a "state of the art" SUV. Time to consider amendments.

The purpose of this article is to discuss some regulatory trouble-spots that may exist in your local ordinance and to discuss some of the recent case law that has clarified (or, in some cases muddied the waters on) the permissible boundaries associated with the regulation of adult oriented businesses. In true Letterman fashion,[2] what follows is the "top 10 list" of things to consider when reviewing your adult oriented business ordinance.

10. **Though the "Message" May Be Unclear, the Court Considers Adult Oriented Businesses to Be Protected by the First Amendment.**

Although probably not necessary, it is sometimes worth reminding people that adult entertainment, i.e., sexually oriented films, books, and live performances, including nude dancing, involves speech, and as such, is protected by the First Amendment. The most re-

Originally published as "The Brave New World of Adult Entertainment Regulation," *Public Law Journal*, Vol. 23, No. 3, Summer 2000, by the Public Law Section of the State Bar of California, San Francisco, CA. Reprinted with permission of the publisher.

cent recitation of this perhaps counter-intuitive conclusion is contained in the Supreme Court's plurality opinion in *City of Erie v. Pap's*: "As we explained in *Barnes*, however, nude dancing of the type at issue here is expressive conduct, although we think it falls only within the outer ambit of the First Amendment's protection."[3] Imbued with this constitutional protection, regulations on adult entertainment are not analyzed under the "rational basis test" associated with most governmental regulation, but under the heightened scrutiny afforded by the intermediate level "time, place, and manner test" (also called the "O'Brien test"[4]) if the regulation is content neutral, and the strict scrutiny test if the regulation is content based.[5]

9. Regulations of Adult Oriented Businesses Are Typically Upheld Only When Those Regulations Are Designed to Reduce the Secondary Effects Adult Oriented Businesses Have Been Demonstrated to Create.

In *City of Renton v. Playtime Theaters, Inc.*,[6] the Supreme Court reaffirmed its prior plurality opinion in *Young v. American Mini Theaters*[7] which found that adult oriented business regulations which are designed to reduce the secondary effects that such businesses have on their surrounding neighborhood are "content neutral" because they are enacted to reduce the businesses' secondary effects rather than suppress whatever message is being conveyed by the entertainers or materials.[8] These secondary effects include, but are not limited to, increased blight, increased criminal activity particularly sexual related crime, depressed property values, and increased vacancy rates for properties in the vicinity of adult oriented businesses. As a content neutral regulation, it will withstand constitutional scrutiny so long as the regulation is within the power of the government to adopt (which it almost always is), is "narrowly tailored" to serve a substantial governmental interest,[9] and leaves open alternative avenues of communication. Courts have

repeatedly held municipalities have a substantial governmental interest in preventing or reducing these secondary effects. As a result, any regulation on adult oriented businesses must be narrowly tailored to reduce the "secondary effects"[10] that the government has a substantial interest in preventing.

8. As Applied to Adult Oriented Businesses, the Term "CUP" Means "Constitutionally Un-Permitted."

Although not a particularly recent development, case law prohibits cities from requiring the "standard" conditional use permit as a precondition to operating a sexually oriented business. Courts have considered such a requirement to be an unconstitutional prior restraint because "the ability to make decisions based on ambiguous criteria such as the 'general welfare' of the community effectively gives the commission the power to make decisions on any basis at all, including an impermissible basis, such as content based regulation of speech." *Smith v. County of Los Angeles*,[11] citing *Dease v. City of Anaheim*.[12]

7. A Municipality Can Require Adult Oriented Business Operators to Obtain a License Prior to Establishing Such a Business Providing the Permit Standards Are Objective.

While the city cannot base its permitting decision on vague and ambiguous standards, it can require a permit as a precondition to operating an adult oriented business **IF** the permitting standards are purely objective.[13] Courts will typically uphold a permitting or licensing system based on "quantifiable standards which the agency charged with deciding individual cases is expected to apply."[14] Such permitting systems do not function as a prior restraint because they prohibit the decision-maker from silencing objectionable speech based on criteria unrelated to the secondary effects the adult oriented businesses tend to create. As an example, a permit system that requires the city to find that the proposed use will not be contrary to the welfare of the community allows the decision maker sufficient discretion to deny the permit based upon a belief that strip clubs are not in the best interests of the community. Such a regulatory system would surely fail as an unconstitutional prior restraint. Alternatively, a finding prohibiting the establishment of a strip club within 500 feet of a children's school is sufficiently objective such that denial cannot be subterfuge, based upon the licensor's objections to the message being conveyed at the strip club. Accordingly, such a licensing system based upon such objective criteria is likely to be upheld.

6. Timeliness Is Next to Godliness.

The obligation to obtain a permit prior to establishing a sex oriented business could also be considered an unconstitutional prior restraint if the ordinance does not provide the proper "procedural safeguards." If a permit is required prior to engaging in expressive activity, the ordinance must mandate: 1) that the decision to issue or deny the permit is made within a brief, specified, and reasonably prompt period of time; and 2) that judicial review of the decision can occur within a short period of time ("prompt judicial review"). In *FW/PBS, Inc. v. City of Dallas*,[15] the Supreme Court invalidated Dallas' licensing system because the ordinance did not guarantee that the city's decision on the permit would be made within a short period of time. Cases have typically held that a city's determination on an ordinance is sufficiently prompt if it is made between 30 to 60 days of the date the application is submitted. (See, e.g., *TK Video, Inc. vs. Denton County.*[16, 17])

In *Baby Tam & Co., Inc. v. City of Las Vegas*,[18] the Ninth Circuit invalidated Las Vegas' adult oriented business permitting system even though Las Vegas' ordinance specifically stated that an applicant can seek judicial review of a decision denying its permit by availing him or herself of Nevada's administrative mandamus process. The court con-

cluded that such a process did not provide prompt judicial review because state law failed to impose upon the court the obligation to actually decide the case within a specified period of time. The court therefore invalidated the ordinance even though it realized that only the state, and not the city, could fix a problem. In response to the *Baby Tam* case, the California Legislature quickly adopted Code of Civil Procedure section 1094.8 which provides that a challenge to a denial or revocation of a permit to engage in expressive activity can be filed within 20 days of the city's decision, and that the court must decide the case within 50 days of the filing of the petition.[19]

5. Look, but Don't Touch.

In *Tily B., Inc. v. City of Newport Beach*,[20] the court found that California cities can prohibit physical contact between patrons and entertainers at sex oriented businesses. The court determined the requirement that "the ordinance further a substantial governmental interest is met because the city enacted these restrictions to combat prostitution, sexually transmitted diseases, criminal activity and the secondary effects of adult entertainment etablishments."[21] The court found this goal was satisfied because "the city could reasonably conclude that separating entertainers from customers reduces the opportunity for prostitution and drug dealing. The restriction is no more than necessary, for the message of the erotic dances is not lessened by allowing customers to look but not touch, and the provision is constitutional."[22] The court similarly upheld a prohibition against patrons handing tips directly to entertainers. "The no-direct tipping rule ... is likewise constitutional." "Preventing the exchange of money between dancers and patrons reduces the likelihood of illicit transactions," and, "while the tipping prohibition may deny a patron one means of expressing pleasure with the dancers' performance, sufficient alterative methods of communication exist for the patron to convey the same message."[23] Finally, the court upheld the requirement that entertainment can only be provided on a stage which is raised 18 inches off the floor and is only occupied by an entertainer when patrons are at least 6 feet from the stage (the "six foot buffer rule"). "The stage height and distance requirements ... furthers the city's interest in crime and disease prevention, they are narrowly tailored to meet the goal, and they are constitutional. 'It is reasonable to conclude that the 6 foot [stage distance] rule would further the state's interests in the prevention of crime and disease.'"[24]

4. It Ought to Be a Crime.

In fact, now it is. There is a long line of authority establishing that the Legislature has preempted cities from adopting criminal prohibitions against sexual activity by occupying the field of criminal sexual relations.[25] Many of the operating regulations contained within an adult oriented business ordinance (i.e., the prohibition against physical contact) could be considered regulations of sexual activity. As a result, some courts have concluded that cities are preempted from criminally prosecuting certain violations of their sex oriented business ordinances. Long ago, however, the Legislature carved out a narrow exception to this general preemption rule when it adopted Penal Code sections 318.5 and 318.6. Those provisions allow the criminal enforcement of regulations applicable to live entertainment at restaurants and bars, but exempted from the exception theaters, concert halls and similar establishments. As adult oriented business owners are able to get "expert" testimony that virtually every live entertainment adult oriented business is considered a "theater, concert hall or similar establishment,"[26] this exception prevented the criminal prosecution of various operational requirements at most adult oriented businesses which provide live entertainment. However, in 1998 the Legislature adopted Assembly Bill 726, which amended Penal Code sections 318.5 and 318.6 by prospectively eliminating the "theater, concert hall and similar establishment" requirement. As

a result, an ordinance can now provide a misdemeanor punishment for a violation of a sex oriented business ordinance in all establishments licensed as theaters, concert halls and similar establishments that began operation after July 9, 1998.

3. The Civil Alternative.

So what do you do about live entertainment establishments which operated as "theaters, concert halls and similar establishments" before July 9, 1998? While you cannot criminally prosecute violations of the ordinance, you can structure your ordinance so that violations of the operational requirements result in a civil revocation of an operator's permit. In *Tily B., Inc. v. City of Newport Beach*, the plaintiff violated numerous provisions of the city's adult oriented business ordinance including the prohibition against direct tipping, raised stage and 6-foot buffer rule, and the prohibition against physical contact between patrons and entertainers. After numerous notices, the city revoked the business's permit and the business sued claiming, in part, that the city was preempted from taking such an action. In rejecting this claim, the court specifically noted "while the state has preempted the criminal aspects of sexually activity,[27] localities remain free to regulate and license such conduct through non-criminal provisions.[28] State law thus does not preempt the Newport Beach ordinance. The city's ordinance is regulatory, not criminal, since permit revocation is the only sanction.... A non-criminal licensing statute aimed at activities expressly left open to local regulation does not conflict with the general law and is valid."[29]

2. The Naked Truth Is That You Cannot Be Naked.

In a series of three separate decisions,[30] courts have provided California cities substantial guidance on whether and to what extent cities can apply a prohibition against nudity to adult oriented businesses. In each of these cases, the court found such regulations to be constitutionally permissible because the regulations were content neutral and satisfied the intermediate level of scrutiny test. Specifically, the court found the prohibition on nudity furthered the city's substantial governmental interest in reducing the pernicious secondary effects adult oriented businesses create. "Because the nude dancing at Kandyland is of the same character as the adult entertainment at issue in *Renton v. Playtime Theatres, Inc.*, 475 U.S. 41, 89 L.Ed.2d 24, 106 S.Ct. 925 (1986), *Young v. American Mini Theaters, Inc.*, 427 U.S. at 51-52, 49 L.Ed.2d 310, 96 S.Ct. 2440 (1976), and *California v. LaRue*, 409 U.S. 109, 34 L.Ed.2d 342, 93 S.Ct. 390 (1972), it was reasonable for *Erie* to conclude that such dancing was likely to produce the same secondary effects."[31]

1. And You Thought Recitals Only Served to Bore You with Bad Piano and Ballet.

And the number one thing to think about in drafting or amending an adult oriented business ordinance is: ... Include a monumental amount of recitals demonstrating how the specific regulations contained within your ordinance are designed to reduce the secondary effects studies have demonstrated adult oriented businesses create. Although the law is in flux with regard to how much evidence the city council must have before it for the court to conclude the regulations are designed to serve a substantial governmental interest, caution dictates that including within your ordinance sufficient recitals to explain why the regulations reduce the blight and crime associated with adult oriented businesses will greatly increase the chance that your ordinance will survive judicial scrutiny.

NOTES

1. *City of Erie v. Pap's A.M. TDBA "Kandyland,"* ____ U.S. ____, 120 S.Ct. 1382, 146 L.Ed.2d 265 (2000).
2. All right, I admit it, this would be a whole lot funnier if Letterman's writers actually wrote it. The *Journal* gave them first crack at the article, but they charge.
3. Id. at 120 S.Ct. 1382.
4. The so called "O'Brien Test" was developed by the Supreme Court in *United States v. O'Brien* (1968) 391 U.S.

367, 88 S.Ct. 1673, 20 L.Ed.2d 672. The test finds a content neutral regulation on expressive conduct (like burning your draft card or, presumably, stripping naked in front of paying strangers) to be constitutional if: 1) the regulation is within the power of the government to enact; 2) it furthers an important or substantial governmental interest; 3) it is unrelated to the suppression of free expression (i.e., it is content neutral); and 4) the incidental restrictions on First Amendment freedoms is not greater than essential to the furtherance of that interest. As the court noted in *Ward v. Rock Against Racism* (1989) 491 U.S. ____, 109 S.Ct. 2746, 105 L.Ed.2d 661, the O'Brien Test and the 3-part "content neutral time, place and manner test" are, in reality the same test. "We have held that the O'Brien Test in the last analysis is little, if any, different from the standard applied to time, place or manner restrictions." (Id., 491 U.S. at 798, 109 S.Ct. at 2757, 105 L.Ed.2d at ____.)
5. If your regulation of adult oriented businesses is content based you might want to save the city coffers the cost of litigation and simply amend your ordinance. Content based regulations almost always lose.
6. *City of Renton v. Playtime Theaters, Inc.* (1986) 475 U.S. 41, 89 L.Ed.2d 29, 106 S.Ct. 925.
7. *Young v. American Mini Theaters* (1976) 427 U.S. 50, 49 L.Ed.2d 310, 96 S.Ct. 2440.
8. It is for this reason that it is very important to include in your ordinance appropriate recital demonstrating that the purpose of the regulations is to combat the increased crime, blight and vacancy rates found to be caused by the establishment of adult oriented businesses.
9. As noted above, one iteration of intermediate scrutiny test applicable to content neutral regulations stated that the regulation be "no greater than essential" to serve the substantial governmental interest of reducing the aforementioned secondary effects. This unfortunate use of words has led adult oriented business owners to argue that the regulation must satisfy the "least restrictive means" analysis typically associated with "content based" regulations. Not so. In *Ward v. Rock Against Racism* (1989) 491 U.S. ____, 109 S.Ct. 2746, 105 L.Ed.2d 661, the court concluded that a regulation is sufficiently "narrowly tailored" so long as the regulation promotes a substantial governmental interest that would be achieved less effectively absent the regulation." (491 U.S. at 798, 109 S.Ct. 2757, 105 L.Ed.2d 661 at 680.)
10. See note 2.
11. *Smith v. County of Los Angeles* (1994) 24 Cal.App.4th 990.
12. *Dease v. City of Anaheim* (C.D. Cal. 1993) 826 F.Supp. 336.
13. In *Smith v. County of Los Angeles* (1994) 24 Cal. App.4th 990, the court did note that discretion is not prohibited, it merely must be constrained to operate within a narrow set of parameters. As a result, the *Smith* court appeared to suggest that the legislative body can delegate discretion to the permit authority providing that "In delegating such authority, the local legislative body must provide criteria which are sufficiently precise to meet the constitutional requirement that they be 'narrow, objective and definite.'" (Id., at 1004.)
14. *Smith, supra*, 24 Cal.App.4th at 103.
15. *FW/PBS, Inc. v. City of Dallas* (1990) 493 U.S. 224, 107 L.Ed.2d 603, 110 S.Ct. 596.
16. *TK Video, Inc. v. Denton County* (5th Cir. 1994) 24 F.3d 705.
17. However, it should be noted that courts evaluate the specified approval period based on the complexity of the approval process. Therefore, ordinances requiring a public hearing can justify a slightly longer period of time than ordinances which establish a ministerial approval process.

18. *Baby Tam & Co., Inc. v. City of Las Vegas* (9th Cir. 1998) 154 F.3d 1097.

19. The U.S. Supreme Court upheld a similar time period as adequate "prompt judicial review." (See, *U.S. v. Thirty-Seven Photographs* (1971) 402 U.S. 363, 28 L.Ed.2d 822, 91 S.Ct. 1416.)

20. *Tily B., Inc. v. City of Newport Beach* (1998) 69 Cal.App.4th 1.

21. Id. at 21.

22. Id. at 22.

23. Id. at 23.

24. Id.

25. See, e.g., In *re Lane* (1962) 52 Cal.2d 99, where the court held that "the Penal Code sections covering the criminal aspects of sexual activity are so extensive in their scope that they clearly show an intention by the Legislature to adopt a general scheme for the regulation of the subject."

26. It has been common for adult oriented business owners to enlist the assistance of a theater arts professors to testify, as experts, that the business is actually "theater."

27. *Lancaster v. Municipal Court* (1972) 6 Cal.3d 805 at 808.

28. *Cohen v. Board of Supervisors* (1985) 40 Cal.3d 227 at 296; *EWAP v. City of Los Angeles* (1979) 97 Cal. 3d 179 at 191 (licensing of peep shows); *Eckel v. Davis* (1975) 51 Cal App.3d at 843 (nudity prohibited in public parks and beaches).

29. *Brix v. City of San Rafael* (1979) 92 Cal.App.3d 47 at 53.

30. See, *Barnes v. Glen Theater, Inc.* (1991) 501 U.S. 560, 111 S.Ct. 2456, 115 L.Ed.2d 504, *City of Erie v. Pap's A.M. TDBA "Kandyland"* (2000) ____ U.S. ____, 120 S.Ct. 1382, 146 L.Ed.2d 265, and *Tily B., Inc. v. City of Newport Beach* (1998) 69 Cal.App.4th 1.

31. A word of caution: With the exception of *Tily B.*, each case was decided on a plurality decision.

Editor's Note:

These chapter notes are listed as they were in the original journal article. Questions concerning the legal citations should be directed to the source, which is listed in the footnote at the bottom of the first page of this chapter.

SECTION II: THE BEST PRACTICES

CHAPTER 5

Albany Officials Provide Cities with Legal Guidelines to Regulate Adult Businesses

Susan L. Watson

Municipal zoning regulation of adult business may be locally popular, but it raises serious constitutional issues when the regulation is directed at free expression protected by the federal and state Constitutions. Non-obscene expression, whether in the form of sexually explicit books, magazines, movies, or dancing, has traditionally been found to be entitled to such constitutional protection. When municipal regulations impinge on an adult business's freedom of expression, they lose the presumption of constitutionality that normally applies to zoning regulations, and the burden shifts to local governments to justify the restrictions.

In order to avoid constitutional problems, zoning regulations pertaining to adult uses must be drafted with skill and precision. Prior to adopting such zoning, a local government must usually show that it conducted or relied upon planning studies evidencing the need to protect neighborhoods from the harmful secondary effects of adult businesses. Some studies have identified such adverse secondary effects as urban blight, decreased retail shopping activity and reduced property values. However, courts will strike down regulations that seek to exclude all adult uses through an outright ban. Therefore, adult uses may be restricted (even substantially) within a community through zoning regulations, but may not be entirely prohibited.

Municipalities drafting adult use zoning legislation typically choose between two zoning techniques, which either: 1) concentrate adult uses in a single geographic area of the locality or 2) disperse adult uses using distance requirements. By concentrating adult uses in a specific area of the community, some municipalities believe these uses will affect fewer neighborhoods and can be avoided by persons who are offended by them. Other municipalities have taken the opposite approach and require that sexually oriented uses be separated from one another or from residential areas. By preventing a concentration of these uses, a municipality may attempt to avoid a "skid-row" effect.

In *City of Renton v Playtime Theaters*, 475 US 41, 89 L Ed 2nd 29, 106 S Ct 925 (1986), the United States Supreme Court [provided] a four (4) part test for determining when it is

Originally published as "Municipal Regulation of Adult Uses," *Legal Memorandum LU03*, 2007, by the Office of the General Counsel, Department of State, State of New York, Albany, NY.

permissible to use zoning to single out adult uses without violating the First Amendment of the US Constitution. In determining the constitutional validity of a zoning regulation, courts must consider whether:

1) The predominant purpose of zoning is to suppress the sexually explicit speech itself, or rather, to eliminate the "secondary effects" of adult uses;
2) The zoning regulation furthers a substantial governmental interest;
3) The zoning regulation is "narrowly tailored" to affect only those uses which produced the unwanted secondary effects; and
4) The zoning regulation leaves open reasonable alternative locations for adult uses.

This paper will focus on two New York Court of Appeals cases — *Stringfellow's* I and II — which applied the federal constitutional test in *Renton* and delineated rules for cases relying on Article 1, Section 8 of the New York State Constitution,[1] the free speech provision.

New York City Cases

In 1993, the New York City Division of City Planning conducted an "Adult Entertainment Study" to determine the nature and the impact that adult businesses had in the City. In addition, the City examined similar studies conducted in nine other localities. The City study concluded that, in the areas where they are concentrated, the presence of adult businesses tends to produce negative secondary effects such as increased crime, decreased property values, and reduced shopping and commercial activities.

In October 1995, in response to this study, the New York City Council amended its zoning regulations to place restrictions on the location and size of adult businesses. The zoning amendments were intended to break the concentration of adult businesses in certain neighborhoods by dispersing them.

The New York City zoning amendment applies to various types of "adult establishments" including adult bookstores, adult theaters, adult restaurants, and other adult commercial establishments. The definition of what is an "adult business is keyed to the character of the activity that takes place in such establishments. If the business regularly features movies, photographs, or live performances that emphasize "specified anatomical areas" or "specified sexual activities" and excludes minors by reason of age, it is considered "adult" and therefore covered by the zoning restrictions.

The New York City zoning amendment does not ban adult establishments outright. Rather, it limits the permissible zones or districts in New York City where they may operate, and terminates those businesses that are not located in those permitted districts. Adult uses are only allowed in a number of commercial and manufacturing districts. The zoning amendment specifically requires that, where permitted, adult establishments: (1) must be located at least 500 feet from a school, house of worship, day care center, or residential district; (2) must be located at least 500 feet from any other adult establishment; (3) must be limited to one establishment per zoning lot; and (4) must not exceed 10,000 square feet of floor space. By confining them to industrial and commercial districts and separating them within those districts, New York City used both concentration and distance requirements to control adult uses.

Any adult establishment operating in a zoning district where adult uses are prohibited must either conform to the new zoning or terminate its business within one year of the amendment's effective date. Narrow exceptions exist to this termination requirement for existing businesses which are not in compliance. Also, adult establishments faced with the one-year termination deadline may apply for an extension to the Board of Standards and Appeals, which may permit the applicant to remain open for a limited time to amortize any substantial and unrecovered costs associated with the adult portion of the establishment.

In the case of *Stringfellow's of New York, Ltd., v City of New York ("Stringfellow's I")*, 91 N.Y. 2d 382 (1998), several adult businesses and their patrons brought three actions, consolidated by the lower court, challenging the NYC zoning regulation pertaining to adult establishments. They contended that since the NYC zoning amendment defines adult establishments as those allowing the exhibition of "specified anatomical areas" or "sexual activities," it is a content-based regulation that unlawfully suppresses expression. They claimed it was presumptively invalid under Article 1, Section 8 of the New York State Constitution.

The New York State Court of Appeals disagreed. While recognizing that municipalities possess considerable authority to enact zoning to improve the quality of their residents' lives, the Court noted that zoning authority is not unfettered. Zoning regulations that aim to curb "adult" uses implicate speech or conduct that is protected by Article 1, Section 8 of the New York State Constitution. Consequently, in weighing the validity of such zoning regulations, courts must consider the constitutional values of free expression.

The Court developed a hybrid test, using state and federal constitutional standards, for determining whether zoning regulations are valid under Article 1, Section 8 of the New York State Constitution.

1) The zoning regulation must be justified by concerns unrelated to speech;
2) It must be "no broader than necessary" to achieve its purpose and
3) It must provide alternative locations for adult use businesses.

When existing adult businesses are rendered non-conforming by subsequent zoning amendments and directed to terminate operations, courts must additionally consider whether the amortization provisions allow for reasonable recoupment of the investment in the business.

1. The Zoning Regulation's Purpose Is Unrelated to Speech

As a threshold issue, the Court focused on whether the City's zoning amendments were purposefully directed at controlling the content of the message conveyed through adult businesses or were instead aimed at an entirely separate societal goal. The federal constitutional analysis requires examination of the ordinance's "predominant purpose," while the State constitutional inquiry focuses on whether there has been "a purposeful attempt to regulate speech." The difference in language between the federal and state tests, however, did not significantly affect the outcome, since it was apparent from the legislative history that eliminating the negative secondary effects of adult uses was the City's goal.

Before enacting the zoning amendment, the City Council assembled an extensive legislative record connecting adult establishments and negative secondary effects, including numerous studies on the effects of adult establishments both within and without New York City. The Court found that New York City properly relied on studies from other jurisdictions:

"While none of the other studies considers a municipality which duplicates New York City in terms of variety of neighborhoods and built conditions, ... the findings of adverse secondary effects and the conditions found in these other studies are relevant to the different neighborhoods of New York City."

In view of the legislative record upon which the City Council rested its decision to regulate adult uses, enactment of the zoning amendment was not an impermissible attempt to regulate the content of expression but rather was aimed at the negative secondary effects caused by adult uses, a legitimate governmental purpose.

As to the content of the City's regulation, the Court said:

Nor is it significant that definitions of adult uses in the Amended Zoning Resolution are based in part on the content of the entertainment offered rather than exclusively on the age of the businesses' clientele (cf., Town of Islip v Caviglia, supra, at 557). *The test under both Islip and Renton is not whether the regulated establishments are defined without reference to content but whether the ordinance's goal is unrelated to suppressing that content.* That test is plainly met here. [Emphasis added.]

2. The Zoning Amendment Is No Broader Than Necessary

The Court next held that the City's zoning amendment represents a coherent regulatory scheme narrowly designed to attack the problems associated with adult establishments. The zoning amendment must set forth explicit standards for those who apply them to preclude arbitrary and discriminatory application. The amended zoning must affect only the category of uses that produces the unwanted negative effects. By preventing adult businesses from locating in residential districts while allowing such establishments to locate in manufacturing and commercial districts, the Court found the amendment protects only those communities and community institutions that are most vulnerable to their adverse impacts. Municipalities may constitutionally bar adult establishments from, or within, a specified distance of residentially-zoned areas and facilities in which families and children congregate. Moreover, zoning regulations may be used to prohibit an adult business from operating within a specified distance of another in order to avoid the undesirable impacts associated with concentration of such uses.

3. Reasonable Alternative Avenues of Communication

To further satisfy constitutional requirements, the City needed to assure reasonable alternative avenues of communication. In particular, there must be (1) ample space available for adult uses after the rezoning and (2) no showing by the challenger that enforcement of the ordinance will either substantially reduce the total number of adult outlets or significantly reduce the accessibility of those outlets to their potential patrons.

In determining whether proposed relocation sites are part of an actual business real estate market, the courts have considered such factors as their accessibility to the general public, the surrounding infrastructure, the likelihood of their ever realistically becoming available and, finally, whether the sites are suitable for "some generic commercial enterprise."

In the case of New York City, the zoning amendment's enforcement will lead to the forced relocation of some 84 percent of the City's 177 adult businesses. Given the extent of the dislocation, it was incumbent upon the City to demonstrate that sufficient alternative sites were available. The City asserted that the space available for adult uses constituted over 11 percent of the City's total land area and about 4 percent when reduced by land encumbered by properties that are unlikely to be developed for commercial use. City officials asserted that the amended zoning code leaves at least 500 potential sites available for adult use relocation. All of the areas in Manhattan zoned for adult use and at least 80 percent of the land area in the other boroughs are within a 10-minute walk from a subway line or a major bus route. The Court concluded that the City satisfied its burden of showing that the space zoned for adult uses is adequate to accommodate the 177 existing adult businesses.

In their response, the adult businesses failed to make concrete allegations as to precisely how many of the 500 potential receptor sites identified by the City were unavailable. The criticisms raised by the adult businesses about various individual sites did not provide an adequate counter to the City's supported claim that, as a whole, there are more than enough receptor sites to accommodate the existing adult entertainment industry. Any further challenge to a similar zoning plan would need to analyze, with particularity and specificity, the sufficiency of alternative locations zoned for adult businesses.

4. Termination and Amortization

Finally, the Court rejected the claim that enforcement of the zoning amendment would lead to an unconstitutional taking because substantial investments in the businesses would be lost if they are required to relocate. The Court said that no taking claim existed because the zoning amendments provide for hardship extensions. Under these provisions, a nonconforming adult establishment may apply to the Board of Standards and Appeals for permission to continue to operate beyond the one-year amortization period set forth in the statue where it can show that it has made substantial expenditures related to the adult use, that such expenditures cannot be recouped within a year and that the requested extension is the minimum period necessary to permit such recoupment.

Stringfellow's II

Some adult businesses have tried some novel approaches to avoid having to comply with New York City's adult zoning restrictions. In a case that generated a good deal of publicity, *City of New York v Stringfellow's of New York, and Ten's World-Class Cabaret* (*"Stringfellow's II"*), 96 N.Y. 2d 51 (2001), the Court of Appeals held that topless entertainment club could not admit minors to avoid being defined as an adult business under the New York City zoning regulations.

Under the City's zoning, a business is considered "adult" if it regularly features movies, photographs, or live performances that emphasize "specified anatomical areas" or "specified sexual activities" and is not customarily open to the general public during such features because *it excludes minors by reason of age.* In order to circumvent the City's zoning law, Ten's Cabaret instituted a policy of *admitting children,* accompanied by a parent, if both sign statements that the child will not smoke or drink alcoholic beverages and will not be harmed by seeing "exposed female breasts." By allowing children onto its premises, Ten's argued it was not an "adult" business.

Supreme Court Justice Crane agreed and ruled that Ten's adult cabaret was not subject to the City's zoning law since it did not exclude minors by reason of age.[2] The Appellate Division reversed Justice Crane[3] and the Court of Appeals affirmed. The Court ruled that Ten's was attempting to make "an end run" around the City zoning law. It said that the letter of a statute will not be slavishly followed when it leads away from the true intent and purpose of the legislation and statutes are not to be read with literalness that destroys meaning, intention, purpose or beneficial end for which the statute has been designed. As a matter of policy, it is certainly highly inappropriate to encourage adult business to allow minors to enter their establishment, simply to circumvent the zoning.

Conclusion

In conclusion, the Court of Appeals held that New York City's effort to address the negative secondary effects of adult establishments is not constitutionally objectionable under any of the applicable federal or state constitutional standards. The *Stringfellow's* decisions are an important adult use case for claims brought under the New York State Constitution.

NOTES

1. Article 1, Section 8 of the New York State Constitution provides in pertinent part: "Every citizen may freely speak, write and publish his sentiments on all subjects, being responsible for the abuse of that right; and no law shall be passed to restrain or abridge the liberty of speech or of the press."

2. *City of New York v Stringfellow's of New York*, 11/10/98 N.Y.L.J. 26 (col. 1).

3. 253 AD 2d 110 (1st Dept. 1999). The matter was remanded to Justice Crane, who subsequently granted the City of New York partial summary judgment on the issue of whether defendant's cabaret falls within the definition of adult eating or drinking establishment contained in New York City Zoning Resolution. On appeal, the Appellate Division affirmed. 268 AD2d 216.

CHAPTER 6

Beckley's Elected Leaders Adopt Zoning Laws to Mitigate the Negative Secondary Impact of SOBs

Emmett S. Pugh III

The City of Beckley's regulation of sexually-oriented businesses is an attempt to mitigate the negative secondary impacts associated with such businesses.

One of the most significant methods of regulating sexually-oriented businesses — and typically the first approach adopted by a community — is to use zoning ordinances to restrict the location of sexually-oriented businesses (SOBs) within the boundaries of the municipality. "Place" regulations are one of the most effective methods of protecting communities from the negative secondary impacts of sexually-oriented businesses. Further study may be required due to the evolving body of law and new studies regarding the negative secondary impacts of SOBs. Retroactive action is generally not possible, requiring a preventative approach in order to effectively resolve SOB issues. Thus, the ordinance must be defensible based on reasonably expected secondary effects.

Because this is a free speech issue, any related litigation takes place at the Federal level, resulting in higher litigation and legal expenses.

The City of Beckley's regulation of sexually-oriented businesses is an attempt to mitigate the negative secondary impacts associated with such businesses. It is recognized that sexually-oriented businesses, due to their nature, have serious objectionable operational characteristics, particularly when they are located in proximity to each other, thereby contributing to urban blight and downgrading the quality of life in the adjacent area. Therefore, the City desires to minimize and control these adverse impacts and thereby protect the health, safety, and welfare of the citizenry, protect the citizens from increased crime, preserve the quality of life, preserve the property values and character of surrounding neighborhoods and deter the spread of urban blight.

Local government's ability to regulate sexually-oriented businesses through zoning regulations that are content-neutral was upheld in the Federal Court case Richland Bookmart, Inc. dba Town and Country v Randall E. Nichols (1998), 137 F.3d 435 (6th Cir.).

In Richland, the Court found substantial government interest in Tennessee's purpose to "reduce crime, open sex and solicita-

Originally published as a portion of Chapter 15 — "Zoning Regulations," *Comprehensive Plan*, August 2002, by the Department of Housing and Community Development, City of Beckley, WV.

tion of sex, and preserving the aesthetic and commercial character of the neighborhood surrounding adult establishments." [Note: In J.L. Spoons, Inc. v City of Brunswick (1998), 18 F.Supp. 2d 782 (E.D. Ohio), the Court did not rule on the government interest, but it noted the government interest was to "regulate sexually oriented businesses in order to promote the health, safety, morals, and general welfare of the citizens of the City, and to establish reasonable and uniform regulations to prevent the deleterious location and concentration of sexually-oriented businesses within the City."]

Distance requirements for sexually-oriented businesses have been established based on studies examining how sexually-oriented businesses impact crime statistics within the immediate area they are located. For instance, a study conducted by the City of Indianapolis, Indiana found that sex-related crimes occur four (4) times more frequently in neighborhoods with a residential character located adjacent to a sex-oriented business than in commercial areas with a sex-oriented business. Other studies have attempted to establish quantitatively how far reaching the secondary impacts of sexually-oriented businesses. The analysis resulting from these studies indicate that additional or expanded sexually-oriented businesses led to significantly increased property (e.g., burglary, theft, auto theft) and personal crimes (e.g., assault, robbery) within a 1,000 foot radius of the sites.

Additionally, where the time frames of operation overlap between sexually-oriented businesses and other facilities (e.g., schools, churches, parks, playgrounds), there is even more potential for harm to legitimate users.

Vulnerable populations that use these facilities are exposed to the potential harm from the secondary impacts of sexually-oriented businesses. This can take the form of personal or property crime, harassment or propositioning of pedestrians. When this occurs, legitimate users and neighborhood residents are typically excluded or driven away by the illicit activity.

Detailed studies, over time, have clearly documented the negative secondary impacts associated with sexually-oriented business. The City of Beckley, in an attempt to protect the health, safety, and welfare of the citizenry, has imposed zoning regulations to reasonably mitigate the negative secondary impacts associated with sexually-oriented businesses.

Within the City of Beckley, sexually-oriented businesses are allowed as conditionally permitted uses in the General Business District (B-2) by a special exception from the board of Zoning Appeals.

The ordinance states that sexually-oriented businesses may not be located within one thousand feet (1,000') of a residential zone, church, school, park, library, or other sexually-oriented business.

> Detailed studies over time have clearly documented the negative secondary impacts associated with sexually-oriented business.

Portions of the City of Beckley's zoning ordinance relate to the regulation of sexually-oriented businesses (SOBs). The regulations were adopted by the City's elected officials on August 13, 2002, and are a part of the community's official zoning regulations. Specifically, Chapter 11 of the City's Comprehensive Plan contains their city-wide zoning requirements for all private businesses, including SOBs.

Those regulations that focus on SOBs include standard definitions, allowable business use districts, supplemental regulations concerning SOBs only and, lastly, a section on the penalties, remedies, and violations associated with these zoning regulations. The highlights of those regulations relating to the City of Beckley's requirements for SOBs are shown below as one example of recent legislation in this area of zoning law.

Details of the Zoning Ordinance

Purpose

This chapter is enacted for the general purpose of dividing the city into zones or districts, restricting and regulating therein the location, erection, construction, reconstruction, alteration, and use of buildings, structures, and land for trade, industry, residence, and other specified uses; to regulate the intensity of the use of lot areas and to regulate and determine the area of open spaces surrounding such buildings; to establish building lines and the location of buildings designed for specified manufacturing, business, residential and other uses within such areas; to fix standards to which buildings or structures shall conform therein; to prohibit uses, buildings, or structures incompatible with the character of such districts, respectively; to prevent additions to and alterations or remodeling of existing buildings or structures in such a way as to avoid the restrictions and limitations lawfully imposed hereunder; to limit congestion in the public streets by providing for the off-street parking and loading and unloading of vehicles; providing for the gradual elimination of nonconforming uses of land, buildings, and structures; and prescribing penalties for the violation of the chapter; to lessen congestion; to provide adequate light and air; to prevent the overcrowding of land; to conserve the taxable value of land and buildings throughout the city; and to promote the public health, safety, and general welfare.

Definitions

For the purpose of this chapter, certain terms and words are hereby defined; words used in the present tense shall include the future; words used in the singular number shall include the plural.

Adult amusement or entertainment: Amusement or entertainment which is distinguished or characterized by an emphasis on acts or material depicting, describing, or relating to specific sexual activities or specified anatomical areas, including, but not limited to, topless or bottomless dancers, exotic dancers, strippers, male or female impersonators, or similar entertainment.

Adult bookstore/adult novelty store/adult video store: An establishment which utilizes ten (10) percent or more of its gross public floor area for the purpose of retail sale, and/or rental, and/or display by image-producing devices, of sexually-oriented material for any consideration; or ten (10) percent or more of the stock-in-trade consists of sexually-oriented materials.

Adult cabaret: A building or portion of a building regularly featuring dancing or other live entertainment if the dancing or entertainment that constitutes the primary live entertainment is distinguished or characterized by an emphasis on the exhibiting of specific sexual activities or specified anatomical areas for observation by patrons therein; or a nightclub, bar, restaurant, or similar commercial establishment that regularly features persons who appear in a state of nudity or semi-nudity; or which exhibit films, motion pictures, video cassettes, slides, or other photographic reproductions that are characterized by the depiction or description of specific sexual activities or specified anatomical areas.

Adult mini motion picture theater: An enclosed building with a capacity of less than fifty (50) persons used for presenting material distinguished or characterized by an emphasis on depicting or describing specific sexual activities or specified anatomical areas.

Adult motel: A hotel, motel, or similar establishment that:

(1) Offers accommodations to the public for any form of consideration and provides patrons with closed circuit television transmissions, films, motion pictures, video cassettes, slides, or other photographic reproductions that are characterized by the depiction of specific sexual activities or specified anatomical areas; and has a sign visible from the public right-of-way that advertised the availability of this adult type of photographic reproductions; or

Nude model studio: Any place where a person who displays specified anatomical areas and is provided to be observed, sketched, drawn, painted, sculptured, photographed or similarly depicted by other persons who pay money or any form of consideration. A nude model studio shall not include a proprietary school licensed by the State of West Virginia or a college, junior college, or university supported entirely or in part by public taxation; a private college or university that maintains and operates educational programs in which credits are transferable to a college, junior college, or university supported entirely or partly by taxation; or in a structure:

(1) That has no sign visible from the exterior of the structure and no other advertising that indicates a model who displays specified anatomical areas is available for viewing; and

(2) Where in order to participate in a class a student must enroll at least three (3) days in advance of the class; and

(3) Where no more than one (1) model displaying specified anatomical areas is on the premises at any one (1) time.

Sexual encounter center: Any building or structure which contains, or is used for, commercial entertainment where the patron, directly or indirectly, is charged a fee to engage in personal contact with, or to allow personal contact by employees, devices or equipment, or by personnel provided by the establishment which appeals to the prurient interest of the patron, to include, but not to be limited to, bath houses, massage parlors, and related or similar activities.

Sexual excitement: Means the condition of the human male or female genitals, when in a state of sexual stimulation or arousal.

Sexually-oriented business: An establishment which advertises or holds itself out in any forum as "XXX," "adult," "sex," or otherwise provides a service or product distinguished or characterized by an emphasis on sexually oriented material, specific sexual activities, or specified anatomical areas. Sexually oriented businesses include the following type of establishments: adult amusement or entertainment, adult bookstore, adult cabaret, adult mini–motion picture theater, adult motel, adult motion picture arcade, adult motion picture theater, adult novelty store, adult theater, adult video store, escort agency, lingerie modeling studio, massage parlor, nude model studio, or sexual encounter center.

Sexually-oriented material: Any media or novelty that is distinguished or characterized by emphasis on matter depicting, describing, or relating to specific sexual activities or specified anatomical areas. Media includes any book, magazine, newspaper, pamphlet, writing, poster, print, drawing, picture, undeveloped picture, pictorial representation, slide, transparency, motion picture film, video cassettes, videotape, videotape production, CD-ROM, DVD, laser disc, figure, image, description, phonograph recording, tape recording, magnetic media, sound recording, game, novelty, or any electrical or electronic reproduction of anything that is or may be used as a means of communication. A sexually oriented novelty includes any instruments, devices, or paraphernalia that are designed as representations of human genital organs or female breast, or designed or marketed primarily for use to stimulate human genital organs, including leather goods marketed or presented in a context to suggest their use for sadomasochistic practices.

Specified anatomical areas: Exhibition, display or depiction of:

(1) The human male genitals in a discernibly turgid state, even if completely and opaquely covered; or

(2) Less than completely and opaquely-covered human genitals, pubic region, buttocks, or a female breast below a point immediately above the top of the areola, but shall not include any portion of the cleavage of the human female breast, exhibited by dress, blouse, skirt, leotard, bathing suit, or other wearing apparel provided the areola is not exposed in whole or in part.

Specific sexual activities: Activities which include:

(1) The fondling or other erotic touching of human genitals, pubic region, buttocks, anus, or female breast; or

(2) Sex acts, normal or perverted, actual or simulated, including sexual excitement, penetration with a finger or male organ into any orifice in another person, oral copulation, masturbation, intercourse, sodomy, or bestiality; or

(3) Offers a sleeping room for rent for a period of time that is less than ten (10) hours; or

(4) Allows a tenant or occupant of a sleeping room to sub-rent the room for a period of time that is less than ten (10) hours.

Adult motion picture arcade: Any place to which the public is permitted or invited wherein coin or slug-operated or electronically, electrically, or mechanically controlled, still or motion picture machines, projectors, or other image-producing devices are maintained to show images to five (5) or fewer persons per machine at any one (1) time, and where the images so displayed are distinguished or characterized by an emphasis on depicting or describing specific sexual activities or specified anatomical areas.

Adult motion picture theater: An enclosed building with a capacity of fifty (50) or more persons used for presenting material distinguished or characterized by an emphasis on depicting or describing specific sexual activities or specific anatomical areas.

Adult novelty store: See "adult bookstore."

Adult theater: A theater, concert hall, auditorium, or similar commercial establishment that regularly features persons who expose specified anatomical areas, or live performances that are characterized by the exposure of specified anatomical areas or by specific sexual activities.

Adult video store: See "adult bookstore."

Use Districts

The city is hereby divided into ten (10) use districts:

(1) R-1 one-family district
(2) R-2 general residential district
(3) R-3 multiple-family district
(4) R-5 multiple-family high rise
(5) R-6 elderly high rise
(6) O/R office/residential transitional district
(7) B-1 neighborhood business district
(8) B-2 general commercial-business district
(9) B-3 "Courthouse Square" central downtown multi-use district
(10) M manufacturing district

General Business District

Permitted use regulations. Permitted uses are:

(1) Agricultural implement sales and service conducted wholly within a completely enclosed building;
(2) Air conditioning and heating sales and services;
(3) Antique shop;
(4) Auction rooms;
(5) Auditoriums;
(6) Auditoriums, indoor;
(7) Auto convenience mart;
(8) Automobile or trailer sales (new or used);
(9) Other uses outlined in the law.

Conditionally Permitted Uses

Conditionally permitted uses. The following uses are permitted as a conditional use and require a conditional use permit in accordance with section 15-5(d).

(1) Cemeteries, crematories, or mausoleums;
(2) Child day care center/nursery school or facility, subject to section 15-24(k);
(3) Churches and accessory buildings used for religious teaching, subject to RLUIPA;

(4) Community or recreational centers;

(5) Dry cleaning plant or facility;

(6) Elderly day care;

(7) Emergency services and service buildings/garages (e.g., ambulance, fire, police, rescue);

(8) Golf and miniature golf courses;

(9) Gymnasiums;

(10) Hospitals or sanitariums;

(11) Kennels, subject to section 15-24(j);

(12) Park/playgrounds (public or private);

(13) Public administration building or any other publicly-owned structure;

(14) Public utility facilities (i.e., filtration plant or pumping station, heat or power plant, transformer station and other similar facilities);

(15) Railroad right-of-way;

(16) Schools, public or private;

(17) Sexually-oriented businesses subject to section 15-24(b);

Sexually-oriented businesses

(1) Sexually-oriented businesses are allowed in a B-2 zoning district by conditional use permit from the board of zoning appeals and that sexually-oriented businesses should not be located within one thousand (1,000) feet of a residential zone, church, school, park or other sexually-oriented business.

(2) Prohibition

  (a) No person shall exercise supervisory control, manager, operate, cause the establishment, or permit the establishment of any of the sexually-oriented businesses as defined in section 15-3. In addition, no person shall exercise supervisory control, manage, operate, cause the establishment, or permit the establishment of any of the sexually-oriented businesses, as defined in section 15-24(b) within:

    1. One thousand (1,000) feet from any other sexually-oriented business. The one thousand (1,000) feet shall be measured in a straight line from the nearest point of the wall of the portion of the building in which a sexually-oriented business is conducted, to the nearest point of the wall of the portion of the building in which another sexually-oriented business is conducted;

    2. One thousand (1,000) [feet] from a church. Church as used herein shall mean all contiguous property owned or leased by a church upon which is located the principal church building or structure, irrespective of any interior lot lines; the one thousand (1,000) feet shall be measured in a straight line from the nearest point of the wall of the portion of the building in which a sexually-oriented business is conducted to the nearest point of the church; provided, however, for a church use located in a building principally used for commercial office purposes (as in a shopping center), the one thousand (1,000) feet shall be measured to the nearest building wall of the portion of the building used for church purposes;

    3. One thousand (1,000) feet from a school of the type which offers a compulsory education curriculum; school as used herein shall mean all contiguous property owned or leased by a school upon which is located the principal school building(s) irrespective of any interior lot lines; the one thousand (1,000) feet shall be measured in a straight line from the nearest point of the wall of the portion of the building in which a sexually-oriented business is conducted to the nearest point of the school;

4. One thousand (1,000) feet from a public park or private park. The one thousand (1,000) feet shall be measured in a straight line from the nearest point of the wall of the portion of the building in which a sexually-oriented business is conducted to the nearest point on the property of the park; and

5. One thousand (1,000) feet from areas zoned residential. The one thousand (1,000) feet shall be measured in a straight line from the nearest point of the wall of the portion of the building in which a sexually-oriented business is conducted, to the nearest point on a residential zoning district boundary line (not including residentially zoned expressway right-of-way).

(b) Provided further that the board of zoning appeals may permit, by conditional use permit, sexually-oriented businesses, as defined in section 15-3 in a B-1 area, subject to the distance limitations set forth under section 15-24(b)(1)a. 1., 2., 3., 4., and 5.

(c) The establishment of a sexually-oriented business shall include the opening of such business as a new business, the relocation of such business, the enlargement of such business in greater scope or area, or the conversion of an existing business location to any of the uses described in section 15-24(b).

(3) Nonconforming sexually-oriented business uses.

(a) Any business lawfully existing as of the effective date of this chapter that is in violation hereof shall be deemed a nonconforming use. Such a nonconforming use will be permitted to continue for a period not to exceed two (2) years, unless sooner terminated for any reason whatsoever or voluntarily discontinued for a period of thirty (30) days or more. Such nonconformity uses shall not be increased, enlarged, extended, or altered except that the use may be changed to a conforming use. In the event that two (2) or more sexually-oriented businesses are within one thousand (1,000) feet of one another and otherwise in a permissible zone, the first such sexually-oriented business licensed and continually operating at a particular location shall be conforming use and the later established business(es) shall be nonconforming.

(b) Any sexually-oriented business lawfully operating as a conforming use is not rendered a nonconforming use by the location of a church, school, park, or residential district within one thousand (1,000) feet of a sexually-oriented business.

Penalties, Remedies, and Violations

(a) *Violation and penalty.* Any person, firm, or corporation who shall violate any provision of this chapter or shall fail to comply with any of the requirements thereof, or who shall excavate for, erect, construct, enlarge, reconstruct, add to, alter, repair, move, maintain, use, and/or occupy any building, other structure, and/or land in violation of an approved plan or directive of the zoning officer, planning commission, board of zoning appeals or common council, or of a building permit or certificate of occupancy shall for each violation, on conviction thereof, pay a fine or penalty of not less than ten dollars ($10.00), nor more than three hundred dollars ($300.00). Each and every day that such violation continues may constitute a separate offense. (Refer to City of Beckley Code Chapter 2, Part 2, section 1-8.)

(b) *Violation as nuisance.* Any building or structure erected, raised, or converted on land or premises used in violation of any of the provisions of this chapter or of any regulations in this chapter or of any regulations made under authority conferred hereby, is hereby declared to be a common nuisance, and the owner of the building, structure, land or premises shall be liable for maintaining a common nuisance.

(c) The planning commission of the city, the board of zoning appeals, common council, or the zoning officer may institute a suit for injunction in the circuit court of this county, to restrain any person, firm, or corporation, or a governmental unit from violating the provisions of this chapter, or of any regulation in this chapter, or any regulation made under authority hereby conferred. The planning commission of the city, the board of zoning appeals, common council, or the zoning officer may institute a suit for a mandatory injunction directing a person, firm or corporation, or a governmental unit to remove a structure erected in violation of the terms of this chapter or of any regulation in this chapter or in violation of any regulation made under authority conferred hereby.

Editor's Note:

The entire Zoning Regulation for the City of Beckley is contained on their website, which is listed in the Regional Resource Directory.

CHAPTER 7

Boston Restores Historic Buildings to Eliminate the Combat Zone

Joe Albanese *and* Scott Martinelli

Preserving and reusing historic buildings renew the economic life of neighborhoods. Boston is a city steeped in tradition. From the Old North Church to the Public Garden, history abounds. Some of Boston's oldest structures are historic commercial buildings that, despite their place in Boston's past, have suffered from years of neglect. A number of factors, including a suburban and office tower building boom in the 1980s and the economic downturn of the early 1990s, dissuaded owners from investing in maintaining or upgrading historic commercial buildings. In extreme cases, buildings stood empty for more than a decade.

In the last five years, however, times have changed. Many of Boston's older commercial buildings are finding new lives as 21st-century office and retail space. After years of inactivity, Boston's original skyscraper — the Custom House — recently was converted into timeshare condominiums. In the city's financial district, a 19th-century granite warehouse located at 163 State Street has been converted into an extended-stay hotel and the art deco Batterymarch Building has been transformed into a mixed-use facility housing retail and food services on the ground floor, a branch of Northeastern University on the podium floors, and a mid-priced hotel on the upper floors.

The recent redevelopment of the Liberty Tree Building is one example of the far-reaching effects that renovated buildings can have on their surroundings. Erected in 1850 near the site of the Liberty Tree, a large elm tree that became a symbol of resistance to British rule prior to the Revolutionary War, the Liberty Tree Building has a long history as part of Boston's commercial and cultural landscape.

The Liberty Tree Building is located in what was once known as Boston's Garment District and later nicknamed the Combat Zone for the hordes of armed forces personnel who used to have their uniforms tailored at area shops. The Garment District thrived for most of the 20th century, but 30 years ago, when the city zoned the area for adult entertainment, the garment industry suffered. A few years later, when the local army and navy bases closed down, the Combat Zone hit rock bottom. Buildings such as the Liberty Tree were either converted into adult entertainment outlets or pool halls or left vacant. For nearly 20 years the Combat Zone was one of Boston's most downtrodden areas.

In the early 1990s, the economy im-

Originally published as "Restoration Renaissance," *Urban Land*, Vol. 57, No. 12, December 1998, by the Urban Land Institute, Washington, DC. Reprinted with permission of the publisher.

proved and the Combat Zone started to heal. Plans to close or tear down strip clubs were drafted. Drug use and prostitution began to drop off. And the Liberty Tree building, vacant since 1988 except for a single adult video store on the first floor, was shopped around Boston by its owner, Kevin Fitzgerald, president of Liberty Tree Associates, as retail and commercial space. In June 1997, the Massachusetts Registry of Motor Vehicles agreed to locate its new Boston branch in the building, and the Liberty Tree reclaimed its lost stature. Reopened this past April after comprehensive renovations by Boston-based Shawmut Design and Construction, the building has renewed economic life in the area as both registry employees and visitors help to revitalize the Combat Zone.

What has sparked this recent trend? And how can a building left partially or completely vacant for years be converted into a modern facility?

The Liberty Tree redevelopment is the result of an ongoing trend in Boston and across the country not only to preserve historic buildings but also to find new uses for them. The force driving this movement is the strong real estate market. In Boston, for example, vacancy rates for commercial space are the lowest in the country and average rental rates for Class A space have soared to more than $40 per square foot.

"The current demand for and cost of renting office and retail space in Boston are very high," says Ira Baline, senior associate at Bergmeyer Associates, a Boston architecture and interior design firm. "Conditions are such that Boston owners are getting an average of $40 per square foot for newer Class A space and $20 to $30 for Class B space. Higher prospective rents help owners convert older, Class C buildings into functioning Class B buildings," he points out. "But the conditions that existed in a depressed marketplace made those conversions difficult to do. Today's strong market allows owners to find tenants willing to relocate into historic buildings and

sign the long-term leases necessary to finance the extensive renovations they require."

While the strong market has enabled owners to view their historic buildings differently, why would a tenant such as the Massachusetts Registry of Motor Vehicles move into a building that requires thousands of dollars and months of renovation rather than move into or construct a new facility?

Desirability. An obvious advantage of historic buildings is that they already exist. Boston is an old city, and finding available buildable lots within the downtown commercial core is increasingly difficult. Ten years ago, migrating to an office park in the suburbs was an attractive option. Today, the philosophy has changed and the desire to be in downtown Boston has increased.

"In the past, public policy encouraged suburban development, but I think we are in the midst of a real turnaround," comments Stanley Smith, director of Historic Boston, Inc., an organization founded in 1960 to preserve Boston's historic buildings. "The hallmark of civilization has been to get people together, and cities like Boston do that," he says.

Not only are tenants trying to get into the city, they are trying to get into older buildings, whose historic charm they find more attractive than the prospect of redeveloping a site. "People are realizing more and more what historic buildings have to offer," observes Michael Cannizzo, an architect with the Boston Landmarks Commission (BLC). "Because of their unique details and characteristics, people want to work and shop in them."

Location. Boston's newer buildings have a difficult time duplicating another attribute: location. "The three basic rules of real estate have always been location, location, location," says Fitzgerald. "Older buildings have it. New buildings have to create it."

Most older buildings in Boston are located on or near one of the city's four subway lines, an advantage to both retail and office tenants because customers have easy access to shops and employees have an alternative means of getting to work. Accessibility was one of the main reasons the state found the Liberty Tree Building so attractive — it sits directly above a subway station. Access to public transportation is a real benefit in any city, but especially in a city as congested as Boston, where the country's largest highway construction project is in progress.

Change in Philosophy. The new interest shown by both owners and tenants is accompanied by a recent change in the philosophy of Boston preservationists that has helped create new opportunities for adaptive uses. When the preservation movement first started, the goal was simply to preserve structures for the sake of preservation. That ideal has evolved into "preservation with a purpose": maintaining the building's historic character but finding a reuse option as well. This is a more realistic approach to preservation because there is a greater change of attracting a tenant and because city governments are more likely to support or fund a project that promises to have a positive impact on the local economy.

Renovation Challenges

Challenging the Boston business community's perceptions of historical buildings was a psychological challenge. The physical challenge comes when these often-dormant 19th-century landmarks are converted into functioning 21st-century office and retail spaces. From upgrading a building's internal mechanical and structural systems to preserving its external façade, there are countless issues associated with adapting buildings for new uses.

Interior Renovation versus Leasable Space. To attract a tenant, an owner must provide modern, amenity-filled spaces where small spaces once existed. Significant alterations are required to modernize a building's interior layout, mechanical systems, and exits. Recouping the capital necessary to finance renovations, however, requires that an owner

first maximize the building's leasable space. The floor plates of historic buildings, especially of some of the smaller buildings in Boston, were not designed for 21st-century uses. Structural support columns and quirky layouts eat into rentable space. Installing new building systems can further reduce leasing space to the point that renovating no longer is cost effective, forcing the development team to devise plans for installations that maximize space.

In the Liberty Tree Building, a stairway leading from the lobby to the second floor was needed to alleviate the passenger load on the elevator system. The existing monumental stairway, located on top of a subway station entrance, did not meet current structural codes. Locating the stairway in another section of the building was not an option because it would take away too much space. The development team was forced to place a stairway in the existing location, without affecting the hundreds of people who enter the subway station daily. With careful planning, a portion of the subway entrance was removed and the new staircase was installed without compromising structural safety or interfering with foot traffic.

Increasing Space. Historic buildings often have large floor-to-ceiling heights, which can allow building of mezzanines. "Mezzanines are a common way to add space within the existing footprint of a structure," says Baline. A mezzanine built on the fourth floor of the Liberty Tree Building added 5 percent, or 2,500 square feet, to the building's 45,000 square feet.

Surprises. While improving exits and upgrading mechanical systems are obvious renovations, there can be "surprises," issues stemming from years of unabated deterioration behind a building's walls. Most surprises are linked to the building's structure and stability, such as load-bearing walls and foundations. These issues cannot be completely determined in a preliminary, noninvasive exploration. Only after the demolition process has begun can the structural system be fully evaluated.

Unseen water damage is a typical surprise. For years, water leaked into the interior of the Liberty Tree Building, severely eroding wood and masonry joints and in many places causing steel to rust and expand, compromising the building's structural integrity.

Hazardous materials — asbestos, lead paint, contaminated soil — are another common surprise. Because records from 100 years ago are not as thorough as they are today, the presence of hazardous materials, such as asbestos, is rarely documented and can be a real obstacle if removal has not been scheduled. In addition, many materials considered toxic today were not known to be harmful when most historic buildings were built. The process is further complicated by new regulations governing the safe removal and disposal of these materials.

Preparing for surprises before a project gets underway is crucial to its success. "Extensive beforehand planning and drawing on the experience of the design/development team as to what to expect are the best ways to anticipate surprises," says Baline. In an empty building with few finishes, such as an old mill, preliminary examinations will reveal most structural problems. But in urban buildings that have had many uses, the original structure will be more difficult to identify and assess.

To ensure that surprises do not delay the project schedule, the owner should set aside a contingency fund — ideally, a single fund instead of separate funds set aside by subcontractors. This helps keep costs down, since the owner can control disbursements. A thorough building exploration should be able to identify 80 to 90 percent of potential problems.

Exterior Renovations. The interior can have energy-efficient lighting, endless computer stations, and modern elevators, but the exterior must represent the building's past. "Identifying the important features of a building and how to preserve them are the keys to renovating the exterior," notes Cannizzo.

One way to accomplish this is to select a period in the building's history and restore the exterior to reflect that period. Although this is not an "authentic" restoration, it is an acceptable method of office building restoration for organizations such as the BLC. For an adaptive use, the goal is to work the essential historical characteristics into the plan as much as possible. "In an adaptive use, it's not necessary to restore the entire exterior to an exact date," says Cannizzo. "Restoring the quintessential elements of the building's character is what's important."

All of the work on the exterior of the Liberty Tree Building was performed in accordance with the BLC's preservation guidelines and the U.S. Department of the Interior's guidelines for rehabilitating historic buildings. The exterior was restored — using a matching brick that was difficult to obtain — primarily to a period in the late 1800s to early 1900s, when the building was a cornerstone of the Garment District. Essential elements, such as a plaque commemorating the location of the Liberty Tree that reads "Sons of Liberty 1766: Independence of their Country, 1776," look today as they did 150 years ago.

Some sections of the Liberty Tree Building's exterior were not restored to the early 1900s. The existing roof was completely replaced with new slate and copper because the slate had exceeded its normal useful life of 100 years. The building's wood windows were modernized by replacing the existing single glazing with insulating glass that meets the requirements of the state's energy code.

Community Impact

For the owner, tenant, and team of architects and builders, bringing about the rebirth of a historic building is a great source of pride. But that is nothing compared with what a building can do for its neighborhood, in both economic and social terms. A renovated building can be a catalyst for change. Even in sections as undesirable as the Combat Zone once was, renovated buildings can spark an economic rebirth that in turn can positively affect the area's social makeup. The key is finding an initial tenant or tenants who have the vision to look past an area's present condition to its future potential. "It's a domino effect," explains Fitzgerald. "Getting the first tenants, and it's not easy, will get the ball rolling for the entire neighborhood."

With a foundation in place, it is just a matter of time before the area begins to reshape itself. Socially, buildings become a source of pride for residents and often result in the renovation of neighboring buildings as local owners try to keep pace; economically, the renovated buildings, whether office or retail space, will greatly increase foot traffic in the area. "Once more people start coming into the area, other tenants will want to be there," says Baline. "The market is where the people are."

The Liberty Tree is one of the first buildings in the Combat Zone to undergo renovation. Along with the recently renovated China Trade Building and the Hayden Building — designed by renowned architect H.H. Richardson in 1875 and, after renovations by Shawmut Design and Construction in 1995, now home to the Penang Restaurant and a branch of the Liberty Bank — the Liberty Tree Building has had a substantial impact on the community as registry employees dine in local restaurants and registry visitors shop in nearby stores.

The renovation of these initial buildings has greatly increased the entire Combat Zone's viability. In the early 1990s, single-digit rental rates (per square foot) were common in the area. Now, as improvements are being made, average rates are in the high teens, allowing owners the opportunity to renovate many older commercial buildings. Nearby Lafayette Place recently was converted into new office space, and two other buildings were renovated for Emerson College — a dormitory and retail space on Boylston Street and a classroom facility on Tremont Street. Another building on Tremont Street now serves as a residence hall for Suffolk University. New construction also has become prevalent in the area, shown by the massive Millennium Place development, a residential, entertainment, and shopping complex that will open in 2000.

Once Boston's black eye, the Combat Zone is beginning to regain its historical prominence. The Massachusetts Registry of Motor Vehicles keeps the Combat Zone buzzing during the day while the Penang Restaurant has become one of Boston's most popular eateries, bringing in patrons seven nights a week. Emerson College and Suffolk University have ensured that the student consumer will be a permanent part of the area's landscape. And once complete, Millennium Place — which includes a Sony theater complex capable of seating 4,500 people, a 6,000-square-foot Reebok store, and an additional 60,000 square feet of retail space — will have a significant effect on the area.

"For the first time in 40 years, the streets around the Combat Zone will have an overwhelming retail theme that will again be attractive to shoppers," says Fitzgerald. "This is quite a turnaround."

CHAPTER 8

Charleston Business Leaders Turned Around Their Downtown

Robert W. Bivens

Charleston, WV, is a city of 51,394 residents in the heart of the Appalachian Mountains. From years of passing the city on Interstate I-64, I was impressed that it appeared to be unusually compact and active, so one day when I toured the downtown and talked with residents, I concluded that something special had been done there. Upon inquiry I learned that in the 1970s, several downtown business leaders met to determine what they could do to reverse the downward spiral that they saw threatening their downtown.

First, a large enclosed downtown mall was built, complete with sheltered parking. In 1982, they formed Charleston Renaissance Corporation to expand downtown improvement efforts. Consultants were engaged and a target program of 16 ambitious projects was conceived. The business community and local government leaders pursued these with rare determination and continuity.

The novel feature of their work was that three top business leaders led the team effort for nearly 15 years. This is no doubt a record for continuity of leadership in private-sector organizations. The Charleston Renaissance board of directors was composed of 60 top business leaders. They joined forces with city officials in a remarkable private-public partnership. Former presidents of the corporation are quick to point out that dedicated cooperation of the mayors and city officials was indispensable.

Among their adopted projects:

- Clearance and redevelopment of a badly blighted section of downtown.
- Development of a financial program of incentives in a "village district" in which businesses were required to restore historic building fronts in order to qualify for financial assistance.
- Sensing that an ill-placed Job Corps facility was an impediment to the redevelopment plan, they worked with the managers and helped relocate the Job Corps to a more fitting campus-type setting.
- An attractive riverfront park was created on the north side of the scenic Kanawha River on the southern part of downtown while at the north end a popular farmer's market was created.
- Their program of creating attractive downtown housing and bringing residents back

Originally published as "Long-Term Business Leadership Is Key to Downtown's Success," *Downtown Idea Exchange*, May 15, 2006, by the Alexander Communications Group, Inc., Boonton, NJ. Reprinted with permission of the publisher.

into the city has been moderately success-ful.

- Overlooking the river, lovely old homes have been converted into offices for lawyers, doctors, accountants, and other profession-als.
- Downtown restaurants are a vital part of their program to keep downtown alive.

The final project of their 16-part plan for downtown was construction of the stunning performing arts center and museum, which was completed in 2002. On a personal tour of this lovely facility in 2004, I saw an outstand-ing structure, the sparkling interior of which would do credit to New York City, Chicago, or San Francisco.

How People Make It Happen

Venerable Senator Robert C. Byrd has been a powerful ally who has participated in this great renaissance. The State, with its capi-tol in Charleston, has also been an active part-ner.

In 2002, former coal company executive (and one of the three Renaissance leaders) Jim Thomas remarked, "One of the most critical roles of the nonprofit coalition of downtown businessmen has been to provide continuity and persistent effort through inevitable polit-ical changes and changes in the dynamics of downtown. Our comprehensive 16-project program has been long term. We are in our seventeenth year and are completing our last project. However, there will be more because downtowns must been continuously nurtured and revitalized to adjust to changing eco-nomic, social, and cultural needs."

The dedication of these leaders and the cooperation of business with government has made a highly visible difference in Charleston. Downtown Charleston held together a 16-project program that extended over a two-decade period and accomplished every one of the projects. To me, that's just phenomenal. Several business leaders saw the threat of de-centralization — of the exodus of business and people — and just got together and decided to do something about it.

Their good work continues to this day under the Charleston Area Alliance, a consol-idated entity of the Charleston Renaissance Corporation, the Charleston Chamber of Commerce, and the Business and Industrial Development Corporation.

From my experience, it's very unusual to have business leaders who will assume that kind of a difficult role for such a long period of time. I don't know what caused their ded-ication, but it was that dedication of the busi-ness leadership that revitalized downtown Charleston. Of course, they worked very closely with all levels of government. But it was the business leadership of the three men who provided the continuity that you need to for long-term projects like downtown revital-ization.

One of the problems today is that most complex projects take a long, long time from start to finish. When you have a turnover of mayors and city councils, it's very difficult to maintain the continuity that's needed.

The key thing to learn from all this is: A strong downtown business organization can provide the continuity that you need for long-term projects.

CHAPTER 9

Columbia Officials Promote Use of Business Licenses to Regulate SOBs

Steffanie Dorn

No, I don't mean what you think; I am talking about Sexually Oriented Businesses. Do you have an ordinance regulating Sexually Oriented Businesses? Has your ordinance been updated lately? It doesn't matter how big or small your town is, you could have a potential problem on your hands. At this year's National Bureau of Business Licensing Officials (NBBLO) meeting, Attorney Scott D. Bergthold, whose entire practice is based on representing local governments with issues related to SOBs, spoke to attendees.

Bergthold gave several tips for items to include in your ordinance so that it may withstand a constitutional challenge. The first item is to be sure that your ordinance not just includes a purpose statement (preventing urban blight, etc.), but has an explanation of findings that led council to pass the ordinance. Another important consideration is the definition of adult businesses. As Bergthold states, "the goal in defining so-called 'adult' businesses is to cast the net wide enough to encompass a broad range of adult business models and at the same time to narrowly tailor the language to affect only that category of [businesses] shown to produce the unwanted secondary effects..." *Renton v. Playtime Theatres, Inc.*, 475 U.S. 41, 53 (1986).

I would hazard to guess that a lot of localities perhaps unknowingly violate the next piece of advice: Have a fixed time for initial permit issuance and avoid "hidden" delays. In *FW/PBS, Inc. v. City of Dallas*, 493 U.S. 215 (1990), the court ruled that although the ordinance required the police chief to approve issuance of a license within 30 days, the ordinance could provide a potential delay because it did not state that a license would be issued even if other departments did not conduct timely inspections. How many of us have an ordinance that requires a Certificate of Occupancy or inspections by the building and fire departments before a license will be issued? If zoning codes have not been altered to provide an expedited procedure for adult businesses, your ordinance could be interpreted as having a hidden delay.

Hopefully none of our ordinances have a provision that allow municipal officials to have "unbridled discretion" to deny a license or permit. Examples include: language that a per-

Originally published as "Are You Protected from SOBs?," *License Examiner*, September 2004, by the Municipal Association of South Carolina, Columbia, SC. Reprinted with permission of the publisher.

mit may be disapproved based on the "potential impact on health, safety and welfare of the community; whether the applicant is of good moral character; failure to define what constitutes a complete application; information shall include, but not be limited to; or a request for any additional information required." These variable language examples give a lot of discretion to whomever is the deciding official in the application process and are subject to unfavorable scrutiny by the courts. If an ordinance is denied, a "fixed timetable during the administrative appeal process" should be provided.

After you have a SOB operating in your boundaries, you must then be careful in any renovation proceedings. Your ordinance should require that an employer must have knowledge of illegal activities being conducted by an employee. Further, a revocation should not necessarily be recommended on the basis of one employee's infractions. To avoid violations of the Fourth Amendment, inspectors should only have access to the same areas as patrons during the same operating hours. During the drafting or review of an SOB ordinance, state law should be carefully reviewed to be sure that it does not preempt a local government's ability to regulate. Sign regulations should be limited and "avoid being content-based in violation of the First Amendment."

In my opinion, the first and most important thing that you need is a good attorney to help draft a SOB ordinance. I hope that by reading this information, everyone realizes the importance of having such an ordinance in place. It is irrelevant the size of your locality; anywhere can become home to these types of businesses. Further, we must remember that rulings from local courts up to the U.S. Supreme Court can have an effect on your local ordinances and cause us to revisit and possibly rewrite them if necessary. We can never be complacent in this area if we want to protect our jurisdictions from having SOBs on every corner! The information from the NBBLO meeting on this subject is available at http://www.masc.sc/programs/knowledge/affiliates.

Business Licensing Suggestions

The top 10 things I learned at the recent National Bureau of Business Licensing Officials (NBBLO) national annual conference in Miami, Florida, are shown below (note item number 2).

10. To determine how best to enforce your license ordinance, know if your goal is compliance or punishment.
9. Be sure that office procedures are reviewed periodically for necessary changes — in other words, don't continue to do things just because they have always been done a certain way.
8. Are ethics a part of employee training? They should be.
7. To help prevent frivolous lawsuits, include a "cost shift" provision in your ordinance. This means that if the city loses, no one pays each other's attorney fees. However if the city wins, the loser pays the city's attorney fees. Although this sounds crazy, it has been tested as legal in court.
6. Always remember that cases in U.S. Supreme Court, S.C. Supreme Court and in the appropriate District Courts can have rulings that impact your jurisdiction.
5. A recent case in Hawaii, *Baker & Taylor v. Kawafuchi*, 83 P.3d 804 (Hawaii 2004), concludes that the Complete Auto Transit test is alive and well!
4. Internet booking of hotel rooms causes a loss in accommodations taxes and business license revenue. Rooms are sold at a discount to Expedia.com, etc., and we don't get the revenue on the actual rate paid by the consumer. Los Angeles, CA just changed the definition of "Operator in Hotel" and is attempting to go after the "dot coms."

3. Your ordinance can be challenged even if an entity has not been "harmed" if it potentially violates the First Amendment.
2. Have a good Sexually Oriented Businesses Ordinance.

1. South Carolina RULES in business licensing!

CHAPTER 10

Columbus Officials Adopt SOB Regulations in Response to Citizens' Initiative

Jim Siegel

Representatives of a conservative Cincinnati-based group pushing for stricter strip-club regulations have assured Ohio lawmakers that eight other states have implemented similar laws. But a check of those states by *The Dispatch* found only one, Tennessee, that has enacted a state law resembling the combination of restrictions proposed by Citizens for Community Values.

Senate Bill 16, created by the group's petition drive, says dancers, both when they're nude and when they've put their clothes back on, must stay at least 6 feet from patrons. It also prohibits nude dancing, or operations of adult bookstores, between midnight and 6 A.M.

The House Judiciary Committee is expected to vote on the bill today, but not before Rep. Louis Blessing, a Cincinnati Republican who is committee chairman, tries to reduce the 6-foot distance requirements. "The distance is ridiculous, and requiring a bubble after they're dressed and fully clothed, I don't know what the purpose is of that," Blessing said, adding that he doesn't think it's constitutional.

Gov. Ted Strickland, speaking about the bill in public for the first time yesterday, said state government has better things to do than to focus on strip clubs. If the bill gets to him, he said, he would have to "conclude for my own satisfaction whether or not there are constitutional issues here that in my own mind could result in me not keeping faith with the oath I took."

The citizens group has argued that the bill is on solid constitutional ground, pointing to a federal circuit court in California that upheld distance requirements. But Blessing, an attorney, said he doesn't think that ruling applies to dancers once they stop their performance and get dressed. If the bill's backers don't agree with the bill's amendments, or if the bill doesn't pass, the group can collect about 120,000 more signatures and put it on the November statewide ballot.

Scott D. Bergthold, a Chattanooga, Tenn., attorney who wrote the bill, said he would be OK with a distance limit of 3 feet, and would accept changes to the "bubble" once women are finished dancing as long as it still prohibits touching. "I think it would still

Originally published as "Strip-Club Bill Outdoes Other States," *The Columbus Dispatch*, May 9, 2007, by The Columbus Dispatch, Columbus, OH. Reprinted with permission of the publisher.

be a good bill and would still serve a regulatory interest," he said. The values group says the bill is aimed at reducing crime associated with strip clubs, including drug use and prostitution. Ohio club owners have said the bill will effectively shut down their $250 million-a-year industry. "We're not breaking any new ground here," David Miller, the citizens group's vice president, said during recent committee testimony. "There are numerous other states, eight different states in the United States, that do have some sort of statewide standard." Barry Sheets, the organization's lobbyist, said states with "similar" laws are Alabama, Arizona, Delaware, Georgia, Illinois, New Jersey, Pennsylvania and Tennessee.

States generally have obscenity and anti-prostitution laws, and many local governments enact adult entertainment restrictions. But Pennsylvania and Georgia have little statewide strip-club regulation, after courts struck down laws in both states. "In the absence of regulation, there is no restriction," said Nil Frederiksen, spokesman for the Pennsylvania attorney general's office. In Georgia, residents amended the state constitution, handing strip-club oversight to counties and municipalities. Delaware says strip clubs must close at 10 P.M.; it's 1 A.M. in Arizona. Neither state spells out a distance between dancers and patrons. Illinois only restricts where a club can be located: 1,000 feet from schools, parks, public housing or churches (3,000 feet in unincorporated areas). New Jersey prohibits nude dancing or "simulation of sexual activity" where alcohol is served. Alabama requires dancers to cover up private parts, but some clubs are using spray-on tanning solution to meet the standard.

Only Tennessee requires a 6-foot distance between dancers and customers, and it prohibits nude dancing after midnight. Unlike Senate Bill 16, Tennessee's 6-foot law applies only when the dancer is performing, and it does not take effect until it is approved by county officials. Senate Bill 16 "would be the most extreme law in America," said Sandy

Theis, spokeswoman for the Buckeye Association of Club Executives.

Phil Burress, president of the citizens group, disagreed, pointing to Delaware's 10 P.M. closing time. "I'm not looking to test something, because we already have great laws that have been upheld," he said, "We only want something passed that is constitutional."

A summary of Senate Bill 16, which passed the 127th General Assembly of the State of Ohio on May 16, 2007, became law on September 4 of the same year it was approved. The bill became law without the Governor's signature. A summary of this piece of legislation, highlights of the prohibitions against sexually oriented businesses, and list of the legal definitions contained in the bill are provided below.

Summary of the Act

- Prohibits a sexually oriented business from being open for business between midnight and 6 A.M., except that a sexually oriented business that holds a liquor permit may remain open until the hour specified in the permit if it does not conduct, offer, or allow any sexually oriented entertainment activity in which the performers appear nude.

- Prohibits a patron of a sexually oriented business who is not a member of the employee's immediate family to knowingly touch any employee of the business while that employee is nude or seminude or touch the clothing of any employee while that employee is nude or seminude.

- Prohibits an employee who regularly appears nude or seminude on the premises of a sexually oriented business, while on the premises and while nude or seminude, from knowingly touching a patron who is not a member of the employee's immediate family or another employee who is not a member of the employee's immediate family or the clothing of a patron who is not a member of the employee's immediate family or another employee who is not a member of the employee's immediate family or allowing a patron who is not a member of the employee's immediate family or another employee who is not a member of the employee's immediate family to touch the employee or the employee's clothing.

- Authorizes the legislative authority of a municipal corporation to request the Attorney General's guidance and assistance in drafting an ordinance regulating adult entertainment establishments and requires the Attorney General to provide that guidance upon request.
- Requires the state to indemnify a township, the trustees of a township, a municipal corporation, and the legislative authority of a municipal corporation that adopts a resolution or ordinance regulating adult entertainment establishments in accordance with the Attorney General's legal guidance from liability incurred in the enforcement of the resolution or ordinance if the court finds the resolution or ordinance unconstitutional or otherwise legally defective but prohibits the state from providing such indemnification for any part of a judgment or settlement covered by insurance, resulting from acts manifestly outside the scope of an officer's or employee's responsibilities or from malicious purpose, bad faith, or wanton or reckless behavior, or that is for punitive damages or any part of a consent judgment or settlement that is unreasonable.

Prohibitions in the Act Related to Sexually-Oriented Businesses

Definitions

The act defines "sexually oriented business" for use in its prohibitions related to such businesses as an adult bookstore, adult video stores, adult cabaret, adult motion picture theater, sexual device shop, or sexual encounter center, but does not include a business solely by reason of its showing, selling, or renting materials rated NC-17 or R by the Motion Picture Association of America.

Hours of Operation

The act prohibits a sexually oriented business from being or remaining open for business between midnight and 6 A.M. on any day. However, if a sexually oriented business holds a liquor permit, it may remain open until the hour specified in the permit if it does not conduct, offer, or allow sexually oriented entertainment activity in which the performers appear nude. A violation of this prohibition is "illegally operating a sexually oriented business," a misdemeanor of the first degree.

"No-Touch" Rule

The act prohibits a patron of a sexually oriented business who is not a member of the employee's immediate family from knowingly touching any employee of the business while that employee is nude or seminude or touch the clothing of any employee while that employee is nude or seminude. The act also prohibits an employee who regularly appears nude or seminude on the premises of a sexually oriented business, while on the premises of that business and while nude or seminude, from knowingly touching a patron who is not a member of the employee's immediate family or another employee who is not a member of the employee's immediate family or the clothing of a patron who is not a member of the employee's immediate family or another employee is who is not a member of the employee's immediate family or allowing a patron who is not a member of the employee's immediate family or another employee who is not a member of the employee's immediate family to touch the employee or the employee's clothing. A violation of either prohibition is "illegal sexually oriented activity in a sexually oriented business" and is a misdemeanor of the first degree if the offender touches a specified anatomical area of the patron or employee or the clothing covering specified anatomical areas (includes human genitals, pubic region, and buttocks and the human female breast below a point immediately above the top of the areola). Otherwise a violation is a misdemeanor of the fourth degree.

Legal Definitions in the Act

"Adult bookstore" or "adult video store" means a commercial establishment that has as a significant or substantial portion of its stock in trade or inventory in, derives a significant or substantial portion of its revenues from, devotes a significant or substantial portion of its interior business or advertising to, or maintains a substantial section of its sales or display space for the sale or rental, for any form of consideration, of books, magazines, periodicals, or other printed matter, or photographs, film, motion pictures, video cassettes, compact discs, slides, or other visual representations, that are characterized by their emphasis upon the exhibition or description of specified sexual activities or specified anatomical areas.

"Adult cabaret" means a nightclub, bar, juice bar, restaurant, bottle club, or other similar commercial establishment, regardless of whether alcoholic beverages are served, that regularly features individuals who appear in a state of nudity or seminudity.

"Adult motion picture theater" means a commercial establishment where films, motion pictures, videocassettes, slides, or similar photographic reproductions that are characterized by their emphasis upon the display of specified sexual activities or specified anatomical areas are regularly shown to more than five individuals for any form of consideration.

"Characterized by" means describing the essential character or quality of an item.

"Employee" means any individual who performs any service on the premises of a sexually oriented business on a full-time, part-time, or contract basis, regardless of whether the individual is denominated an employee, independent contractor, agent, or otherwise, but does not include an individual exclusively on the premises for repair or maintenance of the premises or for the delivery of goods to the premises.

"Nudity," "nude," or "state of nudity" has the same meaning as the Revised Code (the showing of the human male or female genitals, pubic area, vulva, anus, anal cleft, or cleavage with less than a fully opaque covering; or the showing of the female breasts with less than a fully opaque covering of any part of the nipple).

"Operator" means any individual on the premises of a sexually oriented business who causes the business to function or who puts or keeps in operation the business or who is authorized to manage the business or exercise overall operational control of the business premises.

"Patron" means any individual on the premises of a sexually oriented business except for any of the following:

(1) An operator or an employee of the sexually oriented business;
(2) An individual who is on the premises exclusively for repair or maintenance of the premises or for the delivery of goods to the premises;
(3) A public employee or a volunteer firefighter/emergency medical services worker acting within the scope of the public employee's or volunteer's duties as a public employee or volunteer.

"Premises" means the real property on which the sexually oriented business is located and all appurtenances to the real property, including, but not limited, to the sexually oriented business, the grounds, private walkways, and parking lots or parking garages adjacent to the real property under the ownership, control, or supervision of the owner or operator of the sexually oriented business.

"Regularly" means consistently or repeatedly.

"Seminude" or "state of seminudity" has the same meaning as the Revised Code (a state of dress in which opaque clothing covers not more than the genitals, pubic region, and nipple of the female breast, as well as portions of the body covered by supporting straps or devices).

"Sexual device" means any three-dimensional object designed and marketed for stimulation of the male or female human genitals or anus or female breasts or for sadomasochistic use or abuse of oneself or others, including, but not limited to, dildos, vibrators, penis pumps, and physical representations of the human genital organs, but not including devices primarily intended for protection against sexually transmitted diseases or for preventing pregnancy.

"Sexual device shop" means a commercial establishment that regularly features sexual devices, but not including any pharmacy, drug store, medical clinic, or establishment primarily dedicated to providing medical or health-care products or services, and not including any commercial establishment that does not restrict access to its premises by reason of age.

"Sexual encounter center" means a business or commercial enterprise that, as one of its principal business purposes, purports to offer for any form of consideration physical contact in the form of wrestling or tumbling between individuals of the opposite sex when one or more of the individuals is nude or seminude.

"Specified sexual activity" means sexual intercourse, oral copulation, masturbation, or sodomy, or excretory functions as a part of or in connection with these activities.

State law defines "adult entertainment establishment" as an adult arcade, adult bookstore, adult novelty store, adult video store, adult cabaret, adult motion picture theater, adult theater, nude or seminude model studio, or sexual encounter establishment, all of which are also defined in that section. The statute expressly excludes from "adult entertainment establishment" an establishment in which a medical practitioner, psychologist, psychiatrist, or similar professional person licensed by the state engages in medically approved and recognized therapy, including, but not limited to, massage therapy.

Editor's Note:

A copy of Senate Bill 16 can be downloaded in its entirety from the State Legislature, State of Ohio, website <www.legislature.state.oh.us>.

CHAPTER 11

Conway Uses Business Licenses to Regulate Adult Businesses

Jeff Bowman

Cities look to businesses to provide community leadership, spur the local economy and keep downtown areas active. But sometimes businesses' operations conflict with a community's ideals — bringing in unsavory clientele, creating loud noise or disturbances, or not following codes.

Business licensing officials have several options for creating safe business communities for their residents.

One option is enforcing the codes on businesses to the point of demanding severe fines and court costs to get them to comply. Another option is using the nuisance statute to close down businesses. A third, more extreme, option is revoking the establishment's business license.

When codes are strictly enforced on businesses, police and code enforcement officers are heavily involved. Most municipalities have building and zoning codes in place to help regulate businesses. Sometimes, however, there are problems with having enough manpower or the desire to enforce the codes, especially in small towns where everyone knows each other, said Danny Crowe, attorney with Turner Padget Graham and Laney, P.A. and former Municipal Association of SC general counsel.

The Town of Irmo recently was involved in a court case with a nightclub. The club attracted a large number of people until early in the morning, creating a disturbance in the nearby residential area. Officers from the Irmo police department were outnumbered by the crowds and had to get assistance form other law enforcement agencies to respond to problems at the club. Faced with heavy fines and court costs, the business owners agreed to shut down in exchange for the town dropping the case against them.

A second option is use of the nuisance statute. This is a quicker process that allows the county solicitor to bring action in circuit court to close down businesses that are public nuisances. Many business license ordinances allow license revocation for a nuisance business, and municipal and county councils have the power to deal with public nuisances under the Home Rule Act.

Horry County, for example, is using the nuisance statute to close the doors on adult entertainment businesses. A municipal ordinance needs to be specific on actions constituting a nuisance, Crowe said. State case law provides a definition of nuisance that is used by most communities, he said. Before resorting

Originally published as "Creating Safe Business Communities," *License Examiner*, January 2007, by the Municipal Association of South Carolina, Columbia, SC. Reprinted with permission of the publisher.

to business license revocation to deal with nuisance businesses, most officials recommend getting an injunction or prosecuting for operation of a common law nuisance.

Business license revocation is a rare and lengthy process — involving the circuit court — that is used only when other options have failed. This was the case in Cayce, where the city revoked the license of a motel. A large number of arrests for illegal drug sales at the motel drew the attention of the police, who worked with business licensing officials to deny the renewal of the motel's business license.

The motel was the first business license revoked by Cayce, but officials recently have denied a license renewal for a bar that has had a number of incidents involving disorderly conduct and noise violations, Crowe said.

The bar was affecting the quality of life for its residential neighbors, said John Sharpe, Cayce administrator. A citizens who lived directly behind the bar testified the noise level disrupted her family's sleep and she feared violence from the crowds gathered in the parking lot after hours.

"The city has made every effort to help the business to understand the citations they were receiving and get them to 'change their ways' to avoid this action," Sharpe said. "But a year later and with little change, the business license was revoked."

That case currently is being appealed, Crowe added.

"Revoking a license can only be done in extreme circumstances, after officials have built an extremely strong case," said MASC Executive Director Howard Duvall. "Closing down a business must be done very carefully. The rights of a property owner need to be protected."

Instead, municipalities need to first "bend over backwards to make sure businesses understand if they don't clean up their act, we will use the full force of the law to get you to comply," Duvall said.

Business License Denial

One recent example of the use of a business license that was denied to an adult entertainment establishment pursuant to an approved Adult Entertainment Moratorium is highlighted below. The following description was taken from the Court of Appeals, State of South Carolina, opinion No. 2004-UP-553 filed on November 1, 2005.

On May 25, 2001, Horry County Business License manager Roddy Dickenson notified Excitement by letter that Horry County was denying its request for the renewal of its business license. The stated reason was that Excitement was in violation of an Horry County ordinance that prohibited the issuance of adult entertainment establishment licenses pursuant to the Adult Entertainment Moratorium.

Additionally, the zoning administrator declined to issue Excitement a certificate of zoning compliance for the business. The basis of the denial was that Excitement's location was within 2000 feet of a residential area and a church in violation of Horry County Code of Ordinances. Excitement appealed the zoning administrator's decision to the Board of Zoning Appeals. At the hearing, the only testimony offered was that of the zoning administrator. The administrator testified that while on a routine fire inspection, he observed that Excitement was operating as an adult entertainment establishment. He based his assessment on the fact that "99 percent of the shelf and wall displays were Triple XXX videos and anatomically correct adult products used for sexual stimulation.... [O]ther than the bathrooms and a drink vending area, adult videos and adult products consumed the gross floor area of the store." Horry County Code of Ordinances, Appendix B, section 526.3 defines an "Adult Video Store" as any enterprise deriving more than fifty percent of its gross revenues from adult materials. The administrator also testified that Excitement did not meet the spacing requirement of 2000 feet from a residential use or a church.

Excitement put forth the argument that natural vegetation created a "buffer zone" that insulated the business from the view of both the church and the residential area. However, the administrator testified Excitement was not in literal compliance with the zoning ordinance, which requires that measurements be taken from one point to another in a straight line. Measurements indicated Excitement was located 1825 feet from a church and 1598 feet from a residential area.

After consideration of the matter, the Board denied the appeal based upon specific findings that Excitement's business was an adult entertainment establishment as defined in Horry County Zoning Ordinance section 526.3 and it was within 2000 feet of a residential area and a church.

Excitement appealed to the circuit court. In addition to the grounds raised in its petition for review, Excitement argued to the circuit court that it did not receive a fair hearing before the Board in violation of its due process rights. The circuit court requested briefs from both sides on the due process issue. After considering the briefs, the circuit court affirmed the Board's decision.

"The fundamental requirement of due process is the opportunity to be heard at a meaningful time and in a meaningful manner." *South Carolina Dep't of Soc. Servs. v. Beeks*, 325 S.C. 243, 246, 481 S.E.2d 703, 705 (1997). "Due process is flexible and calls for such procedural protections as the particular situation demands." *Stono River Envtl. Protection Ass'n v. South Carolina Dep't of Health and Envtl. Control*, 305 S.C. 90, 94, 406 S.E.2d 340, 342 (1991).

Excitement contends it did not receive a fair hearing because the chairman of the Board interrupted its attorney as he attempted to cross-examine the zoning administrator on the presence of a buffer between the business and nearby church and residences. Our review of the record reveals that the Chairman interrupted Excitement's attorney's cross-examination of the zoning administrator only to in-

form him that the administrator's determination as to the adequacy of a buffer was not relevant as he was limited to enforcing the zoning ordinance as written. Excitement's attorney was in fact able to question the administrator about the existence of vegetation providing a buffer and receive the administrator's answers. Excitement was also allowed to submit into evidence pictures of the alleged buffer and make its argument on this issue. In addition, Excitement was able to question the administrator on the basis for his determination that the business was in violation of the ordinance by having more than fifty percent of its revenue derived from the sale of adult products and to present its argument that the burden was on the administrator to prove this violation.

Near the conclusion of the hearing, the following exchange occurred between the Chairman and Excitement's attorney:

> [ATTORNEY]: I've got it in the record, and I'm done. That's all I wanted to do.
>
> THE CHAIRMAN: Okay.
>
> [ATTORNEY]: That's all I wanted to do. Thank you. We'll rest with the record as it is.
>
> THE CHAIRMAN: Okay. Do we have any other statement from you?
>
> [ATTORNEY]: No. I believe that I have created my record. I can't argue the measurements.

It is clear from the record that Excitement was given sufficient opportunity to present its case. It never complained about the interruptions or asked for the opportunity to question the witness further. In addition, Excitement failed to present evidence or make further argument when given the opportunity. If Excitement's attorney thought that the hearing was conducted in a manner that did not present Excitement with the opportunity to be heard in a meaningful manner in violation of the dictates of due process, then he should have made a statement at that time.

We agree with the circuit court that Excitement has failed to prove a violation of its right to due process.

Editor's Note:

For a complete copy of this Court of Appeals decision, the reader should refer to *Excitement Video Inc., Appellant, v. Board of Zoning Appeals*, Horry County, South Carolina, Respondent, Unpublished Opinion No. 2004-UP-553, Submitted October 1, 2004, and filed on November 1, 2004.

CHAPTER 12

Delaware Officials Advise Their Cities on How to Regulate Adult Businesses

Philip C. Laurien

As with all regulation of land use, there must be a legitimate government interest to regulate adult entertainment. Since there is a significant body of law that deals with the treatment of adult entertainment uses under zoning, I have selected the most often-cited cases.

Young v. American Mini Theatres Inc. (427 U.S. 50, 96 S. Ct. 2440, 49 L. Ed 310, 1976)

The U.S. Supreme Court found that Detroit's prohibition of locating an adult theater within 1000 feet of any two other "regulated uses" or within 500 feet of any residential zone did not violate the First and Fourteenth amendments. Further, the zoning ordinance was designed to combat the undesirable "secondary effects" of adult businesses, which Detroit had extensively shown to occur in their city. These regulations were acceptable as long as they were "content-neutral," setting standards for time, place and manner of operation.

Renton v. Playtime Theaters, Inc. (106 S. St. 925, 1986)

Renton, Washington passed a zoning ordinance that prohibited adult motion picture theaters from locating within 1000 feet of any residential zone, single or multiple family dwelling, church, park, or school. The court found the regulations to be content neutral with regard to the time, place, and manner of regulation "and *acceptable so long as they are designed to serve a substantial governmental interest and do not unreasonably limit alternative avenues of communication.*"

The ordinance was not aimed at the content of the adult films but at the "**secondary effects**" of the theaters on the surrounding community. Renton did not perform its own studies of secondary effects since it had no adult theaters in the city when it adopted the ordinance so it had no experience to draw on. It relied on studies performed by the city of Seattle aimed at preventing adverse secondary effects of locating adult theaters in residential areas of the city.

The Court held that "Renton was entitled to rely on the experiences of Seattle and other

Originally published as *How to Regulate Adult Entertainment by Zoning*, January 2002, by the Delaware County Regional Planning Commission, Delaware, OH.

cities, and in particular on the detailed findings summarized in the Washington Supreme Court's Northend Cinema opinion."

The Court found that Renton allowed for "alternative avenues of communication" because the ordinance allowed for 520 acres of commercial and industrial land, or 5 percent of the city, open to use as adult theater sites.

This land was "ample, accessible real estate, acreage in all stages of development from raw land to developed, industrial, warehouse, office and shopping space that is criss-crossed by freeways, highways and roads." Further, "respondents must fend for themselves in the real estate market" even if there were not any directly available theater sites in this area.

FW/PBS, Inc v. City of Dallas, 492 U.S. 215 (1990)

In FW, the Court expanded its previous theories to deal with a *licensing procedure* developed by the city of Dallas to regulate adult businesses. The court found that challenges to licensing procedures may be made under the First Amendment "where the scheme vests unbridled discretion in the decision maker and where the regulation is challenged as overbroad." *Two tests* were created to determine if a *regulation creates censorship* that imposes a restraint prior to judicial review:

a) Any restraint prior to judicial review can be imposed only for a specified brief period during which time the status quo must be maintained;
b) Expeditious judicial review of that decision must be available, "like a censorship system, a licensing scheme creates the possibility that constitutionally protected speech will be suppressed where there are inadequate procedural safeguards to ensure prompt issuance of the license."

Thus "the license for a First Amendment–protected business must be issued in a reasonable period of time, and, the first two Freedman safeguards are essential." Since Dallas's ordinance failed to provide an effective time limitation on the licensing decision, and it also failed to provide an avenue for prompt judicial review so as to minimize suppression of speech in the event of a license denial, its licensing requirement was unconstitutional.

Since pornography is not obscenity, and since Dallas did not argue this case as obscenity, *the court found that the right to sell this material was a constitutionally protected right.*

Topanga Press v. City of Los Angeles, 989 F.2d 1524 (9th Circuit, 1993)

The city intended to *move* adult businesses from non-conforming locations to conforming locations over a period of time. This, plus *the exclusionary nature of the distance buffers* resulted in the court finding that the city had excluded adult businesses by creating standards which could not be met by the "**relevant real estate market.**"

Los Angeles issued a study in 1977 that documented adverse secondary effects of concentrations of adult businesses. The adoption of the initial distance requirements in 1978 seems, on its face, to follow the Renton guidelines.

In 1983 the city adopted an additional provision that each adult business was considered to be a separate business even if it operated under one roof with another similar business.

The ordinance allowed multiple adult businesses established on or after 9/78 to continue until March 1985. In March 1986 the city expanded their distance requirements (previously 500' from churches, schools, parks or 1000' of other businesses) to include a 500' separation from residential zones.

The 1986 ordinance also provided for the extinction of adult businesses by March 1988 within 500' of a residential zone, with the allowance for continuation of adult businesses within 500' of a residential zone after 3/88 whenever "a site consistent with 12.70C is not reasonably available elsewhere in the City for the establishment or relocation of the subject adult establishment business."

A business existing in 3/86 could continue to operate until 3/91 if the business could establish undue financial hardship based on investment or the existence of a written lease extending past 3/88.

The constitutionality of the zoning ordinance was challenged. The court cited Renton as determinative in finding whether adult businesses' First Amendment rights are threatened and whether a local government has effectively denied a reasonable opportunity to open and operate. This case redefines the "reasonable opportunity" clause.

The court may determine whether a site is "part of a *relevant real estate market*" in deciding whether the local government had provided reasonable opportunities for local adult businesses to locate. In doing so, there are *two tests* that must be met:

1. Whether relocation sites provided to adult businesses may be considered part of an *actual* business real estate market.
2. Whether, after excluding those sites that may not properly be considered to be part of the relevant real estate market, there are an adequate number of potential relocation sites for already existing adult businesses.

In Renton, 5 percent of the city's land area, or 520 acres, was available for adult businesses (although there was an oil tank farm, a sewage treatment plan and a horse race track already there). Subsequent to Renton, in *Alexander v. City of Minneapolis*, 928 F 2d 278, 283 (8th Cir., 1991) that court considered the availability of *commercial land. Basiardanes v. Galveston*, 682 F.2d 1203, 1214 (5th Cir. 1982) held that areas located among warehouses, shipyards, undeveloped areas and swamps did not provide adult businesses reasonable opportunity to relocate.

Accordingly, *in Topanga the court made the following test for what constitutes a relevant real estate market*:

1. Property is not potentially available when it is unreasonable to believe that it would ever

become available to any commercial enterprise.
2. Relocation sites that are reasonably accessible to the general public may also be part of the market.
3. Areas in manufacturing zones, which have a proper infrastructure such as sidewalks, roads and lighting may be included in the market.
4. Potential sites for relocation of adult businesses must be reasonable sites for some commercial business. A warehouse, swamp, or sewage treatment plant site are not examples of reasonable commercial sites.
5. Sites that are commercially zoned are part of the relevant market.

With regard to the relevant real estate market, the court found that of 11,600 "allegedly available" acres for adult business relocation, there was not much truly available. Thousands of acres were beneath the Pacific ocean; some of the land was used as landing strips at Los Angeles Airport; 200 acres were used as a landfill; 600 acres were used as the Van Nuys airport; 4,400 acres were used as oil refineries or by the Port of Los Angeles; 230 acres were used for petroleum gas storage; additional land was used for a Defense plant, a General Motors plant, a portion of a children's hospital.

Out of 11,613 acres "definitionally" available, only 7440 were realistically available, and *only .18 percent of that land was zoned commercial.*

There were 102 adult businesses affected, 95–100 of which needed to be relocated. The city noted 120 sites they believed were practically available. However, they did not take into account the 500' buffer analysis from residential zones!

Once the 1000' distance requirement *between* adult businesses was enforced, it was clear that the first handful of adult businesses to legally relocate would prevent any others from moving into the relevant areas available around them, since every 1000' radius condemned 72 acres around it to no other adult business use.

To relocate 100 adult businesses would thus require 7200 acres of land as buffer zones or over 11 square miles of territory, with the center of that territory having to be available for adult businesses under the five point test.

It was an impossible criterion to meet. As a result the court concluded that the city "may not have provided the adult businesses with reasonable avenues of expression. The court considers zoning ordinance cases such as this to present complex constitutional problems."

General Rules for Regulating Adult Entertainment

The fall 1994 American Planning Association *PLANNING AND LAW* newsletter contained an article by Alan C. Weinstein, professor of law and planning at Cleveland State University's Cleveland-Marshall College of Law. Professor Weinstein's guidelines for regulating adult businesses are:

- *First, and most critically*, officials must recognize that the only permissible goal of adult business regulation is the reduction of their undesirable "secondary effects," and that the courts will not hesitate to invalidate zoning restrictions and other forms of regulation — including restrictions on nude erotic dancing — when they are merely a pretext for eliminating or unduly restricting adult businesses.
- *Local officials must exercise caution* if they choose to rely on the finding of other communities, rather than documenting the negative impacts of "secondary effects" in their own community. Courts are now requiring officials to demonstrate that they gave a reasonable degree of consideration to such findings prior to enacting their own restrictions.
- *Judges are also examining* to what degree any

given local adult business may differ from the businesses in the community whose documented "secondary effects" were used by local officials to justify their own regulations.
- *Local officials must expect* that their locational restrictions will be reviewed under the "relevant real estate market" standard, [so] they should insure that their regulations leave adult businesses with an adequate number of sites that are either zoned for commercial development or, if zoned otherwise, are generally suitable for some form of commercial enterprise.
- *Courts will give local officials* significant leeway, but not total license, when enacting regulations to address the public health concerns raised by adult businesses, such as restrictions which seek to prevent patrons from engaging in sexual activity on the premises.

How to Construct Zoning for Adult Entertainment

Step A. Declare the Purpose Is to Avoid Adverse Secondary Effects

Use language in the purpose and adoption of the ordinance that describes the potential adverse secondary effects of adult businesses near residential districts, and the need for dispersion of such adult entertainment to avoid these adverse secondary effects.

Step B. Define Adult Entertainment in the Zoning Ordinance

Language similar to the following text should be placed in the zoning ordinance glossary.

DEFINITION OF WORDS — **Except** where specifically defined herein, all words used in this Zoning Resolution shall carry their customary meanings. Words used in the present tense include the future tense; the singular number includes the plural; the word structure includes the word building; the word lot includes the word plot or parcel; the term "shall" is always mandatory; the words "used" or "occupied," as applied to any land or structure shall be construed to include the words "intended, arranged or designed to be used or occupied."

Specially defined words — The following listed words are specifically defined for use in this Zoning Resolution.

ADULT — An individual eighteen years of age or older.

ADULT BOOK STORE — Adult book store means an establishment deriving a majority of its gross income from the sale or rental of, or having a majority of its stock in trade in book, magazines or other periodicals, films, or mechanical or non-mechanical devices, which constitute adult materials.

ADULT MATERIALS — **Adult** materials means any book, magazine, newspaper, pamphlet, poster, print, picture, slide, transparency, figure, image, description, motion picture film, phonographic record or tape, other tangible thing, or any service, capable of arousing interest through sight, sound, or touch, and:

1. which material is distinguished or characterized by an emphasis on matter displaying, describing, or representing sexual activity, masturbation, sexual excitement, nudity, bestiality, or human bodily functions of elimination; or
2. which service is distinguished or characterized by an emphasis on sexual activity, masturbation, sexual excitement, nudity, bestiality, or human bodily functions of elimination.

ADULT MOTION PICTURE THEATER — Adult motion picture theater means an enclosed motion picture theater or motion picture drive-in theater used for presenting, and deriving a majority of its gross income from, adult material for observation by patrons therein.

ADULTS ONLY ENTERTAINMENT

ESTABLISHMENT — Adults only entertainment establishment means an establishment which features services which constitute adult material, or which features exhibitions of persons totally nude, or topless, bottomless, strippers, male or female impersonators, or similar entertainment which constitute adult material.

BOTTOMLESS — Bottomless means less than full opaque covering of male or female genitals, pubic area or buttocks.

NUDE (NUDITY) — Nude (nudity) means the showing, representation, or depiction of human male or female genitals, pubic area, or buttocks with less than full, opaque covering of any portion thereof, or female breast(s) with less than a full, opaque covering of any portion thereof below the top of the nipple, or of covered male genitals in a discernibly turgid state.

SEXUAL ACTIVITY — Sexual activity means sexual conduct or sexual contact, or both.

SEXUAL CONDUCT — Sexual conduct means vaginal intercourse between a male and a female, and anal intercourse, fellatio, and cunnilingus between persons regardless of sex. Penetration, however slight, is sufficient to complete vaginal or anal intercourse.

SEXUAL CONTACT — Sexual contact means any touching of an erogenous zone of another, including without limitation the thigh, genitals, buttock, pubic region, or, if the person is a female, a breast, for the purpose of sexually arousing or gratifying either person.

SEXUAL EXCITEMENT — Sexual excitement means the condition of human male or female genitals, when in a state of sexual stimulation or arousal.

TOPLESS — Topless means the showing of a female breast with less than a full opaque covering of any portion thereof below the top of the nipple.

Step C. Adopt Rules of Application

Language similar to the following text should be placed in the forward to the zoning ordinance or resolution

Article III
Standard District Regulations

Section 300 Adoption of the Standard Zoning District Regulations and Rules of Application

300.01 Regulation of the Use and Development of Land and Structures

Regulations pertaining to the use of land and/or structures are hereby adopted or amended.

300.02 Rules of Application

The Standard District Regulations set forth in this ARTICLE III shall be interpreted and enforced according to the following rules:

300.021 Identification of Uses

Listed uses are to be defined by their customary name or identification, except where they are specifically defined or limited in this Zoning Resolution.

The full text of the listings in the North American Industry Classification System (NAICS), Executive Office of the President, Bureau of the Budget, 1997 edition shall be a part of the definition of the use listed in this Zoning Resolution and is hereby adopted as a part of this article.

300.022 Permitted Uses

Only a use designated as a Permitted Use shall be allowed as matter of right in a Zoning District and any use not so designated shall be prohibited except, when in character with the Zoning District, such additional use may be added to the Permitted Uses of the Zoning District by amendment of this Resolution.

300.023 Conditional Use

A use designated as a Conditional Use shall be allowed in a Zoning District when such specific conditions as are stipulated in Section 815 of this ordinance are found to be met by the Board of Zoning Appeals.

300.024 Development Standards

The Development Standards set forth shall be the minimum allowed for development in a Zoning District. If the Development Standards are in conflict with the requirements of any other lawfully adopted rules, regulations or laws, the more restrictive or higher standard shall govern.

Section D. Identify Which Zones Permit Adult Entertainment

I suggest that adult entertainment be treated as a permitted use in a commercial and/or industrial district that attracts regional traffic, subject to meeting certain standards. Adult entertainment should not be placed in neighborhood commercial districts.

Note: Classifying adult entertainment as conditional uses may run afoul of the FW/PBS v. Dallas case, as conditional use hearing by the BZA may constitute an open-ended process with delays and deferrals.

The best zoning ordinances identify permitted land uses by the North American Industrial Classification System. Using such a system, a regional commercial district might appear as follows:

(Sample) General Commercial District

Permitted Uses

Retail stores, personal services, business and professional offices as listed below. Residential uses are permitted if ancillary to a permitted commercial use.

NAICS Code

44412	Paint, Wallpaper, Glass Stores
444130	Hardware Stores
444220	Nursery and Garden Centers
445	Food Stores
448	Clothing Stores
72211	**Eating and Drinking Places (except those establishments offering or feature entertainment including totally nude, topless, bottomless, strippers, male or female impersonators, or similar entertainment or services as defined herein)**

NAICS Code

44611	Drug Stores and Proprietary Stores
44531	Liquor Stores
45110	Sporting Goods
445291	Baked Goods
451211	**Book Store (but not Adult Book stores as defined herein)**
45112	Hobby and toy shops
421410	Camera and photo supply shops
453110	Florists
453991	Tobacco stores
451212	News Dealers (except Adult Books)
9999*	**Adult entertainment — sale of adult books, magazines, videos, and adult performances (including nude dancing) provided the following standards are met and the required zoning compliance is applied for:**

A. Such use shall not be permitted within 1000 feet of:
　　1) **Church**
　　2) **School**
　　3) **Park or playground**
　　4) **Residence or residential district**
B. Such use shall not be permitted within 1000 feet of another adult entertainment use.

In subsequent years since the issuance of this report, some of the member communities of the Delaware County Regional Planning Commission have adopted these suggested zoning guidelines for regulating adult entertainment businesses in their respective communities.

*Since the North American Industrial Classification System (NAICS) for land uses has no code for adult entertainment uses, this number of arbitrarily chosen (i.e., Suggested NAICA Code Number 9999).

CHAPTER 13

Detroit Considers Law to Preclude SOBs from Their Central Business District

Helena Varnavas

Detroit has been working hard to revive the city and bring residential growth to the downtown area.[1] Millions of dollars have gone into renovating historic buildings, creating new public transportation, reviving the riverfront and building residential lofts in the Central Business District area.[2] Detroit wants to prove that, "the growing population can support and sustain retail and grocery development," for its current and future residents.[3] New casinos and stadiums have also enhanced the city's cultural atmosphere while attracting a wave of young professionals.[4] Issues will arise, however, when the city tries to achieve this vision of a "better Detroit" by imposing ordinances and regulations on businesses that it deems problematic to their ideal. In particular, the city of Detroit has targeted the adult entertainment business as an industry they would like to see zoned out.

Legal Issues for Detroit's Adult Entertainment Industry

The adult entertainment industry has been hit particularly hard by these new city ordinances and regulations. The Detroit City Council has commenced its efforts to phase these businesses out altogether by changing the zoning ordinance in 1999 to preclude new adult entertainment establishments from being opened in the Central Business District.[5] Local laws allow such modifications to zoning regulations because the city of Detroit does not need to wait for an area to deteriorate before applying a zoning remedy.[6] The city may also rely on sociological experiences of other cities in enacting legislation as long as doing so is not completely unreasonable.[7]

The City Planning Commission deemed this phase-out of adult entertainment businesses reasonable because "the B6 zoning district classification in this area may have made sense in the late 1960s when there were still wholesale and freight operations on the east side of the [Central Business District]. The

Originally published as "Zoning and Regulation of Detroit's Adult Entertainment Businesses: Has It Gone Too Far?," *The Illinois Law Journal*, November 19, 2008, by the Business Law Society, College of Law, University of Illinois, Champaign, IL. Reprinted with permission of the publisher.

subsequent development of Greektown and Bricktown, however, has rendered B6 inappropriate."[8] In addition, all zoning ordinances must bear a substantial relation to the public health, safety, morals or general welfare in order to be valid.[9] The city of Detroit seems to think that it is for the good of the general welfare that this new zoning ordinance be enacted.

Many adult entertainment business owners, including the proprietors of Déjà vu and the Zoo Club, believe that various provisions of this ordinance unfairly prevent them from operating a legitimate business enterprise.[10] They have brought suit against the city of Detroit and asked the court to determine that the adult use provisions of the city's ordinance are unconstitutional.[11] It is also their view that, "such provisions vest a constitutionally defiant discretionary authority in the hands of the city officials, who have no time constraint imposed upon them to evaluate an application in order to render a decision."[12] The city of Detroit has dragged this case out over several years in order to avoid having to make a decision that would violate the adult entertainment business owners' right to engage in free speech under the First Amendment.[13] The court recently decided that the city's treatment of the plaintiffs in that matter was unconstitutional because of its failure to make a decision on the plaintiff's application within a reasonable amount of time. Nevertheless, it went on to hold that the city of Detroit's ordinances are not unconstitutional on their face and are still applicable to all other adult entertainment business owners in the Central Business District.[14] On appeal, the plaintiffs have asked that the city of Detroit be permanently enjoined from enforcing the adult use provisions of the Detroit Zoning Ordinance and that their operation of adult entertainment businesses be identified as a lawful conforming use of zoning purposes. This case is pending and is sure to impact all of Detroit's adult entertainment businesses currently conflicting with the city's adult provisions of the zoning ordinance.

Other American Cities' Regulations and Zoning Ordinances

Detroit is not the first and likely not the last municipality to employ zoning ordinances to phase-out the adult entertainment businesses. City and county governments around the nation are currently enacting the same types of legislation to bring down established adult entertainment businesses.[15] These legislative bodies normally develop an initial ordinance, update an outdated regulation, or attempt to argue for zoning and licensing restrictions in court to accomplish these shutdowns.[16] They may even try to enact laws that prescribe zoning requirements and land use regulations of areas previously zoned for adult entertainment and give the power to a review board to deny a business for lack of "wholesomeness."[17] Such tactics clearly evince an effort to legislate morality based upon personal opinions of what is "right." Cities may enact these types of legislation as long as they have a factual basis for their regulations, and plaintiffs can challenge by demonstrating that the government's evidence does not support the regulations they are seeking to enact.[18]

Not everyone thinks that the adult entertainment business should be phased-out. Organizations such as the First Amendment Lawyers' Association, the American Civil Liberties Union, People for the American Way, National Coalition Against Censorship, Coalition for Free Expression, Free Speech Coalition, Thomas Jefferson Center for the Protection of Free Expression and the Association of Performing Arts Presenters are all defenders of exotic dancing in the adult entertainment industry.[19]

Conclusion

The city of Detroit wants to grow, shed its negative image and become a desirable place for relocation. Although the city considers tourists to be very important, its attempts are aimed at stimulating population growth within the downtown business area. The general population seems to feel that the adult entertainment industry is a nuisance to their community and a barrier in the way of a "better Detroit."[20] For adult entertainment business owners, this means that their rights may be compromised and will be continually diminished by adult entertainment provisions to the zoning regulations. It is uncertain as to whether the city of Detroit has gone too far with their zoning ordinances and regulations, but at this point, the city's efforts have clearly had an effect on the downtown adult entertainment industry's ability to run business going forward.

NOTES

1. Ruby L. Bailey, *The D Is a Draw: Most Suburbanites Are Repeat Visitors*, The "D" Spot, Aug. 22, 2007, Detroit Free Press, *http://teamowens313.wordpress.com/2007/08/22/if-you-build-a new-detroit-they-will-come/* (last visited September 30, 2008).

2. Robert Sharoff, National Perspectives; *Wave of Renovations Helping Downtown Detroit*, N.Y. Times, Jan. 30, 2005, *available at http://query.nytimes.com/gst/fullpage.html?res=9F01E1DA173BF933A05752C0A9639C8B63&sec=%spon=&pagewanted=1.*

3. Sheena Harrison, *DEGC Enlists Help to Spur Detroit Retail*, Crain's Detroit Bus., Jun. 25, 2007 *available at* http://www.crainsdetroit.com/apps/pbcs.dll/article?AID=/20070625/SUB/70623003/-1/newsletter02.

4. Patty Salkin, *Adult Use Provisions of Detroit's Zoning Ordinance Deemed Unconstitutional*, Law of the Land, Sept. 3, 2007, http://lawoftheland.wordpress.com/2007/09/03/adult-use-provisions-of-detroit%E2%80%99s-zoning-ordinance-deemed-unconstitutional/ (last visited October 1, 2008).

5. *H.D.V.— Greektown, LLC v. City of Detroit*, No. 06-11282, 2007 U.S. Dist. LEXIS 56951 (E.D. Mich. Aug. 6, 2007).

6. *15192 Thirteen Mile Rd., Inc. v. Warren*, 626 F. Supp. 803, 825 (E.D. Mich. 1985).

7. *Id.*

8. *H.D.V.— Greektown, LLC v. City of Detroit*, No. 06-11282, 2008 U.S. Dist. LEXIS 10940 (E.D. Mich. Feb. 14, 2008).

9. *Davis v. Sails*, 318 So. 2d 214, 218 (Fla. Dist. Ct. App. 1975).

10. *H.D.V.— Greektown, LLC v. City of Detroit*, No. 06-11282, 2008 U.S. Dist. LEXIS 10940, at *1 (E.D. Mich. Feb. 14, 2008).

11. *H.D.V.— Greektown, LLC v. City of Detroit*, No. 06-11282, 2007 U.S. Dist. LEXIS 56951, at *2 (E.D. Mich. Aug. 6, 2007).

12. *H.D.V.— Greektown, LLC v. City of Detroit*, No. 06-11282, 2008 U.S. Dist. LEXIS 10940, at *17 (E.D. Mich. Feb. 14, 2008).

13. *Id.* at *30.

14. *Id.*

15. Drew Ruble, *The People v. Jenna Jameson*, Biz. Tenn., Dec. 2005, *http://www.businesstn.com/content/people-v-jenna-jameson* (last visited November 18, 2008).

16. *Id.* at *2.

17. Judith Kynn Hannah, Woodhull Freedom Foundation, *Exotic Dance Adult Entertainment: A Guide for Planners and Policy Makers* (2005), *http://www.woodhullfoundation.org/content/otherpublications/JPL11-05-116-134.pdf.*

18. *Id.* at *11.

19. *Id.*

20. Bob Davenport, Cityscape Detroit (2007), *http://www.cityscapedetroit.org/advocacy/BSE._no_strip_club.pdf.*

CHAPTER 14

Erie's Public Indecency Ordinance Is Upheld by the Supreme Court

Scott D. Bergthold

The Supreme Court's decision in *Pap's A.M. v. City of Erie*[1] has been presented by the media as an inconsequential restatement of the Court's prior holding in *Barnes v. Glen Theatre*.[2] However, some proponents of sexually oriented businesses view the decision as a severe blow to the industry. "This ruling is a catastrophe," said attorney Jeffrey Douglas of the Free Speech Coalition, a California-based porn lobby group. He described the Court's decision as "a knife in the heart."[3] This dismayed response from the industry is merited, because in addition to reinforcing its holding in *Barnes*, the Court clarified the power of local governments to regulate adult businesses as a whole. Cases decided since *Pap's* was handed down show that the Court's rejection of certain arguments from the industry is aiding cities in the defense of their ordinances.[4]

Background

In 1994, the City of Erie, Pennsylvania passed a public indecency ordinance modeled after the statute upheld in *Barnes*. Pap's A.M., a corporation that operated a nude dancing establishment ("Kandyland"), brought suit in state court to enjoin enforcement of the ordinance on First Amendment grounds. The trial court entered a permanent injunction and the City appealed. On appeal, the Pennsylvania Commonwealth Court reversed. Following *Marks v. United States*,[5] the court found that Justice Souter's concurrence constituted the holding in *Barnes* and, finding *Barnes* directly on point, upheld the ordinance as constitutional.

The Pennsylvania Supreme Court reversed the Commonwealth Court and invalidated the City's ordinance. Disagreeing with the lower court and several federal courts of appeal,[6] the court determined that no binding precedent could be discerned from the Supreme Court's decision in *Barnes*. Having decided that it was not bound by *Barnes*, the Pennsylvania Supreme Court determined that Erie's ordinance was content-based because it had, in addition to a secondary effects justification, an "unmentioned purpose" to negatively impact the erotic message.[7] This was based on the preamble, which recited the ordinance's purpose of "limiting a recent increase in nude live entertainment within the City,

Originally published as "City of Erie v. Pap's A.M. and the Future of Sexually Oriented Business Regulation," *Municipal Lawyer*, Vol. 41, No. 5, September/October 2000, by the International Municipal Lawyers Association, Washington, DC. Reprinted with permission of the publisher.

which activity adversely impacts and threatens to impact on the public health, safety and welfare by providing an atmosphere conducive to violence, sexual harassment, public intoxication, prostitution, the spread of sexually transmitted diseases and other deleterious effects."[8] Relying upon this statement and Justice White's dissent in *Barnes*, the court went on to rule that as content-based restriction on speech, the ordinance failed strict scrutiny.

The Supreme Court's Opinion

The Supreme Court reversed the ruling of the Pennsylvania Supreme Court. Justice O'Connor authored the plurality opinion, and was joined by Chief Justice Rehnquist and Justices Kennedy and Breyer in holding that the law was constitutional under *O'Brien* and the Court's prior sex business cases. Justice Scalia, joined by Justice Thomas, concurred on broader grounds, noting that because the law on its face targeted conduct, not expression, it need only satisfy rational basis review.

After resolving an initial justiciability question,[9] Justice O'Connor examined whether the Erie ordinance was content-based or content-neutral. She reiterated that while being "in a state of nudity" is not an inherently expressive condition, nude dancing is expressive conduct within the outer ambit of the First Amendment. However, if the government's purpose is to prevent the negative secondary effects associated with a form or manner of expression, and not the expression itself, then the law is deemed content-neutral and will be sustained if it satisfies intermediate scrutiny.[10] The Court ruled that Erie's ordinance, almost identical to the statute upheld in *Barnes*, is similarly content-neutral because its purpose is unrelated to the suppression of free expression. The Court stated that, on its face, the ordinance is a general prohibition of public nude conduct, regardless of whether that conduct is accompanied by expression. Pap's argued that, nevertheless, the ordinance's preamble,

and statements by the city attorney that the ban would not apply to "legitimate" theater productions, made the law content-based.

"Mixed Motive" Cases Get Intermediate Scrutiny

Justice O'Connor rejected the content-based argument, noting that the Pennsylvania Supreme Court construed the preamble language to mean that "one purpose of the ordinance was to 'combat secondary effects.'"[11] She explained that the law does not seek to control the primary effects of the expression (such as the psychological impact of nude dancing on audiences) but rather, the secondary effects on public health, safety, and welfare, which the Court has previously recognized as caused by sexually oriented businesses.[12] In an important development for local governments, the Court also rejected the lower court's conclusion that a second "unmentioned" purpose, to negatively impact the message of eroticism, meant that the ordinance must be treated as content-based. This type of attack on the legislative record, Justice O'Connor stated, "is really an argument that the city council also had an illicit motive in enacting the ordinance. As we have said before, however, this Court will not strike down an otherwise constitutional statute on the basis of an alleged illicit motive."[13] The Court's deference to Erie's legislative record seems to reflect in a practical way what the Court has consistently stated since *Young*[14]— that sexually graphic expression occupies a subordinate position among First Amendment interests.

Justice O'Connor concluded her discussion of content-neutrality by stating, as Justice Souter had previously stated in *Barnes*, that the government's interest in preventing crime and other harmful effects caused by the presence of adult establishments is totally unrelated to the suppression of free expression. Even if Erie's ordinance has a small effect on an erotic message, the dancers at Kandyland are free to do erotic performances wearing only pasties and G-strings.[15] Any effect on the overall expression is *de minimis*, and "if States are to be able to regulate secondary effects, then *de minimis* intrusions on expression such as those at issue here cannot be sufficient to render the ordinance content based."[16]

O'Brien *Is Satisfied with the City's Expert Judgment*

The Court went on to apply the four-part *O'Brien* test and concluded that the Erie ordinance satisfied that test. Applying the first *O'Brien* factor, Justice O'Connor stated that the law is within the constitutional power of the government, since protecting public health and safety are clearly within the city's police powers. Second, the regulation must further an important or substantial government interest. The Court noted, as it has in prior cases, that preventing harmful secondary effects is an undeniably important interest. It was reasonable for Erie to conclude from the Court's prior cases that nude dancing in Erie is likely to produce similar secondary effects. Additionally, the city relied on its own findings that immoral activities carried on in public places promote secondary effects. The Court accepted Erie's determination, giving a refreshing dose of deference to the legislative judgment of cities dealing with the admittedly serious problems of sexually oriented businesses:

> The city council members, familiar with commercial downtown Erie, are the individuals who would likely have had first-hand knowledge of what took place at and around nude dancing establishments in Erie, and can make particularized, expert judgments about the resulting harmful secondary effects.[17]

Justice O'Connor next stated that since the law is content-neutral, it satisfies *O'Brien's* third requirement that the regulation be unrelated to suppression of expression. Last, the Court reaffirmed its prior holding that the

pasties and G-string requirement is narrowly tailored and that least restrictive means analysis is not required for content-neutral regulations.

The Court Answers an Important Question, but Another Remains

In *Pap's*, the Court answered — or at last restated with greater clarity its prior answer — an important question regarding the proper constitutional scrutiny to be applied to adult business regulations. However, another important question regarding overbreadth, which was not before the Court, remains unanswered, and cities must therefore exercise caution when drafting general public indecency ordinances or prohibitions on nudity in sexually oriented businesses.

"Heightened" Intermediate Scrutiny Is Not the Law

Justice Souter, who provided the fifth vote in *Barnes*, dissented on the grounds that while the Court was correct in applying *O'Brien* analysis to the Erie ordinance, it was wrong in its conclusion that *O'Brien* was satisfied. Specifically, he argued that under intermediate scrutiny as described in *Turner Broadcasting, Inc. v. F.C.C.*,[18] Erie's ordinance lacked a sufficient evidentiary record to sustain its regulation of nude dancing. Justice Souter basically adopted a position that he eschewed in *Barnes*— that the legislative record must demonstrate a precise nexus between the city's adult business regulations and the targeted harms in order to survive intermediate scrutiny. On this point, he was persuaded by the *amicus* brief filed by the First Amendment Lawyers Association (FALA), a group of adult business attorneys who submitted an affidavit attacking the validity of the land use studies documenting crime and other deleterious activities near sexually oriented businesses. Justice O'Connor was quick to point out the discrepancy between this position and Justice Souter's statement that the *O'Brien* standard applies to Erie's regulation of conduct, noting that *O'Brien* "required no evidentiary showing at all that the threatened harm was real."[19] Citing the Court's recent pronouncement in *Nixon v. Shrink Missouri Government PAC*, Justice O'Connor concluded that rigorous, scientific studies are not required to justify adult business regulations.[20] Rather, the standard is the rule enunciated in *Renton v. Playtime Theatres*— that the city may rely on its own experience or the experience of other cities, as long as that experience is relevant to the problem the city seeks to address.[21] Additionally, that experience may consist (as it did in *Renton*) of prior judicial opinions describing the evidentiary basis on which the city relies.[22]

When Is a Public Nudity Prohibition Overbroad?

As in *Barnes*, this question was not before the Court, but will likely be answered on remand to the Pennsylvania Supreme Court.[23] The cases seem to teach that there are two categories of public nudity which can be prohibited: (1) where no expression is taking place, and (2) where marginally protected expression is taking place in a context associated with secondary effects. To comply with *Barnes* and its progeny, including *Pap's*, cities drafting ordinances to prevent secondary effects must enact nudity prohibitions that are both generally applicable (i.e., content neutral) and narrowly tailored (i.e., not overly broad). Thus, the law must not be targeted at suppressing any particularly expression, but also must be sufficiently targeted to address negative secondary effects.

Perhaps the best way to accomplish this is not through a general public indecency ordinance (though these have been upheld on numerous occasions[24]), but instead, by drafting a prohibition of public nudity that applies only on the premises[25] of sexually oriented businesses. A prohibition of all nudity (expressive or not) by employees or patrons at a class of establishments empirically associated with secondary effects is both content-neutral and narrowly tailored to address substantial government interests. This is the approach already taken by many cities and suggested in the model ordinances available from the International Municipal Lawyers Association and various leagues of cities. This preference reflects the fact that in the current body of case law, it is easier to win the content-based argument than the overbreadth argument, which has been decided on far fewer occasions.

Conclusion

The Supreme Court's decision in *Pap's A.M. v. City of Erie* solidifies the ability of local governments to prohibit public nudity, and also gives them substantial latitude in regulating sex businesses as a whole. However, the decision still does not answer a serious overbreadth question that has remained unresolved since *Barnes*. Additionally, the plurality's failure to reiterate the public order and morality rationale for public indecency laws (which the same plurality — minus Justice Breyer — relied on in *Barnes*) raises the question of whether this justification is still a substantial government interest under *O'Brien*. The existence of these unanswered questions counsels against merely adopting verbatim the *Erie* ordinance or any other stock language for use in adult business ordinances. Courts in various jurisdictions have applied a myriad of nuances to the analysis of sex business restrictions, and such approaches require jurisdiction-specific research and drafting. One thing, however, is clear; the commercial sex industry's growth and its rapid expansion into smaller and smaller communities will require cities to take proactive steps to update and implement constitutionally sound ordinances.

NOTES

1. 120 S. Ct. 1382 (2000).

2. 501 U.S. 560 (1990). *See, e.g., Nude Dancing Limits Tightened,* Miami Herald, Mar. 30, 2000, at 19A. ("The Court failed in the Indiana case to settle on a standard, and did only marginally better Wednesday as Justice David Souter changed his mind on the amount of evidence cities needed in order to justify a ban on nude dancing.")

3. *Supreme Court Upholds Erie Nudity Ban,* Adult Video News (Mar. 29, 2000) <http://www.avn.com/ng/query. cig?act=detail&template=news&event_id=1664>.

4. *See, e.g.,* Nightclub Mgmt. v. City of Cannon Falls, 95 F. Supp 2d 1027 (D. Minn. 2000) (upholding public nudity ban under *Pap's*); Harris v. Fitchville Twp. Trustees, 99 F. Supp. 2d 837, 842 (N.D. Ohio 2000) (citing *Pap's* holding that alleged "impermissible motive" by local officials does not invalidate adult business regulations); Urmanski v. Town of Bradley, 2000 Wisc. App. LEXIS 473 (Wisc. Ct. App. 2000) ("In [*Pap's*], a majority of the court clarified that the government's interest in preventing the negative secondary effects — justified any *de minimis* intrusions on the expression inherent in nude dancing."). *But see* Alameda Books, Inc. v. City of Los Angeles, 2000 U.S. App. LEXIS 18059, *22 n.7 (9th Cir. 2000) (holding that *Pap's* reasonable reliance standard was not met when city relied on a general study to support prohibition on more than one adult use in the same building).

5. 430 U.S. 188 (1977).

6. Since *Barnes,* courts have consistently held that Justice Souter's concurrence constituted the holding of the case. *See, e.g.,* DLS, Inc. v. City of Chattanooga, 107 F. 3d 403, 408 (6th Cir. 1997); Farkas v. Miller, 151 F. 3d 900, 904 (8th Cir. 1998); J & B Entertainment v. City of Jackson, 152 F. 3d 362, 370 (5th Cir. 1998); International Eateries of Am., Inc. v. Broward County, 941 F. 2d 1157, 1160-61 (11th Cir. 1991).

7. Pap's A.M. v. City of Erie, 719 A.2d 273, 279 (1998).

8. *Id.*

9. Pap's sought to have the case dismissed as moot because its nude dancing establishment had closed and the owner stated that he did not intend to open another. Justice O'Connor opined that the corporation could feasibly reenter the nude dancing business and that Pap's was seeking to insulate its lower court victory from further review. Justices Scalia and Thomas disagreed and contended that the case was moot.

10. United States v. O'Brien, 391 U.S. 367 (1968).

11. *Pap's,* 120 S. Ct. at 1392 (quoting Pap's A.M. v. City of Erie, 719 A.2d at 279).

12. *Id.,* citing Renton v. Playtime Theatres, Inc., 475 U.S. 41 (1986).

13. *Id.* at 1392 93 (citing *O'Brien* 391 U.S. at 382–83, and Renton v. Playtime Theatres, Inc., 475 U.S. at 47–8).

14. Young v. American Mini Theatres, Inc., 427 U.S. 50 (1976).

15. *Pap's,* 120 S. Ct. at 1392.

16. *Id.* at 1394.

17. *Id.* at 1396.

18. *Pap's,* 120 S. Ct. at 1403 (Souter, J., concurring) ("[The government] must demonstrate that the recited harms are real, not merely conjectural, and that the regulation will in fact alleviate those harms in a direct and material way" (quoting Turner Broadcasting, Inc. v. F.C.C., 512 U.S. 622, 664 (1994) (Turner I).

19. *Id.* at 1396.

20. 120 S. Ct. 897, 903 (2000) (citing Nixon v. Shrink Missouri Government PAC, 528 U.S. _____ (2000) (slip op., at 14–5), for the proposition that the "invocation of academic studies said to indicate" that the threatened harms are not real is insufficient to reject local governments' experiences).

21. Note that even after *Pap's, Renton's* reasonable reliance standard is not assumed to be met. *See* Alameda Books, Inc. v. City of Los Angeles, 2000 U.S. Appl. LEXIS 18059, *17 (9th Cir. 2000) (striking prohibition on multiple adult uses in same building and emphasizing that "[t]his deference to legislative decision making is not unbounded.").

22. *Renton,* 475 U.S. at 51–2.

23. On remand, the Pennsylvania high court has asked the parties to brief (1) whether the case is moot, (2) whether Art. 1, Sec. 7 of the Pennsylvania Constitution provides greater protection to nude dancing than the First Amendment, and (3) whether the ordinance is overbroad.

24. *See, e.g.,* In re Tennessee Pub. Indecency Statute (Déjà vu v. Metro Gov't), 1999 U.S. App. LEXIS 535 (6th Cir. 1999); J & B Entertainment v. City of Jackson, 152 F. 3d 362 (5th Cir. 1998).

25. The definition of "premises" may be expansive if a sexually oriented business operates in multiple locations. *See, e.g.,* Currence v. City of Cincinnati, No. C-1-97-725, slip op. at 26-8 (S.D. Ohio July 13, 2000) (extending *Pap's* secondary effects rationale to apply to a nude outcall dancing business which traveled to residence).

Editor's Note:

These chapter notes are listed as they were in the original journal article. Questions concerning the legal citations should be directed to the source, which is listed in the footnote at the bottom of the first page of this chapter.

CHAPTER 15

Forest Park, Like Many Small Towns, Had No Laws to Regulate Adult Businesses

Ed Brock

The First Amendment's free speech protection makes banning sexually oriented businesses, such as adult video stores and strip bars, nearly impossible for local governments. In response, many cities are creating sexually oriented business overlay districts (SOBODs), to control where the clubs and shops can locate.

When the Crazy Horse Saloon, a strip club, began operating in Forest Park, Ga., in the early 1990s, many residents organized a movement to stop it. But, that was impossible, says Mayor Corine Deyton who was a councilmember at the time. "We didn't have an ordinance to keep them out. It was that simple," Deyton says. "We consulted with our attorneys, and we just didn't have the money to fight it. It takes a lot of money to fight [sexually oriented businesses]."

So, the city created an SOBOD along a four-lane state highway lined with shopping centers and restaurants, and a second SOBOD in an isolated part of the city, in case the Crazy Horse Saloon wanted to open another location, However, when the bar's owners requested a second permit to open another club

in 2001, city officials, apparently unaware of the existence of the second zone, created a third, 447.4-acre parcel on a service road fronting an interstate and away from residential areas. But, Deyton says, the third zone was too large and too close to churches and the Atlanta State Farmer's Market, where many families shop. So, in 2006, the city reduced that SOBOD to 347 acres.

In many cities, zoning laws, such as SOBODs, are the first line of defense in regulating sexually oriented businesses, says Eric Kelly, a professor of urban planning at Ball State University in Muncie, Ind., in "Everything You Ever Wanted to Know about Regulating Sex Businesses," a report for the Washington-based American Planning Association. Along with designating specific parts of a city where sexually oriented businesses may locate, SOBODs often set separation requirements between the adult businesses and residential or family-oriented areas, such as churches and schools.

Sometimes, SOBODs can be used with other laws to regulate adult businesses. Duncanville, Texas, a Dallas suburb with 38,000

Originally published as "Sex Industry Sets Up Shop in Small Towns," *American City & County*, Vol. 123, No. 5, May 2008, by Penton Media, Inc., Atlanta, GA. Reprinted with permission of the publisher.

residents, created an SOBOD nearly two decades ago, though no sexually oriented business has yet applied for a permit to operate in the city, However, in 2000, city officials discovered the Cherry Pit, an apparent sex club, operating illegally out of a resident's home, says City Manager Kent Cagle. "We knew [the club was operating illegally], but proving it was another thing." So, in 2007, the city passed a new ordinance to augment the SOBOD and ban any business that advertises an opportunity for people to view live sexual acts. Cagle says the new law gave them "extra ammunition" to regulate the Cherry Pit.

Cherry Pit owner Thomas Trulock filed suit in Dallas County Court seeking an injunction to prevent the city from enforcing the ordinance, but the city countersued. Although the complaint was later dismissed because the court did not have jurisdiction in the case, Cagle says the city is moving forward with its lawsuit to force Trulock to cease business operations. The city also has issued tickets to Trulock for violating the sexually oriented business zoning law and violating the new ordinance.

Some experts had expected adult businesses to decline because of the availability of sexually related Web sites on the Internet, Kelly says, but actually the businesses are expanding into smaller communities that have no existing regulations and are slow to pass them. "They often don't adopt them until after the first business comes in," Kelly says. By then, he says, it may be too late.

Editor's Note:

It is not uncommon for small cities and town to adopt regulations for sexually-oriented businesses after they come to the community to seek approval to operate. This oftentimes results in expensive lawsuits lasting several years. Public officials should be proactive and have such regulation on the books before such businesses apply for permission to operate. Such laws regulate the location, distance from other land uses, and other desirable conditions typically recommended by professional planners, through appropriate municipal advisory bodies, before being considered and approved by elected officials.

CHAPTER 16

Harrisburg Officials Include Chapter on Adult Business Regulations in Their Municipal Briefing Booklet

Robert D. Robbins

Public officials are sometimes faced with the prospect of adult-oriented businesses (AOBs) locating in a community and the result outcry of constituents. These businesses often target communities that have little or no municipal AOB regulation. Yet, citizens want to know what tools are available to municipalities to minimize the real or perceived effects[1] such businesses may have on the community. Below is an abbreviated list of some methods by which AOBs may be regulated. As the discussions below indicate, each of these regulatory methods presents certain legal challenges[2] that require research and, in all cases, careful drafting and review by a municipality's solicitor.

Regulation of AOBs through Zoning[3]

Zoning is arguably the most prevalent means of controlling AOBs. Zoning that dis-

tinguishes AOBs from other commercial uses has consistently been upheld by courts provided it is done within certain constitutional constraints.[4] There are two primary methods of zoning AOBs: "dispersion zoning," otherwise known as "anti–skid row" regulation, is exemplified in regulations that prohibit the operation of an AOB "within 1000 feet of any other such establishment or within 500 feet of a residential area"[5]; alternatively, "concentration zoning," also known as "red light district" regulations, whereby a particular use is prohibited from locating anywhere except in a specific portion of the municipality. Both methods have been held to be constitutionally permissible as legitimate "time, place, and manner" restrictions of protected speech.[6] It is also true, however, that in distinguishing AOBs for zoning purposes, both "dispersion zoning" and "red light district" regulations are subject to a three-prong constitutional test. Under this test, a regulation must be (1) unrelated to suppressing speech; (2) narrowly tai-

Originally published as "Municipal Regulation of Adult-Oriented Businesses," *Pennsylvania Legislator's Municipal Deskbook*, Third Edition, September 2006, by the Local Government Commission, General Assembly of the Commonwealth of Pennsylvania, Harrisburg, PA. Reprinted with permission of the publisher.

lored to serve a substantial governmental interest, and; (3) permit reasonable alternate channels of communication.[7] The nuances of each prong of this test are complex. It is also important to know what zoning *cannot* do:

- *Zoning cannot completely eliminate AOBs from the municipal or jointly zoned area.*[8]
- *Zoning cannot exclusively permit AOBs in an area that is "commercially unavailable."*[9]
- *Zoning cannot force preexisting AOBs to cease operation and relocate.*[10]

Municipal Licensing of AOBs

Subject to certain constitutional and statutory restraints,[11] Pennsylvania courts have upheld a municipality's ability to enact and enforce licensing requirements for AOBs and their employees.[12] These regulations have involved hours of operation, imposed a minimal distance between erotic dancers and patrons, required employee background checks, and provided for warrantless inspections of AOBs during business hours as well as reasonable administrative fees.[13] It is important for licensing regulations to provide clear and explicit standards and a ready means for court review. These requirements are necessary because these types of regulations involve obtaining governmental approval prior to engaging in "protected speech" and, thus, are typically considered "prior restraint" regulations. As such, there is a rebuttable presumption that the regulations are unconstitutional.[14] This presumption is overcome when the regulation is determined to provide clear standards to guide the decision making official, and prompt judicial review of the decision during which time the status quo must be maintained.[15] As with zoning regulation of AOBs, courts will require that any given licensing requirement have a logical correlation to preventing an "adverse secondary effect" of the AOB.

State Regulations and Municipal Nuisance Ordinances

In 1996, the General Assembly passed Act 120, which added Chapter 55 (Adult-Oriented Establishments) to Title 68 (Real Property) of the Pennsylvania Consolidated Statutes. In the legislative intent provisions of this statute, the General Assembly recognized the evidence of a "number of adult-oriented establishments which require special regulation by law and supervision by public safety agencies in order to protect and preserve the health, safety and welfare of patrons of these establishments, as well as the health, safety and welfare of the citizens of this Commonwealth."[16] The law provides standards for the illumination, physical configuration, restriction on the presence of minors, and ownership liability for the conduct of employees of defined "adult-oriented establishments." Furthermore, the act provides civil remedies and penalties that may be pursued by municipalities, the county district attorney or the Attorney General.[17] Municipalities facing the prospect of an incoming or existing AOB should familiarize themselves with these provisions.

As discussed elsewhere in this publication,[18] municipalities may prohibit the unreasonable interference with the public health, safety, peace, comfort, or convenience. Many municipalities have nuisance ordinances that, under certain circumstances, could possibly be used to shut down AOBs, or force them to abate any conduct or condition that constitutes the nuisance. Furthermore, the Pennsylvania "Use of Property Act"[19] provides that the use of a building for the purpose of "fornication, lewdness, assignation, and/or prostitution is ... declared to be a common nuisance."[20] The district attorney of any county wherein the nuisance lies may bring an action to abate the nuisance or prosecute under the act.[21] It is important to note that *the content* of any adult materials or pornographic speech cannot constitute a nuisance in and of itself.[22] In essence, it is the "secondary effects" of the

AOBs, i.e., sexual activity, indecent exposure, noise, drug activity, etc., that establish the nuisance for purposes of municipal ordinances or, where appropriate, state law.

Specific Issues

1. Difficulties Regulating Nude Dancing in Pennsylvania

As previously discussed, municipal regulation through zoning of the location of businesses featuring nude dancing often withstands constitutional challenges. In light of recent case law, however, it may prove significantly more difficult for a municipality in Pennsylvania to totally prohibit nude dancing in "public places" through operation of "public indecency" ordinances. In *Pap's A.M. v. The City of Erie*,[23] the Pennsylvania Supreme Court held that Article 1, Section 7 of the Pennsylvania Constitution provides greater protection to speech than the First Amendment to the United States Constitution, and, therefore, a total ban on "expressive conduct," such as nude dancing, must satisfy a "less intrusive means" test.[24] Where municipalities seek to ban expressive conduct, they must not only prove that there is a compelling governmental interest in doing so, but they must also prove that governmental goals may not be accomplished by "a narrower, less intrusive method than the total ban on expression."[25]

An ordinance having the effect of totally barring nude dancing faces invalidation under the Pennsylvania Constitution because the goals of combating the "secondary effects" of nude dancing may be accomplished, in the Pennsylvania Supreme Court's opinion, by methods such as zoning, more stringent civil and criminal enforcement mechanisms, and hours-of-operation restrictions. Municipalities seeking to restrict nude dancing by way of public indecency or nudity ordinances should be very aware of the *Pap's A.M.* case and the fact that the Pennsylvania Supreme Court has articulated an extremely strict test for the legitimacy of regulations that regulate "expressive conduct" based on the message the conduct conveys.

2. Sexually-Oriented Conduct in Establishments with Liquor Licenses

The language in the Pennsylvania Liquor Code prohibits licensed establishments from permitting any "lewd, immoral or improper entertainment" on the premises.[26] Two recent federal court decisions, however, have rendered this phrase unconstitutional, thus effectively prohibiting any enforcement of the provision.[27] Prior to these decisions, Pennsylvania case law provided that nude dancing in public bars constituted a violation of this provision,[28] and entertainers in licensed establishments offering any type of exotic dancing, in addition to being required to wear appropriate covering on their bodies, were further required to refrain from certain interaction with patrons.[29] In the Third Circuit decision interpreting this provision, *Conchatta v. Miller*,[30] the court held that the term "lewd" as used in Section 4-493(10) of the Liquor Code is unconstitutionally overbroad.[31] The court noted that "[t]he statutory language clearly could have been drafted more narrowly to specifically target secondary effects associated with nude or topless dancing."[32] The court's language appears to indicate the overbreadth issue could be alleviated by an appropriate revision of the Liquor Code.

The Pennsylvania State Police through its Bureau of Liquor Control Enforcement has a "nuisance bar" program that targets bars that disrupt the community or, until the recent court decisions, violated the decency provisions of the Liquor Code. Citizens can file complaints with either the Bureau or their local police if they have reason to believe the Liquor Code is being or has been violated. It is important to note that the provisions relating to the nuisance bar program would not apply to "bottle clubs," i.e., establishments where alcohol is not sold, but where patrons may bring their own alcohol.

Use of Restrictive Covenants: Community Involvement

A property owner whose property could possibly be used for an AOB has an often overlooked method of combating AOBs. With the advice of legal counsel, a property owner could explore imposing conditions on leases and deeds, known as restrictive covenants, that would limit or restrict the use of property for AOBs. Furthermore, citizens should become familiar with the appropriate state and local enactments that regulate businesses, nuisances, and obscenity, and participate in local government if they feel their community is inadequately protected.

NOTES

1. These effects, known in the legal parlance as the "secondary effects" of adult uses, relate to statistically-supported increases in crime and nuisances and are important factors in establishing the legal justification for regulating AOBs.

2. Often, when methods of municipal regulation of AOBs are challenged, it is on the basis that they impinge on "speech" entitled to protection under the First Amendment to the United States Constitution, and the analogous provision of the Pennsylvania Constitution, Article 1, Section 7.

3. In Pennsylvania, zoning, as discussed *infra*, primarily dictates the *location* of defined uses of property. Subdivision and land development ordinances (SLDOs) essentially regulate the manner in which property is used. SLDO provisions, often in concert with zoning ordinances, can provide for screening, and window and sign restriction that minimize the impact of the AOB on the appearance of the community without running afoul of constitutional limitations. *See also, infra*, text accompanying notes 16 and 17.

4. *See, e.g., City of Renton v. Playtime Theatres*, 475 U.S. 41 (1986), *Young v. American Mini Theatres, Inc.*, 427 U.S. 50 (1976).

5. *See Young*, 427 U.S. at 54.

6. *See City of Renton*, 475 U.S. at 52. *See also*, 427 U.S. at 63, n. 18.

7. *See* 475 U.S. at 49–51.

8. *See Schad v. Borough of Mount Ephraim*, 452 U.S. 61 (1981).

9. There is little Pennsylvania state or Third Circuit federal court authority on this specific issue in the context of the "time, place, and manner" test. Other federal appellate courts use tests that suggest that the land must be both physically available (appropriate for development) and legally available (not excluding adult uses).

10. *See Northwestern Distributors, Inc. v. ZHB (Tp. Of*

Moon), 584 A.2d 1372 (Pa. 1991). In this case, the Pennsylvania Supreme Court held that this practice, called "amortization of a nonconforming use," amounted to a confiscation of property without compensation and thus violated Article 1, Section 1 of the Pennsylvania Constitution.

11. Some questions may be raised as to whether particular types of municipalities, i.e., boroughs, townships, towns, or cities, may have proper statutory authorization to license AOBs.

12. *See, e.g., Paitek v. Pulaski Township*, 828 A.2d 1164 (Pa. Cmwlth. 2003); *Pennsylvania Pride, Inc. v. Southampton Township*, 78 F. Supp. 2d 359 (M.D. Pa. 1999).

13. *See* 828 A.2d at 1167.

14. *See Southeastern Promotions, Ltd. V. Conrad*, 420 U.S. 546 (1975).

15. *See Freedman v. Maryland*, 380 U.S. 51 (1965).

16. 68 Pa.C.S. § 5501 (a).

17. *See* 68 Pa.C.S. § 5506.

18. *See* related *Deskbook* article, "Public Nuisances."

19. 68 P.S. §§ 467–473.

20. 68 P.S. § 467.

21. For the use of this statute in the abatement of nuisances, *see Commonwealth ex rel. Preate v. Danny's New Adam & Eve Bookstore*, 625 A.2d 119 (Pa. Cmwlth. 1993); *Commonwealth ex rel. Lewis v. Allouwill Realty Corp.*, 475 A.2d 1334 (Pa. Super. 1984).

22. "...It has been held that obscenity cannot at once be defined and enjoined under the common law of public nuisance, because nuisance law provides too vague a standard for determining the line between protected and unprotected speech." *Ranck v. Bonal Enterprises, Inc.*, 359 A.2d 748 (Pa. 1976).

23. 812 A.2d 591 (Pa. 2002). This case was the Pennsylvania Supreme Court decision issued after remand from the United States Supreme Court decision *City of Erie v. Pap's A.M.*, 529 U.S. 277 (2000). While the United States Supreme Court upheld the constitutionality of relevant provisions of the City of Erie's public decency ordinance under federal law, the Pennsylvania Supreme Court, on remand, found that the ordinance violated a heightened protection for speech contained in Article 1, Section 7 of the Pennsylvania Constitution.

24. *See* 812 A.2d at 612.

25. *Id.*

26. *See* 47 P.S. § 4-493(10). Section 7329 of the Pennsylvania Crimes Code (18 Pa.C.S. § 7329) uses the same language as Section 4-493(10) of the Liquor Code, i.e. "lewd, immoral or improper entertainment," but applies only in the contest of "bottle clubs" rather than licensed establishments. In light of the federal court decisions in *Conchatta, Inc. v. Evanko* and *Conchatta, Inc. v. Miller* (*see infra* note 27), the constitutional status of Section 7329 could be challenged.

27. The federal District Court for the Eastern District of Pennsylvania, in *Conchatta, Inc. v. Evanko*, Slip Copy, 2005 WL 426452 (E.D. Pa. Feb. 23, 2005), held that the terms "immoral or improper" were unconstitutionally vague as used in the Liquor Code.

28. *See, e.g., Purple Orchid, Inc. v. Pennsylvania State Police, Bureau of Liquor Control Enforcement*, 813 A.2d 801 (Pa. 2002); *Rising Sun Entertainment, Inc. v. Commonwealth*, 829 A.2d 1214 (Pa. Cmwlth. 2003). *But see Conchatta, Inc. v. Evanko*, Slip Copy, 2005 WL 426452 (E.D. Pa. Feb 23, 2005).

29. 40 Pa. Code § 5.32(c).

30. — F.3d —, 2006 WL 2347649 (3d Cir. 2006).

31. *See id.* at *7.

32. *Conchatta*, 2006 WL 2347649 at *7.

Editor's Note:

Some of the above footnotes contain more detailed legal explanations, legal references, and additional citations. To see the above notes in their entirety, please refer to the Local Government Commission, General Assembly of the Commonwealth of Pennsylvania, Harrisburg, PA, website <http://www.lgc.state.pas.us>. This information is contained in Land Use Section of the *Pennsylvania Legislator's Municipal Handbook* (pages 129–134), which is online and a part of the Commission's website.

CHAPTER 17

Hartford Officials Review Adult Entertainment Laws in Connecticut Cities

Christopher Reinhart

A member of the State's legislature inquired about the status of recent ordinances of communities in the State of Connecticut dealing with adult entertainment businesses, and if the State can assist their cities to facilitate their efforts to regulate these businesses. The following report was prepared by the Office of Legislative Research in response to this legislative inquiry.

Summary

We surveyed ordinances regulating adult entertainment businesses in several Connecticut communities including Farmington, Hartford, Milford, New London, Plainfield, Rocky Hill, Tolland, Wallingford, and West Hartford. Most ordinances begin with a list of findings, the ordinance's purposes, and the adverse effects it addresses. They also specifically define the different forms of adult businesses. These ordinances regulate adult businesses in a few different ways: (1) allowing them only in specific zoning district; (2) placing restrictions on how close they can be to schools, parks, day care centers, residential areas, and other adult businesses; (3) requiring that all booths and rooms be well-lighted and visible from the common areas of the premises; and (4) imposing licensing requirements. In addition, Plainfield last year banned public nudity, prohibited businesses from allowing sexually explicit nudity, and required adult businesses to maintain a list of state sex offenders and check the identification of patrons. The ordinances are being challenged in federal court.

Ordinances also include other requirements such as prohibitions of loitering by minors and intoxicated people in the establishment and its parking lot, limits on hours of operation, making owners responsible for employee violations of the ordinances, requiring businesses to be open to inspection, and requiring registration with a town official. Some towns (such as West Hartford) also regulate signs and displays and require that the entertainment not be visible outside the building. Farmington prohibits establishments from employing a person convicted within the past three years of moral turpitude, prostitution, obscenity, sex-related crimes, and drug offenses in any jurisdiction.

Originally published as "Adult Entertainment Ordinances," *OLR Research Report*, No. 99-R-1263, December 10, 1999, by the Office of Legislative Research, State of Connecticut, Hartford, CT.

The state grants municipalities powers that allow them to regulate adult businesses, including police powers and zoning powers. The state obscenity statutes also limit the type of activities that can occur at adult businesses (§ 53a-193 et seq.). The nuisance abatement law could affect adult businesses if criminal conduct occurs there (§ 19a-343a et seq.).

Copies of ordinances from several Connecticut towns, and a sample ordinance from the Connecticut Conference of Municipalities, and OLR Report 98-R-0073 were attached but are not included here.

Zoning Requirements

Hartford provides an example of zoning requirements imposed on adult businesses (Hartford Mun. Code § 35-921). Adult businesses are permitted in districts zoned for industry and cannot be within 1,000 feet of a lot used for (1) single or multi family residences; (2) school or education facilities attended by minors (including after school programs, children's museums, camps, and athletic leagues); (3) churches and religious facilities or institutions; (4) public parks; and (5) other adult establishments.

Licensing

Farmington's ordinance provides an example of licensing requirements (Farmington Code § 73-4 et seq.). All adult-oriented establishments must have a license from the police chief. The town can license only one adult-oriented establishment at a fixed place. The license cannot be sold, assigned, or transferred and applies only to the licensee and a specific location.

An applicant must pay a fee of $650 and post a sign on the business site describing the application. The application requires information about the applicant and his employees, the nature of the entertainment to be pro-

vided, the applicant's permit or license history in other places, and any criminal convictions of the applicant, employee, operator, or anyone directly involved in the establishment. The police chief confirms the applicant's qualifications and inspects the premises for compliance with local and state laws. The chief must issue a license within 75 days unless the applicant:

1. does not comply with building, health, housing, zoning, and fire laws;
2. was convicted of a crime of moral turpitude, prostitution, sex-related crimes, or drug offenses in any jurisdiction within the past three years or an obscenity offense within two years;
3. made false statements or misrepresentations on the application; or
4. violated the adult business ordinances within the past five years.

Licenses are valid for one year and require a $400 renewal fee. Licenses are renewable unless there are (1) uncorrected violations of the adult business ordinances or health, fire, or safety laws, or (2) at least two violations of the ban on live performance of sexual activity (as defined in the ordinance) or at least one violation of the adult business ordinances for over 60 days. A license holder denied renewal cannot get a license for five years.

The chief can suspend or revoke a license for up to 30 days for violation of the ordinances. The suspension or revocation terminates if the violation is corrected. Licenses are revoked for (1) providing false or misleading information on the application, (2) failing to pay a required cost or fee, (3) conviction of the crimes that make a person ineligible for a license, (4) two or more violations of certain provisions in the ordinances, (5) one or more uncorrected violations for over 60 days, (6) failure to correct violations within 30 days of a license suspension, and (7) transfer of the license or an interest in it. The holder of a revoked license is not eligible for a new license for five years.

Well-Lighted and Visible

Tolland provides an example of an ordinance regulating the interior of adult entertainment establishments (Tolland Code § 51-2). All adult-oriented establishments must be well-lighted at all times and physically arranged so that the entire interior of booths, cubicles, rooms, or stalls are visible from the common areas of the premises. Doors, curtains, partitions, drapes, or other obstructions cannot block visibility. Installing enclosed booths, cubicles, rooms, or stalls within adult-oriented establishments for any purpose is illegal.

All operators must provide that rooms and areas for viewing adult movies or other live adult entertainment are well lighted and readily accessible for all times and continuously open to view. The ordinance specifies the amount of overhead light required when patrons are present.

State Grant of Powers to Municipalities

CGS § 7-148 establishes the scope of municipal powers, and generally requires municipalities to exercise their powers by ordinances which establish rules or regulations of general application, the violation of which may result in the imposition of a fine or other penalty, or create a permanent local law of general applicability. Among those powers, municipalities can:

1. regulate how buildings are used, for the purpose of promoting the safety, health, morals and general welfare of people who live in the municipality;
2. define, prohibit and abate all nuisances and their causes, and "all things detrimental to the health, morals, safety, convenience and welfare of its inhabitants";
3. make and enforce police, sanitary, or other similar regulations and protect or promote "the peace, safety, good government and welfare of the municipality and its inhabitants" (CGS §§ 7-148(c)(7).

Zoning

CGS § 8-2(a) establishes the regulatory authority of zoning commissions. Among other things, it allows them to regulate "the location and use of buildings, structures and land for trade, industry, residence or other purposes...." It allows zoning commissions to divide their municipalities into districts, and within each district, to regulate the "use of buildings or structures and the use of land." It requires such regulations to be uniform for each class or kind of buildings, structures, or land use throughout each district. It allows them to provide that certain kinds of buildings, structures, or land use are permitted only after obtaining a special permit or exception, subject to standards set forth in the regulations and conditions necessary to protect the public health, safety, convenience and property values. It requires the regulations to "be made in accordance with a comprehensive plan," and to "be designed to ... promote health and the general welfare...."

CHAPTER 18

Hastings Adopts Laws to Further Restrict the Operations of Adult Businesses

Daniel J. Fluegel

In drafting and enacting an Adult Use Ordinance, the City must taken into account legal authority from numerous sources including the First Amendment to the Constitution of the United States, federal and state judicial rulings, state statutes and other local ordinances that impact the adult uses being regulated. Because the legal authority is so extensive, I will attempt to provide some guidance on the general legal concepts that govern adult use restrictions and also respond to some of the questions and comments that have been raised by individuals in the community. I am providing information on the following three topic areas: (1) Application of First Amendment Rulings to Adult Uses; (2) Minnesota Statutes §617.242 Adult Entertainment Establishments; and (3) Distinction between Obscenity and Protected Adult Uses.

Application for First Amendment to Adult Uses

The Supreme Court of the United States has determined that many forms of adult uses constitute expressive speech or conduct which is subject to free speech protections under the First Amendment. There is a distinction between these protected activities and "obscene" activities or content and that distinction is discussed in more detail below. When government regulations are enacted for the purpose of restraining speech or expressive conduct *based on its content*, those restrictions are presumed to violate the First Amendment. Regulations that prohibit constitutionally protected adult uses based on the content of speech (or activity) will almost always be found unconstitutional and unenforceable.

Cities have been successful by imposing restrictions that are not intended to directly regulate the speech or expressive activity, but instead are intended to prevent the negative secondary effects that have been proven to result from these adult uses. Undesirable secondary effects of adult uses have been found to include increased crime, declining property values, declining retail trade, and a negative impact on the quality of life in the community. Because a city has a substantial governmental interest in preventing these undesirable sec-

Originally published as "Memorandum on Adult Uses," *Report to the Honorable Mayor and City Council Members*, April 3, 2008, by the City of Hastings, MN.

ondary effects of adult uses, the city may impose *content-neutral* restrictions on the time, place and manner in which the adult uses can be conducted. However, in imposing those restrictions, the regulations must always provide business owners reasonable opportunities to open and operate adult use businesses within the city. If no reasonable alternative avenues for this constitutionally protected speech or conduct are available within a city, the ordinance imposing the restrictions will likely be found unconstitutional. Defining what activities fall within the definition of constitutionally protected free speech can be difficult but generally if the adult use does not constitute obscene activity as discussed below, it will most likely be considered a constitutionally protected activity.

It is therefore my opinion that any city ordinance which, as applied, prevents all reasonable opportunities for an adult use business to locate within the City, will be found unconstitutional and unenforceable if challenged.

The current Adult Use Ordinance for the City of Hastings allows adult use-principal by special use permit within the C-4 Regional Shopping Center zoning district. Adult use-principal is a prohibited use in all other zoning districts within the City. The normal requirements of an application for a special use permit apply and there are additional proximity restrictions on adult uses in the current Ordinance. A public hearing is required before issuance of any special use permit. In addition, businesses must obtain a license from the City before operating an adult use. Also, the current City Ordinance regulating alcoholic beverages and liquor licenses prohibits nudity within any premises licensed for liquor sale or distribution.

If the interim ordinance (moratorium) currently before the City Council is enacted, no special use permits for adult uses may be issued during the term of the moratorium.

The current planning process relating to the adult use ordinance began many months ago after staff questioned whether or not the C-4 zoning district was an appropriate area in which to allow adult uses. I know there have been numerous and very legitimate ideas discussed which suggest some areas may be more appropriate than others for this type of use. Initially, staff believed there may be benefit from keeping these types of uses away from the Highway 55 corridor as a major roadway. There have also been discussions suggesting that having the adult uses in a more visible location would be preferred. That is probably a political question and not a legal question.

As part of these discussions, staff researched the question of how much area would be needed where adult uses are allowed to satisfy the reasonable opportunity requirement. As part of that process, I gave to the Planning Department an opinion that the area where adult uses are allowed should probably not be less than 6 to 7 percent of the total commercial property contained within the City; I based the opinion on my review of many federal and Minnesota judicial decisions. There is no "bright line" test to determine how much area must be allowed for these uses within a city. However, the various cases suggest that restricting adult uses to less than 5 percent of commercial area within the City may not be considered as allowing reasonable opportunity for a business to locate within the City. There are cases that specifically found ordinances allowing adult uses in approximately 6 percent to 7 percent of the commercial areas are enforceable. Again, the exact percentage is not a "safe harbor" for ordinances. Instead, a court would look at whether the ordinance allows a reasonable opportunity for a new business to locate within the City based on the ordinance restrictions as well as factors including proximity restrictions, limited access, lack of utility services, proximity to heavy industrial uses, and other factors that would practically prevent a business from selecting a viable location for an adult use within the allowed areas.

Based on the foregoing, it is my opinion and recommendation to the City Council that any adult use ordinance needs to allow constitutionally protected adult uses within some location in the City of Hastings and application of the ordinance, including application of all proximity requirements, needs to allow adult use business owners a reasonable and viable opportunity to locate adult use businesses within the City.

Minnesota Statutes §617.242 — Adult Entertainment Establishments

I know Dave Osberg forwarded to the Council the Minnesota League of Cities Memorandum on regulation of adult uses which very clearly describes the serious doubts that exist on this Statute's constitutionality. I am attaching a copy of that Memorandum and the statute for any parties who did not receive it. Essentially, this statute became effective May 2006 and established under state law certain restrictions for adult entertainment establishments. The statute does not regulate all adult uses but instead only adult entertainment establishments which generally would include live performances that depict sexual conduct or nudity.

After the statute became effective, an adult entertainment establishment filed a motion in federal court seeking an injunction preventing the City of Duluth from enforcing its own ordinance as well as the Minnesota Statute regulating adult entertainment establishments. The opinion of the federal court (copy attached) was issued in August 2006 and the court issued an injunction prohibiting the City of Duluth from enforcing provisions of this statute. Although the opinion does not in itself strike down the statute altogether and the statute has not since been repealed, there are serious doubts about the statute's constitutionality and as noted in the Memorandum from the League, cities should not rely on the statute to regulate adult use establishments. There are specific statements in the federal

court opinion indicating that nude dancing is expressive conduct protected by the First Amendment. Through the application of either the city ordinance or the state statute, there were not sites available for location of an adult entertainment establishment within the city. The business then faced the choice of abandoning its constitutionally protected activity or facing possible criminal prosecution. With no reasonable alternative avenues for the constitutionally protected activity, the ordinance and the statute likely violated the First Amendment protections.

Based on the foregoing, my review of the authorities cited, and the opinion provided from the Minnesota League of Cities and other attorneys, I recommend that any adult use ordinance enacted by the City of Hastings not rely on the provisions of Minnesota Statutes §617.242 and that any new ordinance specifically "opt out" of regulations under the Statute.

Distinction between Obscene Acts and Constitutionally Protected Adult Uses

I think it is important that the Council and members of the community keep in mind that activities and materials which fall within the definition of obscenity can be *completely prohibited* and are not subject to the First Amendment protections. Minnesota Statutes §617.241 makes it a crime to exhibit, sell, print, offer to sell, give away, circulate, publish, distribute or attempt to distribute any obscene material or to produce, present, participate in, or direct an obscene performance. The definition of obscene is also included in that statute (a copy attached). As you will see, it is difficult to apply the definition of obscene. The definition incorporates application of "contemporary community standards" and I saw that phrase referenced in one of the recent emails from a member of the community. While the concept of contemporary community standards would apply in a trial against a person charged with displaying obscene materials or performances, I caution the City Council on blending this concept into the City's ability to regulate adult uses. An attempt by a governing body to expand the definition of obscenity so that nearly all adult uses and adult entertainment activities would be prohibited would, in my opinion, likely be overturned if challenged. Federal and state courts have consistently determined that many adult uses, including live entertainment, simply do not constitute obscene material or performances.

Summary

It is my opinion that the City proceed with enacting the interim ordinance (moratorium) to allow additional time for the planning process. Throughout the process, additional input can be obtained from the public. Based on that input and all other information available, staff and the Council can proceed with examining the existing Adult Use Ordinance to determine if any changes should or should not be made. If the Council considers changing the locations where adult uses will be allowed, it is my recommendation that specific findings be made confirming the restrictions will allow a reasonable opportunity for adult use businesses to locate within the City. The Council may wish to consider modification to the Ordinance adding specific restrictions on live performances and I know the Planning Department is compiling information on possible restrictions from other city ordinances. I strongly recommend the City not rely on the provisions of Minnesota Statutes §617.242.

Background

The various stages of development that the proposed changes to the City of Hasting's Adult Use Ordinance followed during the year of its adoption are highlighted below. The several steps involved, including the role of advisory bodies to the Mayor and City Council, took almost a year and one-half to complete.

- **Potential Adult Use Inquiry — November 2006.** The City of Hastings received questions from a potential adult use operator within a vacant storefront of Westview Shopping Center, a C-4 zone property. Under City Code, adult uses are allowed by a special use permit only within the C-4 — Regional Shopping Center District.
- **Adult Use Moratorium Enacted — December 2006.** The City Council enacted a one year moratorium on the issuance of special use permits for adult uses. Staff is directed to research the issue and review ordinance changes with the Planning Commission.
- **Planning Commission Review — Fall 2007 — Spring 2008.** The Planning Commission met several times to review potential changes to the City Code regarding adult uses. Eliminating adult uses from the C-4 district and adding them to the I-2 — Industrial Park Storage/Service District is recommended.
- **Industrial Park Rezoning — March 2008.** The Planning Commission conducted a public hearing to consider amending the City Code to eliminate adult uses from the C-4 district and add them to the I-2 District. The public hearing was attended by approximately 40 individuals. Those in attendance did not support the changes. The Planning Commission tabled action on the ordinance change and directed staff to recommend adoption of a moratorium to continue research and discussion.
- **Adult Use Moratorium Adopted — April 2008.** The City council adopted a new moratorium ordinance establishing a one year prohibition on issuance of special use permits for adult uses in the C-4 district.
- **Adult Use Public Meeting — April 2008.** The City held a public meeting to review

the legal obligations for allowing adult uses. Approximately 60 people attended the meeting. Those in attendance questioned the need to allow adult uses anywhere within the City.

- **Referred to Planning Committee of City Council — May 2008.** Mayor Hicks directed the Planning Committee of City Council to review potential ordinance changes and report back to the City Council.

Proposed Adult Use Ordinance

The City's elected officials, the Mayor and members of the City Council, voted to amend the City of Hasting's Adult Use Ordinance in September of 2008. A copy of the proposed changes, taken from a staff report from the Planning Director, is shown below:

- **Accessory Adult Use**
  - <=10 percent of floor area (350SqFt max)
  - <=20 percent of gross receipts
  - Do not involve any activity except sale or rental of merchandise
  - Separate room in clear view of manager
  - No internal or external advertising of materials or products
- **Hours of Operation**
  - Prohibited from 1 A.M. to 8 A.M. Monday through Saturday
  - Prohibited from 1 A.M. and 12 noon on Sunday
  - *(Further restrictions on hours were reviewed and not recommended based on increased difficulty in proving harmful secondary effects different than a liquor license.)*
- **Off Site Viewing**
  - Must prevent off site viewing of materials and activities
- **Signage**
  - No message or images which identify sexual activities or anatomical areas
  - No merchandise, photos or pictures of products
  - No window displays

- Activities and products cannot be visible outside
- **Liquor**
  - Sale and consumption prohibited
- **Nudity**
  - Full nudity is only allowed in a modeling class which meets the requirements
- **Layout**
  - Customer entrances must be visible from right-of-way
  - Must be designed so management must be able to see patrons at all time
  - Illumination must be adequate to observe location and activities
- **Contact**
  - No soliciting, payments, exchange of gratuity, exchange of money or any other items between performers, patrons, or others involved in live entertainment
  - No fondling, caressing, or contact of any type between performers and patrons
  - 10' between performer and patron
  - Performer must be on a stage/platform elevated at least 2'
- **Booths**
  - Booths, partitions, and curtains are prohibited
- **Operators License**
  - Required for all owners and spouses
    - Ownership description
    - Prior names
    - Current and prior addresses
    - All businesses within 2 years
    - Convictions of a felony, crime or violation of ordinance (except traffic)
    - Copy of partnership agreement
    - Name of manager, proprietors and agents
    - Site plan
    - Floor plan
    - Revocation of previous adult licenses
    - Transfer of license prohibited
  - Denial if owners or spouse:
    - Under 21
    - Non proprietor of business
    - Violation of adult ordinance in last year

- ♦ Inadequate info
- ♦ False info
- ♦ Convictions for gross misdemeanor or felony related to sex offenses, obscenity or adult establishments
- ♦ Denial, suspension, or revocation of license in other MN City in last 12 mo.
- ♦ Not zoned correctly
- ♦ Current license as a tanning, tattoo, pawnshop, liquor establishment, or therapeutic massage
- ♦ Failure to pay fee
- ♦ Not U.S. Citizen
- ○ 60 day suspension
  - ♦ Violation of ordinance or state law
  - ♦ Sale of alcohol
  - ♦ Refusal of inspection
  - ♦ Gambling
  - ♦ Delinquent taxes
  - ♦ Delinquent fees
- ○ Revocation
  - ♦ Suspended in last 14 months
  - ♦ False info
  - ♦ Use or sale of controlled substances
  - ♦ Prostitution
  - ♦ Illegal distribution of obscene materials
  - ♦ Operation during suspension
  - ♦ Certain convictions
  - ♦ Two or more certain offenses within a 12 month period

- ♦ Allowed specified sexual activities
- ○ Fees
  - ♦ $2,000 annually plus escrow for costs incurred to research and perform background checks
- **Employee License**
  - ○ Proof of age
  - ○ Background check
  - ○ Fee
  - ○ License revoked if caused an operator license to be suspended or revoked
- **Where allowable**
  - ○ C-4 Regional Shopping center
    - ♦ Setbacks
      * 500' from residentially zoned property
      * 500' from church, school, library, park/public recreation (**750 foot setback was reviewed; available land would not meet the five percent availability of commercial land**)
      * 500' from another adult use

Editor's Note:

The above information concerning the Background and Proposed Adult Use Ordinance was contained in a letter from John Hinzman, Planning Director, addressed to Mayor Hicks and City Council, City of Hastings, MN, on September 15, 2008.

CHAPTER 19

Lemont Village Officials Update Their Adult Business Ordinance

James A. Brown

Sexually-oriented business (SOBs), or "adult uses," have generated a tremendous amount of zoning litigation over the past decades. (Throughout this memorandum I use "SOB" and "adult uses" interchangeably). Decisions in various state and federal courts, as well as the U.S. Supreme Court, have made the following clear:

- Adult uses, e.g. nude dancing, is a form of expression that is entitled to free speech protection under U.S. Constitution's First Amendment;
- Municipalities' zoning codes *must* provide for areas within their corporate limits where adult uses could reasonably locate;
- Municipalities may place limits on areas where SOBs may be established so long as such limits serve a substantial governmental interest and do not unreasonably limit alternate avenues of communication.
- The "secondary effects" of SOBS on their surrounding areas justify enactment of regulations that either (1) disperse such

uses, or (2) concentrate them in specific areas.
- A municipality, before enacting any such regulation, does not need to conduct new studies on the harmful effects of SOBs, but may instead rely on studies generated by other municipalities, provided that such studies are reasonably believed to be relevant.

Neither the Zoning Commission nor I believe that our current ordinance adequately addresses adult uses. At its November 13th meeting, the Zoning Commission decided immediate amendments to the Lemont Zoning Ordinance concerning adult uses are warranted. The Zoning Commission intends to hold a public hearing at its next regularly scheduled meeting on an adult use text amendment. Because the Zoning Commission and I feel an urgency to amend the ordinance, the Commission and I suggest that the Village Board consider passing the text amendment at the Board's meeting that immediately follows the public hearing.

Originally published as "Regulating SOBs (Sexually-Oriented Businesses)," *Report No. 257-06 from the Director of the Community Development Department*, November 17, 2006, by the Community Development Department, Village of Lemont, IL.

Several studies that examine the harmful effects of SOBs were also given to the Village Board of Trustees. Board members were encouraged to review these studies before voting on the zoning amendments concerning SOBs.

Adult Uses and the First Amendment

Zoning controls frequently implicate First Amendment rights. The U.S. Supreme Court has stated that "when a zoning law infringes upon a protected liberty, it must be narrowly drawn and must further a sufficiently substantial government interest." Adult videos and disrobing dancers are forms of expression that have been ruled to be protected under the First Amendment, and thus municipal officials may not seek to suppress such expression simply because they do not like them. In 1976 the Supreme Court heard *Young v. American Mini Theatres, Inc.* In this case an adult theater had challenged a Detroit zoning provision. The ordinance had various licensing requirements and prevented adult theaters from locating within 1,000 feet of one another or 500 feet of a residential zone. The plaintiff claimed the ordinance was a content-based law that targeted businesses because officials did not like the expressive messages conveyed. The Supreme Court, however, ruled that the law had been passed not to silence any particular form of expression, but rather to prevent the deterioration of neighborhoods. This court decision gave government officials greater leeway in regulating SOBs if they are concerned with the harmful side effects associated with such establishments. Such harmful side effects may include increased crime, prostitution, decreased property values, and blight. The court ruled that the city's interest in planning and regulating commercial property was clearly adequate to justify the locational requirements placed on adult theaters.

A decade later, in *City of Renton v. Play-time Theaters, Inc.*, the Supreme Court refined its decision in *Young* and the "secondary effects" doctrine. Like Detroit, the City of Renton (WA) did not aim its ordinance at the content of the adult films, but rather at the secondary effects of adult theaters on the surrounding neighborhood. And the Supreme Court again found that the city, in pursuit of its zoning interests, did not squash free speech.

Most important, the Supreme Court held that "Renton was entitled to rely on the experiences of Seattle and other cities in enacting its adult theater ordinance. The First Amendment does not require a city, before enacting such an ordinance, to conduct new studies or produce evidence independent of that already generated by other cities, so long as whatever evidence the city relies upon is reasonably believed to be relevant to the problem that the city addresses."

Adult Use Ordinances

Since Renton, many municipalities have linked their adult use ordinances to any number of various studies — conducted by other municipalities — demonstrating the harmful secondary effects of SOBs. First Amendment advocates claim that the secondary effects doctrine "has proven to be fertile ground for abuse because it enables government officials to conceal their thinly disguised dislike for adult entertainment behind claims of harmful effect."[1]

Land use lawyers I have heard speak at various seminars and conferences have always strongly recommended that a municipality cite specific secondary-effects studies when passing adult use ordinances. Moreover, it is not enough to merely mention the studies — municipal officials should actually review such studies prior to enacting the zoning restrictions.

There are two approaches used by municipalities to restrict SOBs and thus reduce or confine their harmful secondary effects: Either disperse the SOBs throughout the community (as Detroit and Renton did), or concentrate the SOBs in specific areas (usually industrial) of the community. The second approach has also withstood court challenges.

What constitutes an adult use? Ordinances should specifically define terms such as "adult bookstore" or "adult entertainment." The Detroit ordinances' definitions related to adult uses, because they withstood Supreme Court scrutiny, have been widely copied. The Detroit ordinance went to great lengths to clearly define "specified sexual activities" and "specified anatomical areas."

Our Zoning Ordinance and SOBs

Under the Lemont Zoning Ordinance, adult uses are permitted only in the M-4 mineral extraction zoning district. Section X — Manufacturing Districts, Paragraph F, lists *inter alia* as permitted uses the following: adult bookstores or video stores; adult movie theaters; and adult entertainment.

No parcels within the Village are zoned M-4. Therefore, someone wanting to establish an SOB would need to petition for a zoning map amendment. Because our zoning map does not readily provide for places where an SOB could locate, it might be considered as achieving the same effect as an overt and illegal closing law — that is, our ordinance could be construed as "effectively denying respondents a reasonable opportunity to open and operate" an SOB (and thus exercise their First Amendment rights) within the Village.

Moreover, the zoning ordinance does not include definitions for terms such as "adult movie theater" or "adult entertainment."

The shortcomings of our ordinance could potentially result in the legal establishment of an SOB in an area that the Village Board and the community would find objectionable.

Zoning Commission Recommendation

The Zoning Commission recommends that the Village Board consider passage of zoning amendments related to adult uses as soon as possible. Specifically, the Commission recommends adult uses be confined to the M-3 manufacturing district. I am preparing text amendments to the relative portions of our current ordinance, including the definitions section. The Zoning Commission intends to hold a public hearing on the proposed changes at its December 2006 meeting.

Because the Village Board also meets this night, and because the Zoning Commission feels immediate passage of the amendments is desirable, I propose that the amendments be placed on the Board's December agenda for a vote.

El Paso SOB Land-Use Study

Sample ordinance definitions were also attached, as well as summaries of SOB Land Use Studies conducted by the National Law Center,[2] and a report from the American Center for Law and Justice[3] on the Secondary Impacts of Sex Oriented Businesses. The only land-use study attached is from a summary of the El Paso, Texas Land Use Study.

A summary of this land use study, prepared by the National Law Center, is shown below. The El Paso Study was one of the most important studies in the field of municipal regulations of adult-oriented businesses.

Overview

This study done by the Department of Planning, Research and Development, the City Attorney's Office, the Police Department Data Processing Division, and New Mexico State University involved one year of studying the impacts of SOBs on the El Paso area. A separate report by the New Mexico State

University on perceived neighborhood problems is also included. The study is in response to resident concern about the negative impacts resulting from the significant growth in SOBs over the past ten years. The study results show that SOBs are an important variable in the deviation from normal rates for real estate market performance or crime. Also included in the study are detailed maps showing the locations of SOBs in El Paso and within the selected study areas.

Findings

In studying the impacts caused by SOBs, three study areas (with SOBs located in the area) and three control areas (similar areas in size and population, but without SOBs) within El Paso were identified and studied. Using the results of the study areas and the attitudes of the residents living near SOBs, the study concluded that the following conditions existed within the study areas: (1) the house base within the study area decreases substantially with the concentration of SOBs; (2) property values decrease for properties located within a 1-block radius of SOBs; (3) there is an increase in listings on the real estate market for properties located near SOBs; (4) the increase of SOBs results in a relative deterioration of the residential area of a neighborhood; (5) there is a significant increase in crime near SOBs; (6) the average crime rate in the study area was 72 percent higher than the rate in the control areas; (7) sex-related crimes occurred more frequently in neighborhoods with even one SOB; (8) residents in the study areas perceived far greater neighborhood problems than residents in control areas; (9) residents in study areas had greater fear of deterioration and crime than residents in control areas.

The study of perceived neighborhood problems done in the New Mexico State University revealed strong concern by residents of the impact of SOBs on children in the neighborhood. In addition, some respondents told survey interviewers they feared retaliation from SOBs if they gave information about problems related to SOBs. Overall, this survey showed a strong, consistent pattern of higher neighborhood crime, resident fear and resident dissatisfaction in the neighborhoods containing SOBs.

Recommendations

The main recommendations included that a zoning ordinance be adopted with distance requirements between SOBs and sensitive uses, that a licensing system be established, that annual inspections be required, that signage regulations be established, and that a penalty/fine section be included for violations.

Legislative Action

The SOB uses remained as they were before, confined to the B-4 District (Business Zone). The zone was not changed, as proposed, to the M-3 District (Industrial Zone). The Village Board of Trustees also added some definitions to their code, which had been previously lacking.[4]

NOTES

1. Hudson, David L., "Secondary-Effects Doctrine" located at the First Amendment Center's website at <*www. firstamendmentcenter.org/speech/adultent/*>.

2. The sample land-use studies may be obtained from the National Law Center's website at <*www.nationallawcenter. org*>.

3. The sample studies on the secondary impacts of SOBs may be obtained from the American Center for Law and Justice's website at <*www.aclj.org*>.

4. The final legislative action of the Board of Village Trustees was communicated to the Editor from the Director of the Community Development Department via email on May 21, 2008.

CHAPTER 20

Littleton Adult Business Distance Rule Is Upheld by the Supreme Court

Scott D. Bergthold

It appears that the third time is a charm — the decision in *City of Littleton v. Z.J. Gifts D-4, L.L.C.*[1] represents the third time in recent history that the Supreme Court has granted certiorari to clarify the kind of judicial review that is required when a city, pursuant to a time, place, and manner ordinance, denies a license to a speech-related entity for content-neutral reasons.[2] Although the first two cases did not reach the issue, the *City of Littleton* case gave the Court a vehicle with which to squarely resolve the wide circuit split over the requirement of "prompt judicial review" from adverse decisions under sexually oriented business licensing ordinances.

The Ordinance and Proceedings in the Lower Courts

In 1993, the *City of Littleton* adopted a comprehensive adult business ordinance that contained requirements addressing both location and licensing. The ordinance requires that any "adult bookstore, adult novelty store or adult video store" — establishments with a "substantial portion" of their inventory, floor space, revenues, or advertising expenditures dedicated to, or deriving from, sexually explicit materials — locate in a specified zoning district, and at least 500 feet away from specified other uses, including churches and day-care centers.[3]

In 1999, Z.J. Gifts, doing business as "Christal's," opened in a location not zoned for adult businesses and within 500 feet of both a church and a day-care center.[4] Without applying for a license, Z.J. brought a preemptive federal suit under 42 U.S.C. § 1983, challenging the city's ordinance as facially invalid under the First Amendment. At the close of discovery, the district court granted summary judgment *in toto* to the city.[5]

The Tenth Circuit affirmed in part, and revised in part.[6] On review of the record, including a videotape of the interior of Z.J.'s business, the Tenth Circuit concluded that Z.J.'s was "unquestionably" an adult business and rejected its claim that the definition of "adult bookstore, adult novelty store or adult

Originally published as "City of Littleton v. Z.J. Gifts: The Supreme Court Gives the Green Light to Sexually Oriented Business Licensing Ordinances," *Municipal Lawyer*, Vol. 45, No. 6, November/December 2004, by the International Municipal Lawyers Association, Washington, DC. Reprinted with permission of the publisher.

video store" was unconstitutionally vague.[7] The court also rejected *Z.J.*'s challenge that the ordinance did not provide sufficient zoning sites for adult businesses.[8]

However, the appellate court reversed the district court on two issues. First, it held that certain provisions of the Littleton ordinance threatened lengthy administrative delay,[9] although this defection was severable from the remainder of the ordinance.[10] Second, the Tenth Circuit surveyed the split in the circuits over the "prompt judicial review" requirement of *FWI PBS, Inc. v. City of Dallas*,[11] and held the First Amendment required the City of Littleton to guarantee, through its ordinance, a prompt *judicial decision* from any license denial.[12] In other words, the appellate court held that, although the city's ordinance was properly aimed at preventing the negative secondary effects of adult businesses — and not the "speech" of such businesses — it was, nevertheless, required to provide the special judicial review procedure mandated for censorship schemes in *Freedman v. Maryland*.[13]

In response to the Tenth Circuit's decision, the city amended its ordinance to cure the administrative delay issue, and then petitioned the Supreme Court to grant certiorari to resolve the confusion over the question of "prompt judicial review" that had split the circuits.[14]

The Supreme Court's Decision: Freedman *Does Not Apply*

In essence, the city made one core argument: *Freedman*'s special judicial review rule did not apply to well-drafted adult business ordinances, like the City of Littleton's, that did not present the dangers of censorship or unbridled discretion in licensing decisions. In a 9–0 decision,[15] the Supreme Court reversed the Tenth Circuit's ruling on the prompt judicial review issue and identified two separate arguments for doing so: First, the *FW/PBS* court's description of the "prompt judicial re-

view" requirement for secondary effects ordinances deviated from the language used to describe that safeguard in the "significantly different" censorship context of *Freedman*. Second, ordinary judicial review under state law provided, in any event, for a sufficiently prompt judicial determination.[16]

While rejecting the city's invitation to interpret *FW/PBS* as modifying the *Freedman* prompt judicial decision requirement, the Court nevertheless embraced the city's core contention that the rationales of *Freedman* simply did not apply to adult business ordinances with time-limited, objective, licensing standards which had nothing to do with the content of speech.[17] Thus, the Court read Justice O'Connor's plurality opinion in *FW/PBS* "as encompassing a prompt judicial decision"[18] but, nevertheless, modify[ing] *FW/PBS*, withdrawing its implication that *Freedman*'s special judicial review rules apply in this case."[19]

The Court presented four reasons for agreeing with the city that *Freedman* was inapposite in this context. First, the Court held that "ordinary court procedural rules and practices, in Colorado as elsewhere, provide reviewing courts with judicial tools sufficient to avoid delay-related First Amendment harm."[20] The Court specifically noted that state trial courts reviewing licensing decisions could accelerate those proceedings, and state appellate courts could expedite review of lower court decisions. Second, in a refreshing statement recognizing the principles of federalism, the Court stated that it had "no reason to doubt the willingness of Colorado's judges to exercise these powers wisely so as to avoid serious threats of delay-induced First Amendment harm."[21] Moreover, the Court noted a lack of any problems of delay in Colorado, and stated that 42 U.S.C. § 1983 provided "an additional safety value" should any such problems arise.[22] Third, embracing the city's analysis, the Court distinguished *Freedman*. *Freedman* involved a law containing "rather subjective standards and where a denial likely meant complete censorship. In contrast, the ordinance at issue here does not seek to *censor* material. And its licensing scheme applies reasonably objective, nondiscretionary criteria unrelated to the content of the expressive materials that an adult business may sell or display."[23] The Court explained:

> These objective criteria are simple enough to apply and their application simple enough to review that their use is unlikely in practice to suppress totally the presence of any specific item of adult material in the Littleton community. Some license applicants will satisfy the criteria even if others do not; hence the community will likely contain outlets that sell protected adult material. A supplier of that material should be able to find outlets; a potential buy should be able to find a seller. Nor should zoning requirements suppress that material, for a constitutional zoning system seeks to determine *where*, not *whether*, protected adult material can be sold. The upshot is that Littleton's "adult business" licensing scheme does "not present the grave dangers of a censorship system." And the simple objective nature of the licensing criteria means that in the ordinary case, judicial review, too, should prove simple, hence expeditious.[24]

Fourth, commenting on how this was to be done, the Court noted "nothing in *FW/PBS* or in *Freedman* requires a city of a State to place judicial review safeguards all in the city ordinance that sets forth a licensing scheme."[25] It recognized the obvious fact, repeated and reiterated by municipalities in the appellate courts for the last decade, that "cities and towns lack the state-law legal authority to impose deadlines on state courts."[26] The Court concluded that adult business licensing decisions made pursuant to "neutral and non-discretionary criteria" do not require "an unusually speedy judicial decision of the *Freedman* type."[27]

The Early Fallout: Rejection of "Prior Restraint" Challenges

Two recent cases, both of which rejected prior restraint challenges to adult business licensing ordinances, demonstrate that the de-

cision in *City of Littleton* is already benefiting municipalities.

In *Annex Books, Inc. v. City of Indianapolis*,[28] the district court had originally granted a preliminary injunction against the enforcement of an Indianapolis adult bookstore licensing requirement on the grounds that it failed to provide for a quasi-judicial administrative hearing.[29] Thus, the court had previously held that the ordinance "deprived the applicant of meaningful access to judicial review because, without a 'quasi-judicial' preceding such as hearing, no record would be produced for a trial court to review. If access to judicial review were stymied by lack of an administrative record, so would be a prompt judicial determination."[30] At summary judgment, Indianapolis cited the *City of Littleton* case and argued that the paper record that would be developed in any license denial — including a letter specifying, pursuant to the ordinance, the objective grounds for denial — was constitutionally sufficient. The court agreed. Noting that the Littleton ordinance and the Indianapolis ordinance both contained "reasonably objective, nondiscretionary criteria unrelated to the 'content' of the expressive materials that an adult business typically sells or displays,"[31] the court held that judicial review of any license denial would be both simple and expeditious. It went on to conclude that, under *City of Littleton*, a quasi-judicial hearing on a license denial was not required for meaningful judicial review. The need for such a hearing was "obviated by the fact that the four grounds for denial [in the ordinance] are objective and ministerial in nature, requiring no exercise of judgment on the part of the government, only an 'up or down' decision on each factor."[32] Accordingly, the court granted summary judgment to the City of Indianapolis on the "prompt judicial review" issue.

A similar result occurred in *Doctor John's, Inc. v. City of Roy*, Utah.[33] In this case, the city's ordinance not only guaranteed a prompt administrative decision based on objective criteria, but also required, in the event of a denial, that a "provisional license" be issued which ensured the continued operation of the adult business until the judicial resolution of any court challenges to the license denial.[34] Under these circumstances, the court held that the issue "present[ed] none of the dangers of prior restraint," finding the scheme constituted "a well-drafted way for the City to deal with the secondary effects of sexually oriented businesses while protecting First Amendment principles."[35]

Conclusion

The Supreme Court's decision in *City of Littleton* has eliminated much confusion in the lower courts over the constitutionality of licensing sexually oriented businesses to prevent the negative secondary effects they generate. This is not to say, however, that the courts will tolerate sloppy draftsmanship or unbridled discretion in licensing criteria. Cities must still be very careful when implementing such ordinances and must ensure that the language they employ is up-to-date, given the ever-changing landscape of adult business regulation. But *City of Littleton* makes it clear that when a municipality denies an adult business license based on objective, content-neutral standards, it no longer does so under the cloud of *Freedman*'s special judicial review requirement.

NOTES

1. 124 S. Ct. 2219 (2004).
2. *See* City News and Novelty, Inc. v. City of Waukesha, 531 U.S. 278 (2001); Thomas v. Chicago Park District, 534 U.S. 316 (2002).
3. 124 S. Ct. at 2222.
4. *Id.*
5. *Id.*
6. Z.J. Gifts D-4, L.L.C. v. City of Littleton, 311 F.3d 1220 (10th Cir. 2002).
7. *Id.* at 1228–30.
8. *Id.* at 1241.
9. *Id.* at 1233–34.
10. *Id.* at 1234.
11. 493 U.S. 215 (1990).
12. Z.J. Gifts D-4, L.L.C. v. City of Littleton, 311 F.3d 1220 (10th Cir. 2002).
13. 380 U.S. 51 (1965).
14. 124 S. Ct. 2219, 2222 (2004).
15. All nine justices voted to reverse the decision of the Tenth Circuit. Justice Scalia concurred in the judgment, but wrote separately to reiterate his position that under *Ginzburg v. United States*, 383 U.S. 463 (1996), Z.J.'s was engaged in pandering sex, an activity that was not protected by the First Amendment. Justice Stevens, concurring in part and concurring in the judgment, refused to join part II-A of the majority opinion, and further wrote to emphasize the need to maintain stringent judicial review requirements for true censorship schemes. 124 S. Ct. at 2226–27. Finally, Justice Souter, joined by Justice Kennedy, concurred in part and concurred in the judgment, declining to join part II-B of the Court's opinion. Justice Souter wrote "to emphasize that the state procedures that make a prompt judicial determination possible need to align with a state judicial practice that provides a prompt disposition in the states courts." *Id.* at 2227.
16. 124 S. Ct. at 2222–23.
17. *Id.* at 2223–24.
18. *Id.* at 2224. The Court noted that the *Freedman* court set forth a "model" of promptness that involved a hearing the day after joinder of issue, and a decision two days after that. *Id.*
19. *Id.*
20. *Id.* at 2224–25.
21. *Id.* at 2225.
22. *Id.*
23. *Id.*
24. *Id.* at 2225–26 (emphasis added; internal citations omitted.
25. *Id.* at 2226.
26. *Id.*
27. *Id.*
28. 333 F. Supp. 2d 773 (S.D. Ind. 2004).
29. *Id.* at 778.
30. *Id.*
31. *Id.* at 781.
32. *Id.*
33. 333 F. Supp. 2d 1168 (D. Utah 2004).
34. *Id.* at 1176.
35. *Id.* at 1181.

CHAPTER 21

Los Angeles Has Its Adult Business Zoning Criteria Reaffirmed by the Supreme Court

Scott D. Bergthold

In *City of Los Angeles v. Alameda Books, Inc., et. al.*,[1] the United States Supreme Court reaffirmed that cities have substantial latitude when zoning to control the adverse impacts of sexually oriented businesses, and that the evidence upon which municipalities rely need only be "reasonably believed to be relevant to the problem the city addresses."[2] The Court remanded the case for trial on whether the City of Los Angeles' secondary effects evidence supported its unique prohibition on "multiple use" adult businesses (those that combined retail and peep show booth uses under one roof). Despite the Court's affirmation of *City of Renton v. Playtime Theatres, Inc.*[3] and its refusal to impose an "empirical proof" requirement for adult business regulations, some adult business operators view the case as a win, and intend to use it to challenge regulations far afield from the specific prohibition at issue in the case.[4] The extent to which such challenges are successful will likely turn on the ability of cities to discern what *Alameda Books* does and does not stand for, and to distinguish the arguments advanced in that case

from the arguments advanced in defense of their own local ordinances.

Background

In 1995, two adult bookstores whose businesses combined retail and peep show booth uses challenged a portion of the City's zoning code. Section 12.70(C), amended in 1983, prohibited more than one adult use from operating in the same building. Defending the ordinance at summary judgment, the City relied *solely* on its 1977 study demonstrating a correlation between geographic concentrations of separate adult businesses, and increases in crimes such as robbery and prostitution. The district court ruled that the study did not support an inference that multiple use adult businesses would produce secondary effects similar to those associated with concentrations of separate adult businesses in a neighborhood. Finding the City's content-neutral justification lacking, the court invalidated the ordinance as a content-based regulation that failed strict scrutiny.

Originally published as "Alameda Reaffirms Renton's Deferential Standard: Impact Evidence 'Reasonably Believed to Be Relevant' Is Sufficient," *Municipal Lawyer*, Vol. 43, No. 5, September/October 2002, by the International Municipal Lawyers Association, Washington, DC. Reprinted with permission of the publisher.

On appeal, the U.S. Court of Appeals for the Ninth Circuit affirmed on different grounds, holding that the ordinance was more properly analyzed as a time, place, and manner regulation because it "[did] not ban adult entertainment establishments altogether."[5] However, the appellate panel concluded that even if the ordinance was content-neutral, the City's study failed to provide evidence that the multiple use prohibition was "designed to serve" the City's substantial interest in abating secondary effects. Critical in the Ninth Circuit's holding was the perceived attribution of secondary effects not to *individual* adult businesses, but only to the *concentration* of separate adult uses in a given vicinity. On this point, the Court of Appeals found that "Los Angeles has presented no evidence that a combination adult bookstore/arcade produces any of the harmful secondary effects identified in the Study."[6] Although the City's local experience included evidence of secondary effects from such combination businesses,[7] the issue was not specifically addressed in the 1977 study, and the panel concluded that "the pertinent findings of the Study focus *solely* on the concentration of separate adult business entities."[8] Therefore, the Ninth Circuit invalidated the City's regulation.

"Empirical Proof" Requirement for Secondary Effects Ordinances Rejected

The United States Supreme Court reversed in favor of the City and remanded the case for further proceedings. The plurality opinion, authored by Justice O'Connor, concluded that "Los Angeles may reasonably rely on a study it conducted some years before enacting the present version of the § 12.70(C) to demonstrate that its ban on multiple-use adult establishments serves its interest in reducing crime."[9] The plurality first explained that the lower court had misapplied *Renton*'s "reasonably believed to be relevant" standard for sec-

ondary effects evidence, and then specifically rejected the dissent's position that such evidence must empirically prove that the regulation will be effective.[10]

While local governments must be "allowed to experiment with solutions to admittedly serious problems," the plurality cautioned against "shoddy data or reasoning," and held that secondary effects evidence must "fairly support the municipality's rationale for its ordinance."[11] If it does, then the plaintiffs bear the burden to "cast direct doubt on this rationale" before the burden will shift back to the municipality to supplement the record with renewed support "for a theory that justifies its ordinance."[12] The plurality reiterated that, on balance, cities' legislative judgments are entitled to deference because "[m]unicipalities will, in general, have greater experience with and understanding of the secondary effects" that flow from sexually oriented businesses.[13]

Kennedy's Concurrence and the Secondary Effects Standard for a Zoning Ordinance

Justice Kennedy concurred in the judgment and provided the fifth vote to reverse the lower court's ruling. Reaffirming the common sense rationale for typical adult use dispersal ordinances, Justice Kennedy explained that "high concentrations of adult businesses can damage the value and the integrity of a neighborhood. The damage is measurable; it is all too real."[14] The lower court, therefore, erred in granting summary judgment against Los Angeles because it was reasonable for the City to conclude that "knocking down the wall between adult businesses does not ameliorate any undesirable secondary effects of their proximity to one another."[15] Accordingly, while the plaintiffs should have an opportunity at trial to prove that the City's conclusion was unsound, the City should not be foreclosed by summary judgment from exercising its zoning authority through the regulation.

Justice Kennedy noted that ordinances directed specifically at the secondary effects of adult uses were technically "content based,"[16] but explained that such a label in no way determined the law's constitutionality. "This sort of singling out is not impermissible content discrimination; it is sensible urban planning."[17] Thus, he explained, "the central holding of *Renton* is sound: A zoning restriction that is designed to decrease secondary effects and not speech should be subject to intermediate rather than strict scrutiny."[18]

Next, Justice Kennedy cautioned against potential expansion of the *Renton* doctrine to justify a zoning ordinance which had a secondary effects rationale based on decreasing the number of sexually oriented businesses. Rather, "a city must advance some basis to show that its regulation has the purpose and effects of suppressing secondary effects, while leaving the quantity and accessibility of speech substantially intact."[19] Adult business attorneys have opined that this language renders some non-zoning restrictions, such as hours of operation regulations in typical adult entertainment ordinances, presumptively unconstitutional.[20] Justice Kennedy's opinion, however, does not claim to address adult business regulations outside the zoning context,[21] and merely establishes that adult use zoning regulations cannot be premised on the elimination of adult businesses. "If two adult businesses are under the same roof, an ordinance requiring them to separate will have one of two results. One business will either move elsewhere or will close. The city's premise cannot be the latter."[22] Thus, the City could not implement a regulation intended to eliminate or ban one or more adult businesses form the community and claim that result as the basis for its secondary effects rationale. "It is true that cutting adult speech in half would probably reduce secondary effects proportionately. But again, a promised proportional reduction does not suffice."[23]

The plurality foresaw the potential confusion that could flow from interpretations of Justice Kennedy's concurrence, and specifically addressed this issue at the end of its opinion. The businesses had argued that the multiple use prohibition was effectively a ban on peep show booths and should be subject to strict scrutiny. The plurality rejected this contention and noted:

> This also appears to be the theme of Justice Kennedy's concurrence. He contends that "[a] city may not assert that it will reduce secondary effects by reducing speech in the same proportion." *Post*, at 7 (opinion concurring in the judgment). We consider that unobjectionable proposition as simply a reformulation of the requirement that an ordinance warrants intermediate scrutiny only if it is a time, place, and manner regulation and not a ban. The Court of Appeals held, however, that the city's prohibition on the combination of adult bookstores and arcades is not a ban and respondents did not petition for review of that determination.[24]

The detrimental impact of this clarification on the adult businesses' position is evidenced by their extraordinary act of asking the Supreme Court to eliminate this paragraph from the plurality opinion. That motion was denied.[25] The court of appeals clearly held that the regulation was not a ban,[26] and neither that opinion nor the Supreme Court's opinion supported the underlying premise of the businesses' "ban" argument — that the constitutionality of an adult business regulation turned on the economic impact it may have on a particular business.[27]

Conclusion

Several aspects of *Alameda Books* stand out. First, each Justice reaffirmed the central holding in *Renton* as sound, although several were concerned about its application to the case due to the perceived lack of evidence and argument about secondary effects caused by individual adult businesses.[28] Thus, cities should demonstrate, from secondary effects reports and factual findings in adult business cases, that their ordinances are, as *Renton* stated, "aimed at preventing the secondary effects caused by the presence of even one such [sexually oriented business] in the neighborhood."[29] Second, while plaintiffs may assert that the secondary effects doctrine has been undermined, both the plurality opinion and Justice Kennedy's concurrence rejected an empirical evidentiary requirement and reaffirmed that the government's legislative judgment was entitled to substantial deference under *Renton*. Moreover, none of the opinions suggest that the results in *Young* or *Renton* would be changed by the Court's analysis of the Los Angeles multiple use prohibition. Finally, *Alameda Books* did not fundamentally alter lower courts' analysis of typical regulations directed at the secondary effects of adult businesses,[30] which should be upheld provided that they are adequately supported by secondary effects evidence and are not designed to eliminate sexually oriented businesses from the community.

Notes

1. 122 S. Ct. 1728 (2002).
2. *Id.* at 1743 (Kennedy, J., concurring in judgment).
3. 475 U.S. 41 (1986).
4. *Attorneys Hopeful After Supreme Court's Opinion in Alameda Books*, Adult Video News, July 2002, at 204–205.
5. Alameda Books, Inc. v. City of Los Angeles, 222 F.3d 719, 723 (2000).
6. *Id.* at 725.
7. *See, e.g.*, E.W.A.P., Inc. v. City of Los Angeles, 65 Cal. Rptr. 2d 325, 328 (Cal. Ct. App. 1997) ("[D]uring the last two and one-half years, one hundred seventeen arrests have been made which are directly attributable to the presence of Le Sex Shoppe."); DeMott v. Bd. Of Police Comm'rs of the City of Los Angeles, 175 Cal. Rptr. 879 (Cal. Ct. App. 1981) (citing unsanitary acts in bookstore/peep show businesses).
8. 222 F.3d at 725.
9. 122 S. Ct. 1728, 1731 (2002) (plurality opinion).

10. *Id.* at 1736 (citations omitted).
11. *Id.*
12. *Id.*
13. *Id.* at 1738.
14. *Id.*
15. *Id.* at 1743.
16. *Id.* at 1741. This dissent opined that adult business ordinances targeting secondary effects were neither categorically content based nor categorically content neutral, but should be labeled "content-correlated." *Id.* at 1746.
17. *Id.* at 1740.
18. *Id.* at 1741. Justice Kennedy failed to acknowledge that *Renton's* "narrow tailoring" analysis requires secondary effects ordinances to be technically "content based" in his sense of that term. There, the Court held that "the *Renton* ordinance is 'narrowly tailored' to affect only that category of theaters shown to produce the unwanted secondary effects...." 475 U.S. at 52.
19. *Id.* at 1742.
20. *Attorneys Hopeful, supra* note 5, at 204.
21. *See, e.g.*, Young v. American Mini Theatres, 427 U.S. 50, 65 (1976) (cautioning against reading a broad legal principal "literally and without regard for the facts of the case in which it was made."); *see also* R.A.V. v. City of St. Paul, 505 U.S. 377, 386 (1992) ("It is of course contrary to all traditions of our jurisprudence to consider the law on this point conclusively resolved by broad language in cases where the issue was not presented or even envisioned").
22. 122 S. Ct. at 1742.
23. *Id.*
24. *Id.* at 1738.
25. City of Los Angeles v. Alameda Books, Inc., 122 S. Ct. 2585 (June 17, 2002).
26. Alameda Books, Inc. v. City of Los Angeles, 222 F.3d 719, 723 (2000).
27. The converse proposition is well settled. *See Renton*, 475 U.S. at 54 ("The inquiry for First Amendment purposes is not concerned with economic impact").
28. 122 S. Ct. at 1747 ("In this case, however, the government has not shown that bookstores containing viewing booths, isolated from other adult establishments, increase crime or produce other negative secondary effects..."). This appears to be a key premise of the dissenting opinion, where it repeatedly surfaces in footnotes 4, 5, 6, and 9.
29. 475 U.S. at 50.
30. *See, e.g.*, Baby Dolls Topless Saloons, Inc. v. City of Dallas, 2002 U.S. Appl. LEXIS 12202, *22 (5th Cir. June 20, 2002); Ky. Restaurant Concepts, Inc., et al. v. City of Louisville, et al., 2002 U.S. Dist. LEXIS 11011, *16 (W.D. Ky. June 14, 2002) (citing *Alameda Books* for the proposition that cities "are entitled to rely upon the studies of their choice and to experiment with their own regulation of secondary effects...").

CHAPTER 22

Lyons Limits Adult Uses to Industrial Zones and the Court Agrees

Roger Huebner *and* Jerry Zarley

The term "Adult Use" (or "Adult Business"), as used in Illinois, actually comprises a large variety of sexually oriented businesses that may include movie theaters, bookstores, video stores, massage parlors, and strip clubs. These sexually oriented businesses (or S.O.B.s as they are sometimes called) can be extremely profitable and, therefore, are increasing in communities. Furthermore, to avoid prosecution and/or more stringent regulations, many businesses are constantly moving from one place to another or to other communities. More specifically, the owners of these businesses like to move their businesses to a community that has less stringent or no regulations for adult uses. Because many municipal ordinances have not considered the possibility of adult use establishments, a community may find itself unprepared when a sexually oriented business comes to town, especially since the activities and/or materials of these businesses may be constitutionally protected by the First Amendment. Therefore, every Illinois municipality should consider enacting ordinances to regulate adult businesses if it would be appropriate for the municipality.

Q: How can a municipality constitutionally regulate adult uses?

A. Municipalities, whether home rule or non–home rule, regulate the location of adult businesses in their respective communities through their zoning powers. Municipalities may directly license, tax, and regulate adult businesses provided the regulation is content-neutral and within the power of the governmental body. The municipality must show it has a substantial governmental interest and that the interest is unrelated to the suppression of free expression. Such regulation must be an incidental restriction on alleged First Amendment freedoms and be no greater than is essential in the furtherance of the municipal interest.

A municipality may determine where adult businesses may be located in its respective community through its power to zone. A non–home rule municipality derives its zoning authority from the Illinois Municipal Code which provides in pertinent part "...the corporate authorities in each municipality have the ... power[] ... to classify, regulate and restrict the location of trades and industries and the location of buildings designed for

Originally published as "Regulating Adult Uses — An Update," *Illinois Municipal Review*, Vol. 21, No. 3, March 2003, by the Illinois Municipal League, Springfield, IL. Reprinted with permission of the publisher.

specified industrial, business, residential, and other uses."[1] A home rule municipality derives additional zoning authority from Article VII, § 6(a) of the Illinois Constitution of 1970 which authorizes a home rule unit to "exercise any power and perform any function pertaining to its government and affairs including, but not limited to, the power to regulate for the protection of the public health, safety, morals and welfare; to license; to tax; and to incur debt." Furthermore, Section 11-5-1.5 of the Illinois Municipal Code provides that "[i]t is prohibited within a municipality to locate an adult entertainment facility within 1,000 feet of the property boundaries of any school, day care center, cemetery, public park, forest preserve, public housing, and place of religious worship."[2] Therefore, a municipality may prescribe where adult businesses are located in its respective community provided such businesses can constitute an "adult use" as defined by the municipal ordinance,[3] and provided the regulation does not totally exclude adult uses within the corporate limits.[4]

For example, in *Dottie's Dress Shop v. Village of Lyons,*[5] the plaintiff wanted to operate a store which the village's zoning board determined was an "adult use" as defined by the village ordinance in a business zoning district. However, the village ordinance only allowed adult use establishments to operate in an industrial zoning district. The plaintiff claimed its establishment was appropriate for the business district because it was not an adult use facility as defined by the village ordinance. The appellate court determined, however, that although the village ordinance did not specify the type of establishment in question, it was specifically aimed at the regulation of adult or sexually oriented businesses. And, because the plaintiff's establishment was predominantly devoted to selling sexual paraphernalia and sexually oriented devices, it was properly defined as an adult use. Therefore, the court held that the zoning board's decision not to award the plaintiff an occupancy permit to operate in the business zoning district was reasonable.

To further regulate sexually oriented businesses, the regulation must be a proper content-neutral time, place and manner restriction. Where the ordinance regulates *conduct* and not speech, it is a content-neutral regulation.[6] If the regulation upon the adult entertainment industry is content-neutral, it must then satisfy the four part test enunciated in *United States v. O'Brien.*[7] To satisfy the *O'Brien* test: (1) the regulation must be within the power of the governmental body; (2) the regulation must further an important or substantial governmental interest; (3) the interest must be unrelated to the suppression of free expression; and (4) the incidental restriction on alleged First Amendment freedoms must be no greater than essential to the furtherance of that interest.[8]

In *City of Erie v. Pap's A.M., tdba "Kandyland,"*[9] for example, the United States Supreme Court examined the city's ban on public nudity and how the ban was applied to totally nude exotic dancers. The Supreme Court determined that because the ordinance banned all public nudity regardless of its expressive activity, it was aimed at combating the secondary effects of adult establishments, and its effect on the overall expression of nudity was minute, it was a content-neutral restriction that was subject to the *O'Brien* test. In comparing the ordinance to the factors in *O'Brien,* the Supreme Court determined: (1) the ordinance was within the city's police power because the city's efforts to protect public health and safety were within its police power; (2) the ordinance furthered the important governmental interests of regulating conduct through a public nudity ban and of combating the harmful secondary effects associated with nude dancing; (3) the ordinance was unrelated to the suppression of free speech; and (4) the restriction was no greater than was essential to achieve that interest because the resulting requirements were a minimal restriction which left ample alternatives for the dancers to convey their erotic message.

Municipalities in Illinois are statutorily

authorized to regulate sexually oriented businesses. Section 11-42-5 of the Illinois Municipal Code provides that "[t]he corporate authorities of each municipality ... may license, tax and regulate all places for eating or amusement."[10] Through a municipality's authority to license, Section 11-60-1 provides that "[t]he corporate authorities of each municipality may fix the amount, terms, and manner of issuing and revoking licenses."[11] Since sexually oriented businesses are obviously for amusement or entertainment, municipalities may license, tax, and regulate all adult use facilities. Municipalities may also regulate the costs and terms of issuing and revoking such licenses.

For example, a few Illinois municipalities have enacted ordinances which refuse a liquor license to any facility or business which may be considered an adult use facility, or prohibit liquor establishments from conducting any adult business. The most common example of regulating the terms, conditions, and/or classifications of licensing is through the regulation of hours of operation. However, such a regulation must be a proper content-neutral regulation (i.e. the regulation must apply to *all* amusement or entertainment establishments), or be directly aimed at combating the harmful secondary effects of an adult entertainment establishment.[12]

Many municipalities require adult use facilities to obtain an adult use license or permit to legally conduct business within their corporate limits. However, licensing schemes are also subject to judicial scrutiny. Licensing schemes require the licensor to make the decision whether to issue the license within a specified and reasonable time period during to maintain the status quo, and prompt judicial review in the event the license is erroneously denied.[13] Maintaining the status quo means "that a business existing at the time the regulation was adopted may not be regulated during the initial licensing process. However, if the application is denied under a valid regulation, the business must then appeal the denial; the regulation need not provide for an automatic stay of denial."[14] As it currently stands, prompt judicial review means "prompt judicial determination."[15]

To show that the regulation furthers an important or substantial governmental interest and that the interest is unrelated to the suppression of free expression it is necessary for municipalities to explicitly state the reasons for regulating adult establishments within the ordinance. For example, an ordinance may consider all the secondary effects that such businesses may have upon a community. The ordinance may also include such things that consider public health and safety such as protecting the community from communicable diseases, and maintaining traffic conditions. The ordinance may further include the consideration of public morals and decency. For example, an ordinance could be enacted prohibiting public nudity which would have the incidental effect of prohibiting nude dancing.[16] All of these things are within a municipality's police power and completely unrelated to the suppression of free expression. However, the incidental regulation on the alleged First Amendment freedoms must be no greater than necessary to further that (those) interest(s).

In conclusion, no one article or column can sufficiently address all the issues relating to the regulation of adult uses. However, the intent of this article was to introduce the methods that municipalities may use to regulate sexually oriented businesses. The techniques are extremely complicated and subject to various limitations. Therefore, municipal officials are strongly encouraged to consult with their municipal attorney before attempting to enact any adult use ordinance. The experience in Illinois and across the nation demonstrates that being prepared for this controversial issue is the best method to address the communities' concerns.

Notes

1. 65 ILCS 5/11-13-1 (West 1998).
2. 65 ILCS 5/11-5-1.5 (West 1998).

3. *See Dottie's Dress Shop v. Village of Lyons*, 313 Ill. App. 3d 70, 729 N.E. 2d1, 246 Ill. Dec. 1 (1st Dist. 2000).

4 *City of Renton v. Playtime Theatres, Inc.* 475 U.S. 41, 106 S. Ct. 925, 89 L. Ed. 2d 29 (1986); *Cochran V. Town of Marcy*, No. 01-CV364 (N.D. N.Y. May 31, 2001). *See also Arts Studio, Inc. vs. City of Grand Rapids*, No. 1:01-CV-196 (W.D. Mich. Aug. 30, 2002); *Jefferson, Ltd. v. City of Columbus*, No. 2002-CV-0055 (S.D. Ohio May 6, 2002); *R.W.B. of Riverview, Inc. v. Stemple*, No. CIV. A. 2:00-0552 (S.D. W. Va. July 25, 2000).

5. 313 Ill. App. 3d 70, 729 N.E. 2d 1, 246 Ill. Dec, 1 (1st Dist. 2000).

6. *See City of Erie v. Pap's A.M., tdba "Kandyland,"* 120 S. Ct. 1382 (2000).

7. 391 U.S. 367 (1968).

8. 391 U.S. at 377.

9. 120 S. Ct. 1382 (2000).

10. 65 ILCS 5/11-42-5 (West 1998).

11. 65 ILCS 5/11-60-1 (West 1998).

12. *See DiMa Corp. v. Town of Hallie*, 185 F. 3d 823 (7th Cir. 1999); *see also Schultz v. City of Cumberland County*, No. 98-4126 (7th Cir. Sept. 26, 2000).

13. *FW/PBS, Inc. v. City of Dallas*, 493 U.S. 215, 110 S. Ct. 596, 107 L. Ed. 2d 603 (1990); *Illusions Too Reality, L.L.C. v. City of Harvey*, No. 02 C 7272 (N.D. Ill. Feb. 4, 2003).

14. Jules B. Gerard. Local Regulation of Adult Businesses, p. 265 (2002 Edition).

15. *Illusions Too Reality, L.L.C. v. City of Harvey*, No. 02 C 7272 (N.D. Ill. Feb. 4, 2003).

16. *See supra*, Note 6.

Editor's Note:

This article appeared as a monthly column that examines issues of general concern to municipal officers, and provided an update to the Legal Q & A article that was published in the February 2001 issue (Vol. 23, No. 2) of the *Illinois Municipal Review*. It is not meant to provide legal advice and is not a substitute for consulting with a municipal attorney. As always, when confronted with a legal question, public officials should contact their municipal attorney as certain unique circumstances may alter any conclusions reached in this article.

CHAPTER 23

Memphis Officials Defer Final Vote on Allowing Beer Sales in Adult Businesses Until After Court Appeal

Bill Dries

Tennessee Attorney General Robert Cooper will help defend the Shelby County ordinance governing Memphis strip clubs in the U.S. District Court. Cooper's office filed a motion Monday to intervene on the side of the city and county in the case filed by seven strip club owners. The suit challenges the constitutionality of the ordinance as well as the state law on which the ordinance is based.

Cooper's request was filed the day before Memphis City Council members voted to table action on a city strip club ordinance to see how the federal court case plays out. Council member Edmund Ford Jr. moved for the delay. "I do not believe that this council right now should make a decision on this matter while it's under pending litigation, especially since we are involved," Ford said. "If we weren't involved, it would be different."

State of Grace

The 7–5 council vote to table the city proposal means the ordinance enacted last year by the Shelby County Board of Commission-ers banning beer sales at the clubs remains in effect for Memphis as well as the unincorporated county. All of the club are in Memphis. The city proposal drafted by the Herenton administration in consultation with club owners would have permitted beer sales.

The county ordinance took effect with the new year. But the ordinance has a 120-day grace period before enforcement to allow for setting up a system of permits and criminal background checks for workers and owners. The grace period runs out at the end of April.

The club owners have filed for a temporary injunction to stop enforcement of the ordinance until the lawsuit is decided. That could take years, because whoever loses at the district court level is expected to appeal.

All sides in the case are to meet before Federal Magistrate Judge Tu M. Pham in one week.

"A Little Disingenuous"

City Attorney Elbert Jefferson pushed for the city proposal right up to the council vote.

Originally published as "Attorney General to Defend Strip Club Ordinance," *The Daily News*, Vol. 123, No. 56, March 20, 2008, by The Daily News Publishing Company, Inc., Memphis, TN. Reprinted with permission of the publisher.

He told Council Chairman Scott McCormick that the proposal was stronger than the county ordinance even after McCormick pointed out that the city proposal would only allow for a maximum $50 fine, while the county ordinance with backing from the state law makes some violations criminal offenses punishable by jail time. "They can get off. They can negotiate a plea. We have the ability to enforce this particular ordinance," Jefferson insisted. "They're not going to allow their dancers to get an extra $25 tip for doing a lap dance and they end up losing their (business) license." McCormick replied that the city now has the power to suspend and permanently revoke beer permits for the clubs through the Memphis Alcohol Commission. "How often are licenses actually revoked?" McCormick asked. Jefferson said he didn't know.

A 2006 report by Duncan Associates consultants of Austin, Texas, could find no record that any strip club had ever had its beer permit permanently revoked. The study by Eric Kelly also concluded that the strip clubs were the wildest he had ever seen in a career in which he's studied strip clubs in numerous American cities. Jefferson cited roughly $2 million in tax revenue the city would lose if there were no beer sales at the clubs.

McCormick accused him of being "a little disingenuous." "You can't judge how much revenue we're going to lose," he said. "I might have a beer at a strip club. If I can't go to the strip club and have a beer, I might have a beer at a local tavern. You can't tell how much revenue we're actually going to lose." "We have received documentation from the owners themselves," Jefferson replied to laughter from the crowd of about 100 gathered to oppose the proposed city ordinance. Council member Myron Lowery condemned the move to delay as "copping out." "You understand all of the implications. ... We are a legislative body. We should not defer to the courts," he said to other council members. "We need to have courage and leadership to state our convictions, whatever they might be."

"Sinful and Wicked"

The decision to table the proposal on what would have been its third and final reading appeared to satisfy neither side in the larger dispute of how to regulate an industry in which three generations of club owners — Art Baldwin, Danny Owens and Ralph Lunati — have been convicted of federal charges that they ran their clubs as criminal enterprises promoting prostitution. Efforts to regulate the clubs out of business by the city over the last 30 years repeatedly have been held unconstitutional by the courts in rulings that make it clear nude or topless dancing, in and of itself, is a form of expression protected by the U.S. Constitution. Backers of the county ordinance, including Shelby County District Attorney General Bill Gibbons, claim it recognizes those constitutional guarantees as it regulates other conduct that isn't protected.

Club owners and their attorneys watched from the council chambers Tuesday but offered no comment as they left after the vote. Business leader Nick Clark, who was among those favoring the county ordinance, said the council should have voted down the Herenton administration proposal once and for all. "The community then is at risk of having the City Council pass an ordinance when certain members who oppose it are absent," Clark said after the vote to table.

Those voting to table the proposed city ordinance were Ford, Bill Boyd, Shea Flinn, Janis Fullilove, Wanda Halbert, Reid Hedgepeth and Barbara Swearengen Ware. Those voting no were Lowery, McCormick, Harold Collins, Bill Morrison and Jim Strickland.

Council member Joe Brown didn't vote at all. Brown has said repeatedly that he won't vote for or against any measure because he considers the strip clubs to be "sinful and wicked."

Note

1. The State's Attorney General's Office, and the County Attorney, are defending the State law used by the County to adopt its ordinance. The State law is entitled the Tennessee Adult-Oriented Establishment Registration Act (TCA 7-51-1101). The Sixth Circuit U.S. Court of Appeals held a hearing on the appeal granted by the lower court in April 2008. The final decision in this case has not yet been rendered.

CHAPTER 24

Middleton Voters Reject Adult Entertainment Business Zone

John Laidler *and* Bella Travaglini

The background of the proposed adult entertainment zone in the Town of Middleton is set forth in the following paragraphs. This historical overview will provide readers with insights leading to this planned change in the Town's zoning regulations. This section of the article was written by John Laidler, correspondent for The Boston Globe.

Middleton voters next year may decide whether to set aside areas in town where adult-oriented businesses could be located.

At a recent meeting of the Board of Selectmen and several other town panels, it was agreed that the Planning Board will develop a zoning proposal for Town Meeting in the spring calling for creation of one or more adult business districts, according to Selectman Timothy P. Houten.

Houten said the proposed bylaw, similar to measures in place in many other communities, is intended as a proactive step to allow the town to regulate the location of any sex-oriented bookstores, entertainment clubs, or other adult businesses that might want to come to Middleton.

Currently, an adult business could locate anywhere in town zoned for the general type of business involved, such as a bookstore, according to Mark Bobrowski, a consultant to Middleton on zoning issues and a professor at the New England School of Law.

Bobrowski noted that the U.S. Supreme Court has held that municipalities cannot prohibit adult businesses from locating in their communities but can restrict them through zoning to specific areas as long as those restrictions are reasonable.

Houten said no adult businesses are currently seeking to locate in town. But he said officials want to be prepared for the possibility.

"What we are worried about is that there are so many empty storefronts on Route 114," he said, adding that an owner of one of those buildings might be willing to sell or lease to an adult business if the offer was right.

Houten said town officials currently envision locating the adult business districts within one or more of its industrially zoned areas, which include areas near the transfer station, off Logbridge Road, and off Sharpner's Pond Road.

Bobrowski, who has consulted with dozens of communities across the state on zon-

Originally published as "Adult Zoning Proposed: Bylaw Would Limit Area for Business" and "Middleton Leaders Hope to Stay Step Ahead of Adult Businesses," *The Boston Globe*, November 6, 2008 and April 30, 2009, by The Boston Globe, Boston, MA. Reprinted with permission of the publisher.

ing issues, estimated about a third have adopted adult zoning districts or made adult businesses an allowable use within existing districts.

He said he advises communities about the "repercussions of being silent" on the subject in their bylaws, referring to the ability of adult businesses — in the absence of any bylaw restrictions — to "go anywhere that generic type of business could go."

Sam Cleaves, senior regional planner with the Metropolitan Area Planning Council, said in Essex County, communities that have established adult business districts or made adult businesses an allowable use within existing districts include: Amesbury, Danvers, Georgetown, Ipswich, Lawrence, Merrimac, Methuen, North Andover, Rowley, Salisbury, Saugus, and West Newbury.

Donald Schmidt, director of the smart growth zoning program for the Massachusetts Department of Housing and Community Development, cautioned that any zoning restrictions that communities enact regarding adult businesses cannot focus on the type of product being sold. He said the Supreme Court has ruled that would be a violation of freedom of speech. Instead, communities must base any restrictions on "secondary effects" associated with those businesses.

"The message should be that we are concerned about property values, we are concerned about increasing crime," he said. "It should not be that we don't like these uses."

Middleton previously discussed adopting an adult business bylaw about five years ago but no proposal was ever put before a town meeting, according to Planning Board chairman Bob Aldenberg.

"But it's a subject matter every town and city has to deal with," he said. "If you don't want it on every street corner, ... you've got to do it."

Houten said the impetus for developing the districts came from the town's Bylaw Review Committee, which has identified the lack of such a measure as a deficiency in the town's zoning rules.

Housten said the town plans to base its bylaw on the one instituted by the western Massachusetts town of Lee, which he noted is comparable with Middleton in land size.

As a first step, he said, Middleton's Planning Board, which is working with the Bylaw Review Committee, will come up with recommendations on where to locate the adult business districts.

Houten predicted some residents might be alarmed by the bylaw proposal, mistakenly assuming that the town is seeking to attract adult businesses. But he said town officials plan to hold educational forums so residents understand that is not the intent.

The electoral defeat of the proposed adult entertainment zone in the Town of Middleton is reviewed in the following paragraphs. It should be kept in mind that this zone was recommended by the Town's Zoning Bylaw Review Committee, the Planning Board, as well as the Board of Selectman. The following portion of this article was written by Bella Travaglini, a correspondent for The Boston Globe.

Could an adult-themed shop open next to Dairy Queen on Route 114 in Middleton? It's possible, under current zoning laws.

And it's that possibility that prompted officials to propose amending Middleton's zoning bylaw by adopting an adult entertainment overlay district for tighter control of where such businesses may operate.

Following an hourlong public hearing April 13, the Planning Board cast a unanimous vote to recommend a location on Sharpners Pond Road for voters' consideration at the May 12 Town Meeting. Town officials think the location is too remote to attract an adult business.

"These types of adult businesses want to

be in big cities or on main thoroughfares. If you zone unattractive parcels, they won't come," said Selectman Timothy Houten, a lawyer who worked on the bylaw committee.

The board had considered two options: that location and another abutting a West Peabody neighborhood on Boston Street. Both sites were recommended by a zoning consultant following a review of the town's zoning bylaw amid concerns adult shops could open in one of an estimated 50 vacant storefronts along high-visibility Route 114.

Several hundred West Peabody residents attended the hearing April 13.

The proposed 40-plus-acre parcel off Sharpners Pond Road, currently zoned for light industrial use, is on the outskirts of town on the North Andover line. It abuts Creighton Pond Summer Camp, run by the Boys and Girls Club of Lynn. North Andover's soccer and baseball fields are just across the street. A handful of residences dot the street and there is a condominium development adjacent on Route 114.

"It's the lesser of two evils," said Christine Lindberg, a Middleton Planning Board member who works as Hamilton's planning coordinator. "We all live in town and I have two young children myself. I know families in that area. But in our professional opinion, it's the least likely place anyone would put anything."

National Grid owns a majority of the lot and the town of Middleton owns a portion, where an electrical substation operates. Four or five smaller lots are privately owned, Lindberg said.

Robert Barker, executive director of the Boys and Girls Club of Lynn, said he is disappointed with the Planning Board's decision and that he plans to bring the matter up at the next board of directors meeting. The club runs an eight-week summer camp for more than 100 children daily on a wooded parcel surrounded by the lot in Middleton. While Barker recognizes the town should designate an adult zone to protect the town at large, he considers the decision to choose the land next to a youth camp "a gamble."

Adult entertainment overlay districts must be established in a "viable area, commercial in nature and large enough to comply with constitutional requirements," said Houten. Both Houten and Lindberg said the Sharpners Pond Road lot meets the legal criteria for such a zone, yet is too wooded, with limited access, making it cost prohibitive for those looking to turn a profit.

Although the town has not received an official applicant, Houten said he has "heard rumblings" of land owners on Route 114 being approached by developers seeking to open adult-themed stores.

Lindberg is concerned that property owners, given tough economic times, may consider leasing storefronts to any legitimate developer out of financial desperation.

Neighboring communities have adopted adult entertainment districts for the same reasons Middleton is facing. North Andover did so in 1996, North Reading in 1999. Neither North Andover or North Reading has an adult-themed business in operation, while each has received only one applicant since the adult zoning was adopted.

North Reading's adult zone is in the middle of high-rent Route 28, said Patricia Romeo, vice chairman of the North Reading Planning Board. North Andover's zone is off Route 125 in a secluded area past Lawrence Municipal Airport, said Curt Bellavance, the town's director of community development.

Both Romeo and Bellavance would like to see more conditions, such as frontage setbacks and proximity to residential, church, and school area restrictions, included in the language of Middleton's proposed adult zoning bylaw.

Amendments to the proposed language can be raised during the vote at Town Meeting, Lindberg said.

"This does not mean that adult entertainment will automatically go in there [Sharpners Pond Road] if the property is sold," Lindberg said.

Editor's Note:

If approved, the proposed adult entertainment zone would recognize the *secondary effects* of adult entertainment businesses within the Town of Middleton. These effects include, but are not limited to, an increase in the crime rate, an adverse impact on the existing business climate, and a negative impact on residential property values. By limiting adult businesses to one designated zone, these impacts would have been mitigated by the allowing them in only one designated geographic area within the municipality.

CHAPTER 25

Minneapolis and Other Cities Use GIS to Regulate the Location of Adult Businesses

American City & County

Dakota County, Minn., and 11 communities within the suburban Minneapolis–St. Paul county have been using Geographic Information Systems (GIS) for nearly a decade and have discovered a wide variety of applications.

Twenty-two of 28 county departments now use GIS in some form, says Gary Stevenson, director of survey and land information. The county has developed its own Intranet to share information, and a pilot program is underway to put the data on the Internet.

Use of GIS technology for hazard response and monitoring of utilities infrastructure is fairly commonplace, but Dakota County and neighboring communities have found other diverse uses.

For example, last year the National Association of Counties presented the county with an Achievement Award for its pesticide education program, under which the county's digitized soil survey was combined with federal data to develop soil maps depicting pesticide leaching potential in different areas.

Also on the pest control front, GIS was employed to mesh data regarding encephalitis-carrying mosquito species with population density data. The objective was to enable the Metro Mosquito Control District and county to better collaborate on an abandoned tire pickup program.

Stevenson says Dakota County appears to be on the cutting edge in its use of GIS. "I definitely think we're one of the more advanced (counties) as far as the detail of our databases," he says.

Individual communities have also found a variety of uses for GIS. Apple Valley, population 46,079, used GIS to regulate location of adult entertainment businesses.

Prospective sites for the businesses were determined based on adherence to a city ordinance that requires a minimum of 1,000 feet between these establishments and schools, libraries and residential areas. The city also employed GIS to develop more efficient snow plow routes and monitor complaints.

Apple Valley does not have a centralized GIS program; instead, separate departments have their own work stations. The city regularly works with an outside consultant to update and improve its GIS applications.

Originally published as "County, Cities Collaborate on Use of GIS Technology," *American City & County*, Vol. 112, No. 6, June 1997, by Penton Media, Inc., Overland Park, KS. Reprinted with permission of the publisher.

Although GIS cost/benefit analyses are usually limited to narrowly defined projects, some experts have maintained that a 10-year payback on investment is the norm.

However, one recent study noted that GIS makes possible things that were impossible or impractical before, according to one of the study's authors, William Craig, assistant director for research at the University of Minnesota's Center for Urban and Regional Affairs.

"Lots of people have the technology, but not many people are getting as many benefits out of it as Dakota County," says Craig. He attributes this to a great deal of stakeholder involvement on the part of Dakota County and other municipal officials, as well as strong outreach effort to train and encourage employees to use GIS.

Two other examples of the use of GIS to determine the potential location of adult businesses include the City of Moreno Valley, California,[1] and the City and County of Honolulu, in Hawaii.[2] Based upon the examples contained in this article, there is a definite national trend for local governments to use GIS to regulate the location of adult businesses in cities and counties throughout the United States. Details regarding these two GIS applications are provided below.

City of Moreno Valley

The basic premise of land-use zoning is to protect property values and prevent new development from harming existing residents and businesses. However, the regulation of land use by government is often contentious. After all, as the argument goes, how can government tell private property owners what they can or cannot do with their land?

Suppose the property owner of a vacant corner lot across the street from the local high school wants to open a 24-hour convenience store on the site. As long as the parcel is zoned for commercial use and the city cannot find a negative impact on surrounding properties resulting from that use, the store will probably be built. But what if, instead of a convenience store, the property owner wants to open an adult bookstore?

Residents typically oppose business or land development that they feel cuts into the social fabric of their community or infringes upon their sense of decency or well-being. However, an adult business's right to operate is often protected under the law This means that cities must somehow designate where adult businesses can and cannot operate within their jurisdiction.

Officials must also consider surrounding property owners who feel that allowing an adult business to operate nearby will negatively impact the quality of their lives and businesses and reduce their property values. It is a balancing act that affects not just land-use policy but also the social fabric of the community.

When a city needs to develop an adult business ordinance, how can GIS help determine where the city can permit that kind of controversial land use?

When cities are put in the awkward position of finding a suitable location for a not-so-respectable business, they need tools that will help them step through a logical, repeatable process and ultimately establish an enforceable ordinance. Many of the components of an adult business ordinance have spatial or geographic elements, like distance, proximity, and adjacency. GIS gives cities the ability to visualize and analyze those elements, which improves the viability of the ordinance.

For example, cities might first determine which land-use zones absolutely do not permit adult businesses, like open space, public facilities, and high-density residential areas. They might also identify land uses sensitive to adult business activities like medium- and low-density residential areas.

Next they could locate land-use types that accept adult business use like commercial and industrial zones. They might also establish a buffer area where adult businesses are not permitted — within a specified distance, say 500 feet, of commercial and industrial zones that are adjacent to sensitive land uses.

In addition to the land-use map, cities can include the parcel map in their analysis. For example, they might determine that no new adult business can be developed within 1,000 feet of a parcel with an existing adult business.

Based on these restrictions, which is essentially a process of elimination, cities can use standard GIS geoprocessing tools to create a map of possible locations where adult business use will have the least negative impact on the community. This process is easily modeled in the GIS. The model can be modified and run against every time changes to the ordinance or land-use and parcels maps are made.

City and County of Honolulu

The City Council of the City and County of Honolulu directed the City Department of Land Utilization (DLU) to draft and initiate a bill for a proposed City ordinance to restrict the location of "adult business" establishments. The bill proposed to limit the locations of these establishments to specific commercial City zoning districts and set a minimum distance requirement from residential districts and public and private schools. GIS technology was used to perform the spatial analysis to identify the proposed areas where these types of establishments would be permitted to locate.

These maps depict the process and data used to perform the analysis. These maps were created using Honolulu Application Programs and Analyses (HAPA) user interface. The DLU and City Council used these maps during public hearings on the proposed ordinance. For the present, the bill has been tabled by the City Council.

NOTES

1. For more information about how the City of Moreno Valley, California, uses GIS applications to regulate adult businesses in their community, please refer to their website at <www.moreno-valley.ca.us>. Janice Nollar, Senior GIS Analyst, and Mike Heslin, GIS Coordinator, worked on the development of this application for their community.

2. For more information about how the City and County of Honolulu, Hawaii, uses GIS applications to regulate adult businesses in their community, please refer to their website at <www.honolulu.gov>. The Department of Land Utilization (DLU) can be accessed via this official website.

CHAPTER 26

Nashville Reinvigorates Downtown by Creating a Network of Property Owners to Plan for the Future

Jim Constantine *and* Hunter Gee

Government and private enterprise have transformed Nashville into a vibrant mixed-use neighborhood.

Downtown Nashville today is a world apart from that of just ten years ago, when the city center labored through the urban schizophrenia of many downtowns. By day, it was a bustling central business district for banking, commerce, law, and government services. By night, it was a place that people fled for their havens in suburbia. Most windows in the city's office towers fell dark after nightfall. The evening cityscape was punctuated by the blinking of a few neon signs along Lower Broadway, a once-proud boulevard tracing west from the Cumberland River that became weighted with pornography shops, souvenir vendors, and honky-tonks.

Now a series of public/private initiatives has produced a virtual renaissance within the city's former fallow core. Downtown streets are active both night and day as people are being drawn to new offerings of entertainment, major league sports, art, music, and education. While Nashville residents may view the change as having happened overnight, it actually has been a long time in the making.

In the late 1980s, the problems of the declining downtown were being attacked on a number of fronts by a variety of public and private groups, all of which recognized the importance of a strong core to a healthy city. One such effort was an economic revitalization program created to preserve the buildings and provide an economic stimulus for the historic areas of Broadway, Second Avenue, and Printers Alley, which became known collectively as the District. The idea for the District originated with the Broadway Committee, an ad hoc group consisting of the mayor's office, the Metropolitan Development and Housing Agency (MDHA), the Metro Historical Commission, the Metro Arts Commission, and Historic Nashville, Inc. Using a four-point revitalization plan, based on the Main Street Program of the National Trust for Historic Preservation, the District program sought to:

- Organize property owners into committees that would increase the downtown community's involvement;
- Establish specific design guidelines that would retain the area's character;

Originally published as "Reactivating Downtown," *Urban Land,* Vol. 61, No. 12, December 2002, by the Urban Land Institute, Washington, DC. Reprinted with permission of the publisher.

- Market vacant properties to business owners and private investors; and
- Restructure the area economically.

Created with an MDHA grant, the program continues today as an active conduit for downtown revitalization.

Initially, confidence was generated by a few pioneer success stories, most notably the preservation of several blocks on historic Second Avenue and the restoration of the Merchant's Hotel, which reopened in 1988 as a restaurant and continues as a popular spot for lunch and dinner. Separately, the Ryman Auditorium, historic home of the Grand Ole Opry, was restored in 1994 and operates today as a world-class music venue and tourist center in the shadow of the 33-story Bell-South Tower, completed the same year.

In many ways, Nashville's renaissance is tied to the city's reorientation to its riverfront. The 68,000-seat, $292 million Adelphia Coliseum, home of the NFL's Tennessee Titans, opened in 1999 on the Cumberland's east bank. Across the river, a battery of public venues has transformed the once-blighted Lower Broadway into a busy center of sports and entertainment for all ages. The new 20,000-seat, $144 million Gaylord Entertainment Center has been the site of performances by the likes of Luciano Pavarotti and Elton John and also is the home of the Nashville Predators, which in 1998–1999 set the record for the highest attendance for a new NHL franchise. Several arts, cultural, and civic projects have opened this year, including the $50 million Frist Center for the Visual Arts, the $37 million Country Music Hall of Fame, and the city's $50 million main library.

"Twenty years ago, Lower Broadway was considered among the seediest spots in the city," notes Gerald Nicely, MDHA director. "The riverfront was a blemish on downtown and, frankly, it was not friendly for pedestrians. By the early 1990s, major retail had marched to the suburbs. There were no whole-

some entertainment venues or decent restaurants to attract families, professionals, or tourists. The buildings there were historic, but many were in decline.

"We realized that to improve the situation in the District, we needed to do more than save buildings," he adds. "We needed to renew the historical significance and sense of place within the entire area. We wanted people to have a feeling of arrival when they were in the District."

Through MDHA grants, federal tax incentives, and intense marketing and recruiting, investment on Lower Broadway and Second Avenue got a shot in the arm. Restaurants and music venues returned. For example, crowds now swarm Riverfront Park for "Dancin' in the District," a weekly free concert series held during summer months.

"It's been amazing to witness the transformation of the area, particularly Lower Broadway, from an unsavory section into a place enjoyed by crowds," says Nicely. "It has positive energy that is evident now on any given night. This is an indication that we can continue to improve the image and outreach of our downtown and make it the destination in Nashville. It also enables us to achieve future quality growth that is balanced and complementary to what the community has created."

There is a reason for such optimism. Mayor Bill Purcell was elected last November by a broad coalition in response to his emphasis on the improvement of neighborhoods throughout Davidson County. Purcell subsequently spearheaded the creation of Nashville's first Civic Design Center, which brings together Vanderbilt University, the University of Tennessee, private sector partners, and leaders in historic preservation. The mayor has assigned his new planning director, Rick Bernhardt, a proponent of new urbanism, to work with the local think tank.

Nashville Urban Venture, LLC, a private sector partnership of developers and investors who understand urban revitalization and historic preservation, currently is focused on a way to complement the downtown progress. One ingredient is missing, they say, if Nashville is to experience a true urban renaissance: a strong residential component in an urban mixed-use neighborhood.

About two years ago, Nashville Urban Venture assembled a planning team including Looney Ricks Kiss (LRK), an architecture, planning, research, and interiors firm in Princeton, New Jersey; Manual Zeitlin, a Nashville-based specialist in restoration architecture; and RPM, Inc., a Nashville-based traffic engineering firm, to focus on a blighted downtown industrial area just south of Nashville's historic Union Station. The area is bounded by Interstate 65 and a large-scale active railroad complex that serves the suburban CSX rail cargo hub in Radnor Yard located miles to the south. Historically known as the Gulch, it is located within a stone's throw of the burgeoning revitalization of the District and the legendary Music Row area.

Topographically, the Gulch is a depression running along the western edge of the old downtown core that has provided a natural lane for rail lines since the 1800s. Over the decades, it housed an asylum and served as a neighborhood for railroad workers and merchants near Union Station. Since the 1950s, the Gulch has become an out-of-sight, out-of-mind place for warehouses, light-industrial manufacturing, and service companies, with a patchwork of low-tax properties and a number of older buildings, some dating to the 1920s.

Working within the concept of an urban plan, the Nashville Urban Venture team designed a $400 million, 30-acre mixed use area to establish the Gulch as a central component in the fabric of the city's downtown renaissance. The development team visited cities with districts similar to the Gulch, conducted a regional market analysis based on demographic data to determine profiles for potential residential and commercial users, and conducted qualitative focus-group re-

search and a design charrette to obtain information on designing and renting condominium products. This assessment proved that there was a strong market in Nashville for a neighborhood that was very urban in character and unlike anything that currently existed. As a result, the team devised highly tailored rental apartment, condominium, and retail concepts; entertainment themes; and workplace opportunities in various locations within the Gulch. The plan has evolved through an ongoing process of detailing and refinement with feedback from various prospective users and marketing consultants. In addition, an extensive financial analysis was conducted to demonstrate the viability of the completed project and its positive impact on the economy of the region as well as on city tax revenues.

The resulting master plan for the Gulch emphasizes neighborhood and a sense of community, and features moderate density residential uses, including affordable housing. It calls for the restoration of old buildings and the development of new structures to provide an array of lofts, flats, rowhouses, and condominiums. High-tech offices with an industrial edge will be located adjacent to and intermixed with the homes, which will have views of the downtown skyline. Parking will be situated along tree-lined streets featuring retail necessities, cafes, and boutiques, all punctuated by green spaces.

Following an initial planning period, Nashville Urban Venture invested private capital in acquiring properties in the area. In the meantime, the group launched the development of specific office properties and apartments, all presently operating or under construction.

Just over a year ago, the team began discussing its plans with MDHA, and after extensive review, they obtained the endorsement of Mayor Purcell. MDHA's board named Nashville Urban Venture as redeveloper of the area this past May, which enabled the group to use tax-increment financing, and the government has indicated its willingness to provide about $7 million in needed infrastructure improvements. To date, Nashville Urban Venture has purchased the 22 acres called for in the plan it submitted to the MDHA and is working with individual property owners to incorporate additional parcels.

"The Gulch will be a centerpiece for individuals, families, and companies moving into Nashville," explains Joe Barker, managing partner of Nashville Urban Venture. "It will appeal to those who have found the urban lifestyle attractive in other cities. The Gulch also will draw residents throughout our region who seek a progressive and distinctive shopping district in a downtown setting, hopefully making a significant dent in reducing suburban sprawl in our region."

According to the plan for the Gulch, there needs to be a balance between glamour and grit, uniting establishments that range from hip to historic. No single architectural style will dominate, and creative design from multiples architects and developers for individual buildings is considered paramount. Established urban design principles will guide the Gulch development, melding Nashville institutions like the Station Inn with new restaurant concepts and entertainment venues. "For many locals and visitors, the Station Inn presently highlights the area and helps define who we are as Nashvillians," comments Bill Barkley, a partner with Armistead Barkley, developers of the Gulch project and partner in Nashville Urban Venture. "It will add a diverse layer of interest to the unique personality of the Gulch."

The skyline of the Gulch is sculpted with three- to five-story buildings, with taller structures placed in carefully planned locations to take advantage of topography and to capture dramatic views of the downtown. Urban residential stoops and more than 120 storefronts are expected to stimulate visual interest along wide sidewalks. Contemporary forms and materials will be juxtaposed with traditional brick warehouses. On-street parking will be provided where possible throughout the district, with parking structures located behind or beside buildings, screened with landscaping, fencing, and/or other structures. Signs will be designed to complement the buildings and not obscure architectural elements or detailing.

At least 20 percent of the residences in the Gulch will be defined as affordable housing, as determined by federal Department of Housing and Urban Development standards. "Diversity is the key to making this project work," stresses Steve Turner, senior partner of Nashville Urban Venture. "We want the Gulch to embody many aspects of a larger city's urban neighborhood, which means different cultural influences in everything from dining to shopping to living. The Gulch is designed to have people interact with one another professionally and socially, forming a vibrant, sustainable community." A network of public green spaces at six locations and plazas will serve as focal points of activity within the Gulch to enhance neighborhood interaction among those who live and work there.

Its location at the center of an active rail complex will allow the Gulch to serve as the hub for commuters to and from the downtown area. Adjacent to the Clement Landport, which serves as a multimodal motor transportation hub, the Gulch is planned to link commuter rail passengers with light-rail transit, buses, and shuttles. A commuter rail line has been proposed along the existing tracks, which could link outlying communities with the Clement Landport.

When completed, the Gulch will offer 350,000 to 400,000 square feet of retail space, 750,000 to 1 million square feet of office space, 100,000 square feet of hospitality space, and 2 million square feet of residential space — making it a district accessible by foot or mass transit where people can live, work, shop, and spend leisure time.

"As the Gulch project progresses, I think people may wonder why an urban neighborhood downtown has not existed before now," Barker adds. "In one sense, we are responding to and expanding upon an existing downtown community. In another sense, we are build-ing something completely new that we think will excite present Nashvillians and newcom-ers."

CHAPTER 27

New York City Cleans Up Times Square by Creating a Business Improvement District

Howard Kozloff

Fueled by the collective energy of public/private sector initiatives, Times Square returns as an icon of American urbanity.

The single event credited by most as marking Times Square's return as a New York landmark was the 1997 reopening by the Walt Disney Company of the New Amsterdam Theater nearly 95 years after it was built and 14 years after it was boarded up. Disney's corporate presence and the vote of confidence it represented helped to encourage others to set up shop in an area that had become best known as an adult-use enclave. Yet, the presence of Disney and other major corporations, such as Ernst & Young, Reuters, Gap, and Morgan Stanley, does not tell the whole story of Times Square's resurgence on the scene. The turnaround in an area once know for prostitution and drug dealing can be attributed to a multipronged approach aimed at safety, aesthetics, and a mix of uses that involved city and state cooperation and the collaboration of a multitude of developers and corporations.

Times Square is technically the triangle north of 42nd Street where Broadway and Seventh Avenue intersect. However, Times Square has come to refer to the neighborhood covered by the Times Square business improvement district (BID) — West 40th to West 53rd Street between Sixth and Eighth avenues, and extending to Ninth Avenue on West 46th Street. The very notion of referring to Times Square as a neighborhood, with the images and notions that word conjures up, is testament to the fact that Times Square has indeed emerged as another New York City success story.

In the early 20th century, the Times Square area, and in particular 42nd Street, became the home of numerous theaters and stages. However, the stock market crash of 1929 and the ensuing Great Depression bankrupted most of the 42nd Street theater owners. Those who remained realized modest profits — not from presenting legitimate performances, but from turning their stages into burlesque houses and movie theaters. The downward trend continued for decades, exacerbated by the post–World War II exodus of the middle class to the city's outlying suburbs. The emigration continued to the point that, by the 1970s, Times Square had become a haven

Originally published as "Times Square's Time," *Urban Land*, Vol. 61, No. 2, February 2002, by the Urban Land Institute, Washington, DC. Reprinted with permission of the publisher.

for prostitution and drug dealing, with streets lined by X-rated movie theaters and storefronts filled with pornographic wares.

The 1980s brought public realization of the state into which Times Square had fallen. Concomitantly, New York City and New York state, realizing the opportunity cost and the revenue potential of Times Square, cosponsored a $2.5 billion redevelopment plan for 42nd Street and Times Square. The 42nd Street Development Project, Inc. (42DP), a subsidiary of New York City's Empire State Development Corporation, is the largest urban renewal project every undertaken in the city. "42nd Street stands today as North America's oldest and newest tourism and entertainment district," says Charles A. Gargano, chairman of 42DP and the Empire State Development Corporation.

The plan called for the construction of four identical postmodern office towers designed by Philip Johnson at the bowtie of Seventh Avenue, Broadway, and 42nd Street. Fortunately for the bright-lights, big-city attitude of Times Square, the late 1980s economic downturn stopped the project. However, the site developers were required to pay $241 million to the city and state regardless of whether the project was actually built. This money proved significant in giving city planners a substantial starting point to identify and condemn properties in Times Square considered counterproductive to the redevelopment plan.

The 42DP effort was instrumental in clearing key sites on 42nd Street, allowed after a two-year court battle won by the state. As critical as obtaining the key sites were zoning amendments that restricted adult-use establishments. New York City passed the zoning legislation in 1995 and it, too, survived a legal battle, being upheld by the New York State Court of Appeals in 1997. As a result, the number of pornography shops has fallen from 50 to fewer than 20. Today, nearly 20 years after the city and state joined forces, 20 million tourists visit Times Square each year, and 1.5 million people pass through the neighborhood every day.

The Times Square neighborhood, as defined by the boundaries of the BID, attracts a mix of residents, businesspeople, and tourists. Not including residential ownership, there are about 400 property owners in the area representing more than 1,500 businesses and organizations employing approximately 231,000 people. There is 21 million square feet of office space, with more than 2 million square feet under construction, and more than 13,000 hotel rooms — one-fifth of the New York City total, with more planned. There also are 27,000 residents and more than 250 restaurants, and nearly $4 billion in private funds have been invested recently in the Times Square neighborhood.

The Times Square BID, overseer of the area's relatively recent success, started operations in 1992 as a 501(c)(3) nonprofit organization. The BID works in tandem with the private businesses, city agencies, community boards, and other not-for-profit organizations already active in the community. Its $6 million annual budget comes from a mandatory assessment of approximately 0.3 percent of the assessed value of commercial buildings. Residential owners contribute $1 per year; an additional $1 million comes from grants and sponsorships.

Public safety has been a primary focus of efforts in Times Square, but so, too, has been the desire to do right by the neighborhood and the city. Times Square arguably strikes a balance between attracting tourists and their money, and the rights and needs of those who work and live in the area. As spelled out by the BID, but applicable to the main public and private players, the organizing principles of Times Square's comeback are public safety, sanitation, public improvements, community services, and tourism.

The Times Square BID deemed safety and cleanliness to be the primary objectives because people are not likely to congregate in places that are unsafe or dirty, let alone both. Therefore, among the first initiatives it undertook was the hiring of public safety officers

(PSOs). In all, a force of 52 unarmed PSOs are on duty more than 14 hours per day, seven days a week. They communicate by radio directly with a dispatcher at New York's public safety headquarters, located on Broadway in Times Square, who is, in turn, linked by radio to the New York Police Department (NYPD). Also there are two police precincts in the neighborhood, one 24-hour NYPD substation, and one fire station.

In 1993, the PSOs first full year of service, crime in the Times Square area dropped 23 percent. Since that year, crime is down nearly 60 percent, illegal peddling has dropped more than 80 percent, and pickpocketing is down nearly 40 percent. Although the BID rightfully receives the bulk of the praise for Times Square's improved conditions, Bob Esposito, acting president/vice president of operations for the BID, is quick to attribute the improvement to the work of the NYPD, which represents the public sector's commitment to the area.

The benefits of reduced crime extend beyond neighborhood boundaries. "The Bryant Park Restoration Corporation had to turn around Bryant Park, which was only one block away from Times Square, when that area was dangerous and depressing," states Dan Biederman, founder of three BIDs that border Times Square. "Now, Bryant Park has no crime. But the improvement of Times Square over the last few years does make our ongoing management role of Bryant Park somewhat easier. 34th Street and Times Square have very little crime."

Complementing the public safety measures taken in Times Square are the sanitation efforts. Even before PSOs were put in place, sanitation services were underway. Some 50 BID employees work seven days a week sweeping, vacuuming, and scrubbing sidewalks and curbsides, emptying trash cans, and removing graffiti. Additionally, more than 2,000 pieces of street furniture are regularly painted, as are light poles, trash cans, and fire hydrants. In 1992, three months after the cleanup was initiated, the mayor's "sanitation scorecard" rated Times Square's sidewalks more than 93 percent clean, up from 55 percent a year earlier. In the ten years since, the sidewalks regularly exceed 90 percent clean.

In addition to improving safety and sanitation, Times Square also has been responsible for an array of public improvements for locals and visitors alike. For example, a public art fence — a curvilinear structure that includes multicolored images on its side — has been erected in the Broadway median between 44th and 46th streets with the support of such major corporations as Bertelsmann, Inc., Bethlehem Steel, and the New York Marriott Marquis Hotel.

Ten subway lines, serving all five New York boroughs, run through the Times Square station. In all, 344,000 riders use the station and 185,000 commuters pass through the Port Authority Bus Terminal near Times Square every day. Annually, 53 million people enter Times Square's subway stations, making it one of New York's top transportation hubs.

To deal with the enormous number of riders, the Metropolitan Transit Authority (MTA) opened a new subway entrance at 42nd Street in July 1997. In addition, an $82.8 million, 45-month rehabilitation program to be completed late this year aims to create better access to the different subway lines by renovating the station and rehabilitating the platform. To complement these and other improvements, a pedestrian passageway project has been undertaken to ease congestion on sidewalks by increasing the use of midblock tunnels and alleyways through better design, lighting, and signs, among other things.

Times Square's redevelopment strategy is not focused solely on those passing through the area as tourists or employees; there also are efforts and programs to look after the community. Many homeless people remain in the area as reminders of the past, but instead of gentrifying the area by driving them out, there are programs to help them.

The Times Square Consortium for the

Homeless (TSC) is one such agency, using $2.6 million raised from federal and state agencies to address the needs of people such as the mentally ill and substance abusers who have refused services in the past and live permanently on the street. Local lead agencies provide on-street therapy and services, with representatives from the TSC working on the streets 16 hours a day, seven days a week. Over three years, more than 70 homeless people were placed in housing. Supplementing the TSC is an effort called Times Square Delivers, which in two years solicited $860,000 in goods from local businesses for delivery to local social service agencies. The BID is active in this arena, too, giving community service grants to local social service providers for public capital improvement projects that benefit both the Times Square community and the respective providers.

Perhaps the most innovative and successful of Times Square's community service efforts is one that, like the BID, addresses issues traditionally handled by the public sector. Begun in 1993, the Midtown Community Court handles quality-of-life offenders in the Times Square neighborhood who otherwise may slip through the legal system because their offenses are minor, such as illegal peddlers, graffiti artists, turnstile jumpers, and some prostitutes and small-time drug dealers. Offenders are sentenced to community service in the Times Square neighborhood; in 1998 alone, more than 1,100 community service assignments were handed out.

Programs also are in place to serve high school students. A number of arts projects pair professional artists with students from the local Graphic Communication Arts High School. For instance, students created a 225-foot-long mural on the back of the Roseland Ballroom on 53rd Street, and three high school student apprentices working with professionals helped complete restoration of local monuments. Further involvement with high school students includes the effort by the Mayor's Commission on Youth Empowerment Services to place students in jobs at local nonprofit organizations for summer internships, and the publication and distribution by the BID of a newsletter listing entry-level job opportunities in Times Square.

In the end, while city and state support and strong local organizations are essential components of Times Square's revival, it is the vote of confidence and accompanying investment by the private sector that makes the area a desirable destination for locals and tourists. The potential in Times Square has turned into real profits for property owners and businesses, making the levying of assessments all the more palatable. Driving those profits are the tourism dollars being spent and the large-scale development taking place throughout the neighborhood. Although the presence of retail and restaurants in the area is substantial, Times Square's historic reputation as the center of New York's theater world is the major tourist attraction.

The city and state were quick to realize this, taking a major part in the first of the historic theater resurrections. With low-interest loans from the city and state covering 75 percent of the costs, the Walt Disney Company completed the $34 million restoration of the New Amsterdam Theater. Disney's foray into Times Square has immediate impact: on 42nd Street, the historic restoration of the Selwyn Theater, and the opening of the New Victory Theater and the Duke on 42nd Street all helped to reinstate Times Square's reputation. The Duke, an 84,000-square-foot, state-of-the-art studio rehearsal facility for the performing arts, was constructed by New 42nd Street Inc., a not-for-profit entity. The facility includes 15 rehearsal studios, supporting office space, and a 199-seat theater. Even MTV has relocated its main broadcast studios to Times Square, symbolizing the area's new image.

The change was significant and swift. In all, 40 theaters — including all 22 landmark Broadway theaters and the Ford Center for the Performing Arts — are open and operating, and in the 2000-2001 season alone, a record

11.9 million Broadway tickets were sold. Broadway theaters are a substantial component of Times Square's overall tourism draw, which nets 26 million tourists, with 3.9 million overnight stays in local hotels annually.

Times Square also has been successful in attracting high-credit tenants to Class A buildings, whether office, residential, hotel, or mixed-use. Although Disney's arrival in Times Square was significant, the high-profile office towers and accompanying tenants arguably have been the most invigorating. Around Times Square itself, there are four new buildings representing nearly 4 million square feet of space. The new Reuters headquarters, 3 Times Square, include 34,000 square feet of Times Square's legendary neon signage at the northwest corner of 42nd Street and Seventh Avenue. A 1.6 million-square-foot office tower at 4 Times Square, developed by the Durst Organization, houses Conde Nast on a site designated for one of the original postmodern office towers not built because of the 1980s economic downturn. Retailers at the ground floor include NASDAQ's Broadcast and Visitors Center and an ESPN Zone restaurant and entertainment center, a 37-story, 1.1 million-square-foot building.

5 Times Square at the southwest corner of Seventh Avenue and 42nd Street is slated for occupancy by this summer. Developed by Boston Properties and designed by Kohn Pederson Fox, it will be Ernst & Young's national headquarters. Next door, between Broadway and Seventh Avenue, is the Skidmore, Owings & Merrill–designed, 47-story Times Square Tower. Also developed by Boston Properties, this 1.2 million-square-foot, Arthur Andersen–occupied building will be completed by the end of next year.

A 1 million-square-foot *New York Times* headquarters at 41st Street and Eighth Avenue is being developed by Forest City Ratner, but it is the developer's high-profile, highly visible mixed-use project on 42nd Street between Seventh and Eighth avenues that adds to Times Square's action. The 350,000-square-foot 42nd Street Retail and Entertainment Complex includes, among other uses, the 60,000-square-foot Madame Tussaud's Wax Museum and a 25-screen AMC Entertainment movie theater. Plus, in keeping with the area's architectural heritage, the project involves restoration of three historic facades, including the Liberty and Empire theaters. In addition, Forest City Ratner is developing and will be owner of a Hilton hotel, built on the complex's air rights. "42nd Street provides that incredible mix of a very strong leisure/tourist market while also being a very strong financial/media market, which continues to grow by the minute," notes Matt Messinger, senior vice president of hotel investments at Forest City Ratner.

The 871,000-square-foot E-Walk complex on 42nd Street between Broadway and Eighth Avenue is another major mixed-use project in Times Square. Developed by Tishman Urban Development Corporation, it includes, among other uses, the 550-seat B.B. King Blues Club and the 860-room Westin New York Hotel. Other hotel developments in Times Square include DoubleTree's 460-room hotel on 41st Street between Seventh and Eighth avenues, and Starwood's 57-story W Hotel, whose Times Square location includes a 400-seat, two-level restaurant facing the action on Broadway.

Two residential towers also demonstrate Times Square's return as a desirable locale. The Gershwin, a 35-story, 550-unit residential tower on Eighth Avenue between 49th and 50th streets, and Longacre House, a 26-story, 290-unit apartment building between 50th and 51st streets on Eighth Avenue, help prevent Times Square from becoming an urban amusement park by installing those who will develop a vested interest in the neighborhood.

In a relatively small area, billions of dollars of development and revitalization have been spent in accordance with an overall vision. The bright lights of Times Square continue to define its image, but *The Lion King* and camera-toting tourists have replaced the former backdrop of prostitutes and drug dealers, while an air of reassurance and hospitality pervades the once-neglected area. With support of and belief in Times Square by the likes of Disney, the *New York Times*, and MTV, and the development of Class A office space and residential units, Times Square has contributed substantially to New York's renaissance.

CHAPTER 28

North Andover Controls Adult Businesses with an Adult Business District

Brad Kane

North Andover wants a vibrant commercial and industrial district to blossom along its newly created Osgood Street business corridor, but that corridor could also be home to something officials would prefer to keep hidden from the rest of town.

Six parcels of land out by the Lawrence Municipal Airport were established as potential islands of impurity long before the Town Meeting in May called for North Andover to diversify its mostly residential economic base by adding businesses along Osgood Street.

Those properties between Holt Road and Clark Street make up the adult business district, the one place in town where strip clubs, adult movie theaters, adult bookstores, and video stores could locate should they ever choose to set up shop in this Essex County community.

"You protect adult entertainment from being exposed to the churches, schools, and residential areas of the town," said Rosemary Connelly Smedile, chairwoman of the North Andover Board of Selectman. "You protect your community and protect people's freedom of speech rights."

The town's adult business district sprang from a 1984 Supreme Judicial Court decision that communities cannot bar adults-only businesses, as it violates First Amendment rights. Instead, Massachusetts cities and towns can regulate these types of business by relegating them to certain areas.

"It is a crapshoot with that type of use coming into town," said Curt Bellavance, director of North Andover Community Development. "The law says if we don't state where we can allow it, it can go anywhere."

North Andover's adult business district, which was last modified in 2003, has only once shown signs of possible life: In 2002, a 475-seat strip club was proposed for Holt Road, but it never came to fruition.

Even though North Andover's hopes of a commercial and industrial revolution now center on the entire Osgood Street corridor, Connelly Smedile said the six parcels that make up the adult business district won't deter the town's growth plans.

"If you look on a map, it is pretty far down Holt Road," Connelly Smedile said.

Originally published as "Town Pushing a Strip, but Not a Certain Kind: North Andover Backs Growth Corridor," *The Boston Globe,* December 7, 2008, by The Boston Globe, Boston, MA. Reprinted with permission of the publisher.

"This is a common practice among communities in Massachusetts."

By putting the adult business district in a remote location, strip clubs and other establishments would be kept a reasonable distance from schools, churches, parks, and playgrounds, Bellavance said.

"That is a general concern that most towns have," Bellavance said.

Even though local control of Massachusetts strip clubs, adult movie theaters, bookstores, and video stores has been around since the 1980s, new adult business districts are constantly being established or reworked, said Mark Racicot, manager of government services for the Boston Metropolitan Area Planning Council.

In Middlesex County, 16 communities have adult business districts, and there are another 12 in Essex County.

The Board of Selectmen for Middleton — North Andover's neighbor to the east — in November decided to ask the Town Meeting whether the town should create an adult business district. The Dedham Town Meeting, which met in November, moved its adult business district to different locations after the town lost a court ruling saying its original district was too remote.

Communities create or modify adult business districts for many reasons, Racicot said. The Massachusetts Zoning Act changes, an adults-only business tries to move in, a neighboring community creates one or a new court decision changes how communities can control adult businesses.

"In many cases, it is the community realizing they don't have it, and they want to get it," Racicot said.

In July, Methuen changed it regulations to create two specific remote adult business districts. Even though Methuen has never had an application for an adult business, the city didn't want a court to find its regulations overly harsh, and therefore allow the business to go anywhere.

"We wanted to make sure that it holds up in court," said Karen Sawyer, Methuen director of economic and community development. "We hope nobody comes knocking on our door."

The latest court ruling changing adult-use regulations was the 2006 case *T & D Video v. City of Revere*. Revere tried to adopt the special permit regulations as T & D's adult video store was being constructed in the Suffolk County city. The Appeals Court of Massachusetts — later backed by the Massachusetts Supreme Judicial Court — found Revere did not adequately list the negative impacts an adult video store would have, so it was not justified in curtailing the business's First Amendment rights.

The U.S. Supreme Court decided in 1976 that adult businesses cannot be prevented from coming into communities but can be controlled inside communities. In a 1985 case, the high court allowed zoning regulation of adults-only businesses.

"It's not particularly new, although there are always court cases," Racicot said. "If you don't define these areas, then they can go anywhere."

In Arlington adult-use regulations act as a prevention to keep those types of businesses from ever coming into the town, as the town had never had an application for one, said Kevin O'Brien, Arlington director of planning.

The town has 19 zoning districts, and the one that allows adult uses is the downtown center. Because it is in the center of town, the most intensively used district, it seems unlikely an adult business would locate there, O'Brien said.

Reading, which adopted its adult-use regulations in 1996, had an adult video store in a strip mall on North Main Street, but it was destroyed in a 2006 fire. The town hasn't had an adult-use application since, said Carol Kowalski, Reading community services director/town planner.

"The purpose of zoning is to plan for smart growth, and the purpose of these districts is to determine what is the least inappropriate place for them to go," Kowalski said.

CHAPTER 29

North Bend and Issaquah Enter into Agreement with Their County on the Placement of Adult Businesses

Ron Sims

In 1995, King County was ordered by King County Superior Court to amend our zoning regulations because they were found to be in violation of the United States Constitution. Across the country, the courts have consistently found that adult entertainment businesses are protected by the "freedom of expression" clause of the First Amendment to the United States Constitution. Local jurisdictions must allow adult entertainment businesses to locate and operate, but our regulations effectively precluded any businesses from locating in unincorporated King County. While we cannot ban such businesses, we can use regulations to protect residents from their potential "secondary effects," such as crime and blight, by requiring these businesses to locate away from residentially-zoned areas, schools, churches and parks. We can also regulate how these businesses operate.

To help us develop new regulations to address the court order, a citizen committee was formed in 1996. The committee studied the issues, facilitated a series of public meetings, and developed a recommended approach. Their primary recommendation was that the burden of providing potential locations for adult entertainment businesses should be spread throughout the county and should not overburden just one or two communities. The committee's recommendations are reflected in the new adopted changes to the King County Zoning Code

Ordinance 13546 specifies that adult entertainment businesses:

- Can locate only in the Community Business (CB), Regional Business (RB) and Office (O) zones;
- Must be at least 330 feet (about one block) away from residentially-zoned property, schools, licensed day care centers, public parks, trails, community centers, public libraries and churches; and
- Must be 3000 feet away from other adult entertainment businesses.

Originally published as "Adult Entertainment Regulations in King County," *News Statement by King County Executive*, June 10, 1999, by the Office of the County Executive, King County, Seattle, WA. Reprinted with permission of the publisher.

King County is in a unique situation because while we have to allow for these businesses, we have very few commercial areas left. Most of our commercial and industrial lands have either been annexed to cities or included in new city incorporations. The Fairwood area, along with White Center, Boulevard Park, the commercial area due north of Issaquah, and the commercial area east of North Bend along I-90 are the last areas in King County with nodes of commercial zoning buffered from residentially-zoned land. There are properties in each of these areas that meet the zoning requirements listed above. There is only one parcel of land in the Fairwood area that could potentially meet these zoning regulations. It is the parcel of land occupied by the westernmost building of Fairwood Center, which includes a Baskin-Robbins, Seattle's Best Coffee and Zi' Pani.

Neither this parcel of land nor the properties in the other listed commercial areas are in any way targeted or planned for adult entertainment businesses; they are merely commercially-zoned properties that meet the locational requirements.

All of the commercial areas noted above are in areas likely to be annexed to a city in the future. In general, the cities of King County do not welcome new adult entertainment businesses in neighborhood business areas that could one day be a gateway to their city limits. Each city must also develop their own policies and regulations determining where such businesses can locate. Further, King County and the cities within King County need to work together to plan for land uses in the areas the cities will likely annex.

Ordinance 13546 also specifies that adult entertainment businesses:

• Will not be permitted to locate in areas identified as likely to annex to a city as long as that city agrees in an interlocal agreement to provide opportunities for such businesses.

King County discussed these issues with all of the cities near the commercial areas listed above. At this time, the cities of Issaquah and North Bend have agreed to adopt interlocal agreements with King County. Ordinance 13547 authorizes the King County Executive to sign the interlocal agreements with Issaquah and North Bend, which indicate that the cities will ensure their regulations allow for sites for adult entertainment businesses to serve the city as well as the nearby unincorporated area. The other affected cities may choose to adopt interlocal agreements with King County in the future.

Finally, **Ordinance 13548** establishes operating procedures for adult entertainment businesses and includes requirements that live dancing may only occur on a stage that is at least ten feet away from patrons. It also sets lighting standards, requires that licensed managers be on site at all times, and sets booth configurations in adult arcades to minimize criminal activity.

A copy of this ordinance, which was approved by the elected officials in the cities of North Bend and Issaquah, is highlighted below. This is one of the few interlocal agreements in the country regulating adult entertainment businesses. This law, Ordinance Number 13547, was approved by a unanimous vote of the King County Council at their meeting on June 7, 1999.

This multi-jurisdictional agreement set forth findings upon which to base this agreement, the authority of the King County Executive to execute this agreement on behalf of the county, and a description of the unincorporated land areas where adult entertainment businesses would be permitted to locate.

Findings

Adult entertainment businesses have a relevant market and draw their customers from a wide area. As regionally oriented commercial businesses, adult entertainment businesses in

King County and its cities serve residents across jurisdictional boundaries. It is appropriate to establish requirements for the location of adult entertainment businesses through a cooperative, regional approach.

A significant portion of King County's commercial land base is within areas identified as likely to annex to nearby cities. The countrywide planning policies call for joint planning of the types of development to be allowed in potential annexation areas; therefore affected cities should play a significant role in determining the location of adult entertainment businesses in the areas of unincorporated King County that are likely to annex to these cities.

The cities of Issaquah and North Bend have adopted policies and regulations that regulate adult entertainment businesses to limit adverse secondary effects on sensitive uses while providing sufficient opportunity for adult entertainment businesses to locate and operate within their respective city limits. The cities of Issaquah and North Bend have reviewed their policies and regulations to ensure that the sufficient opportunities for adult entertainment businesses within their city limits permitted by these policies and regulations will also provide sufficient opportunities for such businesses to serve the market of the areas likely to annex to each city.

Authorization

The county executive is hereby authorized to execute an interlocal agreement, substantially in the forms attached, with the cities of Issaquah and North Bend to honor the cities' policies regarding the location of new adult entertainment businesses. Each interlocal agreement shall state that King County will not permit new adult entertainment businesses in the areas identified as likely to annex to the respective city as long as the city maintains regulations that provide sufficient opportunities for adult entertainment businesses to operate within their city limits to serve the market for the city and the areas likely to annex to the city.

Zones Where Permitted

All properties zoned RB (Regional Business), CB (Community Business) and O (Office) within the areas likely to annex to the cities of Issaquah and North Bend as identified on the maps attached to the interlocal agreements shall be flagged on the Department of Development and Environmental Services' property tracking systems to ensure permit applications for new adult entertainment businesses will not be processed for these properties as long as the interlocal agreements remain in effect. A copy of each of the interlocal agreements and their attached maps shall be maintained on file at the Department of Development and Environmental Services.

CHAPTER 30

Oakley, a New City, Approves Its First Adult Business Regulations

Alison A. Barratt-Green *and* Rebecca Willis

On January 22, 2008, the City Council adopted an interim urgency ordinance temporarily prohibiting the establishment and operation of adult businesses within the City. The purpose of this moratorium was to provide the City with a reasonable period of time in which to complete studies and adopt appropriate regulations regarding the location, licensing and operation of adult businesses. On February 26, 2008, after a public hearing, the City Council extended the interim ordinance for an additional 10 months and 15 days, as allowed by Government Code. The extended moratorium on adult businesses expires on January 10, 2009.

Since the adoption of these ordinances, staff has continued to study adult businesses and prepared the attached draft ordinance to regulate such businesses in Oakley. The proposed ordinance includes licensing and operational regulations for adult businesses. The ordinance also adds a new section to the City's Zoning Code limiting adult businesses to the City's Light Industrial zone and requiring that minimum distances be maintained between adult businesses and certain sensitive uses, and between the two adult businesses. Because the proposed ordinance includes an amendment to the City's Zoning Code, the proposed ordinance was presented to the Planning Commission on November 3, 2008, and the Planning Commission commented on the ordinance and recommended that the City Council approve it. Staff recommends that the City Council adopt the ordinance.

Background and Analysis

Several months ago, staff identified that the City does not have current regulations related to adult businesses, and that the lack of appropriate and lawful adult business regulations could allow an adult business to become established in Oakley in a manner that would be detrimental to the community. In addition, staff and the City Council recognized that an "after-the-fact" attempt to regulate such businesses could preclude the City from exercising the local control and protection of sensitive land uses that the City desires.

Originally published as "Introduction of an Ordinance Establishing Licensing, Operational Standards, and Zoning Requirements for Adult Businesses," *Joint Memorandum from the City Attorney & Community Development Director*, November 19, 2008, by the City of Oakley, CA.

When the City Council adopted the moratorium, it also directed staff to study this issue in order to develop a permanent regulatory zoning scheme applicable to adult businesses. Staff collected information and studies from other jurisdictions which outline the many negative secondary effects of adult businesses and the regulatory strategies that have been utilized to address these effects. Staff has studied the General Plan land use plan and considered potential options for locating adult businesses within the City, including appropriate zoning and distance requirements, to ensure that these businesses do not locate close to one another or to sensitive uses such as schools, churches and residential uses. On September 15, 2008, staff also held a workshop with the Planning Commission to discuss adult business regulations. Through this process, staff developed the recommended ordinance.

General Legal Background

The subject of these regulations are businesses that provide legal, adult-oriented entertainment which is not obscene. It is important to note that lawful adult businesses involve protected First Amendment activities and therefore enjoy certain constitutional protections. Under current case law, these adult businesses must be allowed to exist and operate within a community regardless of one's feelings about them. However, the City may impose reasonable time, place and manner restrictions on adult businesses for the purpose of addressing the various adverse secondary effects. These adverse secondary side effects are discussed more fully below.

It is also important to note that the proposed ordinance is not intended to prohibit or otherwise regulate child pornography or obscenity. Such material is not now nor has it ever been granted constitutional protection. Furthermore, local regulation of this material has been preempted by state and federal law.

Legal and Factual Basis for Zoning Regulations

There are a number of California and United States Supreme Court cases which have held that cities may adopt land use regulations applicable to adult businesses, such as limiting adult businesses to specified areas of the community and requiring them to be a specified distance from certain uses such as schools, churches, and playgrounds, so long as these restrictions are not aimed at suppressing the content of protected free speech. *See, e.g., Young v. American Mini Theaters, Inc.,* 427 U.S. 50 (1976); *Renton v. Playtime Theaters, Inc.,* 475 U.S. 41 (1986); *City of National City v. Wiener,* 3 Cal 4th 832 (1992). The concept behind any regulatory zoning approach is that the regulations are designed to address the adverse secondary side effects that adult businesses create. The adverse secondary side effects include urban blight, increased crime, and decreased property values. They also contribute to the deterioration of the neighborhoods in which they are located.

It is not necessary for a city to conduct its own studies to demonstrate the presence of negative secondary effects associated with adult businesses. Cities may rely on the experiences and studies of other cities in making these conclusions. In formulating the proposed ordinance, City staff obtained copies and/or summaries of adult business studies conducted in at least 46 cities. Copies of studies conducted by the City of Kansas City, Missouri (1998) and the City of Garden Grove, California (1991), were provided to the City Council in connection with adoption of the moratoriums. Copies of studies conducted by the City of Los Angeles (2007), Centralia (2004), the City of Fort Worth, Texas (2004), Toledo, Ohio (2002), and Bellevue, Washington (1998) and summaries of numerous other studies were provided with this report. Copies and/or summaries of all studies referenced in this report or in the Ordinance are on file with the City Attorney's office and are available for review upon request.

These studies and others reflect the well-documented experiences of other cities with the adverse secondary side effects created by the establishment and proliferation of adult businesses within a community. They also demonstrate that adult businesses in general create the negative secondary effects identified above and that without appropriate zoning and regulations, an adult business could locate in the City of Oakley in a manner that is inconsistent with the City's goals for our community. Finally, they provide meaningful guidance and examples of successful approaches that some cities have taken to address such effects.

Establishing Available Sites

While courts have held that locational restrictions are a permissible form of regulation, they have also determined that restrictive zoning regulations must allow for "reasonable alternative channels of communication." As a practical matter, this means that adult business regulations cannot be so restrictive that they result in a "de facto" prohibition because separation requirements or other restrictions overly limit the number of sites where adult businesses may locate.

The courts have not provided a set formula which offers cities guidance as to how many locations must be available for adult businesses. Instead, cases focus on the reasonable availability of sites for adult businesses and whether the regulatory scheme provides a genuine opportunity for adult businesses to establish and operate in the City. This does not mean that the City must secure sites or ensure that land owners will rent to the owners or operators of adult businesses. However, our locational requirements cannot rule out all reasonable locations where adult businesses might exist and compete in the marketplace. For property in industrial zones to be considered potentially available, such sites must be reasonably accessible to the general public, they must have reasonable access to infrastruc-

ture and must be reasonable for some commercial enterprise.

Given the adverse secondary effects which have been shown to result from adult businesses, staff recommends that adult businesses in Oakley be restricted to the City's Light Industrial (LI) Zone. Residential zones are completely inappropriate for adult businesses because of the overwhelming presence of sensitive residential uses in those zones, including homes, parks, and schools. Since residential zones in Oakley tend to be located in close proximity to commercial areas in the City, staff determined that it would not be desirable to allow adult businesses to locate in commercial zones.

Traditionally, zoning schemes require that adult entertainment businesses be prohibited from locating in close proximity to certain sensitive uses. The traditional approach also includes distance requirements between adult businesses in order to prevent adverse secondary effects related to the over-concentration of adult businesses in a small area. The recommended ordinance follows this traditional approach and requires adult businesses to locate no closer than:

1. 1,000 feet from the property line of a school, park, church, or residential zones,
2. 500 feet from front door to front door of another adult business, and
3. 250 feet from the building wall to a legal non-conforming residence located in a non-residential zone.

There are three different areas within the City's General Plan that are designated as Light Industrial areas. The first is the northwest quadrant, which is the area bordered by the BNSF Railroad to the south, Bridgehead Road to the west, the Delta to the north, and Big Break Road to the east. This area includes the Dupont site. The City is currently preparing a specific plan for the Dupont site and anticipates that this area will be rezoned for business park, light industrial, and open space. The Dupont site is not yet ready for development as it does not have appropriate entitlements or adequate infrastructure to serve a reasonable commercial enterprise. It is premature to count this area as part of the current site analysis, although it could produce available sites in the future. The second area is located on Highway 4, east of District Way, and is the current location of the Ironhouse Sanitary District administrative offices and the sanitation facility. This location is in close proximity to residentially zoned properties and is unlikely to produce any available sites because of the minimum distance requirements in the proposed Ordinance (see below).

The third area is bordered by Highway 41/Highway 160 to the west, Main Street/Highway 4 to the north and the west, and Oakley Road to the south. This area is in proximity to residentially zoned land, existing legal non-conforming residences, and established commercial and industrial uses. This area has been the focus of the Adult Business Site Analysis as it contains sixty-nine parcels, provides appropriate buffers between sensitive uses and adult businesses, and results in viable alternatives for adult businesses that meet state and federal legal requirements. In preparing the site analysis, staff recognized that there are some existing homes within this Light Industrial area. It is anticipated that over time these existing homes will be converted to light industrial uses consistent with the current General Plan. In the interim, the proposed ordinance provides for a 250-foot buffer for these homes in order to give the existing residents some protection until such time as their nonconforming uses cease.

The Adult Business Site Analysis demonstrates that the application of the proposed Ordinance satisfies the legal requirements set forth above and will not effectively prohibit or preclude an adult business from locating within the city. Staff analyzed a combination of distance requirements to confirm that the recommended requirements would result in a reasonable number of alternative sites for adult businesses. The analysis took into account

three factors: (1) the total number of development parcels and potential sites within the designated zone; (2) the number of potential available sites that could be identified given the minimum distance requirements in the Ordinance; and (3) the potential concentration of adult businesses. The site analysis evaluates the location of the existing sensitive uses in relationship to the potential sites, and balances the City's desire to maximize the buffer area between potential adult businesses and sensitive land uses against the minimum legal requirements for maintaining available sites. Applying the legal criteria set forth above and the recommended distance requirements in the proposed Ordinance, staff has identified at least six potential sites that could accommodate up to a maximum of three adult businesses. Since the City does not currently have any adult businesses, staff believes that these potential sites will satisfy minimum legal requirements for a city the size of Oakley and will be legally defensible.

Licensing and Operational Regulations

As demonstrated by the studies from other cities, locational criteria alone do not adequately protect communities from the adverse secondary effects of adult businesses. In addition to zoning regulations, cities across the country have employed other regulatory measures to cope with the adverse secondary effects associated with adult businesses. For the same reason that local governments can enact zoning regulations that are applicable only to adult businesses, licensing and operational requirements applicable to adult uses are also valid.

As with zoning regulations, licensing and operational regulations applicable to adult businesses will not be valid if the only apparent reason for them is to suppress "adult" speech. The City must have legitimate public policy reasons to justify these regulations, particularly when they are only imposed on adult businesses. There are a number of legitimate reasons to enact these kinds of regulations. Fist they facilitate the enforcement of locational and distance requirements under the zoning ordinance. Second, they ensure that adult businesses do not violate criminal laws, such as those that prohibit prostitution, obscenity, drug sales, the employment of minors as nude dancers, or building code requirements. Finally, they mitigate the adverse secondary side effects that the United States Supreme Court has acknowledged these businesses create.

Nevertheless, care must be taken when drafting these kinds of regulations. Permit or licensing requirements for free speech activities can be viewed as a "prior restraint" on speech, which is generally prohibited. To avoid this legal issue, the City's ordinance must provide that the City make the decision on whether or not to issue the license within a specified reasonable time period during which the status quo is maintained. In addition, the applicant must have an opportunity for prompt judicial review in the event that the license is erroneously denied. The recommended ordinance satisfies these requirements.

1. Permit Requirement

The Ordinance establishes a permit requirement for the owners and operators of adult businesses and adult business performers. Applications for a permit can be denied under various circumstances. For instance, an application for an adult business regulatory permit can be denied if the proposed business does not satisfy the locational requirements for the ordinance. Applications for performer permits can be denied if the applicant has been convicted of prostitution-related offenses. A permit issued to the operator of an adult business can be revoked if the operator allows unlawful sexual activity to occur on the premises or if the operator allows any activity to occur on the premises that violates the Ordinance. Similarly, a permit issued to an adult entertainment business performer can be revoked if the performer engages in unlawful

sexual activity on the premises of an adult business or engages in any activity which violates the Ordinance. The studies on the adverse secondary effects associated with adult businesses show that these businesses are frequently used for sexual activities including but not limited to prostitution, and that AIDS and other sexually transmitted diseases are the frequent result of such casual sexual liaisons. Therefore, there are strong public policy reasons to ensure that such activity is not allowed to occur. Many of the regulatory provisions of the Ordinance are intended to address this problem.

2. Business Development and Performance Standards

The proposed Ordinance also includes comprehensive design and performance standards. Once again, the purpose of these regulations is to mitigate the adverse secondary effects that are created by adult businesses. The Ordinance includes provisions which prohibit the display of adult oriented material where it is visible outside the building in which the adult business is located; require illumination of off-street parking and sound absorbing insulation; prohibit the admission of persons under the age of 18 years; require separate restroom facilities for male patrons and employees and female patrons and employees; and require that all interior areas be open to view by the management at all times.

Adult businesses which feature live entertainment pose special problems. Unless appropriately regulated, these businesses can provide an environment which facilitates prostitution and drug dealing. The more potential there is for contact between a live performer and the patron, the greater the potential for these crimes. The proposed Ordinance contains several provisions to address this concern including requirements that the performer be on a stage at least 24 inches high and separated by at least 10 feet from any patron; separate dressing room facilities be maintained for entertainers; performers have separate exits and entrances from the patrons; physical contact between patrons and entertainers is prohibited; and direct tipping is prohibited. In a further attempt to mitigate the adverse secondary effects associated with live entertainment in adult businesses, especially prostitution, the ordinance prohibits complete nudity in adult businesses. All of these types of regulations have been upheld by the courts.

Planning Commission Recommendation

On November 3, the Planning Commission reviewed the proposed Ordinance. The majority of the Commission recommended that the City Council adopt the ordinance as originally presented, subject to minor staff corrections presented at the hearing and the following additional modifications.

1. That an application for an adult business regulatory license be signed by the owner of the business or his/her authorized representative.

    The ordinance contemplates that the legal owner of an adult business is the person responsible for applying for and holding the license for that business. To clarify this, the proposed ordinance has been amended to require a signed and verified statement that the license applicant is the legal owner of the business.

2. That an adult business owner can be prohibited from providing board or shelter for any employee or independent contractor who works for the business.

    As stated in the various studies that staff has cited, adult businesses often facilitate prostitution and other criminal activities. At the Planning Commission hearing, Commissioner Huerta noted the increasing concern among many law enforcement agencies regarding the rise in criminal "sex slave" operations and prostitution rings involving minors and/or illegal immigrants that may be disguised as otherwise legal

forms of businesses such as adult businesses. In most cases, the operators of these illicit prostitution rings will provide board and shelter to the individuals who "work" for them. This practice enhances the operator's ability to exert dominance and control over his/her victims which leads to an atmosphere of dependence and enslavement of the individuals involved. This is yet another potential adverse secondary effect which an adult business can create.

To mitigate this potential impact, the Commission recommended that an adult business owner be prohibited from providing board and shelter to any employee or independent contractor of the business. The Ordinance has been amended to specifically prohibit owners and operators from providing such board and shelter either directly or indirectly (e.g., by using an intermediary or by simply agreeing to pay for an individual's room or board) and to require that all license applicants provide a signed and verified statement acknowledging that they will not provide board or shelter to such individuals.

3. That hearings regarding the proposed revocation or suspension of an adult business license be heard by a third party hearing officer rather than the City Manager.

    The proposed ordinance has been amended to provide that license revocation or suspension hearings will be heard by a third party hearing officer rather than the City Manager (see Section 5.9.114). Staff agrees that using an independent hearing officer to conduct such revocation or suspension hearings would provide additional due process protection to the licensee. For similar reasons, the Council has already chosen to use independent hearing officers for the processing of appeals related to the issuance of administrative citations; therefore, the same hearing officers could be utilized for this purpose as well. There will be some additional cost associated with using a third party hearing officer; however, it is anticipated that this process will rarely, if ever, be necessary so the overall cost to the program should be small.

A copy of the Planning Commission's resolution was attached to the report given to the City Council. In addition, those changes made to the Ordinance by the Commission were highlighted for the benefit of the City's elected officials and citizens who attended the public meeting.

In addition to the above action, the Commission raised concerns that 1) the studies being relied upon by the City were not "current" and 2) the proposed ordinance is inconsistent with the City's existing zoning to the extent that it could allow adult hotels and motels in the Light Industrial area. Staff has also reviewed these concerns and provides the following responses:

1. With regard to the studies, the staff report provided to the Commission included a 2004 study from Fort Worth, Texas, and the original draft ordinance relies on studies as recent as 2006. These studies represent some of the most current and relevant information available. It is true that many of the other studies identified in the documents were done a number of years ago, although this is simply a reflection of the time period over which cities have been grappling with the regulation of adult businesses. Despite the age of these studies, however, they continue to provide concrete and reliable information and guidance on which the City may reasonably rely for its conclusions. Although staff believes the information and studies previously provided are a sufficient basis for the findings and regulations contained in the Ordinance, staff has included a few additional studies, dated between 2004 and 2007, as part of this report. These studies further strengthen the City's record regarding the adverse secondary effects that adult businesses can create and demonstrate that in the over 20 years that cities have been studying such effects, the potential impacts of such businesses have not changed.

2. With respect to the zoning issue, staff has confirmed that hotels and motels are permitted uses in the Light Industrial zone. Therefore, adoption of this ordinance would not change the list of uses that are already permitted in the Light Industrial zone or introduce a new type of use (i.e., hotels and motels) to the Light Industrial (LI) zone. It would simply provide appropriate regulations for an adult hotel or motel and mitigate potential impacts of such a business should one choose to establish itself in this zone.

Conclusion

Staff recommends that the City Council waive the first reading and introduce the Ordinance Amending the Oakley Municipal Code to Establish Licensing and Operational Standards for Adult Businesses and to Establish Zoning Requirements for Adult Businesses.

Editor's Notes:

1. The City of Oakley is one of the newest cities in California, being incorporated on July 1, 1999 — merely a decade ago.

2. The interim ordinance on adult businesses was continued by the City Council on December 9, 2008, pending consideration of the final ordinance, which was approved by the City Council on February 24, 2009.

3. The various reports provided to the City's elected officials, and made available to the public, may be reviewed and/or obtained via the City of Oakley's website, which is listed in the Appendix of this volume under the section titled *Regional Resource Directory*.

CHAPTER 31

Orlando Changes Its Adult Business Code to Set Distances from Other Land Uses

Jason Burton *and* Kyle Shephard

The City's Land Development Code (the "LDC") currently prohibits adult entertainment facilities in all zoning districts except for the General Industrial District ("I-G") where such uses may be allowed by Conditional Use Permit.

The LDC defines "Adult Entertainment Facility" as "[a]ny adult bookstore, adult dancing establishment or adult motion picture theater as defined in Chapter 31A, 37, and 43 of the City Code; or any commercial physical contact establishment as defined by this Chapter; of any body art shop where procedures conducted on specified anatomical areas as defined by Section 3701(f) of the City Code are viewed by persons other than the artist and one other person with the consent of the client."

Additionally, section 58.702, Orlando City Code, establishes minimum separation standards between proposed adult entertainment facilities and certain other specified existing uses. New or substantially enlarged adult entertainment facilities are prohibited within 1,000 feet of (1) another adult entertainment facility, (2) a church or other religious institution, (3) public parks, libraries, elementary, junior high, and high schools, (4) residential zoning districts (including planned development districts with residential uses), and (5) any establishment serving alcoholic beverages for onsite consumption.

Proposed Code Amendment

The City Attorney's Office and the City Planning Division recommends two immediate amendments to the City's Land Development Code related to adult entertainment facilities.

The first proposed amendment is to amend Figure 2B.LDC ("Table of allowable uses in zoning districts inside the traditional city.") and Figure 2D.LDC ("Table of allowable uses in zoning districts outside the traditional city.") in Chapter 58, Orlando City Code, to permit adult entertainment facilities within the I-G district and the Industrial Park District ("I-P"), subject to the minimum separation requirements of section 58,702, Orlando City Code, and other applicable provisions of law.

Originally published as "Proposed LDC Text Amendment for Adult Entertainment Facilities," *Joint Report from the Assistant City Attorney and Chief Planner*, April 21, 2009, by the Municipal Planning Board, City of Orlando, FL.

The second proposed amendment is to amend section 58.702, Orlando City Code, to extend the current minimum separation between existing elementary, junior high, and high schools, and newly proposed adult entertainment facilities or proposed substantial enlargements of existing adult entertainments, from the existing 1,000 feet minimum separation to 2,500 feet minimum separation.

Legal Analysis Overview

The First Amendment to the United States Constitution (the "First Amendment") states that "Congress shall make no law respecting an establishment of religion, or prohibiting the free exercise thereof; or abridging the freedom of speech, or of the press; or the right of the people peaceably to assemble, and to petition the Government for a redress of grievances."

The First Amendment applies to the states and local governments by virtue of the Fourteenth Amendment to the United States Constitution.

In general terms, the First Amendment constrains government suppression of expression based on the government's disagreement with the content, ideas, or subject matter of the expression. This general rule is not absolute, and certain forms of expression receive less protection from the First Amendment than others.

As a general rule, the time, place, and manner of non-obscene erotic expression may be regulated by local governments. A local government may not, however, completely zone adult entertainment uses out of their jurisdiction. Current case law interprets the First and Fourteenth Amendments to require that local government land use and zoning regulations permit adequate avenues for non-obscene commercial erotic expression.

Current Conditions

The LDC currently prohibits adult entertainment facilities in all zoning districts except for the I-G district where such uses may be allowed by Conditional Use Permit.

This staff report depicts locations within the City where adult entertainment facilities may currently be allowed for conditional use permit. This includes the current 1,000 feet minimum separation buffer around each (1) existing adult entertainment facility, (2) church or other religious institution, (3) public park, library, elementary, junior high, and high school, (4) residential zoning district (including planned development districts with residential uses), and (5) establishment serving alcoholic beverages for onsite consumption.

This is for general illustrative purposes only and is based on currently available GIS data that may or may not accurately reflect actual or grandfathered uses. Site specific analysis may result in the discovery of actual or grandfathered uses within the minimum separation buffers.

Currently there is only one adult entertainment facility within the jurisdictional limits of the City of Orlando. This facility, the "Fairvilla Mega Store," located at 1740 N. Orange Blossom Trail, is considered an "adult bookstore" under the definitions contained in the LDC and other parts of the Orlando City Code. A number of adult entertainment facilities, particularly adult dancing establishments, are just outside the City's jurisdiction in unincorporated Orange County, including, for example, (1) "Rachel's South," located at 8701 S. Orlando Ave., (2) "Dancers Royale," located at 5221 E. Colonial Dr., and (3) several adult bookstores and dancing establishments along S. Orange Blossom Trail.

Proposed Conditions

Based upon current case law interpreting the First and Fourteenth Amendments, the proposed text amendment would permit adult entertainment facilities within the I-G and I-P districts. The proposed amendment would also extend the current minimum separation between schools and adult entertainment facilities from 1,000 feet to 2,500 feet.

This staff report depicts locations with the City where adult entertainment facilities would be allowed by right. This includes the current 1,000 feet minimum separation buffer around each (1) existing adult entertainment facility, (2) church or other religious institution, (3) public park and library, (4) residential zoning district (including planned development districts with residential uses), and (5) establishment serving alcoholic beverages for onsite consumption, and 2,500 feet minimum separation buffer around each existing elementary, junior high, and high school.

This is for general illustrative purposes only and is based on currently available GIS data that may or may not accurately reflect actual or grandfathered uses. Site specific analysis may result in the discovery of actual or grandfathered uses within the minimum separation buffers.

Negative Secondary Effects

In general terms, First and Fourteenth Amendment jurisprudence requires that local government regulation of non-obscene adult entertainment facilities be predicated entirely on a sincere and demonstrable effort to combat the negative secondary effects associated with adult entertainment facilities that the City desires to mitigate or avoid by the reasonable land use and zoning regulation of such uses.

Crime

The activities within adult uses provide an opportunity for crime, such as the arrangement of sex acts (prostitution) either within or outside the establishment. This crime po-

tential also includes the attraction of "soft targets"— a person that could be impaired by a reaction to certain stimuli, either due to the reaction to the erotic environment, or decreased awareness for personal safety.

For example, persons can become soft targets for potential thefts or assaults when the focus of the establishment is on excitement, causing a decreased awareness for personal safety. Further, victims of crimes at such establishments may be more reluctant to report crime incidents than a victim at a conventional establishment, such as a shopping mall.

Property Values

Surveys of real estate professionals indicate that adult uses have a measurable negative effect on the value of nearby properties, which exceed even the implications on property values for adjacent pawn shops, bars or salvage yards.

Additionally, the location of an adult use also provides the opportunity for illegal or suspicious activity outside the business and elsewhere in nearby areas. Selling and renting of properties may potentially be more difficult due to the location of a nearby adult use.

Overview of Selected Negative Secondary Effects Studies

Due to the limited amount of adult entertainment establishments within City of Orlando limits — limited to one adult bookstore — the City's analysis of secondary effects relies on analysis conducted in several other jurisdictions and government agencies that are relevant to the City of Orlando, including Orange County. Summaries of these reports, studies and analysis include:

Land Use Study, Austin, Texas, May 19, 1986

Overview: The report was the basis for developing an amendment to existing sexually oriented business ordinances. At the time, 49 such businesses operated in Austin, mostly adult bookstore, theaters, massage parlors and topless bars. The study examined crime rates, property values and trade area characteristics.

The report focused on sexually related crimes in four study areas (with sexually oriented businesses) and four control areas (close to study areas and similar). Two study areas had only sexually oriented business and the others had two such businesses. To determine the effects of those businesses on property values, the city sent surveys to 120 real estate appraising or lending firms (nearly half responded). For trade area characteristics, three businesses (a bookstore, theater and topless bar) were observed on a weekend night to determine customer addresses.

Crime: Sexually related crime ranged from 177 to 482 percent higher in the four study areas than city average. In the two study areas containing two sexually oriented businesses, the rate was 66 percent higher than in the study areas with one such business. All control areas had crime rates near the city average.

Real Estate: 88 percent of survey respondents said that a sexually oriented business within one block of a residential area decreases the value of the homes, with over a third saying that the depreciation would be at least 20 percent. Respondents also said that such a business is a sign of a neighborhood in decline, making underwriters hesitant to approve the 90–95 percent financing that most home buyers require. They said commercial property is also negatively affected by such businesses.

Trade Area Characteristics: Of 81 license plates for owner address, only three lived within one mile of the sexually oriented business; 44 percent were from outside the city.

"A Summary of a National Survey of Real Estate Appraisers Regarding the Effect of Adult Bookstore on Property Values," conducted by the Division of Planning, Department of Metropolitan Development, Indianapolis, January 1984.

Overview: After a ten year growth in the number of sexually oriented businesses (to a total of 68 on 43 sites) and numerous citizen complaints of decreasing property values and rising crime, the city compared six sexually oriented business "study" areas and six "control" locations with each other and with the city as a whole. The study and control areas had high population, low income and older residences. In order to develop a best professional opinion, the city collaborated with Indiana University on a national survey of real estate appraisers to determine valuation effects of sexually oriented businesses on adjacent properties.

Crime: From 1978 to 1982, crime increases in the study areas were 23 percent higher than the control areas (46 percent higher than the city as a whole). Sex crimes in the study areas increased more than 20 percent over the control areas. Residential locations in the study areas had a 56 percent greater crime increase than commercial study areas. Sex related crimes were four times more common in residential study areas than commercial study areas with sexually oriented businesses.

Real Estate: Homes in the study areas appreciated at only half the rate of homes in control areas, and one-third the rate of the city. "Pressures within the study areas" caused a slight increase in real estate listings, while the city as a whole had a 50 percent decrease, denoting high occupancy turnover. Appraisers responding to the survey said one sexually oriented business within one block of residences and businesses decreased their value and half of the respondents said the immediate depreciation exceeded 10 percent. Appraisers also noted that value depreciation on residential areas near sexually oriented businesses is greater than commercial locations.

The report concludes, "the best professional judgment available indicates overwhelmingly that adult entertainment businesses — even a relatively passive use as an adult bookstore — have a serious negative effect on their immediate environs.

Los Angeles Municipal Code, Section 12.70, Ord. 156509, 1982.

Overview: The Department of City Planning studied the effects of the concentration of sexually oriented businesses on surrounding properties for the years 1969–75 (a time of proliferation of such businesses). The report focuses on five areas with the greatest concentration of these businesses — compared to five "control" areas — and cites data from property assessments/sales, public meeting testimony, and responses from two questionnaires (one to business/residential owners within a 500-foot radius of the five study areas and a second to realtors/real estate appraisers and lenders). Crime statistics in the study areas were compared to the city as a whole. Also included: a chart of sexually oriented business regulations in eleven major cities, details of current regulations available under state/municipal law, and appendices with samples of questionnaires, letters, and other study materials.

Property: While empirical data from 1969 to 1975 did not conclusively show the relation of property values to the concentration of sexually oriented businesses, more than 90 percent of realtors, real estate appraisers and lenders responding to the city questionnaires said that a grouping of such businesses within 500–1,000 feet of residential property decreases the market value of the homes. Also, testimony from residents and business people at two public meetings spoke overwhelmingly against the presence of sexually oriented businesses citing fear, concern for children, loss of customers and difficulty in hiring employees at non-adult businesses, and the necessity for churches to provide guards for their parking lots.

Crime: More crime occurred in areas of sexually oriented business concentration. Compared to city-wide statistics for 1969 to 1975, areas with several such businesses experienced greater increases in pandering (340 percent), murder (42.3 percent), aggravated assault (45.2 percent), robbery (52.6 percent), and purse snatching (17 percent). Street robberies, where the criminal has face-to-face contact with his victim, increased almost 70 percent more in the study areas. A second category of crime, included other assaults, forgery, fraud, counterfeiting, embezzlement, stolen property, prostitution, narcotics, liquor laws, and gambling increased 42 percent more in the study areas over the city as a whole.

Survey, Findings and Recommendations of Sexually Oriented Businesses, Toledo, OH, August 26, 2002.

Overview: The City of Toledo ("Toledo") determined it needed to address adult entertainment uses as a result of litigation over its zoning ordinance. Additionally, the City was experiencing an increased number of taverns that were featuring adult entertainment in violations of the City's zoning ordinance. At the time of the study, the City was only regulating adult entertainment through zoning, it did not have a licensing mechanism. The City defined "adult entertainment" as massage parlors, operated by anyone not licensed as a medical doctor, chiropractor, osteopath, nurse, physical therapist, or a person practicing massage of the face and hands in a beauty parlor or barber shop licensed by the City; adult bookstores, adult motion picture theaters, adult mini–motion picture theaters or adult entertainment cabarets. When the study was conducted the City had six adult cabarets, one adult theater that rented videos, eight adult bookstores, two retail shops, four massage parlors, a bathhouse and a lingerie modeling establishment.

Crime: The consultants reviewed police calls to adult entertainment establishments and provided an analysis of crime. Five adult businesses were clustered in one area of the City and accounted for 39 percent of the crime for that area, but only accounted for 20 percent of the total businesses in the area. Additionally, the consultants noted significant differences in the number of police calls to different types of adult businesses. While adult cabarets comprised only 20 percent of the businesses included in the crime study, they were involved in 44 percent of the total police calls. The consultants concluded that adult entertainment establishments which feature live entertainment are likely to have the greatest adverse impact with respect to the number of incidents which require a police response.

Property Values: To address concerns of the effect of adult businesses on property values, the consultants relied on studies conducted in other cities. A study from Rochester, NY, showed that: bars with nude servers and live entertainment have a negative impact on property values; sexually oriented businesses have measurable negative impact on property values; there is more of a negative impact on residential property than on commercial uses; the greatest impact on property values is those residences located on the same block as the adult use; the negative impact decreases with distance, and stops somewhere between 1,000 and 1,500 feet. Also cited the previous Indianapolis study.

Garden Grove, CA, Land Use Study, October 1991.

Overview: The report by independent consultants summarizes statistical analyses to determine a basis for adult business regulations because of their negative impact on the community in terms of crime, decreased property values and diminished quality of life. Statistics were measured from 1981 to 1990 and included crime data, and surveys of real estate professionals and city residents. Garden Grove Boulevard, with seven adult businesses, was selected as the study area. The study incorporated many control factors to insure accurate results. The report includes a brief legal history of adult business regulation and an extensive appendix with samples, materials and a proposed statute.

Crime: Crime increases significantly with the opening of an adult business or with the expansion of an existing business or the addi-

tion of a bar nearby. The rise was greatest in "serious" offenses (homicides, rape, robbery, assault, burglary, theft and auto theft). On Garden Grove Blvd., the seven adult businesses accounted for 36 percent of all crime in the area. In one case, a bar opened less than 500 feet from an adult business, and serious crime within 1,000 feet of that business rose more than 300 percent in the course of one year.

Real Estate: Overwhelmingly, respondents said that adult businesses within 200–500 feet of residential and commercial property depreciate the property value. The greatest impact was on single family homes. The chief factor cited for the depreciation was the increased crime associated with adult businesses.

Household Surveys: 118 calls were completed in a random sample of households in the Garden Grove Blvd. vicinity. The public consensus was that adult businesses on Garden Grove Blvd. were a serious problem. Nearly 25 percent of the surveyed individuals lived within 1,000 feet of an adult business. More than 21 percent cited specific personal experiences or problems relating to these businesses, including crime, noise, litter, and general quality of life. 80 percent said they would want to move if an adult business opened in their neighborhood, 60 percent said they "would move" or "probably would move," 85 percent supported city regulation of the locations of adult businesses, and 78 percent strongly advocated the prohibition of adult businesses within 500 feet of a residential area, school or church. Women commonly expressed fear for themselves and their children because of the presence of adult businesses.

The United States Attorney General's Commission on Pornography (1986) — the "Meese Report."

Overview: A citizen's right to free speech is guaranteed under the First Amendment to the United States Constitution; this right can compete with the rights of others. To avoid these pitfalls, citizens are encouraged to be vigorous, well-informed, but responsible advocates and to exercise self-restraint so that in exercising their rights they do not prevent other citizens from exercising theirs — especially when dealing with issues relating to the adult entertainment industry.

Citizens concerned about pornography in their community should initially determine the nature and availability of pornographic materials in their community, existing prosecution policies, law enforcement practices and judicial attitudes in the community. They should inquire whether these enforcement mechanisms are adequately utilized. They should determine whether the official perception of the current community standards is truly a reflection of public opinion, if enforcement mechanisms appear inadequate or ineffective, if legislative change is necessary to enhance the effectiveness of the criminal justice system, or if the volume of pornography or offensive material is a particular problem in the community, citizens should consider developing a community action program.

Recommended Findings

In light of the constraints placed on government by the First and Fourteenth Amendments to the United States Constitution, the City Attorney and the City Planning Division recommend that the Municipal Planning Board make the following findings in relation to the proposed text amendments described in this report:

1. The proposed text amendments are consistent with all applicable policies of the City's adopted Growth Management Plan.

2. The proposed text amendments do not conflict with the public interest and are in harmony with the purpose and intent of the City's Land Development Code.
3. The proposed text amendments will not result in any incompatible land uses.
4. The proposed text amendments will result in orderly and logical development patterns and will minimize negative effects on such patterns.

Action Taken by Planning Board

This item was actually listed on the Planning Board's minutes as a "request to amend the Land Development Code to designate adult entertainment uses as permitted uses only in the IG and IP zoning districts and to require 1,000 foot separation distance from all residential zoning district, public parks, libraries, religious institutions, alcohol serving establishments and other adult uses and a 2,500 foot separation distance from all schools and prohibiting such uses in the South Downtown Vision Plan Subarea Policy Area."

This code change was unanimously approved by the members of the Planning Board at their meeting of April 21, 2009. The City's staff was directed to incorporate this change into ordinance form for the City Council's consideration in the future.

Editor's Note:

The various maps and reports provided to the City's Planning Board, and made available to the public, may be reviewed and/or obtained via the City of Orlando's website, which is listed in the Appendix of this volume under the section entitled *Regional Resource Directory*.

CHAPTER 32

Providence Uses Enforcement to Clean Up Its Downtown

Ellen Perlman

The town of Johnston, Rhode Island, concedes it was bamboozled by Mario's, a low-key Italian restaurant, when the owner asked for an entertainment license early last year. The restaurant said it wanted to offer soft dinner music to patrons. The council members thought it was a reasonable request and granted the license.

But Mario's hadn't exactly revealed all. Once it had the license in hand, the unexpected form of entertainment started up: women dancing naked. The windows were blacked out and the name of the restaurant was changed to Mario's Show Place. Johnston, a quiet suburb of 30,000 bordering Providence, had unwittingly permitted its first topless bar.

Three weeks after Mario's went topless, the council, shocked by what had transpired, passed an ordinance prohibiting nudity in places that serve alcohol. But the law is under challenge, and while the decision is pending, the strip shows go on.

Even worse from Johnston's point of view, the Mario's episode gave other people ideas. Early this year, El Marocco's, a banquet facility three-tenths of a mile from town hall

on a commercial strip lined with gas stations and fast food places, decided to open as Marocco's Gentlemen's Show Club. It, too, took the local government to court over the anti–strip club law.

But that still wasn't the end of it for Johnston. The town got four calls from adult entertainment clubs in Providence, a five-minute drive away, asking about locating within town limits. This was at a time when those clubs were feeling the heat at their existing locations. Providence had started cracking down on bars that offered nude dancing. It was monitoring them closely, shutting them down for any violations it could find and putting pressure on those still operating. Startled town leaders in Johnston scrambled to figure out how they could slow or halt what they worried might become a tide of adult entertainment businesses heading their way.

If it's any consolation to Johnston — and it probably isn't — dozens, if not hundreds, of municipalities of all sizes are grappling with what to do about SOBs — sexually oriented businesses. Larger cities that have been home to X-rated businesses for years have been looking for ways to put a clamp on lewd entertain-

Originally published as "Pornosprawl: X-Rated Businesses are Leaving the City for the Suburbs. The Suburbs Aren't Ready," *Governing*, Vol. 10, No. 10, October 1997, by Congressional Quarterly, Inc., Washington, DC. Reprinted with permission of the publisher.

ment and move it to the fringes, if not out of the city completely. Smaller municipalities that have never had the problem are trying to fix it so they never do. But like Johnston, they are finding it a difficult task. They are up against the complexities of Pornosprawl.

The fundamental problem is that cities that try to prohibit strip clubs outright typically find themselves on the losing end of a court challenge. "They open up, residents scream outrage about the things they observe, the things the children see," says Jan LaRue, senior counsel for the National Law Center for Children and Families. "The city scrambles, screams, 'What do we do?' But if they try to deny a permit to keep them from opening, they find in court it doesn't hold up."

The law is quite murky when it comes to what's allowed to go on in these clubs once they open up. The U.S. Supreme Court ruled more than 20 years ago that nude dancing can be a protected form of expression under the First Amendment, the same as, say, nudity during a theater production of *Oh! Calcutta!* But in 1991, the court said localities could require dancers to cover up at least a little. It held that an Indiana indecency law requiring erotic dancers to wear pasties and G-strings was constitutional. Since then, other cities have been passing laws against completely nude dancing. In many cases, courts have upheld ordinances that require the dancers to put on some covering. But writing these ordinances to survive a legal challenge and then trying to enforce them in minute detail is more of a burden than many communities want to take on.

Rather than regulate what goes on in the clubs, many cities attempt to use zoning to control where the clubs locate. Although the courts will not let local governments ban SOBs altogether, they have held that cities can zone and regulate them so as to minimize their "secondary effects" — crime, decreased property values and tax revenues, traffic, noise, litter and the spread of sexually transmitted diseases. But there have been challenges to some

of those laws as well. Civil liberties lawyers have argued that it is impossible for cities to prove negative secondary effects from strip clubs.

For all the legal difficulty, most communities find it is best to have some form of SOB zoning ordinance on the books. When there is no zoning law, strip clubs that want to put down roots have the pick of the place. When one town passes restrictive laws, SOBs seek out others with lenient regulations or, even better, no regulations. "If neighboring smaller cities don't have ordinances, these businesses do pop up in strip malls," says LaRue. "And the problem with strip malls is there's usually a residential area right behind the parking lot."

But whatever legal steps a local government may be able to think up, it has become clear that sexually oriented businesses are heading for suburbia. When a big city such as Providence goes after these businesses, it creates a chain reaction that makes surrounding towns vulnerable. The larger cities are, indeed, cracking down. For decades, peep shows, topless bars and adult book, video and sexual gadget stores have been accepted as inevitable — if not wholeheartedly welcomed — by the multitudes in many urban areas. But tolerance for a seamy side of town is waning as mayors and councils wake up to the fact that adult businesses drag down sections that have the potential to be something better, and more appealing to a wider constituency.

Providence is a perfect example. Two decades ago, when it was a grimy industrial city in decline, few paid much attention to the skin shows scattered about town. But central Providence is making a comeback. Rivers that were buried under asphalt have been brought back to the surface, and railroad tracks have been moved underground. New hotels are being built and an arts district has been set up to entice artists to live and work in the city. In all, there's been $1.5 billion in public and private investment. Nude dance joints just don't fit into the city's vision of its economic picture. Strip clubs "do nothing but tear us down and begin the process of decay," says Mayor Vincent A. Cianci Jr. "I have no room for that. It doesn't enhance our image."

Like the rest of the communities in America, Providence did not have the option of simply declaring that nude dancing was bad for the city and sending notices to the clubs to go away. The Supreme Court precluded that. But Providence did have the constitutional right to scrutinize what was going on inside the clubs, and that is what it began doing. During undercover sting operations, police found plenty to work with. There were clubs offering nude dancing that didn't have adult entertainment licenses. There were clubs with adult entertainment licenses where the dancers were flashing much more than was allowed under the local definition of acceptable nudity, which precludes total exposure of the buttocks. In three cases, officers found evidence of prostitution. Altogether, police have made more than 25 arrests at clubs in Providence during the past year.

By strictly enforcing its laws, Providence was able to shut down Cherry's, Tramps and Cabana Girls without too much difficulty. A little intimidation didn't hurt. Uniformed police officers hung around inside and in front of Cabana Girls, sometimes taking pictures of the customers. The American Civil Liberties Union protested this tactic. Cianci says the clubs dug their own graves. "If they didn't violate the law, we probably would not have cause to go in there," he says. "We have people hitting each other with mallets, oral sex going on in back rooms in some places, chains, whips. This thing was getting out of hand."

While Cianci has been seeking to harass strip clubs out of Providence, nearby Boston has been focusing a bright light on the Combat Zone, a 10-square-block neon sanctuary for porn stores and strip joints created in 1974 to keep all adult business in a single section of town. At one time, about 30 adult entertainment establishments vied for customers in the Combat Zone.

But the area is within walking distance of downtown shopping, parks, historic sites and government buildings, and the city administrations of the 1990s have been eager to see SOBs fade away. In an effort to kill off the Combat Zone for good, Boston decided to invest $8 million in lighting and infrastructure improvements. As in Providence, the campaign has been helped by a healthy economy. Real estate values have shot up. Investors are searching for downtown locations. Building owners who don't renew leases of adult businesses are more likely than in the past to find respectable tenants willing to come in. And Mayor Thomas M. Menino is promoting the whole changeover. The sex business entrepreneurs complain that the city is twisting the arms of building owners not to renew licenses of sexually oriented businesses.

In any case, the Combat Zone is shriveling up. A branch of the state Registry of Motor Vehicles is about to move into the historic Liberty Tree building on Washington Street, next door to the Liberty Book II, which advertises "25 cent peeps, live nude girls, total privacy and XXX videos" on its yellow opaque windows. Nearby, a Malaysian restaurant named Penang stands next to a hard-core adult porno shop, and yet lines for the restaurant snake out the door on weekend nights. "There's no more Combat Zone," boasts Jimmy Toh, manager of Penang. Toh is exaggerating a little. There still is a Combat Zone. But it is coming to consist of a handful of sex establishments and a few ghosts — like the rusted out sign on a brick wall around the corner from Penang's, announcing "Mini–Peep Booths." It hangs above doors that are locked shut. It is only a matter of time before politics of Pornosprawl play out in many places around the country where sexual businesses are gradually being forced beyond the city limits.

In Washington, D.C., a stretch of 14th Street formerly home to strip clubs and triple-X video stores now is lined with boutique shops and gourmet food and cappuccino establishments. New York's Times Square has ceased to be a haven for hard-core pornographic businesses and has become home to a multiplex cinema, a Disney Store, and a Virgin Megastore, the world's largest music emporium. Even Baltimore is seeking to sanitize its infamous Block, where Blaze Starr once performed, suspending adult-entertainment licenses for violations of the law, and sending police undercover to find prostitution among club employees.

Not all of the change is a result of government harassment. Natural market forces of gentrification are responsible for part of it; so is the technology that allows people to view pornography in private. "With technology, people don't have to leave home," say s Kelley Quinn of the Boston Redevelopment Authority. "With the advent of VCRs, 1-900 numbers and the Internet, some of these people are going out of business."

But not ALL of them are going out of business, and the ones that stay in operation have to locate somewhere, even if all they want to do is sell X-rated videos. Increasingly, the new target is a community that never saw it coming, never envisioned being a victim of the dispersal process.

Towns that find themselves unprepared for Pornosprawl essentially have two basic choices in deciding how to deal with it. One is to do as Boston did 20 years ago, concentrating SOBs in one place so few other neighborhoods are affected. But the area selected never likes it. "When they're allowed to cluster, the adverse effects exponentially increase," says LaRue.

The other method is to disperse the businesses around town, keeping them apart from schools, churches and each other. That usually leaves industrial, manufacturing or agricultural areas as target locations. This creates problems of its own.

The town of Johnston thought it had found a solution by planning to zone future adult businesses along a three-acre strip within sniffing distance of the Central Landfill, the trash dump for the entire state of Rhode Island. Johnston figured the area would not be economically feasible or palatable to the proprietors of adult businesses.

But the local council didn't take into account the feelings of the residents whose homes were near the landfill. They had learned to live with one blight. That didn't mean they wanted another one dumped on them. "It was done with good thought, but there's no way I was going to consent," says Mary Cerra, the district's councilwoman. "You don't give me the landfill and then give the people in my district Skid Row as well." The idea was dropped.

Given the headaches of trying to fight SOBs with zoning, some communities have looked for more creative tactics to regulate and clamp down on adult entertainment. Lexington, Kentucky, besides trying to ban nudity, passed a law requiring a license fee of $6,000 for the clubs and $100 for any employee who has contact with patrons. Three of the city's 10 strip clubs have challenged the constitutionality of the law. Other towns have been reduced to regulating how many feet away dancers must stay from the patrons. Those distance limits essentially put a stop to couch, lap and table dancing and to customers leaning toward dancers with dollar bills to tuck into G-strings.

Still others have decreed that no establishment may offer both liquor and nude entertainment. That reduces some of the rowdiness connected with drunken patrons, but it doesn't necessarily shut down clubs or provide an Ozzie-and-Harriet-like neighborhood for nearby residents. Instead, such regulations have spawned a category of strip joints that provide nude dancers and nonalcoholic beverages. "They serve soft drinks and orange juice and charge a cover," says LaRue. "You might be paying $10 for a glass of orange juice."

When Silhouettes Restaurant, a topless club in New Haven, Connecticut, lost its liquor license, it opened up as a juice bar and went totally nude. Since liquor was no longer being served, the age of admission dropped from 21 to 18, and since the club was no longer regulated by liquor laws, it could stay open later than bars. Last year, New Haven passed a zoning ordinance to control where any adult business can locate, but the law has been challenged, and the case is pending.

Governments that lose in court can be forced to live with some unpalatable consequences. That's what happened in Portland, Oregon, after courts in that state all but eliminated local authority to regulate where strip clubs could and couldn't locate.

The city used to have an ordinance keeping adult entertainment a certain number of feet away from schools and residences, and another one banning nude dancing in bars serving liquor. Both were overturned by the state Supreme Court in the late 1980s. The court ruled the ordinances were overly broad and violated the state constitution's protection of free expression.

Portland did not attempt to draft a new version. When the city rewrote its zoning code in 1991 to align it with the court's ruling, it left out all specific references to adult businesses. The current code considers a pornographic video store to be a retail establishment like any other. It treats all bars the same whether they feature nude dancing or not.

In Portland, explains Mike Hayakawa, a senior city planner, "a bar is a bar whether someone is dancing with clothes on or someone is dancing without clothes on. If it's retail sales and service, whether they're selling bagels, or books, or books with certain content, they're regulated the same way." They only thing Portland can do is regulate for litter and noise.

As a result, sexually oriented businesses now can be found near homes, schools, and grocery stores all over Portland. In some parts of the town where adult businesses have congregated, the quality of the neighborhoods has deteriorated markedly.

"Once you have a lingerie business next door to an adult video store and a nudie joint, it begins to erode the sense of community to have men come in for all that action," admits Mike Sanderson, regulatory specialist with the city's Bureau of Licensing. Property values drop, and the area becomes vulnerable to being turned over to the sex industry completely. Prostitutes come in, Sanderson says, because the sex trade has served to "centralize a basket of customers."

No community in the country would want to be stuck with Portland's Pornosprawl problem. For most towns, the best option may simply be to have something on the books before the clubs arrive, as a way of at least placing an obstacle in their path.

Grafton, a Massachusetts town of 4,800, less than an hour from Boston, may or may not have been thinking about Pornosprawl and the Combat Zone when it recently proposed to restrict the location of adult businesses and require them to get a special permit — even though there are currently no such businesses in town. The plan will be voted on later this month. Grafton is not the only Massachusetts town that has been moving in that direction. In recent months, the nearby towns of Shrewsbury, Westboro and Northboro have all passed similar laws.

In retrospect, the town of Johnston admits that it probably should have done something like that before this past January, before Mario's ever applied for its entertainment license. Other Rhode Island towns — Burrillville, Foster, North Providence, Scituate and Smithfield — have acted preemptively to try to ward off the establishment of SOBs.

But somehow, naively as it seems now, Johnston never expected a strip club to move in. "Issues pop up all the time around the country," says Milan Azar, the city solicitor. "It's hard to anticipate what might come up while you have real problems sitting on the desk."

At the moment, however, strip clubs are a very real problem sitting on the solicitor's desk. Despite the passage of three separate anti-pornography ordinances — one forbidding nudity where liquor is served, one zoning strip clubs away from schools and churches, and one requiring a special "adult entertainment" license — the topless dancing at Mario's goes on, featuring entertainment in a "nude room," while legal challenges proceed in Superior Court.

If he could go back in time, Azar says, he would have made sure Johnston acted sooner to protect itself, before Mario's metamorphosed into a "show place" with the windows blacked out. "We didn't get around to it," Azar says, "until the wolf was at the door."

CHAPTER 33

Raleigh and Other Cities Have Their Laws Challenged by Adult Businesses

David W. Owens

The North Carolina General Assembly recently enacted major legislation to clarify the options available to local governments regarding regulation of sexually oriented businesses. There has also been significant ongoing litigation on this topic, both within North Carolina and nationally. This bulletin summarizes these recent developments.[1]

N.C. Legislation

A variety of factors converged in the past several years to prompt legislative attention to the question of local regulation of sexually oriented businesses.

In most of the state's larger cities, controversies and litigation have arisen over the location and operation of adult businesses. A bookstore in Charlotte with a substantial amount of adult material contested the city's definition of adult businesses.[2] In Raleigh, a topless bar proposed to be located in a prominent location near the Raleigh-Durham International Airport challenged the city's de-

nial of approval[3] and an adult cabaret downtown challenged application of adult business standards to a club featuring female impersonators.[4]

A nonconforming topless bar in Greensboro challenged the city's limits on its expansion.[5] Durham's restriction of a topless bar adjacent to the Research Triangle Park was challenged. Other highly publicized controversies involved facilities that were heretofore "exotic" for North Carolina in more than one sense, including a sado-masochistic parlor in Raleigh and a nude juice bar and erotic car wash in the Triad.

Significantly, adult business issues also have arisen in the state's smaller cities, rural areas, and resort communities. A federal court ordered that a topless bar be allowed to open in a restaurant in Roanoke Rapids. A widely publicized topless dance club opened adjacent to I-95 in rural Harnett County.[6] Onslow County's authority to adopt restrictions as a general police power ordinance was challenged by a topless bar and its dancers.[7] Topless bars were opened or proposed in a number of the

Originally published as "Recent Developments Regarding Local Regulation of Sexually Oriented Businesses," *Planning and Zoning Bulletin*, No. 10, August 1998, by the Institute of Government, The University of North Carolina, Chapel Hill, NC. Reprinted with permission of the publisher.

state's low density, "family oriented" resort areas, ranging from Currituck County at the northern entrance to the Outer Banks to Calabash on the southern coast and to Maggie Valley in the mountains.

As these and similar uses were proposed, an increasing number of local governments enacted regulations of their location and operation. Not surprisingly, litigation often ensued. One result of the litigation was to identify the uncertainty regarding the exact scope of authority of local governments to regulate sexually oriented businesses. A federal district court held the state statute on adult establishments preempted any local separation requirements, a decision that was subsequently vacated by the Fourth Circuit Court of Appeals on the basis that this was an unsettled area of state law. The state court of appeals subsequently held this statute preempted local dispersion requirements for adult businesses.[8]

In November 1996, Sen. Marc Basnight, the President Pro Tem of the Senate, organized a town meeting in Nags Head to discuss the authority of local governments to regulate sexually oriented businesses and the need for potential state legislation on the subject. The discussion at the meeting included reviews of current state laws, constitutional protections for free speech, and citizens' concerns about the impacts of adult businesses. Early in the 1997 session of the General Assembly, Sen. Basnight asked the chair of the Senate Judiciary Committee, Sen. Roy Cooper, to further review this question and to develop legislative proposals to address identified concerns. Sen. Cooper introduced Senate bill 452 (S. 452) in March 1997 to clarify state law on the question of the scope of local regulatory authority regarding sexually oriented businesses and to provide additional options for localities concerned with these issues. The bill was adopted by the state Senate in April 1997 and the state House of Representatives in July 1998.[9] It became effective upon signature by Governor Hunt on July 15, 1998.[10] The key provisions of the bill are summarized below.

Preemption

One of the principal objectives of S. 452 was to remove any question on whether the legislature intended to allow local regulation of sexually oriented businesses. Local governments may do so even though the state government also continues to regulate certain aspects of adult businesses.

Several judicial opinions had concluded that state statutes preempted local regulation. The statute limiting adult establishments to one per structure had been held to preclude local separation requirements.[11] The statute on indecent exposure had been held to limit regulation of topless dancers.[12] Statutes regulating alcohol sales had been held to limit local regulation of bars.[13]

S. 452 amended several key statutes to provide expressly that these statutes do not preclude local regulation of sexually oriented businesses. These statutes include those prohibiting obscenity (G.S. 14-190.1), prohibiting indecent exposure (G.S. 14-190.9), limiting adult establishments to one per structure (G.S. 14-202.11), and regulating facilities with alcohol sales (G.S. 18B-904). Importantly, each of the amended statutes explicitly provides that local regulations must be consistent with constitutional protections afforded free speech.

Clarification that state laws do not prohibit local regulation clears the way for a variety of provisions that might otherwise have been invalid. Local governments can, for example, set specific hours of operation for adult facilities with alcohol licenses, rather than being limited to the uniform 2:00 A.M. time established by state ABC closing laws. There is no longer a question as to the validity of dispersal requirements between sexually oriented businesses.

Range of Regulatory Options

S. 452 creates G.S. 160A-181.1 to set out the range of regulatory options available to cities and counties in regulating sexually oriented businesses. These regulations are to be directed toward the reduction of adverse secondary impacts of these businesses. Regulations can include restrictions on location and operation of the facilities, licensing requirements, and reasonable fees. The regulations can be included in zoning regulations, licensing requirements, or other appropriate local ordinances.

Among the specific regulatory tools authorized by the law are:

1. Limits on location, including restrictions to specified zoning districts and minimum separation requirements.
2. Limits on operations, including restrictions on hours of operation, requirements that all viewing booths be open and visible to managers, limits on exterior advertising and noise, restrictions on ages of patrons and employees, requirements on separations between patrons and performers, and clothing requirements for masseuses, servers, and entertainers.
3. Licensing, disclosure, and registration requirements, including restricting ownership of employment of those who have criminal records for offenses reasonably related to the legal operation of sexually oriented business;
4. Moratoria on new facilities or expansions while studies are conducted and ordinances debated[14];
5. Amortization requirements for nonconforming sexually oriented businesses; and
6. Interlocal agreements whereby local governments within an interrelated geographic area can provide alternative sites for sexually oriented businesses without the necessity of each unit of government providing sites.[15]

Local governments are also authorized to adopt their own detailed definitions of "sexually oriented businesses" to set precisely the scope of local regulations.

S. 452 also adds a new enforcement tool for local governments. It amends G.S. 19–1 to allow this public nuisance statute to be used against those businesses that repeatedly violate local ordinances on sexually oriented businesses in such a way as to create adverse secondary impacts. This is a powerful tool that can be used by private citizens as well as units of government.[16] It allows injunctions to prohibit continued misuse of the building[17] and allows attorney fees and other costs to be awarded to the prevailing party.[18]

Constitutional Foundation

S. 452 dos not relieve governments of the need to establish a strong constitutional foundation for any regulation of sexually oriented businesses. The U.S. Supreme Court has held that non-obscene but sexually explicit speech is entitled to First Amendment protection and any local regulation must be consistent with those constitutional limitations.

It is a political reality that sexually oriented businesses are unwelcome in many communities. Citizens and local elected officials alike may have strong opposition to the content of sexually explicit performances and materials. Such concern, however, can not be the basis of regulation. Sexually explicit but non-obscene material is protected by the First Amendment's free speech guarantees. Consistent with these cases,[19] S. 452 notes that the purpose of local regulation must be to prevent undue secondary impacts from the inappropriate location or operation of sexually oriented businesses. The regulations must be directed toward preventing negative impacts on neighboring property values and reducing the potential for increased crime, rather than toward suppression of protected speech.[20]

A local government should undertake the following steps to establish a proper constitutional foundation for its regulations of sexually oriented businesses. The courts have held that cities and counties have the burden of establishing that these steps have been undertaken.[21] The steps include:

1. Study the potential adverse secondary impacts to be prevented.[22] This does not require a formal technical study, but some thoughtful, explicit consideration of these impacts while the regulations are being framed is needed. This can include a review of studies conducted in other localities, reports from the planning, police, and other local staff on potential impacts, and testimony from concerned citizens at public meetings and hearings.

2. Conduct an analysis of the adequacy of sites available for location of sexually oriented businesses. The regulations can not have the practical effect of totally excluding constitutionally protected speech. The adopting unit of government needs to establish prior to adoption that the ordinance will leave reasonable alternative avenues for expression open. The sites available do not have to be those most desirable or profitable for the owners, nor do they have to be currently available for sale or rent. But they do need to be sites that could realistically be put to some commercial use and be of a sufficient number to meet anticipated demand.

3. Consider how each proposed regulation will advance the purpose of reducing adverse secondary impacts. Regulations need to be narrowly tailored to meet legitimate objectives.

4. Establish clear and definite standards for decisions and set adequate procedural safeguards to ensure prompt decisions and judicial review if permits or licenses are required prior to operation.

Recent Litigation Regarding Management Options

The courts in North Carolina and around the country have continued to review a variety of local government regulations of sexually oriented businesses. The overview below summarizes some of the more notable judicial developments over the past few years regarding management tools used by local governments to regulate sexually oriented businesses.

Adequacy of Alternative Sites Available

A local ordinance regulating sexually oriented businesses must provide reasonable alternatives for the dissemination of protected speech. It is not permissible to completely prohibit all sexually oriented businesses.

Courts examine the application of all of the restrictions imposed and determine whether the regulations have realistic sites available within the jurisdiction's commercial real estate market that could be used for protected adult speech.[23] There is no need to show that adult uses could be profitably operated at alternative sites, that the sites are currently being offered for sale or rent, or that owners are willing to make them available for adult uses.[24] However, a site cannot be considered to be "available" if the costs of improvements necessary to make the site suitable for any commercial use are so high as to be prohibitive.[25]

Courts increasingly examine the number of potential sites available as opposed to looking at a percentage of the city's land area.[26] Of particular importance is whether the potential supply of sites is proportional to estimated demand for sites.[27] Even a relatively small number of potentially available sites will be deemed adequate if that clearly exceeds past demand for sites in that locality. Some courts have also examined the ratio of the number of potential sites relative to the city's total population as an indicator of whether a "reasonable" number of alternatives are available.[28] This suggests that once a local government makes a "fair share" of its jurisdiction available, additional potential sites are not required.

Where there are no sites available when the totality of the jurisdiction's restrictions are applied, the regulation is invalid.[29] Also, an ordinance that sets minimum setbacks from sensitive land uses (such as places of worship, schools, playgrounds, or residences) and allows a new sensitive land use to be established during the pendency of consideration of an adult use application, thereby "knocking out" the pending adult use, has been held invalid.[30]

Special/Conditional Use Permit Requirements

Many local governments allow adult uses by right in specified zoning districts provided the objective standards set in the ordinance are met. Other local governments require a special or conditional use permit for all adult businesses in order to provide a detailed case by case review for compliance with standards. Such an approach may be unconstitutional.

A special or conditional use permit (as well as adult business license requirements) can effectively serve as a prior restraint on speech protected by the First Amendment. Any prior restraint—a government regulation that restricts the speech before it is made—must have clear and definite standards for decisions and must have adequate procedural safeguards to ensure prompt decisions and judicial review.[31]

Some courts have held that a special or conditional use permit requirement that applies to all similar uses (for example, all bars or retail establishments, not just topless bars or adult bookstores) is a content neutral land use rule that is not subject to a prior restraint analysis.[32] As noted below, however, a number of other courts have applied a prior restraint analysis even to these requirements.

The principal problem with employing a special or conditional use process to regulate adult businesses is the discretionary nature of the standards to be used. If the standards to be applied are objective, there is no need to require a special or conditional use permit.[33] If the standards involve judgment and discretion, they may well be invalid if the special use

permit requirement is considered a prior restraint. Standards that have been invalidated as too broad include:

- that the use be "essential or desirable" and not detrimental"[34];
- that the use be consistent with the purpose of the ordinance, its appearance not have an adverse effect on adjacent properties, and it be reasonably related to existing land uses[35];
- that the site be adequate in size, not adversely affect a place of worship or park, be sufficiently buffered from residential uses, not have an exterior inconsistent with nearby commercial uses, be consistent with the comprehensive and other city plans, and be adequately served by highways of sufficient width and other public services[36]; and,
- that the council may impose "more restrictive requirements and conditions on applications than are provided in the Zoning Code."[37]

If a special or conditional use permit requirement is subject to a prior restraint analysis, many of the general standards commonly used in North Carolina zoning ordinances could not be employed. For example, standards that the use be compatible with the surrounding neighborhoods or that it not cause a significant adverse impact on neighboring property values would likely involve too much discretion to survive prior restraint analysis.

In addition to definite standards, a regulation that is a prior restraint must provide for both prompt decisions and prompt judicial review, which often can not be assured with a special or conditional use process.[38]

An alternative that may hold some promise for local governments that propose to use a special or conditional use review would be to allow protected speech in some geographic areas or in certain circumstances by right and by special/conditional use in other situations. For example, New Haven, Connecticut, adopted an ordinance that required all adult cabarets to obtain a special exception permit, but allowed topless dancing as a use by right in other adult establishments that do not also provide food or drink. The court held that since the expressive speech involved (topless dancing) could be conducted without a special exception permit in part of the jurisdiction, requiring a special exception permit in other parts of the city is a content neutral time, place and manner regulation, and a prior restraint analysis would be inappropriate.[39]

Alcohol Prohibitions

An increasingly popular management tool used by local governments is a prohibition of alcohol sales at sexually oriented businesses. The validity of such restrictions was called into question by *44 Liquormart, Inc. v. Rhode Island*,[40] a 1996 Supreme Court case striking down restrictions on advertising retail prices of alcoholic beverages. The Court had previously implied[41] that additional restrictions on adult entertainment may be imposed on the authority of the Twenty-first Amendment's grant of authority to regulate alcohol sales. *44 Liquormart* disavowed that reasoning. The Court held that while the Twenty-first Amendment grants states authority to regulate commerce regarding the use of alcohol, it in no way reduces the protections afforded by the First Amendment.

Early cases decided subsequent to *44 Liquormart* indicate that alcohol restrictions for sexually oriented businesses will be upheld if the local government carefully establishes the proper constitutional foundation regarding secondary impacts. In 1994 Georgia amended its state constitution to authorize local governments to enact ordinances "regulating, restricting, or prohibiting the exhibition of nudity, partial nudity, or depictions of nudity in connection with the sale or consumption of alcoholic beverages."[42] The Georgia supreme court upheld an ordinance banning alcohol sales at topless bars.[43] The court found the ordinance to be a content neutral regulation

aimed at preventing adverse secondary impacts. A Mobile, Alabama ordinance prohibiting alcohol at adult establishments was upheld by a federal court under the same rationale.[44]

Also, it should be noted that a facility with a North Carolina ABC license that violates the terms of a local ordinance regulating sexually oriented businesses would be subject to state penalties[45] as well as local enforcement.

Clothing Requirements

Among the management tools specifically authorized by G.S. 160A-181.1 are clothing restrictions for masseuses, for servers of alcoholic beverages, and for entertainers. Regulation of clothing for the first two categories pose few legal issues. Providing massages and serving beverages involve conduct, not speech. Thus no First Amendment considerations limit local government clothing standards for these persons. Entertainment, however, usually involves protected expressive speech. Clothing requirements for entertainers such as exotic dancers must be consistent with First Amendment protections.

Local regulations can prohibit obscenity and indecent exposure. Thus exposure of the genitals — "totally nude" or "bottomless" dancing — can be prohibited.[46] This is the case regardless of whether alcohol is being sold on site or whether the entertainment is provided at a "private club" to which the public is invited. The more difficult question arises with proposals to prohibit topless dancing. In 1991 the Supreme Court in *Barnes v. Glen Theater, Inc.*,[47] upheld an Indiana statute that required dancers to wear minimal costumes. Justice Souter's narrowly drawn concurring opinion upheld the statute in the context of regulating secondary impacts. As the narrowest portion of the *Barnes* decision,[48] Justice Souter's opinion has been influential in subsequent decisions.

Courts have upheld several ordinances around the country that impose "bikini top" requirements.[49] Where the proper constitutional foundation has not been established, such requirements have been invalidated.[50] For communities to ban topless dancing altogether in a manner consistent with the *Barnes* decision, it is necessary to establish negative secondary impacts from establishments with topless dancing, as opposed to simply prohibiting topless dancing *per se*, and that the regulation is narrowly drawn to prevent those negative impacts. In this context, the exact amount of clothing that may be necessary to prevent adverse secondary impacts may differ in family resort areas such as Maggie Valley or Nags Head as compared with uptown Charlotte. A local government considering restrictions on topless dancing would be well advised to develop carefully a complete hearing record on two points — the adverse secondary impacts that are anticipated and that the clothing requirement imposed is the least restrictive measure needed to combat those impacts.

Definitions of Adult Entertainment

To avoid constitutional problems of vagueness, local ordinances regulating sexually oriented businesses must carefully define which businesses are subject to the regulations. However, once a definition is set, attempts by business owners to circumvent the regulations by contending a particular business is not included within the definition is not uncommon.

A case in point arose in Charlotte. The Charlotte ordinance established separation requirements between adult establishments and other sensitive land uses. The question presented was whether the petitioner's facility was an adult establishment. The ordinance defined these to include bookstores where a "preponderance of its publications, books, magazines, and other periodicals" were devoted to adult materials. In *South Blvd. Video & News, Inc. v. Charlotte Zoning Board of Adjustment*,[51] the court held that "preponderance" did not require that more than fifty percent of the materials be devoted to adult material, but rather

that adult materials were given a predominant and far greater emphasis in display within the store and in importance to the store's overall business. The court held that videotapes could be considered within the "publications" subject to this definition. The court also upheld a contempt citation based on the efforts to circumvent court orders regarding the business.

Others

Hours of operations. A Vineland, New Jersey, requirement limiting sexually oriented businesses' hours of operation to 8:00 A.M. to 10:00 P.M. Monday through Saturday and requiring open viewing booths was upheld.[52] A similar Tennessee statute that limited adult establishments to operations between 8:00 A.M. and midnight Monday through Saturday and required open viewing booths was also upheld.[53] Less restrictive ordinances setting closing times closer to the hours established by North Carolina ABC laws have also been upheld, including those in Jacksonville, Florida,[54] West Allis, Wisconsin,[55] and Newport, Kentucky.[56] On the other hand, a federal district court in Rhode Island invalidated a ban on the sale or rental of adult videos on Sundays and holidays.[57] While finding the ordinance was not preempted by state Sunday closing laws, the court held the regulation was content-based (no secondary impacts were established). A strict scrutiny analysis was applied and no compelling interest was presented for the restriction.

Advertising. A Minneapolis ordinance that limited on-site outdoor advertising for an adult bookstore to flat wall signs only, limited sign area to one square foot per foot of lot frontage, prohibited pictures or displays on window areas visible from the sidewalk, and limited opaque windows was upheld.[58]

Patron separations. Courts have continued to uphold reasonable requirements of separations between patrons and entertainers. Among the requirements upheld were a Chattanooga ordinance requiring a six foot minimum separation between dancers and patrons,[59] a Bellevue, Washington ordinance requiring a separation of eight feet for stage dancers and four feet for performers off the stage,[60] and an Arlington, Texas, ordinance prohibiting any contact between dancers and patrons.[61]

Space limitation. The Third Circuit Court of Appeals invalidated a requirement that a video store limit its adult material to ten percent of the structure's floor area.[62]

Access by minors. The Ninth Circuit Court of Appeals upheld a California statute prohibiting distribution of adult material (defined similarly to obscenity) in vending machines in which minors have access.[63] The court held this was a content-based regulation as the purpose was to prevent distribution of harmful materials to minors rather than addressing secondary impacts. The court therefore applied a strict scrutiny review, but held the restriction valid as it directly advanced a compelling governmental interest (preventing distribution of sexually explicit material to minors) and employed the least restrictive alternative available to do so. There are, however, limits to regulations limiting access to sexually oriented businesses on the basis of age. A Georgia statute raised the age requirement from eighteen to twenty-one for those attending performances featuring nudity by live performers. The Georgia Supreme Court invalidated the statute, holding it to be a content-based restriction subject to strict scrutiny and finding no compelling state interest in restricting access by adults who were eighteen, nineteen, and twenty years old.[64]

Amortization. Regulations that require existing sexually oriented businesses to come into compliance after a reasonable grace period continue to be upheld. In North Carolina, Onslow County's two year amortization provision was upheld.[65] A Jacksonville, Florida, provision requiring compliance in fifteen to nineteen months was upheld.[66] New York City's one year amortization provision was also upheld, even when the city's newly adopted locational standards required an estimated 84 percent of the city's 177 adult businesses to close or relocate.[67]

Conclusions

In adopting S. 452, the General Assembly has confirmed significant authority for North Carolina cities and counties to regulate sexually oriented businesses. State laws continue to prohibit obscenity, indecent exposure, and multiple adult businesses within a single building, as well as regulating alcohol sales. Local governments may, however, impose additional regulations in order to protect surrounding neighborhoods. Standards may be set on where and how these businesses may be operated.

Local regulatory power is not unlimited. Under the First Amendment, non-obscene but sexually explicit speech cannot be banned. All regulation of protected speech — which includes adult books, videos, movies, and exotic dancing — must be directed toward preventing secondary impacts, not toward suppressing unpopular speech.

As part of its consideration of regulations, each local government must carefully establish a proper constitutional foundation for its action. The courts have not imposed a particularly onerous burden on local governments in this respect. Lengthy, detailed, and expensive studies are not required. Studies from other jurisdictions, citizen comments, and common experience and judgment can and should be considered. Yet some diligence in this area is necessary. Undue haste or cavalier treatment of these constitutional requirements will result in invalidation of the regulations.

Therefore, the prudent local government will take several steps when devising regulations on sexually oriented businesses. It will engage in a focused discussion of what is to be accomplished by the regulations. What secondary impacts are being addressed? What types of businesses need to be regulated? How will the specific regulations proposed address these adverse impacts? The government also must document that adequate alternative avenues for expression will be provided. How many sites can meet the restrictions? Is this a reasonable number considering the number of current such businesses in operation, the number of applications received, the population and nature of the jurisdiction?

Some management tools are widely used and regularly approved by the courts provided this basic constitutional foundation has been set. These include: minimum separations from sensitive land uses and other sexually oriented businesses, usually in the 500 to 1,500 feet range; limitations to specified zoning districts; limitations on late night operation; limitations on physical contact between entertainers and patrons; and open booth and lighting requirements. Other regulations, such as prohibitions on sale or consumption of alcohol at sexually oriented businesses, requiring a special or conditional use permit for all sexually oriented businesses, and bikini top requirements for dancers, have a mixed record in the courts. Local governments proposing such additional restrictions need to take extra care to consider and document how such restrictions comply with First Amendment protections.

Application of these guidelines will not satisfy all citizens. Some will be upset that there is not a total prohibition of activity they find offensive, immoral, and demeaning. Others will feel their rights as adults to decide for themselves what to pay to see are being unduly impaired. The First Amendment and North Carolina's statutes require that local governments balance these concerns. Reasonable steps can be taken to prevent crime and harm to neighboring property values, but this must be done in a manner that respects others' right to provide and see sexually explicit material.

Editor's Note:

The footnotes to the above article provide very detailed legal explanations, many legal references, and numerous court citations. These footnotes were several pages in length and, due to their detailed nature, are not included with this article. To see these footnotes in their entirety, please refer to the website of the School of Government (SOG), The University of North Carolina, Chapel Hill, NC. All of the footnotes for this research can be found at this SOG website <www.sog.unc.edu/organizations/planning/pdfs/pzb10.pdf>.

CHAPTER 34

Renton and Other Cities Base Their Regulations on the Possible Negative Impact of Adult Businesses

Alan C. Weinstein

In eight decisions since 1976, the U.S. Supreme Court has consistently affirmed that local governments could legitimately seek to safeguard their communities against the negative "secondary effects" associated with adult entertainment businesses.[1] These decisions, and the hundreds of lower court decisions interpreting and applying them, have made it clear that local governments may lawfully regulate such businesses —*provided* that regulations are drafted, enacted, and administered with exacting precision. That proviso is critical because adult entertainment regulations are frequently challenged — often successfully.[2] Adult businesses are lucrative and can hire attorneys who specialize in civil rights or First Amendment litigation. Municipal attorneys, by contrast, are less likely to have the same expertise. Over time, however, this advantage has eroded as municipal lawyers have learned to avoid the legal pitfalls in regulating adult businesses.

Recently, adult business attorneys, assisted by academic experts, have begun raising new challenges that target the claim that

local governments regulate adult businesses to control their negative secondary effects. Some of these challenges claim that the secondary effects studies cited by regulators are methodologically flawed and thus cannot reasonably be relied upon[3]; they also often claim that their expert's study of the jurisdiction in question shows no evidence of secondary effects.[4] Others argue that the jurisdiction has no evidence that a particular type of adult business is associated with negative secondary effects.[5] This article discusses the nature of these challenges, analyzes how they've fared in the courts, and suggests how local governments should respond when faced with these new claims.

The "Methodological" Challenge

The methodological challenge debuted five years ago in *City of Erie v. Pap's A.M.*[6] Although the U.S. Supreme Court upheld the city's anti-nudity ordinance, Justice Souter wrote separately to question whether "the city

Originally published as "Responding to the Adult Industry's Claim About 'No Secondary Effect,'" *Municipal Lawyer*, Vol. 46, No. 5, September/October 2005, by the International Municipal Lawyers Association, Washington, DC. Reprinted with permission of the publisher.

has made a sufficient evidentiary showing to sustain its regulations,"[7] citing an *amicus* brief filed on behalf of the adult business that argued "scientifically sound studies show no ... correlation" between adult businesses and negative secondary effects.[8]

One year later, the argument in that *amicus* brief was set out in detail in a law review article.[9] Co-authored by Daniel Linz, a professor in the Department of Communication at the University of California, Santa Barbara,[10] the article argued that the secondary effects studies relied upon by local governments constituted "scientific evidence" subject to the rigors of the *Daubert* test.[11] Professor Linz then applied the *Daubert* standards he claimed were relevant to the "ten most frequently referenced studies."[12] He concluded that "the scientific validity of the most frequently used studies [was] questionable and the methods are seriously and often fatally flawed," and "[t]hose studies that are scientifically credible demonstrate either no negative secondary effects associated with adult businesses or a reversal of the presumed negative effects."[13]

Professor Linz has since appeared several times as an expert witness on behalf of adult businesses,[14] usually seeking to discredit the secondary effects studies cited by the regulating jurisdiction and claiming that his own study shows no evidence of negative secondary effects in that community.[15] While he enjoyed initial success,[16] his more recent efforts have met with mixed results, due largely to how the lower courts have interpreted *City of Los Angeles v. Alameda Books, Inc.*,[17] the U.S. Supreme Court's 2002 case that grappled with the issue of how much evidence of secondary effects was necessary to sustain an adult business ordinance.

As often happens with the Court's First Amendment rulings, there was no clear majority in *Alameda Books*. Justice O'Connor's plurality opinion qualified the Court's earlier statement in *City of Renton v. Playtime Theaters, Inc.* (that a municipality may rely on evidence of secondary effects that is "reasonably believed to be relevant"[18]) by cautioning that a city cannot "get away with shoddy data or reasoning;" rather, its "evidence must fairly support the municipality's rationale for its ordinance."[19] Justice Kennedy's concurring opinion, however, expressed concern that the plurality had subtly expanded what *Renton* permitted.[20] He contended that adult business cases raised two evidentiary questions: "First, what proposition does a city need to advance in order to sustain a secondary-effects ordinance? Second, how much evidence is required to support the proposition?"[21] He argued that the plurality answered only the second question and, while he believed that answer was correct, in his view more attention needed to be paid to the first.[22] The critical inquiry that Justice Kennedy believed the plurality skipped was "how speech will fare under the city's ordinance."[23] According to him, a "city may not assert that it will reduce secondary effects by reducing speech in the same property proportion."[24] In short, "[t]he rationale of the ordinance must be that it will suppress secondary-effects — and not by suppressing speech."[25] That said, he, along with the plurality, argued for significant deference to local government fact-finding in making this inquiry. Cities "must have latitude to experiment, at least at the outset, and that very little evidence is required" to support the proposition,[26] and he cautioned that "[a]s a general matter, courts should not be in the business of second-guessing the fact-bound empirical assessments of city planners."[27]

The "Methodological" Challenge *After* Alameda Books

After *Alameda Books*, the adult entertainment industry strenuously urged lower courts to view the case as authorizing a far more probing judicial inquiry into the rationale and supporting evidence that local governments offered in support of adult business regulations. As discussed below, in several of these cases, Professor Linz's testimony challenged either the rationale for the regulations, or the evidence in support of the rationale. Generally, courts continued to show significant deference to local government effects to regulate adult businesses so long as there was some reliable evidence of negative secondary effects and the rationale for regulation was plausible; some courts, however, have been strongly influenced by Linz's claims.

Recent decisions illustrate why some of these challenges fail while others succeed. In *G.M. Enterprises, Inc. v. Town of St. Joseph, Wis.*,[28] the U.S. Court of Appeals for the Seventh Circuit upheld ordinances regulating nude dancing. After first ruling the ordinances did not impermissibly reduce expression in attempting to minimize secondary effects, the court considered whether the plaintiffs had "cast doubt" on the city's rationale for regulation or the evidence supporting that rationale.[29] The court noted that Professor Linz's testimony "arguably" showed that the city "might have reached a different and equally reasonable conclusion regarding the relationship between adverse secondary effects and sexually oriented businesses,"[30] but the court found that this was insufficient to shift the burden of proof back to the city, as it viewed *Alameda Books* as having left intact *Renton*'s deferential standard.[31] Critically, the court rejected, as "completely unfounded," Linz's claim that a city could not meet *Renton*'s "reasonable belief" standard unless its studies would be admissible under *Daubert*.[32] The court noted that a "requirement of *Daubert*-quality evidence would impose an unreasonable burden on the legislative process, and further[,] would be logical only if *Alameda Books* required a regulating body to prove that its regulation would — undeniably — reduce adverse secondary effects. *Alameda Books* clearly did not impose such a requirement."[33]

Other cases also found that Professor Linz's testimony was insufficient to cast doubt on a defendant city's rationale. In *Annex Books, Inc. v. City of Indianapolis*,[34] the court ruled that Linz's negative assessment of the city's studies, and his own studies claiming to show no evidence of negative secondary effects, were rebutted by the evidence of actual effects caused by plaintiff's establishments, as shown by arrest records.[35] More recently, in *Fantasyland Video, Inc. et al. v. County of San Diego*,[36] the county retained its own expert witness, Richard McCleary, Professor of Social Ecology at University of California–Irvine, both to critique and to rebut Professor Linz's testimony, a role Professor McCleary has carried out for several other jurisdictions.[37]

It is important to note, however, that in the absence of such countervailing expert testimony, some courts have been strongly influenced by Professor Linz's claims. In *J.L. Spoons, Inc. v. Morckel*,[38] involving a challenge to a state liquor control commission's regulation of erotic dancing, the court contrasted the state's reliance on a single out-of-state study with Linz's "thorough investigation of crime rates (and contributing factors to the crime rates)"[39] and described his study as "more persuasive, if counterintuitive, evidence" than that presented by the state.[40]

In *R.V.S., L.L.C. v. City of Rockford*,[41] the Seventh Circuit found that the city's evidence did not support the rationale for regulation of "exotic dancing nightclubs," defined as venues where dancers performed a "striptease" or "erotic dance" while wearing full opaque clothing over the pubic area, buttocks and breasts.[42] The court found that the city had neither conducted its own studies of such businesses nor relied on any studies conducted by other cities, and the city's only pre-enactment "evidence" consisted of unsupported conclusory statements by two city officials.[43] In contrast, Professor Linz presented evidence that no studies demonstrated adverse secondary effects from establishments featuring clothed dancers, nor did he and another expert believe such effects could be found.[44] While acknowledging that courts should not be "second-guessing" the assessments of local government planners, the Seventh Circuit found that it would not have been reasonable for the city to believe, based on the scanty evidence before it, that there was a connection between negative secondary effects and these types of establishments.[45]

Obviously, regardless of expert witnesses, courts will uphold challenges to adult business regulations where evidence to support the government's rationale is wholly lacking. In *Peek-A-Boo Lounge of Bradenton, Inc. v. Manatee County, Fla.*,[46] for example, the U.S. Court of Appeals for the Eleventh Circuit found that the county had not considered *any* evidence prior to the enactment of an adult entertainment ordinance. The case of *Flanigan's Enterprises, Inc. of Georgia v. Fulton County, Ga.*,[47] decided before *Alameda Books*, is also instructive. In *Flanigan's*, after the county's own study showed no evidence of adverse secondary effects, the county sought to justify its regulation of nude dancing establishments based on studies from other jurisdictions. The court ruled that it was not reasonable for the county to ignore relevant local studies and rely instead upon "remote foreign studies" in determining whether adverse secondary effects were attributable to the adult businesses.[48]

The "On-Site" vs. "Off-Site" Challenge

In the adult entertainment context, "on-site" refers to businesses which offer entertainment to be viewed on the premises, as opposed to "off-site" or "take-home" businesses, consisting of adult bookstores and video stores that do not have viewing booths or do not permit on-site viewing.

Adult businesses are claiming that evidence of secondary effects associated with "on-site" adult businesses does not support regulation of "off-site" businesses. In *Encore Videos, Inc. v. City of San Antonio*,[49] the U.S. Court of Appeals for the Fifth Circuit ruled that the city had not met its evidentiary burden for a

zoning ordinance that treated "off-site" businesses with as little as 20 percent of adult material as sexually oriented businesses. The court criticized the city's studies because they had either entirely excluded "take-home" businesses, or did not differentiate the data collected from "take-home" businesses from that of "on-site" businesses.[50] In the court's view, "off-site" businesses differed from "on-site" ones: it was "only reasonable to assume that the former [were] less likely to create harmful secondary effects" as customers would not linger in the area and engage in undesirable behavior if they couldn't view the materials at that location.[51] The court's view on the evidentiary issue was significantly colored, however, by the fact that the 20 percent regulatory threshold could potentially ensnare "mainstream" businesses with adult sections.[52]

In contrast, the U.S. Court of Appeals for the Ninth Circuit upheld a restriction on "off-site" businesses in *World Wide Video of Washington, Inc. v. City of Spokane*, despite the fact that the Plaintiff's expert demonstrated that the city's studies did not deal exclusively with "take-out" businesses and provided his own studies showing that such businesses did not cause negative secondary effects in Spokane.[53] The court ruled that the plaintiff, despite its expert's findings, had not met its burden of "casting doubt" on the city's rationale or supporting evidence. This was because, in addition to the studies from other cities, the city had relied on citizen testimony linking "off-site" businesses with pornographic litter and public lewdness, and this evidence, "standing alone, was sufficient to meet the 'very little' evidence standard of *Alameda Books*."[54]

Conclusion

The "methodological" challenges being mounted by adult businesses should not be treated lightly. In the absence of such a challenge, a court will normally find that government has satisfied its evidentiary burden under *Renton* and *Alameda Books* merely by citing studies of secondary effects from other jurisdictions. That is decidedly not the case when the adult business brings a "methodological" challenge that disputes the validity of the studies relied upon or provides an expert's study showing no negative secondary effects in the challenged jurisdiction. In the face of such a challenge, local government must either introduce evidence to support the validity of the studies relied upon, or provide evidence of actual secondary effects associated with adult businesses in the jurisdiction. Some courts have held that police crime reports, or even personal testimony, are sufficient to demonstrate the existence of negative secondary effects; however, if the adult business has offered expert witness testimony along the lines described above, the challenged jurisdiction should seriously consider retaining its own expert to refute those claims.

NOTES

1. Young v. American Mini Theatres, Inc. 427 U.S. 50 (1976); Schad v. Borough of Mount Ephraim, 452 U.S. 61 (1981); City of Renton v. Playtime Theatres, Inc., 475 U.S. 41 (1986); FW/PBS, Inc. v. Dallas, 493 U.S. 215 (1990); Barnes v. Glen Theatre, Inc., 501 U.S. 560 (1991); City of Erie v. Pap's A.M., 529 U.S. 277 (2000); City of Los Angeles v. Alameda Books, Inc., 535 U.S. 425 (2002); City of Littleton, Colorado v. Z.J. Gifts D-4 L.L.C., 541 U.S. 774 (2004).

2. Author's June 2005 Westlaw search in ALLCASES database listed 1,351 adult entertainment cases since 1976.

3. *See, e.g.*, Nite Moves Entertainment, Inc. v. City of Boise, 153 F. Supp. 2d 1998, 1201–02 (D. Idaho 2001) (claiming city's land use studies and crime reports were fundamentally flawed and did not comply with the standards for expert testimony in Daubert v. Merrell Dow Pharmaceuticals, Inc., 509 U.S. 579 (1993); *see also* R.V.S., L.L.C. v. City of Rockford, 361 F. 3d 402 (7th Cir. 2004); J.L. Spoons, Inc. v. Morckel, 314 F. Supp. 2d 746 (N.D. Ohio 2004).

4. *See, e.g.*, Fantasyland Video, Inc. v. County of San Diego, 373 F. Supp. 2d 1094 (S.D. Cal. 2005).

5. *See, e.g.*, Encore Videos, Inc. v. City of San Antonio, 330 F. 3d 288 (5th Cir. 2003).

6. 529 U.S. 277 (2000).

7. *Id.* at 310–11 (emphasis added).

8. *Id.* at 315, n.3.

9. Bryant Paul, Daniel Linz & Bradley J. Shafer, *Government Regulation of "Adult" Businesses Through Zoning and Anti-Nudity Ordinances; Debunking the Legal Myth of Negative Secondary Effects*, 6 Comm. L. & Pol'y 355 (2001) (thereafter "*Linz*").

10. Linz's co-authors, Paul and Shafer, are, respectively, one of Linz's Ph.D. students and a Michigan adult business attorney.

11. In Daubert v. Merrell Dow Pharmaceuticals Inc., 509 U.S. 579 (1993), the Court outlined the standards for "reliability" governing the admissibility of expert scientific evidence in federal courts.

12. *Linz, supra* note 9 at 369–75.

13. *Id.* at 386–87.

14. *See, e.g.*, Fantasyland Nite Moves Entertainment, Inc. v. City of Boise, 153 F. Supp. 2d 1198 (D. Idaho 2001); G.M. Enterprises, Inc. v. Town of St. Joseph, Wis., 350 F. 3d 631 (7th Cir. 2003); R.V.S., L.L.C. v. City of Rockford, 361 F. 3d 402 (7th Cir. 2004); J.L. Spoons, Inc. v. Morckel, 314 F. Supp. 2d 746 (N.D. Ohio 2004); Annex Books, Inc. v. City of Indianapolis, 333 F. Supp. 2d 773 (S.D. Ind. 2004); Fantasyland Video, Inc. v. County of San Diego, 373 F. Supp. 2d 1094 (S.D. Cal. 2005).

15. *See, e.g.*, *Fantasyland Video, Inc.*, 373 F. Supp. 2d 1094.

16. *Id.*

17. City of Los Angeles v. Alameda Books, Inc., 535 U.S. 425 (2002).

18. 475 U.S. 41, 51–52 (1986).

19. *Alameda Books, Inc.*, 535 U.S. at 438–39.

20. Because there was no majority opinion, Justice Kennedy's concurrence is the narrowest opinion joining the judgment of the Court and is controlling authority under Marks v. United States, 430 U.S. 188 (1977). *See, e.g.*, G.M. Enterprises, Inc. v. Town of St. Joseph, Wis., 350 F. 3d 631, 637 (7th Cir. 2003).

21. Alameda Books, Inc., 535 U.S. at 449.

22. *Id.*

23. *Id.* at 450.

24. *Id.* at 449.

25. *Id.* at 449–50.

26. *Id.* at 451.

27. *Id.* at 451–52.

28. 350 F. 3d 631 (7th Cir. 2003).

29. *Id.* at 639

30. *Id.*

31. *Id.* at 639–40.

32. *Id.* at 640. The court also noted that both the plurality and Justice Kennedy had "bluntly rejected" Justice Souter's suggestion that a city be required to produce empirical data in support of its rationale for regulation, on the ground that "such a contention would go too far in undermining our settled position that municipalities must be given a 'reasonable opportunity to experiment with solutions' to address the secondary effects of protected speech." *Id.*, quoting *Alameda Books*, 535 U.S. at 439. *See also* Center for Fair Public Policy v. Maricopa County, 336 F. 13d 1153 (9th Cir. 2003) (rejecting claim that government must support its rationale with empirical data).

33. *G.M. Enterprises, Inc.*, 350 F. 3d at 640.

34. 333 F. Supp. 2d 773 (S.D. Ind. 2004).

35. *Id.* at 786–87.

36. Fantasyland Video, Inc. v. County of San Diego, 373 F. Supp. 2d 1094 (S.D. Cal. 2005).

37. Correspondence with Professor McCleary (May 27, 2004) (on file with author).

38. 814 F. Supp. 2d 746 (N.D. Ohio 2004).

39. *Id.* at 756.

40. *Id.*

41. R.V.S., L.L.C. v. City of Rockford, 361 F. 3d 402 (7th Cir. 2004).

42. *Id.* at 405.

43. *Id.* at 405–06.

44. *Id.* at 406–07.

45. *Id.* at 410–12.

46. 337 F. 3d 1251 (11th Cir. 2003).

47. 242 F. 3d 976 (11th Cir. 2001).

48. *Id.* at 986–87 ("We simply cannot find it reasonable for a government entity to conduct studies on specific areas and then to reject the conclusions thereof in favor of studies from different cities and different time periods." *Id.* at 987).

49. 330 F. 3d 288 (5th Cir. 2003).

50. *Id.* at 294–95.

51. *Id.* The court noted that the Washington Supreme Court had reached a similar conclusion in World Wide Video, Inc. v. City of Tukwila, 816 P.2d 18 (Wash. 1991), but that two federal circuits disagreed that the distinction between on-site and off-site businesses held any legal meaning; *see* Z.J. Gifts, D-2 L.L.C. v. City of Aurora, 136 F. 3d 683 (10th Cir. 1998) and ILQ Investments, Inc. v. City of Rochester, 25 F. 3d 1413 (8th Cir. 1994).

52. *Id.* at 295. *See also* Giggles World Corp. v. Town of Wappinger, 341 F. Supp. 2d 427 (S.D.N.Y. 2004) (questioning, on motion of summary judgment, secondary effects basis for ordinance regulation businesses with only 20 percent adult material).

53. 368 F. 3d 1186 (9th Cir. 2004).

54. *Id.* at 1195.

CHAPTER 35

San Antonio Involves Citizens in the Planning and Renewal of Their Neighborhoods

J. Rolando Bono

The City of San Antonio adopted the Community Building and Neighborhood Planning (CBNP) Program in October 1998 to preserve, protect and enhance the integrity, economic viability and livability of San Antonio's neighborhoods. The program's primary purpose is to strengthen neighborhoods as self-sustaining communities working towards improved quality of life. It is designed to foster community-based partnerships with businesses, nonprofits, schools, public agencies, and other groups. Equally important, the program empowers neighborhoods to articulate community values, and, subsequently, the adopted neighborhood plans are actively used as guides by public and private entities in community development decisions.

The CBNP program consists of four service components: Building Capacity, Focusing on the Issues, Master Planning, and Implementing Incentives. Building Capacity is designed to support successful, sustainable, informed organizations working to improve neighborhoods through neighborhood registration, self-help workbooks, and special seminars addressing membership, resource mapping, newsletters, the city's budget process, and capital improvements funding.

The Focusing on the Issues component helps neighborhoods prioritize action strategies to address current issues and work collaboratively with community partners. The product is a Goals and Strategies Report or Special Study that is distributed to the Mayor, City Council members, and appropriate City Departments. Most Focusing on the Issues recipients proceed to developing a Master Plan. Special studies have focused on economic development, corridor land use, revitalization, and historic preservation.

The Master Planning component encourages the development of Neighborhood Plans with a range in population from 2,000 to 10,000, Community Plans (20,000–80,000 persons) and Perimeter Plans that coincide with annexation and thoroughfare plan amendments. The plans incorporate extensive public involvement through community meetings and work sessions that address land use, community facilities and transportation networks using a strategic planning methodology. The draft plan is considered by the

Originally published as "Community Building and Neighborhood Planning Program," *Application for Program Excellence Award for Citizen Involvement*, 2005, by the Office of the City Manager, City of San Antonio, TX.

Planning Commission and forwarded to City Council for adoption as a component of the City's Master Plan.

A citizen's Planning Team is created to support the outreach efforts and coordinate meetings. The public meetings and workshops, which take place over a nine-month period, involve a spectrum of stakeholders, such as residents, neighborhood associations, nonprofits, school, universities, chambers of commerce, property owners, and business owners. Participants determine strengths and weaknesses and develop plan goals and objectives. Designed as action plans, time frames, responsible parties, and potential funding sources are outlined to poise the plan for implementation.

The CBNP's fourth service component promotes implementation. A plan coordinating committee is formed to keep stakeholders involved in future decisions relating to capital improvements, zoning, and public and private programs that deliver services. The city's Neighborhood Improvement Challenge Program provided funds to neighborhoods for tree planting projects, small improvement projects, and seed grants to build capacity.

Measurable Outcomes/Results

Major benefits to San Antonio neighborhoods that participate in the Community and Neighborhood Planning Process are empowerment, collaborative partnerships with city departments, public agencies and non-profit organizations, and involvement in the land development process. Today, a total of 26 Neighborhood, Community and Perimeter Plans cover 259 square miles, and a population of 400,000 persons. Recent projects resulting from Master Plan adoption have entailed several large area-wide comprehensive rezonings; implementation of neighborhood conservation districts and corridor overlay districts; a study by the United States Army Corps of Engineers of the restoration of the Olmos Creek

ecosystem; a $475,000 Texas Department of Transportation project to install medians on Austin Highway, and the funding of a number of capital improvements and bond projects.

A neighborhood and community organization registration program has resulted in the listing of 380 neighborhood associations and 57 community organizations. Registered neighborhoods cover 40 percent of the city's area and 18 percent of the extraterritorial jurisdiction. The benefits of neighborhood registration include notification to neighborhoods within 200 feet of the site of public hearings concerning rezoning, major plats, demolitions of historic buildings, and board of adjustment appeals. This enables neighborhoods to have considerable input into the development process.

Through the Neighborhood Improvement Challenge program, community groups in all parts of the city planted more than 979 trees. Thirty-six community groups were awarded a total of $215,000 and provided a match of $80,366 to implement landscaping, murals, pavilions, entrance signs, and other improvement projects. Finally, one recent study on the rehabilitation of the late 19th Century Hays Street Bridge led to the development of an application for State Transportation Enhancement Program funds which resulted in an award of $2.9 million and a pledge of $110,000 in private funds. The donation of the bridge to the City by Union Pacific Railroad is anticipated in April, and the design phase is underway.

Lessons Learned

A major lesson learned is the importance of extensive outreach in the Master Planning process. The dissemination and collection of information in both English and Spanish was essential to engage the community. Outreach methods ranged from targeted mailings of postcards and newsletters; press releases; newspaper inserts; posters; logos; appearances on

Spanish talk radio; kitchen table discussions; notices in church bulletins, and surveys sent home with elementary school children. Kick-off events including press conferences, kite flying and picnics in the parks, and a traditional Tex-Mex lunch buffet with mariachi music oriented citizens on the benefits of community planning.

The Community Building and Neighborhood Planning (CBNP) Program has involved thousands of citizens in the creation of a comprehensive land use plan for the City of San Antonio while addressing goals and objectives specific to neighborhoods. It continues to promote grass-roots involvement, to engage citizens in the development process, and to identify funding that has launched many special projects to improve the health, safety, and welfare of San Antonio's citizens.

Editor's Notes:

1. The award the City of San Antonio applied for was for cities with a population of 50,000 or greater. This is one of several categories of awards made available to cities and counties throughout the U.S. annually by the International City/County Management Association (ICMA), Washington, DC. Readers can learn more about ICMA by referring to their entry in the National Resources Directory listed in the Appendix of this volume.

2. The 2005 Program Excellence Award for Citizen Involvement in the above category was awarded to the current and former City Manager of San Antonio, TX. At the time, the award was presented, J. Rolando Bono was City Manger and Alex Briseno was the former City Manager.

3. Involving citizens in the planning process leads to the best mix of land uses, as well as achieving community's goals consistent with the wishes of residents who live there.

CHAPTER 36

Saratoga Springs Planning Board Reviews Its Adult Use Laws

Jaclyn Hakes

In early 2007 Mayor Keehn has asked the Planning Board to develop some proposed amendments to the zoning ordinance relating to adult uses. The Mayor has specifically asked that the Planning Board "undertake a study of the potential secondary effects of adult uses in the City and produce recommendations for amendments to the City Code for the suitable siting, land use and zoning standards and control therefor."

In this report the Planning Board will summarize the following:

- Legal basis for regulating adult oriented businesses
- Review of the secondary impacts studies conducted in other communities
- Survey of existing regulations and conditions in the City of Saratoga Springs
- Finding and recommendations.

Legal Basis for Regulating Adult Oriented Businesses

The Planning Board asked City Attorney Michael Englert to provide an analysis of the legal basis for regulation of adult oriented

businesses, and he provided the following analysis:

Although the City May Regulate "Adult Uses" Pursuant to Its Municipal Police Power, It May Not Flatly Prohibit Such Uses.

- Both the 1st Amendment of the U.S. Constitution and Article 1, Section 8 of the New York State Constitution provide for the protection of every citizen's right to the freedom of speech and expression.
- Municipalities are therefore not permitted to enact local regulations that totally suppress the freedom of expression associated with adult use activities, and such uses must be allowed within any and all municipalities.
- It should be noted, however, that constitutional protections do not cover activities or material deemed to be obscene, and these materials and activities may be banned altogether by municipalities.
- Adult entertainment use can range from bookstores and/or video stores carrying a significant number of sexually-oriented materials, to modeling studios, massage parlors and strip clubs. Many of the common adult entertainment activities, such as adult

Originally published as "Secondary Effects Study of Adult Oriented Businesses," *Report of the Planning Board*, March 7, 2007, by the Planning Board, City of Saratoga Springs, N.Y.

book and video and nude dancing establishments, while sexually explicit are not considered obscene, and are protected by the First Amendment.

Permitted Regulations of Adult Use Is to Mitigate "Secondary Impacts" of Adult Use Establishments.

In *City of Renton v Playtime Theaters*, 475 U.S. 41, 89 L Ed 2d 29, 106 S Ct 925 (1986), the U.S. Supreme Court established a four-part test to determine when zoning regulations for adult businesses do not violate the First Amendment:

- Whether the predominant purpose of the zoning is to suppress the sexually explicit speech itself, or rather, to eliminate the "secondary effects" of adult uses;
- Whether the zoning regulation furthers a substantial governmental interest;
- Whether the zoning regulation is "narrowly tailored" to affect only those uses which produce the unwanted secondary effects; and
- Whether the zoning regulations leave open reasonable alternative locations for adult uses. In the New York case of the *Town of Islip v Caviglia*, 73 N.Y. 2d 544 (1989), the court upheld Islip's regulations allowing adult uses only in an area zoned for industrial use, which the court found provided ample space for the development of such uses.

Hence, the federal and state constitutions protect the *content* of adult entertainment activity.

- Police power justifying zoning regulations cannot be aimed at suppressing or limiting the *content* of the use.
- "When municipal regulations impinge on an adult business's freedom of expression, they lose the presumption of constitutionality that normally applies to zoning regulations, and the burden shifts to local government to justify its restrictions." New York State Department of State Counsel's

Office, Opinions of Counsel: Municipal Regulation of Adult Uses After the *Stringfellow's* Decision.

- Municipal regulations cannot focus on regulating adult uses because of what those uses contain, whether it be sexually explicit printed material, videos, or nude dancing.

Municipalities, however, are allowed to regulate adult uses in a manner that seeks to mitigate the potential *secondary impacts* (increase in crime, drug use, lowering of property values, etc.) often associated with adult entertainment uses.

In the case of *Stringfellow's of New York, Ltd., v City of New York*, the New York State Court of Appeals developed a test for determining the validity of zoning regulations under Article 1, Section 8 of the New York State Constitution, which includes:

- The zoning regulation must be justified by concerns unrelated to speech; i.e. secondary impacts;
- It must be "no broader than necessary" to achieve its purpose:
  — the adult use law should be a coherent regulatory scheme narrowly designed to attack the problems associated with adult establishments;
  — set forth explicit standards for those who apply them to preclude arbitrary and discriminatory application;
  — *affect only the category of uses that produce the unwanted negative effects*; and

The zoning regulation must provide alternative locations for adult uses businesses.

- By preventing adult businesses from locating in residential districts while allowing such establishments to locate in manufacturing and commercial districts, the *Stringfellows* court found the amendment protects only those communities and community institutions that are most vulnerable to their adverse impacts.
- Municipalities may constitutionally bar

adult establishments from, or within, a specified distance of residentially-zoned areas and facilities in which families and children congregate, and may prohibit adult businesses from operating within a specified distance of one another to avoid the undesirable impacts associated with concentration of such uses.

Necessity of Planning Study to Evaluate Secondary Impacts

To justify zoning regulations for adult businesses, municipalities must show that the regulations are not directed at the content of the use, but at the elimination of the negative secondary impacts resulting from that use. These are often demonstrated through secondary effects (or impacts) studies. Based on potential impacts identified in the study, a municipality can then recommend land use controls to regulate these types of uses.

Prior to adopting adult entertainment regulations, a municipal government must therefore demonstrate that it has conducted or relied upon planning studies illustrating the need to protect certain areas of the municipality from the negative secondary impacts associated with adult businesses.

In *Renton v Playtime Theaters*, the Court stated "that the city did not have to produce its own studies ... but must reasonably believe (on the record) that the studies were relevant to its concerns."

While secondary effect studies can take various forms, there are certain elements that should be included in any study. *The Secondary Effects Study of Adult Entertainment Uses* from the Village of Scotia (funded by the New York Planning Federation, and released in September 1999), can be used as a model for how communities prepare these studies and their format.

For its study, the Village of Scotia reviewed studies from Austin and El Paso, Texas; Newport News, Virginia; Garden Grove, Cal-ifornia; Islip and the City of New Rochelle, New York; and Indianapolis, Indiana.

- Research methods included:
  - a comparison of areas that contained adult uses with areas that did not (control areas),
  - a survey of professionals and residents,
  - and gathering statistical data.
- Secondary effects studied included crime rates, impacts on real estate, traffic, noise and general neighborhood appearance.

Based on the review of these studies, the Village of Scotia concluded that all supported the existence of a number of negative secondary effects of adult entertainment uses, such as an increase in crime rates, decline in property values, and a general deterioration, both in reality and perception, of the neighborhoods in which these uses are located. Scotia also found that the studies were relevant to the Village since the studies did not focus on the community as a whole, but on much smaller areas. In addition, the impacts of adult uses on the study area were found to be independent of the size of the municipality.

The Village of Scotia findings that were especially applicable to them included:

- The smaller the commercial district, the larger the impact because the "negative halo" will affect a larger proportion of the municipality's business than it would in a larger city;
- Because of the small size of commercial districts, the probability of substantial impacts of sexually oriented businesses upon residential areas increases, and;
- Smaller places are more likely to have fewer days and hours of commercial activity than larger cities. This increases the likelihood that an adult business will have a larger impact on the area in which it is situated during off-hours for other business increases.

Regulation Recommendation and Local Law

The next step after establishing the potential secondary impacts which adult entertainment uses may have on a community is to identity how best to regulate these uses to minimize the negative impacts on residents and businesses within the municipality.

Before choosing a regulatory method, the Village of Scotia:

- *Reviewed current zoning:* The Village identified which zoning districts would currently allow adult entertainment businesses to locate as a permitted use, siting some of the undefined permitted uses within the Village zoning that an adult entertainment establishment may argue are appropriate classifications for their use. These included, but were not limited to, retail stores and shops, restaurants, theaters, membership clubs, drinking establishments and personal services stores.
- Identified land uses sensitive to potential negative impacts: The Village identified sensitive areas "as possessing characteristics that are essential to the Village's character, quality of life, and economic success." These areas include residential neighborhoods, the central business district, places of worship, schools, childcare facilities, recreation areas, parks and playgrounds, and civic and cultural facilities.
- Reviewed legal considerations and regulatory options: An overview of legal considerations and regulatory options was presented to outline major court decisions that impact local regulation of adult entertainment uses. Regulatory methods of licensing, concentration (which concentrates adult uses within a specific zone), dispersion (which seeks to prevent the concentration of adult uses), and the hybrid method (which concentrates adult uses within a certain zone and additionally restricts adult uses from locating within a certain

distance of identified sensitive areas) were presented as options available. *Id.* at 14–16.

Based on the above analysis, the Village of Scotia decided to adopt a local law regulating adult entertainment uses for the purpose of mitigating the negative secondary impacts potentially caused by such uses. Adult entertainment uses are permitted only in industrial zones within the Village and further restricted from being within a minimum of 500 feet from identified sensitive areas. A minimum separation of 500 feet between adult uses is included, as are signage restrictions.

Summary: When faced with regulating adult entertainment uses, municipalities should remember the following:

- Identify the issues — what causes concern? Adult entertainment uses are often controversial and the issue or issues a municipality is most concerned with should be clearly identified and stated, ideally first addressed in a municipal comprehensive plan. As with any issue, communities should specifically identify what causes concern.
- Identify possible solutions/tools as municipal options — While municipal police power is limited in terms of prohibiting adult entertainment uses, municipalities do have control over where these uses can be located to mitigate possible negative secondary impacts.
- Conduct a Secondary Study — A secondary study is required before drafting any adult use regulations. While there is no required format for secondary studies, municipalities should include secondary impacts, current regulations/zoning, sensitive land uses and legal and regulatory options.
- Draft and implement regulations — Based on the secondary study and municipal options for regulation, draft and implement regulations that best suit the character of your municipality and best address municipal concerns.

- Involve the public — Involving the public throughout the planning and regulatory process helps build a constituency regarding the issues of concern for this community. When dealing with a potentially controversial issue, involving the public can also help educate the community on all aspects of the issue.

Review of Secondary Impacts Studies

Since the City of Saratoga Springs does not have any existing adult oriented businesses, the Planning Board could not undertake its own study of the potential negative secondary impacts that adult use might have. Therefore, the Planning Board relied on existing studies of secondary impacts of adult oriented businesses that were conducted in other communities:

The Planning Board reviewed the following original studies:

- "Secondary Effects Analysis of Adult Oriented Businesses in the Town of Wilton, New York" (1998)
- "Secondary Effects Study of Adult Entertainment Uses" Village of Scotia, New York (1999)

The Village of Scotia report provided a detailed summary of similar studies that had been undertaken in the following communities:

- Austin, Texas
- El Paso, Texas
- Newport News, Virginia
- Garden Grove, California
- Islip, New York
- Indianapolis, Indiana, and
- Rochester, New York.

After the review of the analysis of studies undertaken in other communities, the Planning Board made the following conclusions:

- Crime rates are higher in areas of adult uses.
- Sex crimes are higher in areas near adult uses.
- Residential property values are decreased when in close proximity to adult uses.
- Physical blight near adult uses.
- Near adult uses residential properties are not well maintained, financial institutions are more hesitant to invest, etc.
- Most patrons of adult oriented businesses do not live within one mile of site.

Regulatory Approaches for Saratoga Springs

The Planning Board examined the following three different regulatory approaches:

- Concentration Method: Under this method adult uses would be concentrated within a specific zoning district or geographic area. The concept would be similar to what the City of Boston once did by creating a "combat zone" where the adult uses were concentrated.
- Dispersion Method: Under this method the adult uses would be dispersed throughout the City to prevent concentration. The dispersion is generally accomplished by requiring separation distances between adult oriented businesses and between "sensitive uses" such as residences, parks, schools, places or worship, etc.
- Hybrid Method: Under this approach a variation of the concentrated model is used, but separation distances are also established.

The Planning Board felt that the hybrid method would be the most applicable to conditions of the City.

Approaches Used by Other Communities in the County

The Planning Board reviewed the following summary of the adult use regulations in the following selected communities with Saratoga County:

- Town of Wilton (1998):
  - Prohibited adult uses if located:
    o Within 1,000 feet of any church, school, park, etc.
    o Within 500 feet of another adult use.
    o Permits adult uses in the C-3 Commercial/Light District upon the issuance of a special use permit.
- Town of Halfmoon (2000):
  - Prohibited adult uses if located:
    o Within 1,000 feet of any residential property, church, park, cemetery, etc.
    o Within 1,500 feet of any school.
    o Within 2,500 feet of any place where alcoholic beverages are sold.
- Town of Moreau (2002):
  - Permits adult uses in a M1A District upon the issuance of special use permit.
  - Prohibited adult uses if located:
    o Within 500 feet of a residential use.
    o Within 2,500 feet of any church, school, park, etc.
    o Within 1,000 feet of another adult use.

Recommendations and Findings

The Planning Board makes the following recommendations to the City Council:

1. It is a constitutional requirement for the City to provide for adult uses somewhere within the community.
   - City can't flatly prohibit all adult uses.
   - City can regulate adult uses to mitigate secondary impacts.
   - City is required to undertake a planning analysis to evaluate secondary impacts.
2. The existing regulations for controlling adult uses are not appropriate and should be abandoned for the following reasons:
   - The definitions are old and not inclusive. Since the ordinance was originally adopted in 1990, the adult use industry has changed.
   - The existing regulations relating to adult uses permit the uses to be dispersed in numerous commercial districts through the City provided they are not within 2,500 feet of a school, library, park, playground or place of worship. This has potential adverse impacts on other sensitive land uses such as residential areas, daycare centers, entranceways, cemeteries, community centers, etc.
   - The three geographic areas that currently meet the requirements are:
     - The Transect -4 area zoning district off of Gick Road near Exit 15 = 5 acres
     - The Transect -4 and Transect -5 area off of Church Street between West Avenue and Kirby Road = 63 acres.
     - Highway General Business District area on Route 50 near Northline Road = 5 acres.
   - The existing regulations that require adult uses to be at least 2,500 feet from "sensitive" land use is likely unconstitutional. Most courts have not accepted a separation distance of greater than 1,500 feet.
3. The City should adopt a new ordinance to regulate adult uses because to not have one that meets the constitutional requirements will likely lead to the following:
   - Expose the City to lawsuits that challenge the constitutionality of the current regulations. Such litigation would:
     - Likely be expensive to defend.
     - Likely result in our existing ordinance being overturned.
     - Likely result in the accuser being awarded the rights to establish an adult use in the location of their

choice, with the resultant adverse impact that the City would be unable to control.

4. The various types of adult uses should be divided into three categories:

   • Class I Adult Uses are those that would likely have minimum adverse impact and should be controlled by developing new standard relating to display of materials.

   • Class II Adult Uses are those that would likely have significant adverse impact and should be controlled as to location and design.

   • Class III Adult Uses are those that would likely have detrimental adverse impacts and should be prohibited throughout the City.

5. No Class II Adult Uses should be permitted in a structure that is within:

   • 500 feet of the property line in which an existing single-family, two-family or multiple family dwelling is located.

   • 1,500 feet from the existing property boundary of any public park, off road public bike path, public playground, cemetery, public indoor recreational facility, public library, public or private school, place of worship, public community center or day care facility.

   • 500 feet from any structure where an existing Class II Adult Use is located therein.

   • Any parcel within the downtown area (T-6 and Congress Park Centre PUD districts).

   • Any parcel that is within 100 feet of the right-of-way boundary of any designated entranceways to the City.

   • A structure that has an existing Class II Adult Use located therein.

6. Class II Adult Uses shall only be permitted within a specifically designated "adult use overlay district" which shall be in the following location:

   • The portion of the Industrial-General (IND-G) zoning district that lies within 400 feet of the right-of-way boundaries of Duplainville Road (County Route 46) and Grande Boulevard (County Route 46). This area is approximately 92 acres and currently involves portions of 12 separate tax parcels.

7. Require special development standards for Class I and Class II Adult Uses:

   • The construction of new Class I Adult Uses will require site plan review approval in commercial zoning districts and will have to comply with strict standards relating to the display of adult materials.

   • The construction of new Class II Adult Uses will require site plan review and architectural review with strict standards on outside signs and display.

The Planning Board reviewed this information, discussed their proposed findings and recommendations, and approved the seven points outlined above at their meeting on March 7, 2007. This matter is presently before their City Council for its consideration.

Editor's Notes:

1. A six-page detailed section of the study, called "Survey of Existing Regulations and Conditions" in the City of Saratoga Springs is not included in the above information. Also excluded was a two-page analysis of proposed adult uses by areas, including street and highway locations.

2. The above land-use analysis included sensitive areas for possible adult uses. These areas of the city included schools (public, private, and parochial), libraries, parks and playgrounds, places of worship (churches, convents, monasteries, mosques, and synagogues), community centers, cemeteries, residential neighborhoods, downtown areas, entranceways to the city, and tourist sites.

3. The main criteria used by the Planning Board is included in the above information. The complete report is available on the City of Saratoga Springs website, the address of which is included in the *Appendix* section of this volume under the *Regional Resource Directory*.

CHAPTER 37

Seattle Defines and Regulates Adult Business Uses

Diane M. Sugimura

In May 2005, the City Council approved a work plan for the Department of Planning and Development (DPD) to prepare, with the assistance of the City's Law Department, a legislative proposal defining and regulating adult cabaret uses in appropriate zones in Seattle. DPD proposes that these uses be allowed within the area bounded by:

South Walker Street on the north;
3rd and 4th Avenues South on the west;
Interstate 5 on the east; and
Duwamish Avenue South on the south.

DPD proposes to define adult cabarets, allowing them subject to certain development standards, including maximum size and limits on on-premise signs.

The purpose of the record is to:

(1) identify the land use impacts of adult cabarets;
(2) recommend appropriate locations for adult cabarets; and
(3) recommend applicable development standards.

There are many perceptions about the impacts adult entertainment uses have on a neighborhood or community. This report, however, focuses on impacts that can be addressed through land use regulations. It does not intend to regulate the activity within adult entertainment establishments. After researching current literature, case law, and studies prepared by other jurisdictions, DPD concludes that in addition to generating conventional land use impacts, adult entertainment establishments have the potential for negatively impacting public safety and welfare, and property values.

Context and Background

Zoning regulation of adult entertainment uses has consistently challenged many communities across the country generally due to the perception that these uses degrade property values and are a threat to public safety. Historically in Seattle these uses were located in the downtown area, the majority of which were located along First Avenue. Many citizens continue to identify adult entertainment with this area. However, it was not until adult entertainment businesses began locating in neighborhoods outside downtown that the City began to specifically identify and regulate them through zoning.

Originally published as "Adult Cabarets in Seattle," *Report of the Director*, March 28, 2006, by the Department of Planning and Development, City of Seattle, WA.

Adult motion picture theaters in Seattle were the first regulated, in 1976. In 1979, adult panorams were identified separately and were only allowed in certain downtown zones: Downtown Office Core 1 and 2 (DOC1 & DOC2), and the Downtown Retail Core (DRC) zones.

Over the years several "strip clubs," or adult cabaret establishments, located outside of the downtown area in Seattle's neighborhood business district. Citizen concerns about these uses prompted the City Council to pass an ordinance requiring adult cabarets to be licensed (Ordinance 114225). The Council also placed a moratorium on the establishment of any new topless dancing establishments in these neighborhoods (Ordinance 114254). Both ordinances were passed in November 1988.

DPD (formerly the Department of Construction and Land Use) was directed to make recommendations for amendments to the Land Use Code that would minimize the adverse impacts of adult cabarets. The City Council Public Safety Committee conducted a public hearing on proposed adult cabaret regulations in April 1989. The concerns expressed at that public hearing prompted the Council to extend the moratorium on adult cabarets (Ordinance 114531). This moratorium continued through its last extension in May 2005. In late 2005, the City's moratorium was overturned by the courts. DPD was once again asked to report back to the Council and propose appropriate locations in which to allow adult cabarets and how to regulate them.

Adult Cabarets

"Adult cabaret" refers to establishments where nude and/or semi-nude dancers perform for adult members of the public. Food and/or beverage may or may not be served. Liquor is generally not sold on the premises due to provisions of state liquor laws.

Adult cabarets, also known as strip clubs, topless dance halls, bars, and/or nightclubs have been regulated as "performing arts the-aters" since the 1986 adoption of the Neighborhood Commercial chapter of the Land Use Code. Before 1986, topless dancing establishments were classified as any one of several different uses. Depending on the type of operation, they may have been classified as restaurants, taverns, dance halls, theaters or indoor places of public assembly. Today, as in the past, topless dancing establishments are prohibited in residential zones, and permitted in all commercial (except NC1), industrial (except for the Duwamish Manufacturing and Industrial Center) and downtown zones.

Of the adult cabarets now in business, one is located in the Downtown Mixed Commercial zone (DMC 125). Some form of adult entertainment use has existed at this location intermittently for many years. This business is also licensed as a panoram location. Two adult cabarets are located in a Neighborhood Commercial 2 (NC2) zone, one of which has been at the same location for over 30 years. The only other adult cabaret is located in a C1 zone.

Regulation of Adult Uses

Over the years, the establishment of adult uses in Seattle's neighborhood commercial areas has generated a number of citizen complaints. Community groups, business associations, and hundreds of individuals have testified at public hearings or through letters and emails, expressing their concerns about: liter; noise; traffic; the decline in property values; increases in insurance rates; and fears about burglary, vandalism, rape, assaults, drugs, and prostitution. Many comments have been received on the overall detrimental influence of adult uses on the community.

Local governments must always be cautious in regulating adult uses. Arts and entertainment uses, regardless of whether they are intended for adult audiences only, involve protected forms of expression under the First Amendment to the United States Constitution. This constitutional amendment is often cited in case law involving regulation of adult entertainment businesses. The First Amendment has been the standard against which regulations affecting adult entertainment uses must be measured.

Licensing is one traditional method used by local governments to regulate adult entertainment uses. This approach often requires owners, operators, and/or employees to provide detailed information. Licensing regulations often specify facility and operational standards. Seattle Municipal Code chapter 6.270 is an example of such a license regulation. This business regulation requires topless dancing establishments to be licensed with the City. Licensing is an effective method for addressing performance-oriented standards. As a general rule, zoning and land use regulation is more effective at addressing locational issues and land use impacts.

In the 1976 landmark decision of *Young v. American Mini Theaters, Inc.*,[1] the U.S. Supreme Court declared that adult entertainment uses can be subject to carefully tailored local regulations. In order for a land use regulation of adult entertainment to be valid, the local jurisdiction must provide adequate opportunities for this type of expression. In other words, zoning cannot be used directly or indirectly to ban adult cabarets, or other forms of adult entertainment.

In summary, the Court determined that regulations can be imposed to minimize adverse land use impacts of adult entertainment establishments. This can be accomplished by specifying the zones where adult entertainment uses are most compatible with the surrounding neighborhood. Another land use regulation is to require that minimum distances be maintained between adult entertainment uses and/or other uses that may be more sensitive to the impacts of adult uses. In this U.S. Supreme Court case, *City of Renton v. Playtime Theaters, Inc.*,[2] it was held that a city is entitled to rely on the experience of other cities in enacting regulatory legislation. Both the *Young* and *Renton* decisions have been used

in many cities to support local zoning regulation of adult entertainment uses.

Seattle, like many other jurisdictions, relied on the Young decision to restrict adult motion picture theaters to downtown. Citing *Young* again in 1979, the City limited the areas where adult panorams could be located. In 1985, Seattle's new Downtown Plan established a policy to encourage downtown residential development. The downtown chapter of the Land Use Code reflected this policy by authorizing adult motion picture theaters and adult panorams only in three non-residential downtown zones: Downtown Office Core 1 (DOC1), Downtown Office Core 2 (DOC2) and the Downtown Retail Core (DRC). To date, adult motion picture theaters and adult panorams are the only two forms of adult entertainment uses identified specifically in Seattle's land use regulations.

Land Use Impacts

Overview

Land use regulation is based on the concept of compatibility. Generally, the City's commercial, industrial, and downtown policies encourage a variety of businesses that are compatible with each other and the residential areas they serve. Some uses, however, have impacts which are not compatible with other uses or create unavoidable impacts on surrounding properties.

Uses such as animal shelters, towing services, or construction yards are examples of commercial uses that have objectionable impacts and are not compatible with residential areas or other neighborhood serving businesses in a pedestrian environment. They are specifically identified in the Land Use Code and allowed only where the impacts they generate are minimized.

Adult motion picture theaters were determined not to be compatible near residential neighborhoods oriented towards families with children. This conclusion was found in a study entitled "Zoning Controls for Adults-Only Theaters" prepared by the City Planning Commission in 1976.[3] In order to determine in what zones adult entertainment uses should be permitted, it is necessary to survey their impacts and determine with what other uses they are compatible.

During the City Council's public hearing on licensing of adult uses, many citizens spoke of their concerns about these businesses in their neighborhoods. Problems with litter, noise, parking and traffic; inappropriate signage; fears about deteriorating property values, attraction of undesirable transients, and increases in crime; potential hazards for children and personal safety were cited. Citizens generally protested that adult entertainment uses interfere with their ability to raise their children in a healthy, family environment.

The decision by the City in 1976 to allow adult motion picture theaters only in the downtown area was based on findings that these same impacts were detrimental to residential areas. This decision was upheld by the Washington State Supreme Court in the Northend Cinema case.[4] In another case, *Village of Belle Terre v. Borass*,[5] the U.S. Supreme Court recognized that local governments have the right to use zoning based on impacts of family values to protect the public welfare.

Many studies prepared by other communities have documented that litter, noise, traffic impacts, public safety impacts (e.g. burglaries, vandalism, assaults, prostitution), and deteriorating property values often occur in association with adult entertainment uses.

Conventional Impacts

Under-represented in many planning studies prepared by other communities are the conventional land use impacts that are often generated by adult entertainment uses. Noise, litter, parking and traffic are impacts commonly associated with adult entertainment businesses.

Because adult entertainment businesses are generally visited late at night, they are often the source of complaints about noise. The noise may come from the starting or idling of cars on or near the premises, and from car sound systems. It may be generated by the business's own sound system, or by disorderly patrons. There may also be secondary noise effects. Noise may be created by police and emergency vehicles called in and around adult entertainment establishments in response to disturbances.

Litter is another common problem cited. Since alcoholic beverages are generally not available at adult entertainment businesses in Seattle, neighbors report that beer bottles/cans and other liquor containers are frequently tossed into nearby yards. Food wrappers, condoms and other refuse were among other items neighbors complained were discarded in and around the vicinity of existing adult establishments.

Generally, adult cabarets are auto-oriented. The observation is made in recognition that these businesses are frequented by patrons who wish some degree of anonymity and ease of access and egress that limits visual contact with surrounding uses and pedestrians. Consequently, these are uses that are not necessarily consistent with pedestrian areas and generate a potentially substantial amount of traffic. In addition, normal traffic flow may be disrupted by police and emergency vehicles that may be called to the scene of a disturbance. On-street parking may be usurped, especially near existing adult cabarets, where little off-street parking is provided.

Secondary Impacts

In a report published by the American Planning Association, *Everything You Wanted to Know about Regulating Sex Businesses* (Kelly and Cooper, Planning Advisory Service Report No. 495-96, Chicago 2000), many major studies were reviewed and the following findings were synthesized from them.[6]

1. Real estate professionals believe that there is a significant negative impact of adult entertainment businesses and other adult-related entertainment businesses (such as bars with live entertainment) on both residential and business properties. The impacts are less if there is a separation between the studied use and the other use. Beyond 1,000 feet there may be some impact but beyond 1,500 feet there is no basis for believing that there will be any impact on property values. (Rochester, Indianapolis, New York City; some supporting data from Denver).

2. The greatest impacts on property values are on other properties on the same block. (Denver, Rochester).

3. The impacts on property values affect residential properties more than nonresidential properties. (Rochester, Indianapolis).

4. The studies showing the most significant impacts of adult entertainment businesses on neighborhoods involved significant numbers of businesses with live entertainment and/or direct interaction between patrons and entertainers or other employees. (Newport News, St. Paul, Whittier).

5. There is a lower correlation of crime incidents with retail adult entertainment businesses than with those that involve on-premises entertainment of any kind. (Denver).

6. Although there is some evidence of an increase in crime, particularly around concentrations of adult entertainment businesses (Phoenix, Denver, Indianapolis, Whittier, St. Paul), the increase is not necessarily in violent crimes. (Phoenix, Denver).

7. At least two cities that studied the issue clearly had prostitution flourishing in some adult businesses. (Denver, Whittier).

PROPERTY VALUES

Decline of adjacent property values is another documented land use impact resulting from adult entertainment uses. A study of appraisers, residents and business owners provides some key information regarding this issue.

Indianapolis, Indiana

In 1984, an analysis of adult entertainment businesses undertaken by the City of Indianapolis was conducted by that city's Department of Metropolitan Development.[7] With the assistance of the Indiana University School of Business, they conducted a national survey of Members of the Appraisal Institute (MAI), and the American Institute of Real Estate Appraisers. This survey was intended to determine the market effect of adult entertainment businesses on nearby land values. It was concluded that "adult entertainment businesses — even a relatively passive one such as an adult bookstore — have serious negative effects on their immediate environment." Next-door properties were most affected, decreasing substantially in order of adjacency. Negative impact on property values was substantiated for properties within three blocks of an adult entertainment use. While respondents felt that both residential and commercial properties were affected, residential properties were more severely impacted.

Fort Worth, Texas

A recent survey of appraisers in the Fort Worth–Dallas Metroplex carefully documented the opinions of these real estate professionals about the effects of sexually oriented businesses on the values of surround properties.[8] In a survey submitted to 186 appraisers who carry the professional MAI certification (Member of the Appraisal Institute) and SRA (Senior Residential Appraiser), with 41 responses, the following conclusions were drawn:

• Appraisers were nearly unanimous in responding that adult-oriented businesses of any kind (stores, arcades, or cabarets) would decrease single-family home property values. Other uses deemed similarly detrimental to property values included homeless shelters, bars, and pawnshops.

- More than 70 percent of the appraisers judged the influence of adult-oriented businesses on property values to extend beyond 3000 feet (or approximately 6 blocks). While a few suggested the influence was not felt quite so far, even the lowest estimates put the distance at 1000 feet. The average distance was between 2700 and 2800 feet. Only homeless shelters were considered to influence property values that far away. Pawnshops, bars, and gas stations were next (2300 to 2500 feet).

- The appraisers considered the property values of community shopping centers to be equally detrimentally affected by the proximity of adult-oriented businesses. More than 7 percent considered adult uses to decrease commercial property values. The only use considered to be comparable in its decreasing of property values was homeless shelters. Pawnshops and bars were next in their impact on lowering appraised values for community shopping centers but to a much lower degree (53 percent and 32 percent, respectively).

- Approximately 50 percent of the appraisers felt adult-oriented businesses impact shopping centers' appraised values beyond 3000 feet. As compared to single-family homes, the distances at which appraised values would no longer be affected by an adult use was somewhat less. Other respondents felt that it only took from 2200 to 2300 feet before an adult use had no impact on the appraised value of a shopping center. Only homeless shelters were suggested to have a further reach (2400 feet). Again, pawnshops and bars were next in their influence on property values within 2000 and 1900 feet, respectively.

- The vast majority of appraisers agreed that a concentration or cluster of detrimental uses had a greater negative impact than isolated uses.

- Three negative uses grouped together were considered by most appraisers to be the level at which the impact was greater. The grouping was considered to occur if uses were within approximately 1000 feet of each other. They felt the concentration ceased to have an impact at an average distance of 3800 feet (as compared to approximately 2300 to 2800 feet single uses).

- Slightly more than 20 percent of appraisers felt that the answers to the survey questions might be influenced by their "personal, moral, or ethical beliefs." This means the findings may be slightly skewed negatively towards adult-oriented businesses.

Because the response rate was lower than in some surveys, the margin of error was 13.7 percent; but, in response to many of the questions, more than 80 percent (and in some cases more than 90 percent) agreed on the nature and extent of the adverse secondary effects of sexually oriented businesses on other properties; thus, even applying the worst-case margin of error to the findings, a significant majority of the appraisers believed that these effects would occur.

Rochester, New York

The City of Rochester, New York, conducted a survey of 39 property appraisers to determine their perceptions of impacts of sexually oriented businesses on residential and commercial property values. This was important since most ordinances deal with sexually oriented businesses by requiring them to be separated by some specified distance (typically between 500 and 1500 feet) from certain categories of land use. The Rochester survey attempted to find a relationship between distance and impacts on property.

Based on the results of the survey, appraisers in the Rochester, Monroe County area have the following views on the impact of sexually oriented businesses:

- Bars with nude servers or live entertainers clearly have the greatest negative impact on surrounding property values;
- Sexually oriented businesses have a measurable negative impact on the value of some neighboring property;
- There is significantly more negative impact on the value of neighboring residential property than on commercial property;
- The greatest impact on property values is on properties located on the same block;
- The impact on property value is less significant if located along the same street than if located on the same block; however, it is of greater significance than any particular distance separation;
- Based on a combination of responses, if two properties are equidistant from the same *studied business*, with one located on the same street as the *studied business* and the other on another street, the property located on the same street as the *studied business* will suffer greater impacts;
- The negative impact decreases with distance and stops somewhere between 1,000 and 1,500 feet.[8]

Public Safety

In the law and planning literature on adult entertainment uses, public safety hazards are the most often cited adverse land use impacts for surrounding neighborhoods. Some evidence indicates that crime rates increase with the presence of adult entertainment uses. The major crimes frequently mentioned include: burglaries, assaults, indecent exposure, and prostitution. The criminal activity is often associated with areas in which a concentration of adult entertainment is allowed to prosper.

New York City police found that serious crime complaints ran almost 70 percent higher on police posts that contained adult uses.[9] The cities of Cleveland, Ohio[11]; Indianapolis, Indiana[7]; Los Angeles, Calfornia[12]; and Austin, Texas[13]; among others have documented that crime rates were anywhere from 15 percent to 77 percent higher in areas containing adult businesses than those areas containing no adult businesses. A study in Phoenix, Arizona,[14] concluded that not only was there a higher rate of sex-related crimes in areas where adult businesses were located, but that rate was significantly higher where there were several adult businesses adjacent to one anther.

Most cities prefer to disperse adult entertainment uses, where adult entertainment uses are allowed throughout the community. There are usually special conditions which require these businesses to maintain a certain distance from each other and from public schools and residential zones. Law enforcement strategies are usually less effective when a dispersed approach is used.

A concentrated approach is one that allow adult entertainment uses in one small compact area. This concentrated approach is often used to contain adult entertainment businesses that are historically concentrated in an area. In such cases studies have shown a higher incidence of crime than other business district in a city.[14] While reports of crime may be comparatively high, it should be noted that in these concentrated or historical "skid row" areas, there are generally many other potentially problematic uses, such as taverns, lounges, and nightclubs, also concentrated in the zone.

Adult entertainment uses are, generally, auto-oriented or destination-type uses attracting a regional clientele. Trade characteristics studies in Bothell, Washington,[16] and Austin, Texas,[13] confirmed that at least one half of all customers frequenting adult businesses came from outside the city limits (one investigation in Bothell found that of 321 vehicles checked, only 8 were registered in their city). In Austin, less than 5 percent were located within a one-mile radius of the establishment.

While there are many businesses that may attract a regional clientele, the fact that adult entertainment uses may have an increased potential for criminal activity makes them more of a public safety risk to a neighborhood. People who patronize these establishments may have no sense of identity with or regard for the neighborhood in which these businesses may be located. They may also be less inhibited in their personal behavior than if they were in their own community.

No known analyses or comparative studies have been conducted in Seattle to verify a correlation between adult entertainment uses and criminal activity. It is assumed that adult entertainment uses in Seattle are not unlike those in other cities. It is also not assumed that all adult uses generate or are involved in criminal conduct. But as evidence in the foregoing discussion, there is enough documentation to demonstrate a link between adult entertainment uses and the potential for increased criminal activity.

The secondary effects of police response to a business have already been noted. The noise from sirens, flashing lights, and traffic hazards created by police and emergency vehicles are disturbances not conducive to healthy business or residential environments. The increased potential for crime, together with these effects, result in impacts that are likely to be more substantial than those of other neighborhood commercial uses, intended to serve the needs of surrounding residents.

Analysis and Recommendation

The recommendation to restrict adult cabaret uses to industrial zones is based on the following analysis. Compared with the potential land use impacts of adult cabarets in different areas of the City, adult cabarets uses would be least intrusive and have substantially fewer impacts in industrial areas. The location of an adult cabaret use shares greater compatibility with surrounding uses in industrial areas, and would not have the same negative influence on property values, or contribute to an escalation of criminal activities in and around residential neighborhoods, and would result in the least negative impacts to pedestrians, particularly to children.

Approximately 12 percent of Seattle's land area is industrially zoned. Of Seattle's industrially-zoned land, more than 90 percent is contained within the City's two manufacturing and industrial centers (MIC): Ballard/Interbay (17 percent) and Duwamish (77 percent). An additional 295 acres is zoned industrial outside of the two centers. Nearly 75 percent of the City's industrially-zoned land is used for industrial purposes (as measured by the King County assessor's office, these include industrial uses, warehousing, transportation/utilities/communications, and institutional/public facilities). About 25 percent of the land is used for non-industrial purposes, including commercial uses, "other" uses (parking, etc.), and open space. Most entertainment uses are permitted in industrial zones. Prior to the moratorium, adult cabarets were permitted in industrial zones; however none have historically chosen to locate in these zones.

The Ballard/Interbay MIC generally abuts commercial and residential neighborhoods around the Magnolia, Queen Anne and Ballard neighborhoods. While much of the Duwamish area is dominated by Port-related industry, transportation and distribution activities, and borders the Pioneer Square and Chinatown/International District neighborhoods. The area also contains the City's major league sport stadia on the north, and is bordered by significant topography and the Interstate 5 freeway on the east. Recognizing that some industrial areas of the city may not be suitable for adult entertainment uses, the DPD was asked to examine the impacts of locating adult entertainment uses in a specific portion of the Duwamish industrial area. Since there are no shoreline designations in this area, preferred water-dependent or water-related uses are not affected. The remainder of the discussion in this section pertains to this sub-area.

Warehousing, transportation, and distribution uses are critical activities in this area. Parcels are generally large, often created by consolidation of half to full blocks. The average lot size is 1.5 acres for unimproved sites and 1.1 acres when improved. The platting pattern and the freight network make the area especially suited for these activities and give it its working industrial identity.

Three major rail corridors subdivide the area and limit local east-west traffic. Buildings are often large, and characteristic of industrial uses, having few openings. Open sites are often devoted to parking or storage. Commercial activity is concentrated along two major arterials, Fourth Avenue South and Airport Way South.

Residential development is currently prohibited in industrial zones with two exceptions: artist's studio/dwellings in existing structures and caretaker's quarters. There are no playgrounds, public or private schools, or other institutions, although some vocational training may take place in this area. The nearest school is located east of Interstate 5, approximately ½ mile from the study area. The nearest residential zones are on Beacon Hill located east of Interstate 5, which provides an effective barrier, and Georgetown to the South.

The Seattle Comprehensive Plan recognizes the importance of industrial businesses to the City's economy, consistent with state and regional growth management objectives, and supports protecting the limited supply of large parcels of land zoned for industrial use in the City from factors that would negatively affect investment in the area. The City's industrial lands policy has historically been able to provide a stable industrial environment and to protect viable industries, and family wage jobs, from competing uses.

While not a residential neighborhood, and not associated with family activity that generally is central to the opposition to adult businesses elsewhere in the city, the Duwamish area possesses some vulnerability to the potentially negative impacts of adult entertainment businesses. Industrial area employers have reported that it can be difficult to recruit employees because of perceived public safety risks that accompany isolated areas. Pedestrian infrastructure is limited and there is often inadequate parking. The public transportation system is limited and does not often address the needs of shift work schedules. Outlying suburban locations often provide more incentives at lower costs. These factors often discourage investment in the area.

Industrial uses are also dependent on certain commercial uses for support. Allowing the location of adult entertainment uses could negatively affect the desirability of those sites for industrial support functions. If permitted, adult entertainment businesses would not necessarily compete directly for sites with industrial uses, but rather for those sites where other commercial businesses in industrial areas prefer to locate.

Public safety issues are a concern in the Duwamish study area, not necessarily because of proximity to residential or neighborhood commercial development, but because the development pattern necessary for industrial activity and its inherent isolation contribute to the more vulnerable appearance of the area. Large lot and block configurations create a platting pattern that makes east-west local access difficult. The combinations of dead end streets, lack of pedestrian lighting, large site layout, outdoor storage of materials, and the lack of oversight provided by pedestrian activity could hamper law enforcement strategies.

Allowing adult entertainment businesses throughout this large area may increase the perception of public safety risks for people working in or visiting the area and property values could be negatively affected, as well. However, the effect on property values is considered far less likely in industrial areas due in large part to the character of the area and the already lower property values associated with industrial activity than would be true downtown or in other mixed used commercial neighborhoods throughout Seattle.

While there is no historical precedent for adult entertainment businesses operating in this area, in the past, concerns were raised about what effects the proximity of adult entertainment uses to traditional trades will have on businesses and their employees.

The economic vitality of the Duwamish industrial areas is dependent on maintaining incentives for industrial businesses and employees to remain in the City. Incentives that encourage employment, customer and support services should not be eroded. Allowing adult entertainment businesses to locate in the study area could negatively impact these incentives and contribute to the out-migration of industrial businesses from the City.

However, the most compelling arguments for limiting adult entertainment uses are to reduce the potential for public safety and property value impacts on the broadest number of citizens, in residential, commercial and mixed use neighborhoods throughout the City, where the majority of citizens live and work. Comparing the land use impacts of adult entertainment uses in the different areas of the City, adult cabaret uses would be least intrusive in industrial areas than in downtown and other Seattle, pedestrian-oriented residential and mixed use neighborhoods.

Recommendations

Adult cabarets are proposed to be prohibited in all zones except that portion of the Duwamish industrial area, and defined generally as:

South Walker Street on the north;
3rd and 4th Avenues South on the west;
Interstate 5 on the east; and
Duwamish Avenue South on the south.

South Walker Street is recommended as the northern boundary because it provides a sufficient distance from the historical and mixed use neighborhoods of Pioneer Square and the Chinatown/International District,

and from frequent events at the city's major sports facilities.

3rd and 4th Avenues South provide a western boundary that distinguishes the area from the retail centers on 1st Avenues South and the Port activity and transportation corridors associated with the Duwamish.

Interstate 5 provides a formidable eastern boundary, limiting mobility between Beacon Hill and the industrial neighborhood to the west. Interstate 5, in combination with a substantial topographic change, effectively protects the single family and mixed use neighborhoods to the east on Beacon Hill.

The proposed southern boundary is defined by the right-of-way for the diagonal rail yards on Duwamish Avenue South. This boundary would provide a necessary buffer in both distance and transition to the residential area of Georgetown, approximately ¼ to ½ mile to the south.

The area recommended in which to allow adult cabarets would provide adequate locational opportunities for adult entertainment uses away from most residential uses, and pedestrian-oriented mixed use neighborhoods.

Definition

"Adult cabaret" is proposed to be defined as a place of public assembly where licensing as "adult entertainment purposes" is required by Seattle Municipal Code 6.270.

Maximum Size of Use

The size of an establishment has some correlation with the potential for impacts associated with the business. The larger the business the greater traffic or parking it is likely to generate, the greater the number of patrons on site at any one time, etc. The City's environmental laws governing traditional project or development-related impacts (SEPA) establishes a threshold for environmental review of establishments that exceed 12,000 square feet of gross floor area in industrial areas. However, non-industrial uses or those that may have unforeseen consequences on industrial uses in the area, such as retail, office or residential, are either limited in size compared to industrial use (e.g. office or retail) or generally prohibited (e.g. residential). Restaurants are limited to 5,000 square feet of gross floor area. Given the secondary impacts associated with adult cabarets, and their general common traits with uses such as restaurants, a common size limit is appropriate.

Two existing adult entertainment establishments in the city are in the range of 4,000 to 6,000 square feet of gross floor area. Generally, facilities in the 4,000 to 7,000 square foot size range appear to be the norm and the proposed maximum size limit, not to exceed 5,000 square feet, is believed to be an economically viable maximum size for an adult cabaret use in Seattle.

Separation from Sensitive Uses

In order to minimize the impact of adult cabarets on sensitive uses, it is proposed that any new or expanding adult cabaret be located no closer than 1,000 feet from any religious institution, childcare facility, or any facility operated by the Seattle Public School System that provides public instruction to children, community center, park, or light rail transit station. Of these uses from which adult cabarets must maintain a minimum distance, only a light rail transit station (passenger service is scheduled to begin in 2009) is currently located within the area in which adult cabarets are proposed to be permitted. Interstate 5 effectively separates the area in which adult cabarets would be allowed from the residential and mixed use neighborhoods adjoining this area to the east.

Nonconforming Uses

DPD recommends that existing uses made nonconforming in their present location be allowed to continue. They may maintain, repair, renovate, or structurally alter the structure to accommodate the elderly or disabled. Once a nonconforming use is discontinued for more than a year, it cannot be reestablished or recommenced.

Signs

DPD also recommends that pole or roof signs that are visible from State Route 99, the Spokane Street Viaduct, or Interstate 5 are not permitted in conjunction with an adult cabaret.

NOTES

1. Young v. American Mini Theaters, Inc. 427 U.S. 50, 49 L. Ed. 2d. 310, 96 S. Ct. 2440 (1976).
2. City of Renton v. Playtime Theaters, Inc., 475 U.S. 41, 89 L. Ed. 2d. 29, 106 S. Ct. 925 (1986).
3. Seattle Department of Community Development, City Planning Commission, Zoning Controls for Adults-Only Theaters; March 11, 1976.
4. Northend Cinema, Inc. v. City of Seattle, 90 Wn. 2nd 709.585 P2nd 1153 (1978).
5. Village of Belle Terre v. Borass, 416 U.S. 1, 39 L. Ed. 2d. 797, 94 S. Ct. 1536 (1974).
6. Bibliography of cited studies on secondary impacts from:

- Kelly and Cooper, *Everything You Wanted to Know about Regulating Sex Businesses*, Planning Advisory Service PAS Report No. 495-96. Chicago: American Planning Association, 2000;
- Newport News: *Adult Use Study*, Newport News Department of Planning and Development, March 1996.
- Rochester: *Survey of Appraisers in Monroe County, New York*, Summer 2000.
- St. Paul: *Effects on Surrounding Area of Adult Entertainment Businesses in Saint Paul*, June 1978, City of Saint Paul Division of Planning, Department of Planning and Management; and Community Crime Prevention Project, Minnesota Crime Control Planning Board.
- Tucson: *The Tucson "study"* actually consists of two memos: one from the Citizens Advisory Planning Committee, addressed to the Mayor and City Council, and dated May 14, 1990; and the other from an Assistant Chief of Police to the City Prosecutor, regarding "Adult Entertainment Ordinance," dated May 1, 1990.
- Denver: *"A Report on the Secondary Impact of Adult Use Businesses in the City of Denver,"* prepared by multiple city departments for Denver City Council, January 1998.
- Whittier: *"Staff Report, Whittier City Planning Commission*; Subject: Adult Business Regulations," July 11, 1994.
- Duncan Associates, Eric Damian Kelly and Connie B. Cooper, Survey of Appraisers, Fort Worth and Dallas: *Effects of Sexually Oriented Businesses on Surrounding Property Values*. Conducted for the City of Fort Worth. September 2004.

7. City of Indianapolis, Indiana, Department of Metropolitan Development, Division of Planning. *Adult Entertainment Businesses in Indianapolis: An Analysis.* 1984.

8. Duncan Associates, Eric Damian Kelly and Connie B. Cooper, Survey of Appraisers, Forth Worth and Dallas: *Effects of Sexually Oriented Businesses on Surrounding Property Values.* Conducted for the City of Forth Worth. September 2004.

9. Kelly and Cooper, *Everything You Wanted to Know about Regulating Sex Businesses,* Planning Advisory Service PAS Report No. 495-96. Chicago: American Planning Association, 2000; pages 51–57.

10. Toner, William. *U.S. Cities Face Combat in the Erogenous Zone, Planning,* Vol. 43. Chicago: American Society of Planning Officials, September 1977.

11. *Regulating Sex Business.* Planning Advisory Service, Report No. 7. Chicago: American Society of Planning Officials, May 1977.

12. City of Cleveland, Ohio, Police Department. Special Investigation Unit Report, August 1977.

13. City of Los Angeles, California, Department of City Planning. *Study of the Effects of the Concentration of Adult Entertainment Establishments in the City of Los Angeles.* June 1977.

14. City of Austin, Texas, Office of Land Development Services. *Report on Adult Oriented Businesses in Austin.* May 1986.

15. City of Phoenix, Arizona, Planning Department. *Adult Business Study.* May 1979.

16. Pratter, Jerome and Connie Hager, "Zoning Laws, Not Obscenity Laws, Offer the Way to Control Adult Entertainment," *Nation's Cities Weekly,* Vol. 3, April 21, 1980.

17. City of Bothell, Police Department Investigations. 1984.

Editor's Note:

While citation number 10 in the Notes is listed as a reference source, it is not listed as a specific citation in the article.

CHAPTER 38

Shoreline Adult Business Group Tries to Change the City Government

Robert Deis *and* Larry Bauman

Special interests are nothing new to local governments. We deal with them all the time and often find ways to balance their interests with those of the wider community. Not all special interests, however, are willing to compromise their narrow agendas for the sake of the community's broader values. This article is about one such case, a case in which a special interest not only decided not to compromise but also pursued a strategy for gaining a decisive role in reshaping the foundation of a newly incorporated city government.

Whenever special interests possess sufficient funding to pursue their causes, they can pose special challenges for city and county management. When they do, they seldom have the power, ingenuity, and desire to attempt to overturn the basic form of a city government. One such group, however, tried to do exactly this in the new incorporated city of Shoreline, Washington, before the city's third anniversary.

Charter Election

This particular special interest was a powerful arm of the region's adult entertainment industry, masking itself as a "good government" cause. When the Shoreline City Council, basing its actions on documented concerns about prostitution and other illegal activities, began a process to regulate so-called "lap dancing" at adult cabarets, this particular business decided to challenge the very foundation of the city. The strategic weapon employed against the city was a charter election.

It was an attempt to gain voter support for a ballot measure that would have eventually imposed a charter on the city, forced the entire current council out of office, and appointed a charter commission charged with designing a brand-new city government and then staging new elections for its leadership.

Fortunately, this charter effort not only went down to defeat but failed by a margin of 80 percent. While to some degree the winning margin was a vindication for the accomplishments of the first two-and-a-half years in this city, the real story is why and how the vote even occurred. The story exemplifies how a wealthy special-interest group can cost a local government money by staging unwanted elections, and also how the narrow interests of one

Originally published as "How a Special Interest Tried to Change Our Form of Governance," *Public Management*, Vol. 81, No. 1, January 1999, by the International City/County Management Association, Washington, DC. Reprinted with permission of the publisher.

business can potentially unravel several years of community self-determination efforts.

This case history shows how special interests can attempt to use the democratic process itself to forward their specific agendas in their efforts to avoid local government regulation and control. Finally, it also demonstrates how a community, when threatened from outside, can coalesce to defend itself and thus can succeed after all.

Incorporation

Shoreline is a largely residential community contiguous to Seattle's northern border, with a population of 52,000. Incorporated in August 1995, this suburban city was pretty much built out in the 1940s through the 1960s, with roughly half of the city developed in older but relatively affluent neighborhoods. The balance of the city consists mainly of relatively modest neighborhoods built right after World War II.

These neighborhoods will require careful attention in the near future to maintain their stability. The major business district in the city is Aurora Avenue (state Highway 99), which was built primarily for automobile use with no pedestrian amenities (no median strips, sidewalks or trees, few protected crosswalks, and so forth).

Aurora Avenue is made up of older buildings, some of which are vacant, with many small to medium-sized retail businesses struggling to stay open. As a result, some of the major goals of the new city have included economic development, reconstruction of the inherited deficient infrastructure, and improvement in overall governmental services.

Incorporation for Shoreline was prompted by several factors: a long-held dissatisfaction with the level of some county services; the sense that local community concerns were not necessarily high priorities for the county government; and the implementation of the state's Growth Management Act, which encouraged all urbanized places within incorporated areas to incorporate or become annexed by adjacent cities. The leaders in Shoreline who mounted the incorporation campaign, after carefully studying the options under state law, chose the council-manager form of government because they believed it would best suit their goal of a professionally administered local government directed by an elected, part-time council.

Before incorporation, along Aurora Avenue, the city had become a venue for prostitutes offering their services within close proximity to schools. After incorporation, the city's new police department was quick in eliminating this activity. The city also has various adult entertainment establishments, including adult video parlors and one adult cabaret (strip club).

Like other localities in the state of Washington, we in Shoreline have documented various illegal activities and ancillary effects on neighboring businesses. As a result, and again like other local governments in the state, Shoreline has adopted some additional regulations to provide more surety that behavior in these businesses would comport with the law. The relatively new council has been careful to recognize that these businesses were protected under the First Amendment; councilmembers simply wanted them to comply with the law.

Lawsuit

In response to the new regulations, an adult entertainment establishment promptly sued the city. The strip club hired a professional firm to gather signatures to place a measure on the ballot that would create a new form of government. Once sufficient signatures had been gathered to place the item on the ballot, citizens began to call city hall.

They protested that they had been misled by the signature gatherers and that, if they had understood what they were signing, they simply would not have signed. Nevertheless,

Shoreline was forced to schedule an election that cost it $35,000 to hold.

Shoreline had originally been formed under the state of Washington's Optional Municipal Code. As a result, the city had received its authority through state law (not a charter) that has some of the strongest language for a council-manager model. On the other hand, the ballot measure, financed by a single strip club, was asking voters to found a charter commission that would be required to draft a charter for the city.

While there always was an option to keep the council-manager form under the new charter, it was fairly evident that the adult entertainment industry wanted to exert more political influence on regulations. It was not clear how this additional influence would have been sought through the new charter.

If the voters had approved the charter commission, another vote would have been required within the following six months to approve or disapprove the new charter written by the commission. In addition, the existing council would have been abolished, and all seven councilmembers would have had to run for office again. This second election would have cost another $35,000.

Added to this cost would have been the impact of a huge distraction to the organization and the community. Note that the entire city council had just recently stood for reelection and had taken office only three months before this new initiative came up. So, within a year of running for and taking office, elected officials could have been forced to run again for the new city government.

City Strategy

As readers might know, the challenge of creating a new city organization is formidable task difficult to overstate. Because of growing pains in the first year, the city had hired its third manager by the close of its first anniversary. Needless to say, a huge amount of organization development was needed to deal with administration turnover.

Barely more than a year after Shoreline's incorporation and before it had begun operating a public works department, the city suffered a devastating washout downstream of 50,000 cubic yards of soil and an arterial-street intersection during a 1997 New Year's Eve storm. Local utilities lost millions of dollars of infrastructure. The damage was so severe that it was featured in *Time* magazine and numerous newspapers throughout the world. Elected officials, including Vice President Al Gore, came to visit Shoreline.

Then, as the storm damage was repaired in record time while the organization also was being rebuilt, the election and its new challenge confronted the city. As key opinion leaders organized to fight this attempt to buy a new form of governance, the council officially opposed the charter measure. While the ballot measure was an additional challenge to an already burdened city, this event had the side benefit of galvanizing a group of citizen supporters who covered the political spectrum. Even against the backdrop of staunch partisan politics that is involved in many Seattle-area local government elections, we saw conservatives and liberals alike meeting weekly to fight this challenge together, as the Vote No Charter Committee.

As the election neared, proponents of the ballot measure hired a polling firm from Denver to solicit community opinions about individuals in the community affiliated with the Vote No Charter Committee. They even went to far as to include survey questions regarding councilmembers' spouses and the city manager. The result of the survey were never divulged, but many of us surmised that the results confirmed that the strip club-financed ballot measure had no chance of passing.

Community Support

Yes, there was a rainbow behind the gray cloud! The results of the election were overwhelming, with 90 percent of the voters axing the idea of a charter commission. It is important to note that the vote was not entirely a vote of confidence for the city's first two-and-a-half years; it also was a strong statement against the local adult entertainment industry.

We made sure that the press and the community knew who was behind the ballot measure. Yet our city council, like any council, was bombarded by the usual small group of critics and wanted to know how the larger community really felt about its work. Ultimately, the pain of this additional challenge (beyond those of the natural disaster and the administrative turnover) had the unintended benefit of blowing a fresh breeze of confidence into the new council: a 90 percent affirmative vote is rare by anyone's standard.

The irony of this series of events cannot be overlooked. The community had overwhelmingly voted to incorporate, with a specific form of governance. Within only three years of this vote, one business alone had financed and spearheaded a campaign to change the governance form, to require a new slate of city council elections, and incidentally to cost the citizens an additional $35,000. But this campaign had gone down to defeat.

A progress report: one of the adult entertainment lawsuits has been dismissed through summary judgment, and we fully expect the other to experience the same demise.

Lessons

Lessons learned from this experience include the need to expect that some special interests, if they feel they have nothing further to lose, will take extreme measure to gain a powerful advantage in dealing with local government. As a result, no local government can be complacent about how well it understands and reflects its community's values while honoring the constitutional rights of minority interests.

Understanding the community's core values can provide a local government with a reserve of support when special interests rise to assert their power. In other words, when challenged by a bully, it's good to know that your friends are behind you.

CHAPTER 39

Southeast Establishes Land-Use Controls to Regulate the Establishment of Adult Businesses

Willis H. Stephens, Jr.

This study was initiated by the Town of Southeast to investigate the need for land use controls to regulate the establishment of adult businesses in the Town. On March 17, 2005 the Town Board passed a resolution imposing a temporary moratorium on approvals for sexually oriented businesses. The purposes of the moratorium were to give the community the opportunity to evaluate the potential effects from the establishment of adult uses and to draft the regulatory changes for the Town Board's consideration.

The current zoning regulations in the Town restrict adult uses with minimum distance requirements. In New York State, the Court of Appeals requires a municipality to conduct a study examining possible secondary effects before adopting regulations of adult uses. In this study, the Town of Southeast has relied upon studies completed by other communities in order to document what secondary impacts can be expected.

The potential secondary effects examined relate to economic impacts, property values, fear of crime, and the negative impact on community character. In areas where commercial and residential land uses are mixed the general quality of life of residents could potentially be affected by the uncontrolled location of adult businesses.

Zoning has been determined the land use control best suited to regulating the location of adult businesses. However, adult businesses can not be entirely prohibited through local zoning. Nor can a municipality base its regulations on the content of materials sold or the nature of the entertainment provided. In order for a zoning law to be effective, adult uses need to be defined in a manner that differentiates them from traditional bookstores and bars. One method has been to use their exclusion of minors as part of the definition.

Local regulations should attempt to minimize secondary impacts to the community rather than completely prohibit them. This study has identified the land uses most sensitive to the adverse effects of adult uses. Residential properties, institutional uses (e.g. schools and houses of worship), and recreational areas were identified. Limiting adult businesses to certain districts where they will have the least effect on the most sensitive land

Originally published as "Adult Use Zoning Planning Report," *Report of the Town Counsel*, August 18, 2005, by the Office of the Town Counsel, Town of Southeast, Brewster, NY.

uses is the most acceptable method of control. Adult uses can be required to first obtain a special use permit. Within the criteria established to receive such a permit key requirements can include:

- Buffers to other land uses identified as being most susceptible to the negative impacts of adult uses
- Dispersion through minimum distances between two adult uses
- Limits on the number of establishments per property
- Requirements for screening and limiting signage.

This study concludes that the possible secondary effects from adult uses to the residential neighborhoods and central business district pose a significant enough threat that zoning amendments should be adopted.

Adult Entertainment Industry

Previous Studies

Potential secondary effects can be assessed by looking at what has happened in other communities. Many communities in New York, and nation-wide, have prepared special studies addressing the secondary effects of adult entertainment establishments.

This study relies on the findings of other adult entertainment studies in New York State. In preparing this study, those documents and their corresponding regulations were reviewed for similarities to the Town of Southeast situation. This was done in order to develop an appropriate strategy for addressing adult uses specific to the Town. While some of the communities reviewed differ greatly from Southeast in size and urban development, the potential effects from adult uses at the neighborhood level is still applicable.

NEW YORK CITY, NY

In New York City, several studies have identified impacts associated with adult enter-tainment establishments. Due to its size, New York City has a large number of establishments to track trends in type and location of new adult businesses. In New York City, the number of adult book and video establishments grew from 29 to 86 between 1984 and 1993. The number of topless and nude bars also grew from 54 to 68 during the same period. In terms of their location, adult entertainment uses have a tendency to concentrate in specific areas. In 1994, surveys done in various business districts were compared. Differences between areas with and without high concentrations of adult entertainment establishments were identified. The Overall Findings and Conclusions of the 1994 NYC Adult Entertainment Study are summarized as follows:

- Adult entertainment uses tend to concentrate; they cluster in central locations.
- In the areas where adult uses have concentrated, the study identified numerous secondary effects. Owners of other types of businesses overwhelmingly believed that their businesses had been adversely affected. A substantially higher incidence of criminal activity was also found in the areas where adult uses were most concentrated.
- Areas with less dense concentrations of adult uses found fewer impacts than the areas with the higher concentrations. However, the community leaders still expressed fear of the results of proliferation.
- In the areas where adult entertainment uses were isolated, other businesses typically reported that the adult uses had not yet adversely affected their neighborhoods.
- Real estate brokers reported that adult entertainment establishments were perceived to negatively affect nearby property values.
- Adult entertainment business signs were found to be generally larger, more often illuminated, and graphic (sexually-oriented) compared with the signs of other nearby commercial uses. Community residents

viewed this signage as out of keeping with neighborhood character and were concerned about the exposure of minors to graphic sexual images.

The consensus among those expressing opposition to the operation of adult uses is that adult entertainment establishments have a negative impact on communities in which they are located. These impacts include: inappropriate exposure of children and teenagers to graphic sexual images, increased crime, diminishing property values, adverse effects upon the climate for other types of commercial activities, and overall negative influences upon community character.

Islip, NY

The study completed by the Town of Islip in 1980 was initiated in part by the public concern when a new adult book store/peep show opened. A case study, including an examination of public resentment through newspaper accounts, and an inventory of other existing adult entertainment businesses was conducted. Similar to the New York City study, the Town of Islip was able to look at the effects from existing adult uses. The case study could then be used to determine what locational factors were responsible for the outpouring of neighborhood residential opposition. The inventory of 15 exciting adult entertainment uses examined zoning conformance, neighboring land use, value (assessed), and building condition. An individual site analysis was prepared for each business. After findings suggested that adult uses could potentially create a "dead zone" and hinder development in areas identified for revitalization, the Islip study encouraged the limitation of adult uses to industrial districts in order to prevent cumulative effects in the Historic Downtown of Islip.

As a result of a 1989 court decision in *Town of Islip v. Caviglia*, a challenge brought by an adult bookstore owner was rejected. The court found that although Islip's regulations allowed adult uses in an area zoned for industrial use, this provided ample space for the development of such uses.

Hyde Park, NY

In Hyde Park, an adult use study was prepared in 1996 for the Town Board by Green Plan, Inc. Hyde Park prepared a secondary effects study although it had neither an adult use nor a proposed adult use. Hyde Park's examination analyzed studies prepared by other municipalities and discovered universal negative secondary impacts associated with adult businesses. The study estimated potential impacts of adult uses on specific land uses and found that because a significant part of the town's economy revolved around tourists attracted to the many historic and scenic sites, adult uses could "irreparably damage" Hyde Park's quality of life, character and tourism trade. The Hyde Park study concluded that adult uses should be regulated differently from other establishments, and that proactive land use regulation should be drafted. Proactive legislation would prevent a situation where adult use regulations are enacted hastily in response to deleterious secondary effects, thereby reducing the likelihood of a legal challenge. The Hyde Park study concluded that it is appropriate for the Town of Hyde Park to regulate adult businesses differently from other commercial establishments. The Town required any proposed adult use to apply for a special permit and added specific adult use criteria, including special dimensional requirements.

Study Conclusions

- Adult uses in close proximity to one another can create a "skid row effect." Regulatory response often involves prohibiting adult use establishments from locating near each other. The Town of Southeast intends to avoid this by establishing minimum distance requirements between two adult use establishments.

- Studies recognize the deleterious effect that adult use establishments can have to nearby residences. In order to control possible secondary effects of such uses on the community, towns and cities restrict such uses from locating within a certain distance from residential uses. These regulations are not intended to control the content of the material purveyed, but are rather to avoid any potential effect on residential neighborhoods. The Town of Southeast intends to establish minimum distance between adult use establishments and residential areas.
- The Islip study indicates that adult use establishments have the possibility of detracting from community revitalization efforts by discouraging private investment in certain areas. In this case, effort was not made to control the content of the material, but to restrict the location of such adult uses in order to avoid a concentration of such establishments. Islip also set minimum distance requirements between adult uses and sensitive land uses such as schools, churches, parks and residential districts. In addition, non-conforming adult uses are amortized according to their capital investment and have the opportunity to appeal to the Zoning Board of Appeals. The Town of Southeast intends to institute minimum distances between adult use establishments and identified sensitive land uses.
- A regulatory response was also employed in Hyde Park which established an "adult use" land use category and restricted them to one zoning district. In addition, Hyde Park established minimum distance requirements, required special use permits and added signage provisions. The Town of Southeast intends to require that an adult use establishment will require a Town Board special permit.

Town of Southeast

The Town of Southeast currently regulates adult uses by listing a number of definitions as "restricted uses." In Local Law No. 7, adopted on April 24, 2003, the Town added minimum distance requirements that apply to these restricted uses. Restricted uses shall not be located closer than one thousand (1,000) feet from any residential district boundary line, school, or house of worship. Also, these uses shall not be located closer than one thousand (1,000) feet from any other restricted use including nightclubs, pawnshops, pool or billiard halls, and tattoo parlors. The Town also requires that any restricted use receive a special permit from the Town Board.

In considering their current zoning, the Town of Southeast, in adopting the temporary moratorium, intends to amend its current regulations in order to more clearly define adult uses and to develop town-specific regulations. In recognition of the findings of the above studies, the Town intends to avoid a concentration of adult uses which have the potential to create a "skid-row" effect and to protect sensitive land uses within the Town.

Potential for Adult Uses

The adult entertainment industry is growing and spreading geographically. In recent years, several adult use establishments have opened in and around the Town.

The Town of Southeast's existing zoning allows commercial/residential mixing in many areas, increasing the potential for conflicts between adult entertainment and sensitive land uses.

Potential Secondary Effects

Previous studies by other municipalities have documented that secondary effects from adult entertainment establishments may include increased crime, decreased property values, negative impact upon other commercial businesses and a deterioration of residential neighborhoods. A common conclusion of those studies has been that if adult entertainment uses are not regulated (with districting and separation distances) the adjoining neighborhoods may decline.

Both the New York State Court of Appeals and the United States Supreme Court have affirmed the right of a community to regulate the location of adult uses based on these secondary effects.

Municipalities can regulate adult entertainment businesses by limiting them to certain zoning districts or neighborhoods where the secondary impacts are minimized. The regulations must leave some reasonable alternatives to where they can locate.

Sensitive Land Uses

There are certain land uses that are more susceptible to the impacts from an adult entertainment neighbor. They include, but are not limited to, residential neighborhoods, schools, churches, public facilities, parks and playgrounds and historic resources at which the public may congregate. Separation distances or buffers can be utilized to mitigate impacts to these most sensitive land uses.

Additional control is available by placing adult entertainment businesses in a land use category that requires review and approval of a special use permit.

- Institutional
  This category includes land devoted to county and local government functions, schools, churches and other social, civic and religious functions of the community. The JFK Elementary School, Henry Wells Middle School and Brewster High School comprise one of the major institutional uses in Southeast. The schools, playing fields, and administration and maintenance buildings form a substantial educational campus. The other significant parcel is Morningthorpe on Turk Hill

Road, a non-profit drug rehabilitation center.

- Recreation Areas, Parks and Play Grounds
  This category includes Scolpino Park, the park at Lake Tonetta and several other Town-owned parcels.
- Residential Neighborhoods
  Residential areas located throughout the Town often within close proximity of commercial areas. For this reason, it is important that the town consider adequate zoning regulations that would protect sensitive land uses from potential adult use establishments.

Proposed Districts and Separation Distances

The Town of Southeast, in support of the findings above, proposes to restrict adult uses as well as other identified restricted uses to two districts within the Town: Highway Commercial HC-1 and Highway Commercial HC-2 Zoning Districts. In order to locate adult uses in areas where their effect on adjoining neighbors will be minimized, minimum separation distances will also be established in order to provide an appropriate buffer between adult uses and those land uses determined to be sensitive to the possible negative secondary effects of adult uses. Minimum separation distances also prevent concentrations of adult uses. The attached map shows the potential location of adult uses in these districts, subject to the proposed minimum distance requirements. Any proposed use would also be subject to the standards defined in the proposed amended zoning below.

Proposed Zoning Amendments

The definitions of the existing land-use ordinances were modified and amended as follows:

- Add: "Adult Cabaret — A building or portion of a building regularly featuring dancing or other live entertainment if the dancing or entertainment that constitutes the primary live entertainment is distinguished or characterized by an emphasis on the exhibiting of special sexual activities or specific anatomical areas for observation by patrons there."

- Add: "Adult Retail Shop — An establishment having as a substantial or significant portion of its stock-in-trade videotapes, digital video disks, compact disks, other electronic formats, films, slides, books, magazines or adult accessories, whether for sale or rent."
- Add: "Adult Use — Any activity covered by the definitions of adult bookstore, adult cabaret, adult motel, adult motion-picture theater, adult retail shop, massage parlor, model studio, or sexual encounter center or any other activity that appeals to the prurient interest of the general public."
- Combine and revise the definitions of "Adult Mini-Motion-Picture Theater" and "Adult Motion-Picture Theater" to read "An enclosed or unenclosed building, structure or portion thereof used for presenting materials distinguished or characterized by primary emphasis on matter depicting, describing or relating to sexual activities or sexual anatomical areas for observation by patrons."

The amendments to "nonresidential districts" were modified in the Commercial Zoning Schedule by listing as "permitted principal uses" adult uses in the HC-1 and HC-2 zones. Adult uses would be allowed in these two zones as "special permit uses."

The restricted uses section of the Town's existing laws was amended to read as follows: No persons shall cause or permit the use, occupancy or establishment of any land, building or structure as or for an adult use, nightclub, pawnshop, pool or billiard hall or tattoo parlor unless a special permit, in accordance with Article X of this chapter, is received from the Town Board, subject to the special standards identified below.

The purpose of the existing land-use legislation was modified and amended to read as follows:

The Town Board finds that certain business activities, by their nature, have serious objectionable operation characteristics which can lead to a significant impact on the surrounding community. The Town Board further finds that the unrestrained proliferation of such business is inconsistent with existing development and future plans for the Town of Southeast in that they often result in influences on the community which increase the crime rate and undermine the economy, moral and social character of the community. To preserve the integrity and character of residential neighborhoods and important natural and human resources of the Town, the Town intends to restrict the proximity of adult use establishments to churches, schools, nursery schools, day-care centers, educational institutions, parks, historic and scenic resources, civic and cultural facilities and residential areas.

The standards of the existing land-use legislation were modified and amended as follows:

Adult uses, nightclubs, pawnshops, pool or billiard halls, and tattoo parlors may be permitted by the Town Board in the HC-1 and HC-2 Districts subject to the following requirements:

(1) No more than one activity constituting an adult use shall be permitted on any lot.

(2) No adult use shall be permitted in any building otherwise used in whole or part for residential purposes.

(3) No adult use shall be permitted on any lot which is located within 1,000 feet of any other lot on which is located an adult use or nightclub, pawnshop, pool or billiard hall, and tattoo parlor. This distance shall be measured from the nearest property line of such use to the nearest property line of the proposed adult use.

(4) No adult use shall be permitted on any lot which is located within 1,000 feet of

any lot in any residential district. This distance shall be measured from the nearest property line of any residential district to the nearest public entrance door of the adult use premises.

(5) No adult use shall be permitted on any lot which is located within 1,000 feet of any lot on which is located a church, community center, funeral home, school, day-care center, hospital, alcoholism center or drug treatment center, counseling or psychiatric treatment facility or public park. The distance shall be measured from the nearest property line of such above use to the nearest public entrance door of the adult use premises.

(6) No adult use shall be permitted on any lot which is located within 1,000 feet of any school bus stop. This distance shall be measured from the nearest school bus stop to the nearest public entrance door of the adult use premises.

(7) No adult use shall be permitted on any lot which is located within 1,000 feet of any commercial enterprise that customarily employs minors.

(8) No adult use shall be permitted on any lot which is located within 1,000 feet of any establishment that sells or serves alcoholic beverages.

(9) The proposed use shall meet all other requirements of the law of the Town of Southeast, including but not limited to district lot and bulk regulations, parking regulations and signage requirements.

(10) It shall be a condition of any special permit issued for an adult use that no person under the age of 18 years shall be permitted into the premises.

(11) Explicit messages or drawing on signs and/or the public display of explicit sexual material associated with any adult entertainment use is prohibited.

(12) The Town Board may impose such terms and conditions upon the issuance of the special permit required hereunder as it deems appropriate to further the aims of this subsection, including but not limited to restrictions on advertising, outdoor displays and the location of merchandise.

The proposed ordinance had the following effect on existing adult uses:

(1) Any adult use lawfully in existence on the date on which the provision of this subsection become effective shall be permitted to continue, provided that such use is registered with the Building Inspector within 30 days of the effective date of this subsection and it is established to the satisfaction of the Building Inspector that such use complies with all the requirements set forth herein.

(2) Any adult use in existence on the date on which the provisions of this subsection become effective which fails to conform to the regulations herein shall be discontinued in accordance with the following amortization schedule:

Amount of Capital Investment

As of the Effective Date of New Law	*Date Before Which Use Shall Terminate*
$0 to $25,000	September 1, 2006
$25,001 to $50,000	September 1, 2007
$50,001 to $75,000	September 1, 2008
$75,501 to $100,000	September 1, 2009
$100,001 or more	September 1, 2010

Although the original report from the Town Attorney was from August of 2005, the Town Board approved the amendments of the existing land-use law relating to adult businesses on March 16, 2006. The amendments and modifications to the existing legislation that are outlined above are now the law in the Town of Southeast.

Editor's Note:

The complete copy of the approved land-use legislation by the Town Board on March 16, 2006 is available from the Town of Southeast's website, which is listed in the *Appendix* section of this volume under *Regional Resource Directory*.

CHAPTER 40

Staunton Adopts Law Limiting Adult Uses to Their Industrial Zone with a Business License and Permit

Deborah A. Lane

After a lengthy process that began with the City's Planning Commission, a legal public hearing on the recommended changes to the regulation of adult businesses was scheduled before the City Council. This meeting consisted of the Mayor, Vice Mayor, and five members of the City Council; the Chair and Vice Chair; as well as three members of the Planning Commission. Those staff in attendance included the City Manager, City Attorney, Director of Planning, and Clerk of the Council.

The following narrative describes the public process that followed, which included a formal presentation, a public hearing to hear citizens who spoke on both sides of this issue, and a final vote of the City's elected officials on those recommendations before them from the City's Planning Commission.

The Director of Planning provided a briefing on this matter. Ms. Angle noted that beginning at its August 16, 2007 meeting, the Planning Commission began a process to try to determine appropriate and legitimate regulations that may be warranted for adult

(sometimes referred to as sexually oriented) businesses in the City of Staunton. The informational process continued with the following meetings:

- September 18, 2007 — Work Session
- September 24, 2007 — Work Session
- October 8, 2007 — Work Session
- October 25, 2007 — Regular Meeting

The City Attorney advised the Planning Commission that, under existing legal precedent, any regulation by the City must be consistent with the free speech protections of the First Amendment to the United States Constitution.

The Planning Commission preliminarily reviewed illustrative studies on the secondary effects of sexually oriented businesses on communities:

1. American Planning Association Study of Adult Uses, Chapter 3.
2. Garden Grove, California
3. New York City, New York

Originally published as "Public Hearing and Consideration of Adoption of an Ordinance to Add and Adopt New Provisions for Adult Businesses," *Minutes of the Staunton City Council*, November 8, 2007, by the Office of the Clerk of the Council, City of Staunton, VA.

These studies, as well as others, document the harmful secondary effects of adult businesses. Various other studies are being made available for review by the Planning Commission and City Council. The studies evidence, among others, the following negative secondary effects of the location of adult businesses in a community:

- Increased crime of various sorts — higher police calls related to crime of assault, robbery, burglary, and theft
- Lower property values for both residential and commercial property in the vicinity of the adult businesses
- Lack of revenue from other stores closing early to avoid the negative secondary effects of these businesses
- Increased costs to other businesses in having to provide private security guards
- Higher turnover of residents

In summary, as shown in studies from other localities which have experienced the location of adult businesses, these businesses have a real adverse impact on the quality of life. Also, adult businesses, by the nature of their operations, pose risks because of health, safety and welfare-related effects.

The Planning Commission also considered various court cases which recognize the harmful secondary effects and illustrate that the courts have allowed regulation when shown that there is a legislative basis tied to the negative secondary effects of adult businesses. The reviewed cases and others also are being made available for formal review by the Planning Commission and City Council.

At the Planning Commission's September 18 work session, members heard from eight (8) members of the public who noted their concern with the negative impacts of adult businesses in the City of Staunton, citing concerns for the community as a whole and for individuals.

After reviewing the studies on the negative secondary impacts of adult businesses and the court cases recognizing those effects and

illustrating legitimate regulation of these businesses, the Planning Commission preliminarily concluded that the City of Staunton does have a substantial governmental interest in the regulation of adult businesses in that we have a City where:

- Schools and churches are located throughout the community
- Property values need to be protected
- Crime needs to be minimized
- Children and residential neighborhoods need to be protected
- We continue to promote and protect our Historic Districts, including our commercial and residential structures and surrounding areas
- Tourism and related venues are an important part of our economic development

The Commission recognized that the objective of regulation is not, consistent with the First Amendment to the Constitution of the United States, to prevent a business from operation altogether, but how to legitimately regulate. The Commission reviewed approaches taken by other localities which considered the use of police power and land use regulations. The Commission looked at ordinances from among the following localities in Virginia:

- Henrico County
- Chesterfield County
- City of Waynesboro
- City of Harrisonburg
- Draft of Augusta County (never adopted)

After review and discussion, the Planning Commission concurred that the approach they would like to see developed was an ordinance which allowed the adult business by right, but where requirements for the business are outlined. This kind of approach was taken by Henrico County but would necessitate, in part, an amendment of Title 5 of the City Code. The Commission also concluded that the adult businesses would be allowed by right in I-1, Light Industrial Districts and, therefore, also in I-2, Heavy Industrial District, with regulation. This approach, too, requires an amendment to the City's Zoning District regulations and is dealt with as a separate draft ordinance to be formally considered jointly by the Planning Commission and City Council. It was determined that utilizing a Special Use Permit process was not an option, as the question is not whether an adult business may locate in the City, but rather where and under what circumstances it can operate.

Ms. Angle stated that the proposed ordinance was drafted in order to add and adopt new provisions, Chapter 5.4, Adult Businesses, of Title 5, Business Licenses and Regulations of the Staunton City Code, to require, for example, that an adult business apply for an annual permit from the Chief of Police to operate an adult business; furnish various background information and references; pay an application fee; provisions for permit revocation; prompt administrative and judicial review and determination procedures; inspection authority of city departments; conditions on the operation of adult entertainment and adult motels; and prohibit transfer of permits.

The City Attorney noted that the two ordinances before Council are a permitting process and a zoning consideration. Mr. Guynn noted that the Chief of Police would be responsible for conducting background checks and issuing, revoking, or denying an application. If this ordinance is adopted by Council, it will require that an existing business must get a permit within 30 days and comply with all the regulations within 90 days.

Mayor King advised the process for conducting the public hearing, noting that all speakers are to come to the microphone and provide their name and address for the clerk's record. All speakers will be limited to a 3 minute time period.

The public hearing was opened.

Speaking in favor of the proposed ordinance were:

- Speaker 1 praised Ms. Angle and the City Attorney for the work they have done on this ordinance.
- Speaker 2 spoke about a personal experience regarding pornography during the time she and her husband ran a child day care center.
- Speaker 3 stated that she was angered when she thought of all the cases of murder, abuse, etc. which stemmed from pornography.
- Speaker 4 stated that he'd done research on this matter, and he asked Council to please deter and control pornography in Staunton.
- Speaker 5 stated that she lives near the pornography shop on Springhill Rd. She stated that because of Council's inaction, her investment is now threatened.
- Speaker 6 stated that he and his wife moved to Staunton because of a better quality of life. He stated that now when potential renters come to look at his investments near Springhill Road, they are discouraged when they see a pornography shop. He stated that the proposed business is a good pro-business ordinance. He requested that Council adopt the ordinance.
- Speaker 7 urged Council to adopt the ordinance for moral reasons and for objective reasons.
- Speaker 8 stated that he was not happy with the pornography shop being on Springhill Rd. near his home. He stated that he used to be a manager of a video store and that he knows what pornography can do to a person's life.
- Speaker 9 urged Council to adopt the ordinances before them. He spoke representing himself and his church. He urged Council to adopt the ordinances to give Staunton's youth a chance.
- Speaker 10 stated that there is a lot of sexual abuse in the Staunton, Waynesboro and Augusta County area, and that pornography fuels the fire.

- Speaker 11 praised the city officials for the research done on these ordinances. He also commended the speakers for sharing their views and stories. He urged the public to vote with their dollars and to avoid those places that distribute pornography.
- Speaker 12 thanked Council on behalf of the Citizens Task Force for its dedication in developing strict ordinances regulating adult businesses. She presented a petition with over 3,000 signatures supporting the adoption of these ordinances.

Speaking in opposition to the proposed ordinance were:

- Speaker 1 observed that prior to tonight's meeting, he visited the After Hours video store and found a very well lighted and clean establishment. The employees were helpful and friendly. He said there was no evidence of prostitutes or drug dealers, and that he could not see any houses from the store. He spoke with regard to the research of harmful, negative, secondary effects. He asked if there is any evidence that the adoption of strict ordinances reverses these effects. He suggested that this matter be tabled for a period of six months until Council has time to thoughtfully consider the outcome.
- Speaker 2 stated that if the existing pornography shop is allowed to stay in Staunton, it will produce negative effects.
- Speaker 3 stated that he wouldn't mind if the pornography shop would close. He stated that local law enforcement should not have to be jumping through hoops because certain citizens want it to jump through hoops.

The public hearing was closed.

Mr. Bell moved to adopt an ordinance adding and ordaining Chapter 5.40, Adult Businesses, of Title 5, Business Licenses and Regulations of the Staunton City Code. The motion was seconded by Mr. Robertson.

Mr. Metz stated that this particular ordinance satisfies the requirements that allow this action to stand up in court. Mr. Metz quoted from *Young v. American Mini Theatres,* "a governmental regulation is sufficiently justified, despite its incidental impact upon First Amendment interest, "if it is within the constitutional power of the Government; if it furthers an important or substantial governmental interest; if the government interest is unrelated to the suppression of free [Page 80] expression; and if the incidental restriction on ... First Amendment freedoms is no greater than is essential to the furtherance of that interest."

The motion carried unanimously by roll call vote.

Editor's Notes:

1. The recommendations of the Planning Commission were unanimously approved by the City Council on November 8, 2007, and are now law in the City of Staunton, VA.

2. Two new laws were approved at this meeting to regulate the location and operation of adult business. They were referenced as Ordinance No. 2007-28 and 2007-29. The former dealt with business licenses and regulations, the latter with limiting adult uses to the City's Industrial Zone.

3. The names and addresses of the citizens speaking in favor and in opposition to the proposed changes to the City's adult business ordinance have been changed to "Speaker 1," "Speaker 2," "Speaker 3," etc. The Editor felt it was important to know what was said, rather than the name and address of the person who said it.

4. Copies of these ordinances, as well as additional information, can be obtained from the City of Staunton's website, which is listed in the *Appendix* of this volume in the section titled *Regional Resource Directory.*

CHAPTER 41

Tampa Ordered by Court to Restore Public Access Channel Closed for Airing Adult Shows

Neil J. Lehto

The First Amendment is coming to hometown cable television.

In the past year, federal courts in Tampa, Florida and Athol, Massachusetts have ordered local government officials to restore public access channels that had been shut down over claims of objectionable programming.[1] In the Tampa case, U.S. District Judge James S. Moody, Jr. granted a preliminary injunction enjoining Hillsborough County's local government from terminating $355,000 in funding to a non-profit corporation that managed the joint City of Tampa/Hillsborough County public access production studio and channel, *Speak Up Tampa Bay*.[2] The *Tampa Tribune* reported that the County Board's attorneys spent upwards of $140,000 defending against the preliminary injunction request, and the County risked being slapped with hundreds of thousands of dollars in plaintiff's legal fees if it lost the First Amendment case.[3]

Meanwhile, some local governments are considering the extent of their own First Amendment rights, asking municipal lawyers whether they can generate new revenue by selling commercial advertising on government access channels despite objections from the local cable television operators. The surprising answer is that, in most states, there is no legal prohibitions against doing so, and that the state laws and administrative rules banning or limiting advertising over public, educational and government channels (for example, in New York, Connecticut, Hawaii and Minnesota) are subject to First Amendment challenge. This article will examine the growing body of First Amendment law affecting the complex relationship between municipal government and cable television.

The Origins of Cable TV's First Amendment Implications

Cable television began in 1948 as an alternative means of delivering television service to viewers in the mountains of Arkansas, Oregon and Pennsylvania, where reception of broadcast TV signals was poor because of the terrain or the remote location.[4] It has since ex-

Originally published as "The First Amendment, Local Government & Cable Television," *Municipal Lawyer*, Vol. 44, No. 1, January/February 2003, by the International Municipal Lawyers Association, Washington, DC. Reprinted with permission of the publisher.

panded into a multi-billion dollar industry serving almost seventy percent of U.S. households.[5] Under common law principles dating back to the fourteenth century,[6] local governments have primarily regulated cable television systems in the same way as other public utilities, which require cable operators to obtain a franchise to install cables on utility poles, or underground along and across the public rights-of-way.

However, the broad local governmental authority over cable television systems has been slowly eroded. On February 2, 1972, the Federal Communications Commission (FCC) took a major swipe at local government regulation of cable television by adopting sweeping new rules on cable television with significant First Amendment implications for local government.[7] In particular, the FCC required that cable television operators set aside channel capacity for one noncommercial public access channel for use by the public on a "first come, first serve" basis.[8] Without requiring noncommercial use, the FCC also required the "set aside" of one channel each for local educational and governmental use ("PEG channels").[9]

The U.S. Supreme Court upheld some of the provisions of the 1972 rules in *United States v. Midwest Video Corp.*[10] Although the Court did not address the First Amendment in deciding the case, it did recognize a legitimate governmental interest in providing local outlets for individual expression. The broad reach of the FCC's rules came under criticism in the concurring opinion by Chief Justice Warren Burger, who suggested "that the Commission's position strains the outer limits of even the open-ended and pervasive jurisdiction that has evolved by decisions of the Commission and the courts."[11] The rules subsequently came under attack by the cable industry as being outside of the FCC's jurisdiction, and in 1979, in *F.C.C. v. Midwest Video Corp.*, the Supreme Court struck them down.[12] Nullifying the FCC preemption of the area, the ruling was interpreted by some as protecting the author-

ity of local government officials to award and renew franchises requiring franchise fees, PEG channels, studios, and production equipment.

Congress Steps In, Repeatedly

The U.S. Cable Communications Act of 1984 added Title VI to the Communications Act of 1934, the first major change in the Communications Act.[13] Congress's principal purpose in enacting the 1984 Act was to establish "a national policy that clarifie[d] the current system of local, state and federal regulation of cable television."[14] This policy continued to rely on the local franchising process as the primary means of cable television regulation, while defining and limiting the authority that a franchising authority could exercise through the franchise process.[15] The 1984 Cable Act adopted the local franchise requirement, and also authorized municipal officials to negotiate franchise terms requiring PEG channels, studios and production equipment, dropping the specific noncommercial limitation language on public access which the FCC had imposed.[16]

Following adoption of the 1984 Cable Act, some in the cable industry responded by bringing a series of constitutional challenges against local governments. The leading cases were filed in the federal district courts in California and dragged out over the next ten years.[17] These cable operators claimed they were First Amendment speakers entitled to a private, unqualified right of access to public rights-of-way. They argued that because they did not use broadcast spectrum, they could not be held to broadcast-type regulations. Rather, they defined themselves as electronic publishers subject to the same level of First Amendment protection awarded to print publishers under *Miami Herald Pub. Co. v. Tornillo*.[18] Their legal theory had two important prongs. First, they argued that attaching a cable system to utility poles did not use the public rights-of-way any differently than the way publishers used the rights-of-way to deliver newspapers. Second, they argued that the public rights-of-way used by cable systems were subject to public forums analysis under the First Amendment as applied in *Tornillo*. This line of attack reached the U.S. Supreme Court in *City of Los Angeles v. Preferred Communications, Inc.*,[19] in which the Court concluded that, while the franchise process implicated protected speech, it "was unwilling to decide the [First Amendment] legal questions posed ... without a more thoroughly developed record of proceedings."[20]

In fact, the U.S. Supreme Court did not recognize First Amendment protection for cable systems under the 1991 case of *Leathers v. Medlock*,[21] involving the taxation of cable system. The Court confirmed, "[c]able television ... is engaged in 'speech' under the First Amendment, and is, in much of its operation, part of the 'press.'"[22] In other cases, the requirement that cable systems set aside PEG channels, a studio, and production equipment have never been successfully challenged, unlike similar requirements in the case of newspaper publishers.[23]

In 1992, Congress enacted the Cable Television Consumer Protection and Competition Act of 1992.[24] Included in the 1992 Act was a provision inviting a constitutional challenge with a direct appeal to the U.S. Supreme Court.[25] The industry took up the invitation, launching a broad attack on numerous provisions of the 1992 Act, and on the 1984 Act as well. In deciding the case, *Turner Broad. Sys. Inc. v. F.C.C.*, the Supreme Court applied the *O'Brien* test[26] of intermediate First Amendment scrutiny to the regulation of cable television.[27] Subsequently, using the intermediate scrutiny standard in *Turner*, the D.C. Circuit Court of Appeals upheld, against constitutional attack under the First Amendment, all of the one-must-carry industry challenges to rate regulation, leased and PEG access, indicating that the standard would be applied to most other First Amendment challenges of cable television regulations.[28]

Are Public Access Channels Protected Public Forums?

In November 2002, the Florida District Judge dealing with the Hillsborough County case invoked *O'Brien* in deciding that the County could not shut down the public access channel: "[w]hile it may be correct that the Constitution does not require government to fund public access, it is clear that once a public forum is created, it may only be eliminated in a manner consistent with the First Amendment."[29] Courts that have decided First Amendment cases involving public access channels have disagreed on whether the channels are protected public forums.[30] For example, a federal district judge declined to apply forum analysis to a city council's moratorium on public access programming, imposed while new programming rules were being considered and adopted.[31] However, a Texas city's decision to drop a public access channel from the line-up in negotiations for a renewed cable television franchise was successfully challenged in *Bunton v. City of Palestine*.[32] There, the court ruled that the public access channel was at least a limited public forum and granted a temporary injunction giving the plaintiff access to the PEG channel.[33] Finally, in *Denver Area Educational Television Consortium, Inc. v. F.C.C.*,[34] the U.S. Supreme Court strongly suggested that a public access channel constituted a public form, although the concurring in part and dissenting in part opinion by Justice Kennedy (joined by Justice Ginsberg) said they are full public forums.[35]

Is Commercial Speech Permitted?

While many cable television franchises around the country specifically prohibit advertising on PEG channels or require that PEG channels be operated on a non-commercial basis, that is not uniformly the case. However, in some states, state law or administrative rules requite that PEG channels be used for non-commercial purposes. New York's rule has been the subject of at least two cases.[36] The Cable Communications Policy Act of 1984, as amended, allows local governments to require cable operators to set aside channel capacity for PEG channel use, but does not preclude advertising.[37] As mentioned earlier, Congress did not import the FCC's noncommercial limitation on public access channels when drafting the 1984 Act.

Cable television franchise agreements which make no prohibition on advertising satisfy what Justice Kennedy noted in his opinion in *Denver Area Educational Television Consortium, Inc. v. FCC*: "Substantive limitations on the types of programming on [PEG] channels ... [are] left to franchise agreements, so long as the channels comport in some sense with the industry practice to which Congress referred in the statutee."[38] The few federal courts that have addressed complaints by cable operators about advertising on governmental access channels have carefully avoided deciding that a government channel can never run advertiser-supported or commercial programming under the First Amendment or the U.S. Cable Communications Policy Act of 1984.[39] Quite to the contrary, the lower court in one case explicitly ruled: "If a municipality determines advertising is useful to fund programming on local government at work or other appropriate PEG programming, [there is] nothing in the Cable Act that would prevent a municipality from doing so."[40] Some legal scholars and most cable television operators argue that advertising on public access channels is contrary to the generally accepted concept on the proper use of these channels. They suggest that past practice argues against allowing advertising, especially by an individual profiting from the free use of public access studios, equipment and channel capacity, and creating competition with the cable operator for advertising dollars. However valid these concerns may be, they do not readily apply to government access channels.

However, it may be legally advisable to limit the types of advertising acceptable for use on the government access channels. A local government which accepts advertising may thereby create a public forum for all kinds of objectionable advertising, unless it exercises care in developing a written policy setting forth, in a manner consistent with First Amendment public forum analysis, what types of advertising it will accept. In doing so, the local government should be careful to avoid creating opportunities for arguments that it is engaged in viewpoint discrimination. Obviously, it is a good idea to involve legal counsel in the process of developing advertising rules. A clearly written policy, well-trained employees, and an established line of authority not only help to prevent violations of the First Amendment, but also send a positive message to the public that the local government is an active participant in the tradition of respecting and upholding the right to free speech. Finally, the local government might choose to adhere as closely as possible to the enhanced underwriting and donor acknowledgment rules followed by public broadcast stations: using logos and slogans which identify rather than promote, and value-neutral descriptions of products and services. Price information is forbidden; and announcements containing a call to action or an inducement to buy, sell, or rent are not permissible.[41] These kinds of policies will help convince cable operators to avoid any court challenge to commercial advertising on the government access channels.

NOTES

1. *See* Speak Up Tampa Bay Public Access Television, Inc. v. Board of Hillsborough County Commissioners, No. 8:02-cv-1762-T-30MSS (M.D. Fla. Nov. 12, 2002); Demarest v. Athol/Orange Community Television, Inc., 188 F. Supp. 2d 82 (D. Mass. 2002).

2. *Speak Up Tampa Bay Public Access Television, Inc.*, No. 8:02-cv-1762-T-30MSS (M.D. Fla. Nov. 12, 2002).

3. Ted Byrd, *Public TV Brouhaha Cost Hits $140,000*, The Tampa Tribune, Nov. 22, 2002 at http://www.tampatrib.com/MGANZPZ6S8D.html.

4. Jim Emerson, *Cable TV Viewers*, Sept. 30, 1998 at http://www.directmag.com/ar/marketing_cable_tv_viewers/ (last accessed on Dec. 17, 2002).

5. U.S. Census Bureau, *USA Statistics in Brief*, at http://www.census.gov/statb/www/part2.html#commo (last accessed Dec. 17, 2002).

6. Proprietors of the Charles River Bridge v. Proprietors of the Warren Bridge, 36 U.S. 420, 432 (1837). An early case recognizing the important municipal role in regulating cable TV systems is TV Pix, Inc., v. Taylor, 304 F. Supp. 459, *aff'd per curiam*, 396 U.S. 566 (1970).

7. In the Matter of Amendment of Part 74, Section 121, 24 Rad. Reg. 2d (P&F) 1501, 36 F.C.C. 2d 141 (released Feb. 3, 1972). (Hereinafter "1972 Cable Television Report and Order").

8. 1972 Cable Television Report and Order, § 76.251 (4).

9. 1972 Cable Television Report and Order, § 76.251 (5) & (6).

10. 406 U.S. 649 (1972).

11. *Id.* at 767.

12. 440 U.S. 689 (1979).

13. 47 U.S.C. § 521 *et seq.* (1984).

14. H.R. REP. NO. 98-934, 19 (1984) *reprinted in* 1984 U.S.C.C.A.N. 4655, 19..

15. H.R. REP. NO. 98-934 at 20–22.

16. 47 U.S.C. § 531.

17. *See* Preferred Communications, Inc., v. City of Los Angeles, 754 F. 2d 1936 (9th Cir. 1985) *remanded by* 476 U.S. 488 (1986); Group W. Cable, Inc., v. City of Santa Cruz, 669 F. Suppl. 954 (N.D. Cal. 1987); Pac. W. Cable Co. v. City of Sacramento, 672 F. Supp. 1322 (E.D. Cal. 1987).

18. 418 U.S. 241 (1974).

19. 476 U.S. 488 (1986).

20. *Id.* at 495

21. 499 U.S. 439 (1991).

22. *Id.* at 444.

23. Time Warner Entm't Co., L.P. v. F.C.C. 93 F. 3d 957 (D.C. Cir. 1996) (per curiam) *reh'g en banc denied*, 105 F. 3d 723 (D.C. Cir. 1997); Telesat Cablevision, Inc., v. City of Rivera Beach, 773 F. Supp. 383, 411–13 (S.D. Fla. 1991).

24. Pub. L. No. 103-385, 106 Stat. 1477 (1992).

25. 47 U.S.C. § 555(c) (1992).

26. U.S. v. O'Brien, 391 U.S. 367 (1968).

27. Turner Broad. Sys. Inc. v. F.C.C., 520 U.S. 180 (1997).

28. Time Warner Entm't Co., L.P. V. F.C.C., 93 F. 3d 957 (D.C. Cir. 1996) per curiam) *reh'g en banc denied*, 105 F. 3d 723) (D.C. Cit. 1977) 13 (S.D. Fla. 1991).

29. Speak Up Tampa Bay Public Access Television, Inc. v. Board of Hillsborough County Commissioners, No. 8:02-cv-1762-T-30MSS (S.D. Fla. Nov. 12, 2002) at 6, *citing* Missouri Knights of the Ku Klux Klan v. Kansas City, Mo., 723 F. Supp. 1347 (W.D. Mo. 1989).

30. *See* Anthony Palange, Jr. v. Denver Community Television, Inc., No. 93 CV 4429 (Colo. Aug. 31, 1994) (public access channel was a public forum); Quincy Cable TV, Inc., v. F.C.C., 768 F. 2d 1434, 1452 (D.C. Cir 1985) (channel was a public forum); Horton v. City of Houston, 179 F. 3d 188 (5th Cir. 1999) (not a public forum).

31. Demarest v. Athol/Orange Community Television, Inc., 188 F. Supp. 2d 82 (D. Mass. 2002).

32. Joe Ed Bunton v. City of Palestine, No. 6:99cv605 (E.D. Tex. June 11, 2000), available at http://www.spiegel mcd.com/archieve/bunton_injunction_order.htm.

33. *Id.*

34. 518 U.S. 727 (1996).

35. *Id.* at 762–63.

36. Time Warner Cable of New York City, a Div. of Time Warner Entm't Co., L.P. v. Bloomberg, L.P., 118 F. 3d 917 (2d Cir. 1997); Goldberg v. Cablevision Systems Corp., 261 F. 3d 318 (2d Cir. 2001).

37. 47 U.S.C. § 531 (a) (1992).

38. *Denver Area Educational Television Consortium*, 518 U.S. at 790.

39. *See, e.g.,* Time Warner Cable v. Bloomberg, 118 F. 3d 917 (2d Cir. 1997).

40. Time Warner Cable of New York City, a Div. of Time Warner Entm't Co., L.P. v. City of New York, 943 F. Supp. 1357, 1387 (S.D.N.Y. 1996).

41. For an example, see the PBS page at http://www.pbs.org/insidepbs/guidelines/howto.html (last accessed on Dec. 17, 2002).

CHAPTER 42

Thousand Oaks Considers Zoning Designations and Regulations for Adult Businesses

Mark G. Sellers

The City Attorney prepared this research report for the City Council. The issue at hand was should the City Council consider the enactment of an ordinance designating certain areas or zones of the City as appropriate for adult entertainment uses or businesses, and establish the various conditions or regulations for that form of commercial enterprise, using a suggested ordinance as a guide.

This report contained a summary of the above issue, a staff recommendation, financial impact statement, and background information for consideration by the City's elected officials. This report is highlighted in the following paragraphs.

Recommendation

The City Council should direct the Planning Commission to consider the ancillary impacts of this type of use, look at the appropriate areas or zones of the City for adult entertainment uses or businesses, consider what conditions or regulations may be required for that form of commercial enterprise, the per-mitting process and provide its recommendation to the City Council, using the attached proposed ordinance as a guide.

Financial Impact

Costs of staff time and work for this type of ordinance and use.

Background

- **First Amendment Rights; No Flat Prohibition**

The regulation of adult entertainment frequently causes tension between a city's land use objectives and the First Amendment rights to view or provide this form of expression. It is a land use subject which has generated a significant amount of litigation. Like many other commercial uses, adult oriented businesses can produce litter, noise, and traffic.

What makes such adult uses different is that they frequently cause neighborhood decay, assist in the transmission of diseases,

Originally published as "Proposed Ordinance for Regulation of Adult Entertainment," *Report from the City Attorney*, December 12, 2000, by the Office of the City Attorney, City of Thousand Oaks, CA.

and are associated with certain criminal activity. Therefore, a city can legally classify this type of business as a unique and separate use, and regulate it in an effort to eliminate those normal ancillary adverse impacts or secondary effects. *Young v. American Mini Theatres,* (1976) 472 U.S. 50, 96 S. Ct. 2440. However, adult uses or establishments[1] cannot be singled out merely in a city effort to create a *de facto* or broad ban on such uses. *Schad v. Borough of Mount Ephraim,* (1981) 452 U.S. 61, 101 S. Ct. 2176 (Court struck down a zoning law which banned live adult entertainment city wide). Nor can a city's regulations focus on the "content" of the adult expressions, which is a form of protected speech. Like it or not, non-obscene adult entertainment is a form of speech entitled to First Amendment protection.

- **Regulate "Secondary Effects" as Goal; Local Time, Place and Manner Restriction Serving Legitimate Governmental Interest**

City regulations focusing on the content of the speech or entertainment, called "content-based" restrictions, will be subject to the demanding "strict scrutiny" standard of review by the courts. Content-based restrictions are justified only if the ordinance is narrowly tailored to serve a "compelling" governmental interest.

On the other hand, a "content-neutral" local ordinance, which regulates the secondary effects or conduct other than what was said [but conduct which may be associated with an act of speech], is subject to a lesser justification or judicial review standard. This type of regulation may be justified if it furthers one of many "substantial" governmental interests and the regulation is tailored to serve that governmental interest. The city's police power is very broad, and consequently goals such as the prevention of crime, the preservation of neighborhoods, avoidance of blight and the regulation of nuisances have long been considered proper objectives of zoning and are "substantial" governmental interests.

A "content-neutral" ordinance can even regulate "the time, place and manner" of communicating the ideas. An ordinance is content-neutral if it is aimed at eliminating or controlling the "secondary effects," such as noise or criminal activity, which can be expected to result from exercising that protected form of expression. In determining whether an ordinance is content-neutral, the court's inquiry is "whether the government has adopted a regulation of speech because of disagreement with the message it conveys" or to prevent a true secondary effect. *Ward v. Rock Against Racism,* (1989) 491 U.S. 491, 109 S. Ct. 2746.

In case of *City of Renton v. Playtime Theaters, Inc.,* (1986) 475 U.S. 41, 106 S. Ct. 925, the Supreme Court upheld the City's adult entertainment ordinance, since the ordinance focused on preventing the "secondary effects" of that type of commercial business, and not on the content of speech allegedly being conducted therein. The court found the legislative purposes of preventing crime (such as prostitution, underage drinking, fights, etc.), curbing blighting influences of certain land uses (such as depressing property values), and limiting identified impacts (noise, late night disturbances, etc.) on nearby uses or properties are proper objectives of zoning and substantial governmental interests. The court indicated an adult use ordinance needs to identify or state its goals and the nature of each regulation enacted must be a reasonable step in achieving those goals. A factual background on the adverse effects and the reasons for the regulation must be presented to support the city council's findings for enacting the ordinance. Therefore, some study or report must be prepared which identifies the adverse secondary effects of unregulated adult businesses. The court, in the City of Renton case held a city could rely on the experiences of other cities and adopt the studies and conclusions of those other cities. A study prepared by the City of Los Angeles was attached.

- **Concentration or Dispersing Use; Adult Businesses Must Be Left with a Reasonable Opportunity to Open and Operate**

In *City of Renton v. Playtime Theaters, Inc.*, the court also held that a city could either (1) concentrate these uses into one location; or (2) disperse them throughout the city (a "noncluster" or "Anti–Skid Row" ordinance designed to discourage development of a "skid row" area).[2] The City of Renton allowed these uses in commercial zones (although "manufacturing" or "industrial" zones are often used), but prohibited such uses within 1000 feet of any residential zone, church, park, or school. Other cities have limited them to certain areas,[3] or have created a specific or unique zone for such uses.

Whatever approach a city takes, it must leave "reasonable alternative avenues of communication" for this form of protected expression, generally accomplished through zoning sufficient areas of the community as acceptable for these establishments. A city must analyze the availability of feasible acreage where these uses will be allowed under a proposed ordinance (prepare a staff report identifying those permissible locations). To be "feasible," the land zoned for adult uses must be part of the "active commercial real estate market." *Topanga Press v. City of Los Angeles* (9th Cir. 1993), 989 F2d 1524. The existence of an ample supply or market for adult entertainment outside the city does not justify the city's suppression of that form of speech and market within its borders.[4] In essence, there should be some type of supply and demand analysis. To be valid, the amount or number of acceptable complying sites, under the ordinance, which are in the community's active commercial real estate market, must be reasonable in light of the expected local demand for such forms of speech. If it is not reasonable based on that demand, the ordinance will be viewed as a *de facto* (and invalid) ban on this form of speech.

A. *Defining Active Commercial Market.*

To qualify as part of the active real property commercial market, a site must have the normally expected minimal level of infrastructure (stubbed out lines for sewers, electric, and street access, etc.). However, a site or space need not be currently available to purchase or lease, nor need it be offered at what some might allege is an affordable commercial rental rate, nor need the land owner be willing to rent space to an adult business.[5] The court looks primarily at the physical characteristics or practical suitability of the land zoned, with a limited inquiry into the costs of improving, altering or developing that land into a viable commercial or industrial site. To date, courts have not required a city to evaluate the possible severe economic impacts of high land costs or lease rates upon the operation of a business (such as the cost of a site will result in lower or no profits and high overhead costs to be commercially unfeasible for an adult business). "Adult businesses must fend for themselves in the real estate market, on an equal footing with other prospective purchasers and lessees." Topanga Press, at 1529.

B. *Adequate Number of Sites.* How much is sufficient? There are no set formulas. The number of adequate sites for a city with unacceptable *existing* adult uses, which are being closed out via a city amortization program, and thus forced to relocate, must be at least greater than the number of those existing adult businesses, plus the number of new businesses seeking, or likely to seek, permission to open. If a city has no present adult businesses and no pending inquiries or applications, the number must be reasonable based generally on the size of the city.

For example, the City of Renton allowed 5 percent of its total land area or 520 acres for this use; the City of Minneapolis zoned 6.6 percent of the city's total acreage then zoned for commercial uses (*Alexander v. City of Minneapolis* (8th Cir. 1991), 928, F.2d 278.[6] In *Walnut Properties, Inc. v. City of Whittier* (9th Cir. 1988), 861 F.2d 1102, the federal court found a zoning ordinance that effectively left only 1.4 percent of the city's land area, for a city of 90,000 people, insufficient. However, the court also noted that the Whittier ordinance, enacted *after* the plaintiff began offering adult entertainment, "would force the only existing adult theater in Whittier to close at its present location with no definite prospect of a place to *relocate*."

Perhaps, a more appropriate general inquiry of land area available is the number of separate feasible sites where an adult business could exist in light of the proposed zoning restrictions. (*BBI Enterprises v. City of Chicago*, (N.D. Ill. 1995) 874 F. Supp. 890 ("more relevant basis for comparison is the relationship between (1) the number of a city's sites that are really available for adult uses and (2) that city's population — a relationship that speaks more directly in supply-and-demand terms."). For example, the federal district court found an ordinance valid where the city showed that with one adult business currently existing in Pasadena, new adult businesses could locate in up to 26 sites in the City of Pasadena, which had a population of 135,000. *3570 East Foothill Boulevard, Inc. v. City of Pasadena*, (C.D. Cal. 1995) 912 F. Supp. 1257); *see also*, *Lakeland Lounge of Jackson, Inc. v. City of Jackson*, (5th Cir. 1992) 973 F. 2d 1255 (10 alternative sites for 5 existing businesses did not limit expression under Renton). Three sites were reasonable for the City of Taft with a population of 19,000 people. *Diamond v. City of Taft*, (9th Cir. 2000) 215 F. 3d 1052.

• **No Discretionary Approval; Need for Defined Clear and Objective Standards or Criteria**

Adult businesses cannot be regulated by means of any "discretionary" entitlement process such a Conditional or Special Use Permit. Discretionary permits give the governing body or administrator too much substantive flexibility, encouraging inquiries into content, and lacking uniform application, thus, this subjective permitting represents an invalid prior restraint on free speech. *Dease v. City of Ana-*

heim, (C.D. Cal. 1993) 826 F. Supp. 336; *Gammoh v. City of Anaheim*, (1999) 73 Cal. App. 4th 186, 86 Cal. Rptr. 194. Any criteria or operational standards must be "narrow, definitive and objective." The use of expansive language or vague phrases such as "the use shall not *adversely affect* the neighborhood," or the "use shall not be *inconsistent* with the other use or structure in the neighborhood," or "the site should be *sufficiently* buffered from nearby resident" leaves too much discretion and subjectivity with the permit granting body or officer. *Smith v. County of Los Angeles*, (1994) 24 Cal. App. 4th 990, 29 Cal. Rptr. 2d 680 [must be a true zoning ordinance, rather than a prior restraint of free speech]. The process should be administrative similar to that for a permitted use in a set zone.

Since free speech is involved, the time for processing and acting on any application for an adult use must be prompt and within a period of days as set forth in the ordinance. A long processing time of 90 or more days has been found to be a form of censorship. Any built-in discretion or authority for the permitting officer to unreasonably delay the processing of an application is a *de facto*, and therefore improper, ban. *FW/PBS, Inc. v. City of Dallas*, (1990) 493 U.S. 215, 110 S. Ct. 596.

• **"Knock Out" Issue: Simi Valley Experience**

Simi Valley's ordinance had a required sensitive "buffer area" from certain other existing or planned uses, so an adult use application had to be denied if for instance a church opened up within the 1000 foot buffer area and the city found that this fact knocked the applicant's site out as a permitted site for city consideration. The federal district court found the Simi Valley ordinance invalid based on this aspect. The appropriate time for measuring the incompatible adjoining uses is at the time of the application, and not later at the hearing.

• **Operational Standards**

To offset the identified secondary effects, a city can prohibit the touching of entertainers and customers, *Hang-On v. City of Arlington*, (5th Cir. 1995) 65 F. 3d 1248; prohibited the "direct" tipping by customers of the entertainers, *Kev, Inc. v. Kitsap County*, (9th Cir. 1986) 793 F2d 1053; set minimum requirements for the stage and seating areas, such as the stage or platform shall be at least twenty-four (24) inches in elevation above the level of the patron seating areas and no adult entertainment by an entertainer shall occur closer than ten (10) feet to any patron. *Colacurio v. City of Kent*, (9th Cir. 1998) 163 F.3d 545, *Tily B., Inc. v. City of Newport Beach* (1999) 69 Cal. App. 4th 1, 81 Cal. Reptr. 2d 6; required a certain level of management supervision. *Spokane Arcade, Inc. v. City of Spokane*, (9th Cir. 1996) 75 F. 3d 663, Colacurcio, (9th Cir. 1998) 163 F. 3d 545; and prohibited total nudity, *City of Erie v. Pap's A.M.*, (2000) 529 U.S. 277, 120 S. Ct. 1382.

Quick Judicial Review of Any Challenge

In *Baby Tam & Co., Inc. v. City of Las Vegas*, (9th Cir. 1998) 154 F. 3d 1097, an adult bookstore owner challenged a Las Vegas ordinance and the Ninth Circuit federal court determined that a Writ of Mandamus under the Nevada state law did not satisfy the required procedural safeguard of a prompt form of judicial review. Since the Baby Tam decision, the California writ of mandate law has been changed by the state legislature to add Section 1094.8 to the state's Code of Civil Procedure. That section now allows for an expedited court judicial review of a city's revocation, suspension, or denial of an adult business permit or any other entitlement for any expressive conduct protected by the First Amendment of the United States Constitution. That state law requires a city to designate, by ordinance or resolution, those city permits or entitlements that should receive expedited judicial review because such permits or entitlements regulate expressive conduct.

• Proposed Ordinance

This office has evaluated a number of adult entertainment ordinances enacted in other cities, as well as a number of model ordinances. We have reviewed the case law in this area. This office has drafted the proposed ordinance which can be used by the Planning Commission in its review of this matter. The ordinance would, among other things, prohibit the transfer of any permit, require employee registration, limit the hours of operation, set lighting levels, establish configuration requirements for stage area and seating, prohibit touching of customers, prohibit tipping and nudity, require security guards, have a time duration for the permit, and set up an administrative permitting process.

NOTES

1. Although defining an "adult" use is sometimes a challenge, the California courts have held an adult "use" need not be one where only "over 50 percent" adult films are shown or products sold. A city may define such a use as one where on a "regular basis" films characterized by an emphasis on the "specified sexual activities" are shown, or where such films constitute a substantial portion of the films or account for a substantial part of the revenues derived from the exhibition of films. People v. Superior Court of Los Angeles County (1989) 49 Cal. 3d 14, 259 Cal. Rptr. 740.

2. The dispersing approach, such as requiring an adult business to be at least 1000 feet from another adult business, requires some speculation as to where the first such use may appear, then the second, third, etc. to see how many could qualify. Therefore, the dispersing approach when added with other distance criteria creates a moving target situation causing some legal concerns in verifying adequate sites are still available in the city.

3. In City of National City v. Wiener, (1992) 3 Cal. 4th 832, 12 Cal. Rptr. 2d 701, the California Supreme Court held that a municipal zoning ordinance, which had a 1500 foot separation restriction on the location of adult entertainment businesses in the commercial area, but which also provided an exception for those businesses to locate within the enclosed regional shopping mall, did not violate the First Amendment even though the mall owner would be unlikely to rent to such businesses.

4. The only way a city can show that there is no need for its contribution to the adult speech market is for the city to open its borders to the speech. If the city's contribution to the market is not needed, then no adult establishments will flourish.

5. Note: presently the issue of whether a city, in meeting its burden of proof regarding the existence of reasonable alternative avenues of communication, must analyze the length and terms of the existing leases of commercial space is uncertain and is being litigated in the federal courts. U.S. Supreme Court certiorari review of the Ninth Circuit court's case of Lim v. City Long Beach, (9th Cir. 2000) 217 F. 3d 1050.

6. The City of Stanton was only 3.5 square miles in size but limited the location of adult businesses to no closer than 1000 feet of each other (together with the other standard separation criteria for schools, parks, residential zones). However, the city planning director could not testify as to square footage of useable land within the city that was available for that use. The Court found this to be a *de facto* ban and invalid. City of Stanton v. Cox, (1989) 207 Cal. App. 3d 1557, 255 Cal. Rptr. 682.

Editor's Note:

In May 2009, the Editor was informed by the City Clerk Department that this ordinance had not yet been adopted by the City Council.

CHAPTER 43

Toledo Carefully Regulates Existing Adult Businesses

Robert Henry

Regulation of sexually oriented businesses became one of the more challenging tasks faced by Toledo, as a balance is required between the concerns of the citizens and the rights of the sexually oriented businesses and their customers to operate within the City of Toledo.

This issue was brought to the forefront with the opening of Priscilla's, a "sex shop," selling racy lingerie, sex toys and gag gifts across the street from an all girls Catholic high school. The City initially allowed the store to open and then after a number of citizen protests attempted to close it because it was located within 500 feet of a school and a church in what the City claimed was a violation of a City zoning ordinance. Priscilla's filed litigation and the City allowed the store to remain open. Citizens believed the City was regulating the locations of these businesses.

In actuality, the City had not been attentive to the issues involving sexually oriented businesses. They had been attempting to regulate these businesses through the use of zoning, which was a good tool for dealing with the issues of location but a poor tool for dealing with the actual operation of the business. The City needed to develop regulations on the

adult entertainment industry that were clearer, more effective and more easily enforced.

It was clear to the City that the regulation of sexually oriented businesses was going to be a challenging task. The concerns of the community and the First Amendment rights of the business and their customers had to be balanced. The City realized they would be in a better legal position if they conducted their own study of the problem instead of relying on the studies conducted in other communities. Therefore, the City decided to hire a nationally known consulting firm of Duncan and Associates to assist with the study.

A review of existing zoning and licensing ordinances as well as state statues and previous and ongoing litigation was conducted. Crime reports were reviewed to better understand the types of complaints occurring at these establishments. On site visits at each establishment were also conducted. A public hearing was also held where citizens talked about the adverse effect on the quality of life in their neighborhoods.

Based upon all the information gathered, several City Ordinances were repealed and new ones enacted to establish reasonable and

Originally published as "Regulating Sexually Oriented Businesses," *SARA Committee Report*, 2003, by the Office of the Chief of Police, Police Department, City of Toledo, OH.

uniform regulations regarding sexually oriented businesses.

Scanning

The regulation of sexually oriented businesses has become one of the more challenging tasks facing communities today. There needs to be a balance between the concerns of the citizens and the rights of the sexually oriented businesses and their customers to operate in the City.

The issue that brought the sexually oriented business to the forefront in Toledo was the opening of Priscilla's, a "sex shop" located opposite the Notre Dame Academy, an all girls Catholic high school. This store sells racy lingerie, sexy toys, gag gifts, adult videos and magazines. The City allowed the store to open, but then after a public outcry attempted to close it based upon its location in the immediate proximity of a school and church. Priscilla's threatened litigation and the City allowed the store to remain open despite the zoning violation. It became quite clear to the community that the City had not been very attentive to the issues surrounding sexually oriented businesses and its duty to regulate them.

A review of these businesses by the Planning Commission revealed three adult clubs had permits to operate as a bar, but were passively allowed, with the City's knowledge, but not official approval, to feature sexually oriented entertainment. Two of the establishments were located too close to residential areas and one was in the wrong zoning district for adult entertainment.

Neighbors were also complaining of the noise coming from the live entertainment until the early morning hours. Others complained of seeing prostitutes walking in the area, though they may not have been associated with any business. There were complaints of finding used condoms and viewing booth tokens in the neighborhoods. Additionally residents were also concerned about the reduction of property values with an adult entertainment venue located in the neighborhood.

Neighborhood complaints were being addressed on an ad hoc basis. The police department would receive a complaint and dispatch a crew. There was no coordinated effort to solve the problem. Occasionally the Vice squad would make an arrest.

Analysis

The City Law Department, Zoning Commission, Police Department and City Council members began to examine what other cities have done to address the problem but soon realized they would be in a better legal position if they conducted their own study regarding sexually oriented businesses instead of relying on one completed for another community. City Council authorized $19,500 for a consultant to provide a fresh and objective look at the sexually oriented businesses and to assist in developing a comprehensive set of recommendations balancing the concerns of the citizens with the rights of the businesses. The City needed regulations that were clear, more effective and easily enforced.

A committee was formed consisting of representatives from City Council, the Zoning Commission, the Toledo–Lucas County Planning Commission, the Law Department and the Police Department to assist the consultant in the study. A review of the existing zoning and licensing ordinances as well as state statutes and previous case law was conducted. Zoning ordinances were reviewed by examining the provisions that directly affect sexually oriented businesses and zoning characteristics of non-residential areas that may provide appropriate locations for these businesses.

Twenty-five sexually oriented businesses were identified in Toledo and were separated into the following categories: Adult cabarets (5), Adult Theater (1), Adult Book Stores (7),

Contact/Encounter Business (6), Sex Shop (1), Byrne Road "strip mall" (5).

Crime reports at these identified sexually oriented businesses were reviewed for the preceding two years to assist in understanding the types of complaints that these establishments were generating. A total of 338 police reports had been taken at 25 separate locations. Forty percent of these reports were at the Byrne Road "strip mall," a shopping plaza that contains four different types of sexually oriented businesses: a sex shop, adult cabaret, adult bookstore and a massage parlor.

Of the 338 reports, 104 were for crimes of violence, 65 involved vehicles, 14 involved sex crimes, 10 involved public indecency, 57 involved a theft offense, 6 involved narcotics complaints, and 82 were miscellaneous reports.

With the exception of the massage parlor, site visits were conducted at each of the identified sexually oriented businesses within Toledo.

The committee looked at two types of data. First were the secondary effects of the business on the surrounding neighborhood. A basic principle of First Amendment law is that protected speech may not be restricted because of its content, but speech can be restricted to reduce the "secondary effects" of the business on the surrounding neighborhood.[1]

Secondly, activities were examined that concerned residents but are not protected by the First Amendment. For example, what a newspaper prints is protected by the First Amendment. However, the location of the building in which it is printed is subject to zoning laws. The First amendment protects the dancers on stage as a form of expression but it does not protect activities such as lap dancing which constitutes interaction between dancers and the public.

The most common secondary effect occurs when the business is located close to a residential area or an area where families frequent. People unwittingly come into contact with the business when used condoms and tokens for viewing booths in their neighbor-

hoods are found. Children finding these items are of particular concern.

It was discovered that one of the adult cabarets was providing transportation for male patrons to a nearby home rented by a dancer from the club. Further investigation yielded enough information for a search warrant to be issued resulting in the subsequent seizure of narcotics. The owner of the residence was notified and the tenant was evicted.

A citywide meeting was organized by the committee for citizens to express their concerns regarding issues related to sexually oriented businesses. The most prominent concerns were the concentration of sexually oriented businesses — especially those with live entertainment — within North Toledo neighborhoods and the negative effect on "legitimate business" when a sexually oriented business moves into a shopping plaza.

Others complained of the noise generated by the live entertainment businesses that stretched into the early morning hours on weekends. One resident expressed concern of children seeing scantily dressed dancers taking breaks behind a club abutting a residential area.

Response

From the site visits, discussions with businesses and residents, and a review and analysis of litigation and judicial decisions in the city and others, the committee decided to repeal current ordinances and implement new ones. It was not the intent of these ordinances to restrict or deny access by adults to sexually oriented materials protected by the First Amendment, or to deny access by the distributors and exhibitors of sexually oriented entertainment to their intended market. Nor did the City with these ordinances condone or legitimize the viewing and distribution of obscene material. The requirements set forth in these new ordinances did not "grandfather" existing businesses.

Chapter 767 entitled Sexually Oriented Businesses was enacted. The first part of the ordinance set forth definitions of terms (which had previously never been defined) such as sexually oriented business, adult media, adult media store, booth, entertainer, gross public floor area, hard core material, lingerie modeling or photography studio, massage, nude, semi nude, sex shop, sexual encounter center, sexually oriented cabaret, cinema and theater and specified sexual activities. The second part of the ordinance regulates sexually oriented businesses by limiting their hours of operation and location of business, specifying requirements for arcades, cabarets, lingerie modeling and photography studios, setting forth the responsibilities of the operators of these businesses, and listing certain prohibitions and unlawful acts such as having physical contact with an entertainer while they are engaged in a performance of live, sexually oriented entertainment. This new ordinance also prohibits a massage parlor from operating. A massage parlor is defined as an establishment not employing persons licensed by the State of Ohio ORC 4731.16. Unlike previous ordinances directed at sexually oriented businesses, this ordinance did not "grandfather" existing businesses but gave them 90 days from the effective date to comply with the provisions of this chapter.

City Council also passed an ordinance that will regulate where a sexually oriented business can locate. Previously they were allowed to operate in areas zoned only C-3 Commercial or C-5 Central Business District. They are now additionally permitted to operate in areas Zoned M-1 Restricted Industrial District and M-2 Industrial District, which actually brought several businesses into compliance. Further restrictions for a sexually oriented business require that they shall not locate within five hundred (500) feet of any residential district, school (K–12), pre school, child care center, religious institution, public park or playground, public library or other use established for minors, or within one thou-

sand (1,000) feet of another existing sexually-oriented business.

A third ordinance was passed repealing previous Massage Parlor licensing provisions. Massage Studios must now operate with a State certified massage therapist under ORC 4731.16 or under the direct supervision of a licensed physician.

With these ordinances Toledo was seeking a balance in regulating land use. The City recognized they can not ban all sexually oriented businesses but made reasonable provisions for sexually oriented businesses to operate. They also did not allow these businesses to offer all the products or activities they might like to offer. With the enforcement of these changes, the negative impact upon residential areas by sexually oriented businesses has been minimized.

Assessment

To assess the impact of the ordinances on sexually oriented businesses, the department has engaged the following techniques:

- Tracking the calls for service at these businesses
- Examining Crime Analysis information for the areas surrounding these establishments
- Direct observation
- Community involvement through Block Watch groups
- Examining advertisements in local newspapers

As a result of this work, massage parlors have been eliminated within the City. Advertisements in the local newspaper are now appearing for massage parlors operating approximately 40 miles from Toledo.

Sexually-oriented businesses not licensed to sell alcoholic beverages are now limited in their hours of operations from 6 A.M. to 2:30 A.M. Monday through Saturday and Noon to 2:30 A.M. on Sunday. This has eliminated many complaints of noise continuing throughout the night.

Sexually oriented businesses licensed to sell alcohol are abiding by the hours of operation permitted by their liquor license.

Random inspections during business hours by the Police Department, Department of Economic Development, the Fire Department, Department of Finance (Licensing Agency) and the Health Department are conducted to ensure compliance with all regulations.

Conclusion

The problem solving initiative was adopted by the entire City. All officers in the police department began to receive training in problem oriented policing in 1995 and are expected to practice it in their daily work. This training has now been incorporated into the Academy curriculum.

A committee selected by the Chief reviews exceptional problem solving projects. The committee examines the problem, the analysis conducted by the officers, their response and the assessment. Awards are then presented to officers who the committee believes exhibited the best response to their problem-solving project.

Officers in the department are trained in the SARA model of problem solving.

City Council authorized $19,500 to hire a consultant to assist with a study of sexually oriented businesses in Toledo.

NOTE

1. Playtime Theatres, Inc. v. City of Renton, 475 U.S. 41, 106 S. Ct. 925, 89 L. Ed. 2d 29 (1986).

Editor's Notes:

1. The SARA problem solving process was developed to build problem-solving partnerships, and consists of a four step decision making model that includes Scanning, Analysis, Response, and Assessment (SARA). It is a part of the Community Policing process and dates back to the late 1970s.

2. The City of Toledo's ordinance regulating sexually oriented businesses was unanimously approved by the City Council on January 21, 2003, and took effect for existing businesses on July 21 of the same year. The regulations contained in this ordinance included requirements for the minimum height of stages, the distance dancers must keep from patrons, the conditions of booths in adult video arcades, requiring an adult business to close between 2:30 and 6:00 A.M. if they have no liquor license, as well as other regulations.

3. Other Community Policing practices that focus on neighborhood problem-solving can be obtained from the Center for Problem-Oriented Policing website <www.popcenter.org>.

CHAPTER 44

Urbana Plans for the Future by Regulating Adult Businesses Before It Has One

Mary M. Farmer

The Town Council, in amending their Town Municipal Code to have regulations for adult entertainment uses, adopted several "legislative findings, intent, and determination" for their decision-making action. The first several paragraphs below list the rationale of the City's elected officials for adopting these additions to their municipal code. These changes included appropriate definitions, the specific activities covered by this law, and local restrictions on adult entertainment businesses. All of these new additions by the City's code are explained below.

The Town of Urbana is a residential community consisting of approximately 2,600 people encompassed within an area of 4.1 square miles. Even though the Town does not currently have an adult business, the possibility exists since it is served by several highways providing easy access from all directions.

It is recognized that there are some uses, which, because of their very nature, have serious objectionable operational characteristics under certain circumstances, thereby producing a deleterious effect upon adjacent areas. Special regulation of these uses is necessary to ensure that their adverse effects will not contribute to the blighting or downgrading of the surrounding residential neighborhoods and sensitive areas. The Town Board of the Town of Urbana finds it in the public interest to enact these regulations.

The unrestrained proliferation and inappropriate location of such businesses is inconsistent with existing development and future plans for the Town of Urbana because, quite often, they result in influences on the community which increase the crime rate and undermine the economic and social welfare of the community. The deleterious effects of these businesses change the economic and social character of the existing community and adversely affect existing businesses and community and family life.

Having no adult entertainment business, the Adult Entertainment Uses Law Advisory Committee relied upon the studies in the Village of Scotia, New York; Village of Savona, New York; Austin, Texas; Newport News, Virginia; Garden Grove, California; Islip, New York, Indianapolis, Indiana, and the City of New Rochelle, New York, to determine if

Originally published as "Adult Entertainment Use Amendments to the Town Municipal Code," *Ordinance Number 1-2004*, April 17, 2007, by the Office of the Town Clerk, Town of Urbana, Hammondsport, NY.

adult entertainment regulations were necessary within the Town's boundaries. After reviewing these studies, the Adult Entertainment Uses Law Advisory Committee determined that the impact of adult entertainment decreased residential property values, deteriorated conditions of the residential neighborhood, attracted the wrong type of clientele, increased traffic, increased noise, increased criminal activity, including sex crime, and threatened the character and general quality of life in a small town. The Committee was also concerned that, because the Town of Urbana is residential and has several sensitive areas, the placement of adult businesses anywhere within its boundaries would most likely result in increased home sales by the elderly, as well as families with children, thus having a negative impact on the Town's growth.

The Town Board recognizes the right for an adult entertainment business to exist. It is not the Board's intent to prohibit such activities but to reasonably regulate their location through the Town's zoning powers. Since the residential district and sensitive areas comprise the largest part of the community, finding an area for adult uses within the Town, and still maintaining the required 1,000 feet from residential district and 1,500 feet from sensitive use areas, was difficult.

The only area determined to be a suitable area for adult entertainment uses is designated to be located along County Route 113, commencing as its intersection with Longwell Road and continuing thereon in a general southerly direction to the borderline of the Town of Bath, to be zoned for adult entertainment uses. By limiting adult entertainment uses to this district, the impact of such a business is minimized while still providing a reasonable area for meeting all of the requisite legal criteria.

Accordingly, the Town Board of Urbana declares that the purpose of this chapter is to prevent or lessen the negative effects of adult entertainment uses and not to inhibit the right of free expression guaranteed by the United States and New York State Constitutions as they may be expressed and presented in the form of goods and services offered by adult-oriented businesses.

Therefore, the Town Board of the Town of Urbana hereby concludes that the health, safety and general welfare of the Town would be protected and promoted, and the overall public interest would best be served, by its enactment of this chapter.

Definitions

As used in this chapter of the code, the following terms shall have those meanings indicated under the heading of "Adult Entertainment Use" in the Town of Urbana's municipal code.

- *Adult Book and/or Video Store*— An establishment having a substantial or significant portion of its stock in trade books, magazines, periodicals, or other printed matter of photographs, films, videos, slides or other visual representations which are characterized by the exposure or emphasis of specified sexual activities or specified anatomical areas, or instruments, devices or paraphernalia which are designed for use in connection with specified sexual activities and which are for sale, rental or viewing on or off the premises.

- *Adult Entertainment Cabaret*— A public or private establishment which regularly presents topless and/or bottomless dancers, strippers, waiters or waitresses, male or female impersonators, lingerie models or exotic dancers, or other similar entertainment or films, motion pictures, videos, slides or other pornographic material, or which utilizes employees who, as part of their employment, regularly expose patrons to specified sexual activities or specified anatomical areas and which has a prevailing practice of excluding minors by virtue of their age.

- *Adult Theater*— A theater, concert hall, auditorium or similar establishment which, for any type of consideration, regularly features live performances characterized by the exposure of specified sexual activities or anatomical areas.

- *Adult Motion Picture Theater*— Any motion-picture theater where, for any type of consideration, films, motion pictures, video cassettes, slides or other photographic reproductions are shown, and in which a substantial portion of the local presentation time is devoted to the showing of material characterized by an emphasis upon the depiction or description of specified sexual activities or specified anatomical areas.

- *Massage Establishment*— Any establishment having a fixed place of business where massages are administered for pay, including but not limited to massage parlors, sauna baths or steam baths. This definition shall not be construed to include a hospital, nursing home or medical clinic or the office of a physician, surgeon, chiropractor, osteopath, duly licensed physical therapist, or duly licensed massage therapist or barbershop or beauty salon, athletic club, health club, school, spa or similar establishment where massage or similar manipulation of the human body is offered as an incidental accessory service.

- *Adult Model Studio*— Any place where a person appearing in a state of nudity or displaying specified anatomical areas is made available for observation or to be sketched, drawn, painted, sculpted, photographed or similarly depicted by other persons who pay money or any other type of consideration therefore.

- *Peep Shows*— A theater which presents materials distinguished or characterized by primary emphasis on matters depicting, describing or relating to specified sexual activities or specified anatomical areas, in the form of live shows, films or videotapes, viewed from an individual enclosure, for which a fee is charged.

Specific Activities Covered

The following two "areas of activity" were also set forth in this new chapter of the Town Code relating to adult entertainment use.

- *Specified Anatomical Areas*— Less than completely and opaquely covered human genitals, pubic region, buttocks and female breasts below a point immediately above the top of the areola; and human male genitals in a discernibly turgid state even if completely and opaquely covered.

- *Specified Sexual Activity*— Human genitals in a state of sexual stimulation or arousal; acts of human masturbation, sexually intercourse or sodomy; or fondling, or other erotic touching of human genitals, pubic region, buttocks or breasts.

Locational Restrictions on Adult Uses

The following locational restrictions were adopted for adult entertainment uses.

- Adult entertainment uses shall be permitted only in that area hereinabove set forth in §34-1F.

- Adult entertainment uses shall be prohibited within a distance of 1,000 feet from the property line of any residence.

- Adult entertainment uses shall be located at a distance of at least 1,500 feet from sensitive use areas wherein is located any private or public schools; or any church or other religious facility or institution; or any public park, public bike path, playground, playing field, cemetery, civic or recreational facility.

- No adult entertainment use shall be permitted to be within 500 feet of another such use, and only one such use shall be located on any lot.

- The distances provided hereinabove shall be measured by following a straight line without regard to intervening buildings, from the nearest point of the property parcel upon which the adult entertainment use is to be located to the nearest point of the parcel of property or the land use district boundary line from which the adult entertainment use is to be separated.

Other Restrictions on Adult Uses

The following list includes other restrictions that were approved for adult entertainment uses, including exterior displays, advertising, the site plan approval process, compliance requirements, and their hours of operation.

• No adult entertainment use shall be conducted in any manner that allows the observation of any material depicting, describing or relating to specified sexual activities or specified anatomical areas from any public way or from any property not containing an adult entertainment use. This provision shall apply to any display, decoration, sign, show, window or other opening.

• There shall be no outdoor sign, display, or advertising of any kind other than one identification sign limited only to the name of the establishment.

• Adult entertainment uses shall be required to obtain site plan approval from the Town Planning Board in accordance with Chapter 88 of the Urbana Town Code.

• Adult entertainment uses shall meet all other regulations of the Town of Urbana, including but not limited to district lot and bulk regulations, parking regulations and signage.

• It shall be unlawful to operate any adult entertainment use between the hours of 12:00 midnight and 8:00 A.M.

The Future

Given the fact that the Town of Urbana had no adult entertainment businesses located in their community, advanced planning such as this avoid potential litigation in the future. It is advantageous to have the "law on the books" before the application is made, rather than "after the fact."

Given the Town's location on a major State of New York highway (Route 54), a well traveled artery in the Finger Lakes Region, the Town's elected officials wanted these laws in place. Other local towns without regulations received applications from adult businesses, and were legally forced to let them in their community.

Editor's Note:

The above section of this chapter, "The Future," was added by the Editor to place the Town's proactive efforts at regulating the location of adult entertainment businesses in perspective.

CHAPTER 45

Waco Works with Citizens and Makes Public Investment to Bring Back a Deteriorated Neighborhood

Michael Morrison

The Jubilee Center, a multi-purpose neighborhood service facility, is located in a deteriorating neighborhood which was once a thriving area of neighborhood retail stores and restaurants surrounded by tree-lined streets with beautiful residential structures. Mission Waco, a local non-profit organization, and neighborhood residents have been working hard to take back their neighborhood, and the Jubilee Center is a focal point of that effort.

Mission Waco, which is coordinating the neighborhood revitalization, assembled the financing for Jubilee Center, with CDBG funding serving as the catalyst for contributions from other organizations and businesses. CDBG provided $125,000 for restoration of the facility and $20,000 for a youth development program. The Enterprise Community Grant provided $51,000. Several local foundations and associations provided $114,000 in grants. Local businesses donated over $110,000 in labor and materials.

The Jubilee Center, formerly a large commercial building that deteriorated into a site for drugs, prostitutes, bars and a porn theater, now includes:

- Wings, a pre- and post-employment job training center for unemployed persons, which provides placement after graduation;
- an after-school tutoring program for children which includes help with homework, reading and language;
- a computer lab, available in the evenings and on weekends, which provides 30 computers loaded with literacy and English/Spanish language training materials;
- Homestore, a discount store, which sells donated housing materials for residents to use in maintaining their homes;
- a pay-station which neighborhood residents can use to pay personal utility and telephone bills and to access financial resources via Western Union, and an automatic teller machine;
- a Business Resource Center which provides incubator assistance to start-up businesses;
- a Theater/Meeting Center which includes a theater for stage presentations, arts training, production training, and seating for meetings and seminars;
- retail space; and

Originally published as "Status Report on the Development of the Jubilee Center," *Community Development Block Grant Success Stories*, 1999, by the Office of the Mayor, City of Waco, TX.

- a teen clubhouse which is open late on weekends for supervised activities.

Working with public and private organizations, educational groups, foundations, churches and neighbors, Mission Waco's efforts have led to other positive developments in the immediate area. Down the block from Jubilee Center, the McLennan Community College has started a small engine repair training center; Kimberly Clark has donated a new playground; and across the street, Habitat for Humanity is building its 45th house.

Downtown Overlay District

It was the unanimous recommendation of the City's Planning Commission that the City Council approve a Public Improvement District (PID), frequently referred to as an "overlay district." This approval was granted by the Planning Commission at their meeting in February 2009, and is being sent on to the City Council for its consideration at a subsequent public meeting.

The overlay district, as its very reason for being considered, states the following. The purpose of the Downtown district is to create a place:

- Where people can live, work, and play within its boundaries,
- That values the architectural history of our community,
- That encourages the best of contemporary design, and
- That encourages human interaction through the development of a physical environment that is vital, attractive, pedestrian friendly, and secure.

The law that creates this overlay district sets forth nearly two dozen definitions: the fact that it is a zoning classification within the City of Waco, that the regulations contained in this ordinance are applicable to all of the proper-

ties located in this area, and a list of suggested prohibited land uses. These prohibited land uses include, but are not limited to, sexually oriented businesses, manufactured homes, television and radio broadcasting towers, car-washing establishments, garages that repair machinery, self-storage warehouses, motor freight and truck service terminals; junkyards, wrecking yards, salvage yards, and scrap operations; and facilities related to the storage or refining of petroleum or its products.

The PID goes on to cover such areas as building forms, which include setbacks, height and width limitations, ground floor levels, entrance locations, loading and service entries, the treatment of facades, private frontage, awnings, windows, and construction materials. Also includes in the proposed overlay district are requirements for parking and access, signage, fencing, and the treatment of public spaces.

There is no doubt that the purpose of the Public Improvement District is to preserve the taxpayers' investment and hard work that has been done over the years. These efforts, as mentioned above, have been undertaken by the City of Waco in its development of the Jubilee Center, other investments made by downtown stakeholders, and the slow but continuous restoration of the neighborhood by the citizens who live there. The stage has been set by the Planning Commission, and there is no doubt that the City Council will want to help achieve this goal.

Editor's Notes:

1. It should be noted that nearly a decade has elapsed from the investment of Community Development Block Grant (CDBG) funds to restore the Jubilee Center, and the approval of the proposed Public Improvement District being recommended by the City's Planning Commission (i.e., 1999 to 2009).

2. A copy of the Proposed Downtown Overlay Zoning District may be obtained from the City of Waco's website, which is listed in the *Appendix* of this volume in the *Regional Resource Directory*.

3. Because of its importance, since it specifically prohibits certain land uses, the discussion "Downtown Overlay District" was added by the Editor.

CHAPTER 46

Wichita Spends Public Funds to Stimulate Private Investment to Revitalize Its Downtown

D. Kay Johnson

Today Old Town, a 40-acre sub-district of downtown Wichita, Kansas, is a blur of activity both day and night. Residents and visitors are drawn to the streets by the compact neighborhood's historic character, its plazas and parks, and a wealth of dining, shopping, cultural, and entertainment options. But Old Town has not always been a vibrant community. Innovative thinking and cooperation among local government, businesses, and citizens have overcome seemingly insurmountable barriers and brought about purposeful change in what was once a blighted area.

Present day *Old Town*, decidedly urban but distinctly Kansan, exemplifies innovative urban planning. The process that brought about Old Town's renaissance, as well as the end result, are reasons that in 2006 the U.S. Environmental Protection Agency (EPA) awarded the *City of Wichita* one of it highest honors for urban planning: the *National Award for Smart Growth Achievement—Built Projects.*

A Forgotten City Center

By the 1980s Wichita's downtown had gone the way of many urban centers. Businesses had moved out or closed leaving buildings vacant and boarded. The life and excitement of Wichita's core area had drained away. Crime rates were up, few restaurants remained, and cultural and entertainment venues were nonexistent. Core areas of the city were underutilized and needed assistance to compete with suburban developments.

Concerned that the situation was affecting the city's ability to advance economic development initiatives, city leaders decided to embark on a bold, large-scale redevelopment plan. The plan would start with the renovation of Old Town, a rundown warehouse district where more than 50 percent of the buildings were vacant.

At the time, Old Town served as an industrial and wholesale distribution location, with turn-of-the-century brick buildings, brick streets, railroad tracks, and several dirt and gravel parking lots. Businesses that had

Originally published as "Wichita's Old Town: A Revitalization Success Story," *Application Information from EPA's National Award for Smart Growth Achievement*, March 20, 2007, by the Department of Environmental Services, City of Wichita, KS.

originally located in the area because of proximity to rail access were no longer compatible with the area and now caused congestion with their heavy truck traffic. The area suffered from a steadily declining image, competition with suburban developments, and a lack of both pedestrians and pedestrian-friendly infrastructure. Old Town was an underutilized area ripe for rehabilitation.

Planning for Redevelopment

In 1988 MarketPlace Properties was selected as the site's preferred private sector developer, and a public-private partnership was solidified. The city's approach was to use public investments to leverage private redevelopment. To that end, the city would coordinate capital improvements, assemble land, and provide public parking facilities. The city established financial incentives, primarily in the form of tax increment financing, to attract private investment. It also offered historic tax credits and living amenities, such as affordable housing and free parking. The city knew that successful revitalization was contingent upon maintaining the historic character of the area and introducing mixed uses that would attract activity beyond the typical nine-to-five cycle.

Decisions regarding rehabilitation of Old Town were made with citizen and stakeholder input. Initial comprehensive studies and plans of the site included citizen input at public meetings. And, prior to development of Old Town Square, area merchants and property owners were surveyed to determine what was included in their vision of Old Town.

Discovery Threatens Redevelopment of Old Town

In 1990 the city started implementation of the first phase of Old Town's redevelopment plan by making initial infrastructure renovations. Then, bad news arrived: The Kansas Department of Health and Environment (KDHE) informed local officials and the public that it had discovered widespread groundwater contamination in an aquifer encompassing 2,600 acres, directly under the downtown area.

After the U.S. EPA Site Investigation Report was made public, all private commercial real estate activity within the contaminated area — dubbed "Gilbert and Mosley" after the intersection of two streets at the heart of the contamination — came to a complete halt. Old Town redevelopment plans appeared doomed by the prospect of a Superfund listing. While public improvements could be started, private contributions had to be put on hold. Some $86 million worth of commercial and residential properties were affected, comprising more than 8,000 individual parcels of land. Financial institutions, wary of liability, discontinued loans in the affected area, and one of Wichita's most important tax bases began to erode. After a funeral home in the area was refused a loan to rebuild following a fire, the city knew it needed to take action. It would do whatever was necessary to prevent the contamination from ruining both the city's redevelopment plans and the existing downtown tax base.

City Takes On Groundwater Contamination

Working quickly, city officials decided to take responsibility for the contaminated area rather than let it become a Superfund site. At the time, this was an unheard of action. Although it lacked a model for how municipalities could play an effective role in site cleanup, the city forged ahead. Committed to expediting the cleanup and protecting innocent property owners from unwarranted liability, the city signed a cleanup agreement with KDHE and hired a nationally recognized consultant to conduct further investigations into the extent and the causes of the contamination.

Key to the city's approach to addressing the contamination was the development of strategic alliances with stakeholder groups. Under the city's leadership, local businesses and property owners, homeowners, lending institutions, real estate companies, environment and health specialists, regulators, and state legislators joined forces. These stakeholders helped the city promote changes to state laws to create a unique funding mechanism (a capped, reverse tax increment financing plan) for the investigation and eventual cleanup, estimated at upwards of $30 million.

To set redevelopment back on track, the city developed and implemented a "Certification and Release of Liability" program. Under the program, the city signed agreements with the lending institutions that ensured these agencies were protected from property liability. This action allowed property values to be maintained and reinstituted loan transactions in the area.

The city knew it was going to be required to make long-term commitments to remove, treat, and dispose of contaminated groundwater. An innovative remediation plan was prepared that included a treatment and education facility, the *Wichita Area Treatment, Education & Remediation (WATER) Center*. This facility would eventually be designed and built to receive and treat groundwater from around the contaminated site, while also creating an environment education facility in a public park.

Private Investment Resumes

Once funding was identified for investigation and remediation of the groundwater contamination and a liability release program was established, phase one of the Old Town's private investment could resume. Over the next decade, more than 60 buildings were rehabilitated for mixed use by the private sec-tor, including specialty restaurants and retail, mixed-use office complexes, apartments and condominiums, an historic hotel, and cultural and entertainment venues.

At the same time, the city carried out the public portion of the project, including construction of parking lots and structures providing over 1,100 parking spaces; renovation of six blocks of brick streets; and construction of entry arches and additional infrastructure. In addition, the city constructed a Farm and Art Market and an adjacent brick plaza.

In 2003 phase two of redevelopment, another public-private partnership, expanded the Old Town area eight acres to the north. This phase, called Old Town Square, included another planned mixed use area, a movie theater, two residential projects, and 90,000 square feet of office and retail space. The city invested in a *CityArts* building that holds gallery exhibitions, art events, and educational programs for children and adults. Additional public investments included a 500-car parking garage and plaza area as well as construction of streets and infrastructure, similar to phase one.

Smart Growth Concepts Increase Livability and Attraction

Comprehensive plans dating back to 1989 stress the importance of reinvestment in and strengthening of existing communities to achieve balance in regional development. Old Town redevelopment has not only established equilibrium with infill development but also encouraged citizen and stakeholder participation in development decisions.

The new *Old Town* — now 93 percent built-out — emphasizes urban living, utilizing compact, mixed use, and pedestrian-friendly design. Private developers took advantage of compact building design, building housing, office, and commercial spaces "up" not "out." Residents have a variety of housing options, including condominiums, lofts, and apartments. More than 100 restaurants, shops, clubs, theaters, museums, and businesses have been established in the area. And the central, downtown location allows for a wider variety of transportation choices than any other area of town.

Inviting plazas and parks entice residents and visitors to step out and enjoy the walkable community. And citizens can learn about the groundwater cleanup at the new *WATER Center.* This facility was constructed in a large city park and features walking paths, large indoor and outdoor aquaria, a constructed wetland for actual treated water disposal, as well as a commitment to public education, so that the care can be taken to prevent future groundwater contamination.

A Successful Transformation

The main goal of the Old Town project was to complete a mixed-use development that would capitalize on the historic beauty of downtown Wichita and foster new life in a declining area. The area has been transformed from a rundown warehouse district to a premier urban community that has an active neighborhood association with loyal and committed residents.

Resident and business owner Joan B. Cole, of Cole Consultants, provides a testimonial for Old Town's livability: "I reside in a third-floor condo of a redeveloped brick and concrete warehouse. My office is on the first floor of the same building, so my commute takes two minutes and costs nothing. Living in the center of downtown is exciting, convenient, and satisfying. I love it."

Old Town has also impacted the area's private development sector. Private investments have exceeded public investment by six times. Phase two alone saw over $14 million invested by the private sector. Since construction, over 80 businesses have located in Old Town, employing more than 900 people. Development has generated $40 million in increased property values. And, significant development continues.

The success of Old Town's redevelopment has spurred other exciting downtown Wichita projects. These include a new riverfront retail development called WaterWalk (a public private partnership between the city of Wichita and WaterWalk LLC) and a new all-purpose 15,000-seat community arena being built by Sedgwick County. Both projects are scheduled to be finished in the next three years.

Innovative leadership by city government, including positive and swift action when faced with a daunting dilemma; full participation by private sector partners; and involvement of citizens and other stakeholders have provided the impetus for a vibrant future for Wichita's downtown core area.

Editor's Notes:

1. A protective Overlay Zone was also added to the Old Town area to preserve its historical character and the type of businesses that locate in this area.

2. The Old Town area was also the recipient of the Ford Foundation Innovation Award, and was recently recognized as one of the top 10 American Planning Association (APA) "Great Neighborhoods for 2008." The APA award acknowledge that "...it was singled out for the city's bold vision, astute planning, collaborative partnerships, and innovative practices that transformed a derelict warehouse and light industrial district into a bustling and successful mixed-use quarter."

3. Today Old Town is home to 130 businesses. Property values have grown more than six-fold since 1992, and a proposal to extend Amtrak passenger service between Oklahoma City and Wichita is presently under consideration.

4. When public officials in a city work with citizens to determine their desires and priorities, then make an investment of public funds, this is one of the best ways that exist to stimulate neighborhood redevelopment.

SECTION III: THE FUTURE

CHAPTER 47

Cities, Adult Businesses, Regulations, and the Law

David L. Hudson, Jr.

Adult-entertainment establishments face a litany of restrictions ranging from licensing to zoning to regulating the content of nude dancing. A common restriction on such businesses limits the hours of operations, prohibiting them from being open during early morning hours. These limits are justified — like nearly all other restrictions on adult businesses — based on the secondary-effects doctrine.

This doctrine provides that government officials have greater leeway to restrict adult businesses and their expressive content if the purpose of the regulation is to combat harmful side (or secondary) effects allegedly associated with such businesses — such as decreased property values and increased crime. The doctrine does not save government limits if the true purpose of the regulation is to suppress free expression. In the federal courts, regulations on adult businesses justified by the secondary-effects doctrine are evaluated under a lower level of review — intermediate scrutiny — rather than the highest form of judicial review — called strict scrutiny.

Many federal courts have upheld hours-of-operations regulations, reasoning that the intent of the laws was to combat crime —

much of which occurs in the early morning hours. However, what if there is more crime committed at a local 24–7 convenience store than at the local adult bookstore? Furthermore, a looming question on the horizon is whether a state Supreme Court might view a restriction on adult businesses with a more critical eye under its state constitution than a federal court would under the First Amendment.

A case in Arizona may serve to be such a test case for hours-of-operation litigation on both counts — whether these restrictions actually combat secondary effects and whether there may be greater relief for free-speech claimants under a state constitution. In *State of Arizona v. Stummer*, the Arizona Supreme Court ruled in October 2008 that a lower court must apply a higher level of scrutiny (or review) to a challenge to an hours-of-operation regulation brought under the Arizona Constitution.

A state Supreme Court is free to interpret its own state constitution's free-speech provision to provide greater protection for individual freedom than the U.S. Supreme Court provides under the federal Constitution's First Amendment.

Originally published as "What's on the Horizon," *Adult Entertainment Issues*, October 2008, by the First Amendment Center, Vanderbilt University, Nashville, TN Reprinted with permission of the publisher.

In the *Strummer* case, the Arizona Supreme Court declined to apply the traditional intermediate-scrutiny standard applied in secondary-effects cases in the federal courts. "Because Arizona's speech provision safeguards the right to speak freely on all topics, our test must more closely scrutinize laws that single out speech for regulation based on its disfavored content," the Arizona high court wrote.

The Arizona high court also questioned whether secondary effects are really greater during late-night or early morning hours. The state high court noted that "the record is devoid of evidence that secondary effects are greater during the hours of forced closure." The state high court added that "the government must establish that, during their early morning operation, adult bookstores disproportionately cause negative secondary effects and that these negative effects are or will be significantly lessened by closure during those hours."

The case is headed back to the lower courts and bears close watching.

CHAPTER 48

Zoning, Land Uses, and the Future of Downtowns

George R. Frantz

Communities across the United States recognize the value of—and continue to invest in — efforts to maintain and reinvigorate their downtowns. One critical aspect of the downtown puzzle that many cities overlook is their municipal zoning code, much of which may be working counter to their vision for downtown.

Zoning in the United States dates back to the early 1900s. Unfortunately for many downtowns, an underlying assumption of zoning, albeit rarely articulated, is that the dense urban pattern that developed in America since colonial times and which marked the typical downtown, is inherently unhealthy. The objectives of good zoning laid out in the Standard State Zoning Enabling Act published by the U.S. Department of Commerce in 1926 — including lessening congestion in the streets, securing safety from fire, providing adequate light and air, and preventing overcrowding — were part of a wider reaction to the perceived ills of America's cities. The rise of zoning also coincided with the rise of the automobile and the new American suburbs, which presented an attractive alternative to life in the city.

Particularly in smaller cities, zoning regulations were written to reflect the new suburban ideal of zoning, which emphasized the accommodation of the automobile and reducing development densities. Front, side, and rear yard setback requirements and lot coverage and building height restrictions ignored the historic American downtown development patterns, which emphasized attached, multistory buildings with zero setbacks from the right-of-way and with no provisions for parking. In many towns across the country, the very downtown properties that create the physical character and atmosphere that residents and visitors cherish do not conform to current zoning regulations.

Although nobody is being forced to tear down buildings that do not conform to zoning, nonconformance can be a major obstacle to downtown revitalization. It is one more risk that investors weighing a downtown project against one on a suburban Greenfield site must factor into the equation. The need to seek special permits, variances, or other municipal approvals for a building that does not conform to zoning may be the added cost, and the roll of the dice, that turns away the prospective investor. Design that meets local downtown

Originally published as "Downtown Revitalization: Is Your Zoning Helping or Hindering It?" *Downtown Idea Exchange*, October 15, 2007, by the Alexander Communications Group, Inc., Boonton, NJ. Reprinted with permission of the publisher.

zoning may well be possible, but more often than not, building with 10- or 20-foot setbacks, keeping to a 30- to 40-percent maximum lot coverage, and providing parking on-site is an economic non-starter.

And in too many instances where new downtown development that conforms to zoning has occurred, it has required heavy government subsidies, including from the pockets of local taxpayers. In most cases, too, the results have not been aesthetically pleasing. Simply setting a building back even just 10 feet from the historic sidewalk edge can have a dramatic visual effect on the character of a downtown commercial block. The traditional row of sidewalk storefronts is disrupted and the downtown pedestrian experience suffers. The impact on downtown character can be particularly adverse when it involved a block of historic commercial buildings.

Unfortunately in many cases, the adverse visual impact of buildings to zoning in the downtown is further exacerbated by the need to provide parking. Too often in smaller downtowns, the parking goes between the new building and the street line, or alongside the building. The hole in the fabric of a downtown gets bigger and bigger, as storefront displays are replaced with a sea of asphalt. The overall aesthetic appeal of the downtown and the quality of the pedestrian experience deteriorate accordingly.

Civic leaders, businesses, and downtown development professionals need to take a close look at their zoning regulations for downtown to ensure that the regulations will support, not impede, their vision for a vibrant downtown. The traditional fabric and historic architecture of the American downtown has weathered the post–World War II suburban development binge fairly well. The zero setbacks from the street line, 100-percent building lot coverage, and four- to five-story height limits are extremely efficient uses of land. These walkable development characteristics promote an attractive pedestrian environment, feature texture, and create an ambience the suburban strip commercial developments can only fantasize about. They are what collectively attracts increasing numbers of people back to the downtown.

Ironically, out in the suburbs, planners and developers have woken up to this very fact. Suburban communities are now adopting neotraditionalist and new urbanist–style zoning regulations that permit developers to mimic the traditional American downtown. Even they have come to recognize a good thing! Make sure your downtown zoning recognizes a good thing as well.

CHAPTER 49

Ten National Trends to Help Plan for and Develop Innovative Downtowns

Bill Ryan

Based on market analysis findings of many communities, coupled with business examples being submitted to the University of Wisconsin–Extension's Innovative Downtown Business online clearinghouse, 10 broad categories of retail are emerging as good fits for downtown. These can include both chains and independents and should be considered when downtown develops its business expansion and recruitment wish list.

1. Lifestyle and wellness retail: An innovative example of a business designed to respond to busy lifestyles is Meal Time in downtown Platteville, WI. This independent business allows busy people to prepare their own healthy meal, take it home to freeze or bake at their convenience. The business creates late afternoon traffic for the nearby wine and cheese store and fitness center.

Ladles to Linens in Winnsboro, TX, a gourmet kitchen shop, allows shoppers to take evening cooking classes. Shoppers are drawn from as far as Dallas, and often end up staying downtown for a visit to the spa and the nearby café.

Earth Rider is a bicycling business in downtown Broadhead, WI that supports a lifestyle of fitness, achievement, wellbeing, and quality of life through cycling. The business combines a retail store, rentals, tour packaging, and a bicycling-inspired inn, providing an escape from urban stress.

2. Community gathering place businesses: Downtown's central place and sense of place make it uniquely suited for people to congregate for social or community purposes.

The Red Mug Coffeehouse in downtown Superior, WI, has carved out a niche not only as a coffee shop, but also as a culturally aware store promoting the arts and organic/fair-trade food. They have become a gathering spot to organize community-oriented events geared toward education and activism.

3. Retailers that celebrate local heritage: The character of traditional downtowns is well suited to businesses that sell products to celebrate the past. While antique shops are common examples of such stores, other retailers also celebrate a community's past.

In Prairie du Chien, WI, the wood counters and floor found in Hamann's Variety Store add to the nostalgic atmosphere of the commu-

Originally published as "Ten Realistic Retail Themes for a Vibrant Downtown," *Downtown Idea Exchange*, June 15, 2008, by the Alexander Communications Group, Inc., Boonton, NJ. Reprinted with permission of the publisher.

nity. Candy purchased at the old wood counter remind many parents of the corner stores of their youth while creating the same kind of memories for their kids.

Sarah Winter Clothworks has helped call attention to the textile-manufacturing heritage in Willimantic, CT. Clothing is designed, cut, dyed, and sewn by hand onsite using natural fibers such as hemp and organic cotton. Because the products they sell are made in their store, the business is creating a connection that celebrates local heritage.

4. *Stores that entertain*: "Shoppertainment" is a concept adopted by certain major chains in recent years. But entertainment can be part of the downtown retail experience on a smaller scale.

The Mustard Museum in downtown Mount Horeb, WI, has become a draw to many visitors because the business promotes inside jokes through products such as "Evaporate Your Eyeballs Hotsauce" and collegiate T-shirts carrying the name "POUPON U." Similarly, Das Wurst Haus in Lanesboro, MN, lures customers in for German deli food (sausages, mustards, breads) with the sound of an accordion and the smell of great food.

5. *Stores that celebrate local arts*: Often people look to downtown as a place where local products are sold. Unlike the regional mall, downtowns often have stores showcasing locally made jewelry, art, and gifts.

Wind, Water and Light in downtown Champaign, IL, features original pieces in a variety of mediums from 180 local and national artists. They developed a reputation as a gallery that educates its customers about the art, the process, and the artists.

6. *Stores that educate*: Businesses that provide the community with education to accompany their products often find downtown the most attractive place to do business.

The Family Piano Co. has played an active role in the revitalization of downtown Waukegan, IL. Not only does it sell and service pianos, but the shop offers tours, lessons, and performances. Scrapbook Attic in Fre-

mont, OH sells scrap-booking essentials, but also offers free workshops.

7. *Stores with a community and global perspective*: A growing segment of the population is interested in supporting businesses that help the local economy and contribute to a better world.

Autumn Leaves has developed a niche in Ithaca, NY, as a used bookstore with the selection and quality of a new bookstore. It participates in the Ithaca HOURS program, a local currency effort in which 600 businesses participate. By participating, these businesses help keep dollars local and promote growth of the Ithaca economy. A quarter of the merchandise at Earth and State, a pottery and gift store in Media, PA, is Fair-Trade certified. The focus at Earth and State is on local artists, but integrated with pottery and pieces from all over the world.

8. *Gift and indulgences stores*: Chocolate Harbor in St. Clair, MI, is committed to the old-fashioned method of making everything from scratch. Customers can watch as they make caramel or fondant in the open kitchen, or view the making of fine German chocolate and hand-dipped truffles.

Evolutions in Design in downtown Wausau, WI, is a full-service floral business with five staff designers to help customers craft their own unique arrangements. The floral business also has a large retail area, where shoppers can buy items ranging from jewelry and gifts to furniture and local artwork.

9. *Unique destination retailers*: Many one-of-a-kind and innovative businesses successfully operate downtown. In Faribault, MN, Burkhartzmeyer Shoes prides itself on its understanding and care of feet. They retain two certified pedorthists (people trained in foot care) to assist customers in finding the perfect shoe. They attract customers from up to 50 miles away and have benefited from physician referrals.

10. *Neighborhood-serving retailers*: The growing downtown housing market requires conveniences to support quality of life.

Town Meat Market in Garden City, NY, is an example of a full-service butcher characterized by high-quality products and exceptional customer service. Their specialty is dry-aged prime beef, but their selection of meats also includes fresh fish, lobster, chicken, pork, veal, lamb, and a variety of sausages. They offer a door-to-door delivery service that operates six days a week.

In Newport, VT, the Pick & Shovel Do It Best store is one of 4,100 independently owned hardware and home improvement retailers that are members of Do It Best Corp., which claims to be the only full-line, full-service buying cooperative in the hardware, lumber, and building materials industry. The Newport store serve the surrounding neighborhoods by filling local product gaps such as pet supplies, storage and organizing, electronics, and office supplies.

Restaurants are also a key component to bringing people back downtown and can contribute to a vibrant retail center. While dining places add to downtown vitality and extend commercial activity into the evening, too many can give the appearance of a food court. Similarly, too many drinking establishments may actually discourage retail development. Accordingly, a balance between retail and food and beverage establishments is necessary.

CHAPTER 50

The Urban Center Is the Future of the American City

Diane Filippi *and* Jim Chappell

As the world evolves into one of the ten-second TV sound bits, as local newspapers lose readership, and as the population becomes increasingly mobile, demand grows for new and better ways to keep citizens informed about development so they can participate in the public process with knowledge, not just with emotion. The urban center can create a destination where the interested public can become informed players in shaping the future of its communities.

One of the earliest urban centers of this kind was the Pavillon de l'Arsenal in Paris, France. Originally founded by the French national government in 1988 to exhibit Les Grands Projets of French President François Mitterand, the Pavillon de l'Arsenal is the center of information about the past, present, and future of the Paris region. It is a nonprofit organization whose board president is the deputy mayor of Paris in charge of urban planning and architecture. Funding comes from both government and private donations. Although French culture is not renowned for participatory local planning, the facility has become a vibrant center for the design and planning community in Paris, and is often crowded. Housed in a historic 19th-century structure,

it has three floors of galleries, two presentation rooms, a small bookstore, and a book and a photo library. With 17,200 square feet (1,600 sq m) of exhibition space, the Pavillon de l'Arsenal has become an international mode for urban centers.

The permanent exhibit, located on the ground floor, features the design history of Paris, from inception through the plan for Paris 2012. The second-floor exhibition, which typically changes three times a year, recently featured European housing types from 1900 through 2007, with photographs, floor plans, site plans, critical text, and video interviews with residents. "Paris is inexhaustible," says Dominique Alba, director general of the Pavillon de l'Arsenal. "There is always more to say about its urban design and architecture."

The second floor also houses the library, with collections of plans and planning books and a photo archive of Paris. Planning data are organized by neighborhood to facilitate meetings of neighborhood organizations, helping them understand how new proposals fit into the existing fabric and into adopted public plans. "All these tools — exhibitions, conferences, debates, and the library — are available to the general public as well as to profession-

Originally published as "New Places for an Informed Public," *Urban Land*, Vol. 67, No. 3, March 2008, by the Urban Land Institute, Washington, DC. Reprinted with permission of the publisher.

als," notes Alba. "Each exhibition can be viewed on several levels, depending on the audience."

Each year the Pavillon de l'Arsenal sponsors 20 urban design, planning, and architectural competitions, the method for awarding most professional commissions in Europe. The third-floor exhibit recently showed entries in a competition to build over the Montrouge railway station and construct a new urban village atop the rail yards. The next exhibit will focus on the redevelopment of the Austerlitz neighborhood in Paris.

Many towns and cities in the Netherlands have some kind of urban center. Architectuurcentrum Amsterdam (more commonly known as ARCAM) is considered one of the most important. ARCAM was founded in 1986, and its board chair is the director of the department of urban development in the Hague. In the Netherlands, as in most European countries, urban planners typically are architects, hence the name.

Not as large as the Pavillon de l'Arsenal, or the Netherlands Architectuur Instituut in Rotterdam, ARCAM is located on Amsterdam's eastern waterfront in a building designed by architect René van Zuuk in 2003. ARCAM's mission is to fuel discussions about urbanism in and around Amsterdam and to involve the greatest possible numbers of the public. Among Dutch planners, it has a reputation for taking on tough urban issues. While this old port city evolves as a key part of a new megaregion encompassing not only the Low Countries, but also extending into northern Germany, new building types and scales must be accommodated. How and where this can be done is the subject of heated debate in the historic city. ARCAM also functions as an information center promoting high-quality architecture through its numerous publications — maps, books, and pamphlets — of interest to local citizens, architectural aficionados, and tourists. A small permanent exhibition, a time line of significant Amsterdam development and architec-

tural history from the year 800 to the present reinforces the fact that cities, no matter how vulnerable, are living organisms that change and develop.

ARCAM's ground-floor gallery typically stages five changing shows per year. An exhibition last fall featured the work of ten young architects to both engage the public in discussions with them and help "start-ups." The current exhibition focuses on Bogotá, Colombia, and is part of a series on megacities. In an era in which more than half of the world's population lives in cities ARCAM realizes it is of increasing significance to understand best practices from around the world. The exhibition documents how, under a series of activist mayors, Bogotá is successfully changing its reputation from an unsafe, unsanitary, deteriorating city, to one that is a model of how to handle growth. With efficient public transit, improved living conditions, and reduced crime, the city is on the road to financial health. This past year, featured cities in the megacities series included Jakarta, Indonesia, and Johannesburg, South Africa.

ARCAM frequently hosts forums and lectures, publishes a print and online newsletter, and conducts a variety of tours of the city and region, all with the goal of developing a better informed populace. With urban centers a feature in most towns, the Netherlands is regarded as a leader in furthering modern architecture and urban design.

In the United States, planners look to the Chicago Architecture Foundation (CAF) and the Center for Architecture in New York as successful examples of urban centers. In the 1950s and 1960s, Chicago was losing several significant architectural landmarks. The Chicago Architecture Foundation was originally founded in 1966 as a vehicle for advocating historic preservation and has since developed a wide variety of educational programs. It provides world-renowned architectural boat tours on the Chicago River, led by expert volunteer docents. Located on the ground floor of the Santa Fe building on South

Michigan Avenue across from Grant Park and the Art Institute of Chicago, CAF occupies a series of spaces centered on the glass-topped atrium in this Daniel Burnham–designed structure. The atrium houses topical and traveling exhibitions; the adjoining CitySpace Gallery designed by Skidmore, Owings & Merrill, contains a model of the city, as well as a variety of other exhibits. A 150-seat lecture hall doubles as a third gallery and a learning center serves both children and adults. As part of the foundation's commitment to education, one gallery is currently devoted to work by students at the University of Illinois at Chicago and the Illinois Institute of Technology, who are examining Chicago's past and future.

The Chicago Architecture Foundation has increased awareness of Chicago's architectural legacy as well as its planning issues and has been instrumental in preserving some of its most important landmarks. "Familiarizing citizens with issues and history specific to Chicago engenders a sense of stewardship and lays the groundwork for future involvement in discussion and debate on planning and policy issues that affect the landscape," says Lynn Osgood, CAF president and CEO, in the fall 2007 issue of *Oculus*, published by the New York Chapter of the American Institute of Architects.

The New York Chapter of the American Institute of Architects operates the New York Center for Architecture, founded in 1990 and located, since 2003, in a multilevel space designed by architect Andrew Berman in Greenwich Village. "Successful public and private collaboration in New York relies upon the Center for Architecture to provide public forums as well as open meetings for citizen activists and agency officials to discuss their projects," according to Frederic Bell, executive director. The center presents programs, for up to 150 participants, in the main hall, with two additional smaller venues. Six gallery spaces hold a variety of exhibitions; one of the current exhibits investigates the search for a new

Chinese national identity as demonstrated by the new generation of Chinese architects. Because of this center, a whole new audience beyond the architectural community is becoming involved in issues regarding the built environment — a more expansive, diverse audience — and architects are also being asked to get involved in many more community issues.

Every urban center is different, reflecting the local culture and often the special circumstances of its founding. The San Francisco Planning and Urban Research Association (SPUR) was founded in 1959 to keep San Francisco's urban core economically, environmentally, and socially healthy. Allied with redevelopment early on, the organization today has become an independent think tank. "For almost 50 years, SPUR has communicated with the public via the written and spoken word," says Gabriel Metcalf, SPUR's executive director. "We added a Web site a decade ago, and now we are developing the urban center as a new tool to really involve the public in understanding and participating in the future of the city through the shared experience that only occurs with the public working side-by-side in a non-adversarial setting."

A nonprofit organization with 3,000 members today, SPUR expects its membership to double with the opening of its urban center a year from now. Designed by San Francisco–based Pfau Architecture, Ltd., the SPUR Urban Center, a 14,500-square-foot (1,300 sq m) facility currently under construction, is located in the burgeoning Yerba Buena arts district in the heart of the expanding downtown core. "We wanted the urban center to be as transparent and open as SPUR is — a place where all the public will feel welcome and will keep coming back," says architect Peter Pfau. "Located on a tight urban site, the two-story glass façade will both attract the passing pedestrian and showcase the work being done."

Opening a year from now, the SPUR Urban Center will feature a large meeting room for 130, several smaller conference spaces, a library, 3,000 square feet (280 sq. m) of galleries, and offices for SPUR's urban research staff. The organization has raised more than $11.5 million to construct the urban center, with the participation of major developers, design professionals, and contractors in the region, as well as philanthropists, foundations, and state government. A public campaign will start this spring to complete fundraising. In a city known for an acrimonious public process, the intent is to build a more informed and democratic process by which to shape the city.

Last fall, the Chicago Architecture Foundation sponsored an organizational meeting for representatives from urban centers. The meeting included delegates from the United States, Canada, Australia, Germany, and Austria sharing insights and best practices on ways they are working to inform the public and open up dialogue and debate on the future of the built environment.

Each of the 15 organizations holds forums, debates, and public lectures; they all host exhibitions; each is in the publishing business to one degree or another; many give tours. Some do community organizing, and others help write school curricula. They see themselves as part of a larger nexus of interests — urban planners, architects, environmentalists, politicians, and grass-roots activists — and use their special programs and exhibitions to translate complex issues to help the public become more effective participants in community dialogue.

Beyond this commonality, the urban centers are as different as the communities that spawned them; they represent the particularities of place. This divergence of organizational structures and approaches is appropriate for the continuing experimentation that is the heart of the urban experience. What is important is that so many communities have found that the urban center provides a significant way to encourage an ongoing dialogue about the future of the urban world.

Editor's Note:

Urban Centers, since they are the location of government, as well as the arts and entertainment, and higher-education, will increasingly require and reflect a substantial public investment in libraries, museums, educational institutions, parks and open space, and related public improvements. Government planning processes in the future will (and must) involve those citizens that reside in these urban areas. Our nation's Urban Centers will provide the ideal forum for such upblic planning processes.

Appendices

Containing A. Periodical Bibliography; B. Regional Resource Directory; C. State Municipal League Directory; D. State Library Directory; E. National Resource Directory; F. U.S. Supreme Court Cases and Adult Business; G. Secondary Effects Land-Use Studies of Adult Businesses in America

A. Periodical Bibliography

This listing includes major periodicals in the United States that focus on contemporary issues in communities, as well as functional disciplines related to the various issues and problems facing municipal governments. The contact information to review, inquire, and order these periodicals is shown below.

American City & County
Penton Media, Inc.
(http://www.americancityandcounty.com/)

California Planner
California Chapter
American Planning Association
(http://www.calapa.org/)

Downtown Idea Exchange
Downtown Research and Development Center
Alexander Communications Group
(http://www.downtowndevelopment.com/)

Economic Development Quarterly
SAGE Publications
(http://edq.sagepub.com/)

Governing
Congressional Quarterly Inc.
(http://www.governing.com/)

Journal of the American Planning Association
American Planning Association
(http://www.planning.org/)

Land and People
The Trust for Public Land (http://www.tpl.org/)

Land Use Law & Zoning Digest
American Planning Association
(http://www.planning.org/)

Municipal Lawyer
International Municipal Lawyers Association
(http://www.imla.org/)

Planning
The American Planning Association
(http://www.planning.org/)

Public Law Journal
The State Bar of California
(http://www.calbar.ca.gov/)

Public Management
American City/County Management Association
(http://www.icma.org/)

Real Estate Economics
American Real Estate and Urban Economics Association
(http://www.areuea.org/)

The Next American City
The Next American City Inc.
(http://www.americancity.org/)

Urban Land
Urban Land Institute
(http://www.uli.org/)

Zoning News
American Planning Association
(http://www.planning.org/)

B. Regional Resource Directory

Local government organizations, including those boroughs, cities, communities, towns, villages, and counties included in the "best practices" section of this volume, are listed below in alphabetical order.

Albany, City of
(http://www.albanyny.org/)

Beckley, City of
(http://www.beckley.org/)

Boston, City of
(http://www.cityofboston.gov/)

Charleston, City of
(http://www.charlestoncity.info/)

Columbia, City of
(http://www.columbiasc.net/)

Columbus, City of
(http://www.cityofcolumbus.org/)

Conway, City of
(http://www.cityofconway.com/)

Delaware, City of
(http://www.delawareohio.net/)

Detroit, City of
(http://www.ci.detroit.mi.us/)

Erie, City of
(http://www.erie.pa.us/)

Forest Park, City of
(http://www.forestparkga.org/)

Harrisburg, City of
(http://www.harrisburgpa.gov/)

Hartford, City of
(http://www.hartford.gov/)

Hastings, City of
(http://www.ci.hastings.mn.us/)

Horry County
(See Conway, City of)

Issaquah, City of
(http://www.ci.issaquah.wa.us/)

King County
(See North Bend, City of)
(See Issaquah, City of)

Lemont, Village of
(http://www.lemont.il.us/)

Littleton, City of
(http://www.littleton.gov.org/)

Los Angeles, City of
(http://www.ci.la.ca.us/)

Lyons, Village of
(http://www.villageoflyons.com/)

Memphis, City of
(http://www.cityofmemphis.org/)

Middleton, Town of
(http://www.townofmiddleton.org/)

Minneapolis, City of
(http://www.ci.minneapolis.mn.us/)

Nashville, City of
(http://www.nashville.gov/)

New York, City of
(http://www.nyc.gov/)

North Andover, Town of
(http://www.townofnorthandover.com/)

North Bend, City of
(http://www.ci.north-bend.wa.us/)

Oakley, City of
(http://www.ci.oakley.ca.us/)

Orlando, City of
(http://www.cityoforlando.net/)

Providence, City of
(http://www.providenceri.com/)

Raleigh, City of
(http://www.raleigh-nc.org/)

Renton, City of
(http://www.rentonwa.gov/)

San Antonio, City of
(http://www.sanantonio.gov/)

Saratoga Springs, City of
(http://www.saratoga-springs.net/)

Seattle, City of
(http://www.seattle.gov/)

Shoreline, City of
(http://www.cityofshoreline.com/)

Southeast, Town of
(http://www.townofsoutheast-ny.com/)

Staunton, City of
(http://www.staunton.va.us/)

Tampa, City of
(http://www.tampagov.net/)

Thousand Oaks, City of
(http://www.ci.thousand-oaks.ca.us/)

Toledo, City of
(http://www.ci.toledo.oh.us/)

Urbana, Town of
(http://www.townofurbana.com/)

Waco, City of
(http://www.waco-texas.com/)

C. State Municipal League Directory

Most states have a municipal league, which serves as a valuable source of information about municipal governments. State leagues frequently have copies of municipal laws and policies, as well as model practices available for public officials to review in their state. The contact information for the various leagues is shown below.

Alabama League of Municipalities
(http://www.alalm.org/)

Alaska Municipal League
(http://www.akml.org/)

League of Arizona Cities and Towns
(http://www.azleague.org/)

Arkansas Municipal League
(http://www.arml.org/)

League of California Cities
(http://www.cacities.org/)

Colorado Municipal League
(http://www.www.cml.org/)

Connecticut Conference of Municipalities
(http://www.ccm-ct.org/)

Delaware League of Local Governments
(http://www.ipa.udel.edu/localgovt/dllg/)

Florida League of Cities
(http://www.flcities.com/)

Georgia Municipal Association
(http://www.gmanet.com/)

Association of Idaho Cities
(http://www.idahocities.org/)

Illinois Municipal League
(http://www.iml.org/)

Indiana Association of Cities and Towns
(http://www.citiesandtowns.org/)

Iowa League of Cities
(http://www.iowaleague.org/)

League of Kansas Municipalities
(http://www.lkm.org/)

Kentucky League of Cities
(http://www.klc.org/)

Louisiana Municipal Association
(http://www.lamunis.org/)

Maine Municipal Association
(http://www.memun.org/)

Maryland Municipal League
(http://www.mdmunicipal.org/)

Massachusetts Municipal Association
(http://www.mma.org/)

Michigan Municipal League
(http://www.mml.org/)

League of Minnesota Cities
(http://www.lmnc.org/)

Mississippi Municipal League
(http://www.mmlonline.com/)

Missouri Municipal League
(http://www.mocities.com/)

Montana League of Cities
(http://www.mlct.org/)

League of Nebraska Municipalities
(http://www.lonm.org/)

Nevada League of Cities and Municipalities
(http://www.nvleague.org/)

New Hampshire Local Government Center
(http://www.nhmunicipal.org/)

New Jersey State League of Municipalities
(http://www.njslom.com/)

New Mexico Municipal League
(http://www.nmml.org/)

New York Conference of Mayors and Municipal Officials
(http://www.nycom.org/)

North Carolina League of Municipalities
(http://www.nclm.org/)

North Dakota League of Cities
(http://www.ndlc.org/)

Ohio Municipal League
(http://www.omunileague.org/)

Oklahoma Municipal League
(http://www.www.oml.org/)

League of Oregon Cities
(http://www.orcities.org/)

Pennsylvania League of Cities and Municipalities
(http://www.plcm.org/)

Rhode Island League of Cities and Towns
(http://www.rileague.org/)

Municipal Association of South Carolina
(http://www.www.masc.sc/)

South Dakota Municipal League
(http://www.sdmunicipalleague.org/)

Tennessee Municipal League
(http://www.tml1.org/)

Texas Municipal League
(http://www.tml.org/)

Utah League of Cities and Towns
(http://ulct.org/)

Vermont League of Cities and Towns
(http://www.vlct.org/)

Virginia Municipal League
(http://vml.org/)

Association of Washington Cities
(http://www.awcnet.org/)

West Virginia Municipal League
(http://www.wvml.org/)

League of Wisconsin Municipalities
(http://www.lwm–info.org/)

Wyoming Association of Municipalities
(http://www.wyomuni.org/)

D. State Library Directory

Most state libraries have copies of state laws, both proposed and adopted, in an on-line database. Many states also have copies of the various laws adopted in those cities and towns within their jurisdiction. They are an excellent resource. The contact information for the various state libraries is shown below.

Alabama
(http://www.apls.state.la.us/)

Alaska
(http://www.library.state.ak.us/)

Arizona
(http://www.lib.az.us/)

Arkansas
(http://www.asl.lib.ar.us/)

California
(http://www.library.ca.gov/)

Colorado
(http://www.cde.state.co.us/)

Connecticut
(http://www.cslib.org/)

Delaware
(http://www.state.lib.de.us/)

District of Columbia
(http://dclibrary.org/)

Florida
(http://dlis.dos.state.fl.us/)

Georgia
(http://www.georgialibraries.org/)

Hawaii
(http://www.librarieshawaii.org/)

Idaho
(http://www.lili.org/)

Illinois
(http://www.cyberdriveillinois.com/departments/library/)

Indiana
(http://www.statelib.lib.in.us/)

Iowa
(http://www.silo.lib.ia.us/)

Kansas
(http://www.skyways.org/KSL/)

Kentucky
(http://www.kdla.ky.gov/)

Louisiana
(http://www.state.lib.la.us/)

Maine
(http://www.state.me.us/msl/)

Maryland
(http://www.sailor.lib.md.us/)

Massachusetts
(http://mass.gov/mblc/)

Michigan
(http://www.michigan.gov/hal/)

Minnesota
(http://www.state.mn.us/libraries/)

Mississippi
(http://www.mlc.lib.ms.us/)

Missouri
(http://www.sos.mo.gov/library/)

Montana
(http://msl.state.mt.us/)

Nebraska
(http://www.nlc.state.ne.us/)

Nevada
(http://dmla.clan.lib.nv.us/)

New Hampshire
(http://www.state.nh.us/nhls/)

New Jersey
(http://www.njstatelib.org/)

New Mexico
(http://www.stlib.state.nm.us/)

New York
(http://www.nysl.nysed.gov/)

North Carolina
(http://statelibrary.dcr.state.nc.us/)

North Dakota
(http://ndsl.lib.state.nd.us/)

Ohio
(http://winslo.state.oh.us/)

Oklahoma
(http://www.odl.state.ok.us/)

Oregon
(http://oregon.gov/OSL/)

Pennsylvania
(http://www.statelibrary.state.pa.us/libraries/)

Rhode Island
(http://www.olis.ri.gov/)

South Carolina
(http://www.statelibrary.sc.gov/)

South Dakota
(http://www.sdstatelibrary.com/)

Tennessee
(http://www.tennessee.gov/tsla/)

Texas
(http://www.tsl.state.tx.us/)

Utah
(http://library.ut.gov/index.html/)

Vermont
(http://dol.state.vt.us/)

Virginia
(http://www.lva.lib.va.us/)

Washington
(http://www.secstate.was.gov/library/)

West Virginia
(http://librarycommission/lib.wv.us/)

Wisconsin
(http://www.dpi.state.wi.us/dltcl/pld/)

Wyoming
(http://www-wsl.state.wy.us/)

E. National Resource Directory

This listing includes major national professional, membership, and research organizations serving public officials, professionals, and citizens. Many of these organizations focus on various issues relating to inner-city, or downtown, development and renewal, and major programs relating to these topics.

Alliance for National Renewal
(http://www.ncl.org/anr/)

American Economic Development Council
(http://www.aedc.org/)

American Planning Association
(http://www.planning.org/)

American Real Estate and Urban Economics Association
(http://www.areuea.org/)

Building Officials and Code Administrators International
(http://www.bocai.org/)

Center for Compatible Economic Development
(http://www.cced.org/)

Committee for Economic Development
(http://www.ced.org/)

Community Defense Counsel
(http://communitydefense.org/)

Community Development Society International
(http://www.comm-dev.org/)

Congress of New Urbanism
(http://www.cnu.org/)

Council for Urban Economic Development
(http://www.cued.org/)

Creative Economy Council
(http://www.creativeeconomy.org/)

Downtown Development and Research Center
(http://www.DowntownDevelopment.com/)

First Amendment Center
(http://www.firstamendmentcenter.org/)

Interactive Economic Development Network
(http://www.iedn.com/)

International City/County Management Association
(http://www.icma.org/)

International Conference of Building Officials
(http://www.icbo.org/)

International Downtown Association
(http://www.ida-downtown.org/)

International Economic Development Council
(http://www.iedconline.org/)

Local Government Commission
(http://www.lgc.org/)

National Association of Counties
(http://www.naco.org/)

National Association of County Administrators
(http://countyadministrators.org/)

National Association of Development Organizations
(http://www.nado.org/)

National Association of Towns and Townships
(http://www.natat.org/)

National Center for the Revitalization of Central Cities
(http://www.uno.edu/~cupa/ncrcc/)

National Civic League
(http://www.ncl.org/)

National Community Development Association
(http://www.ncdaonline.org/)

National Bureau of Business Licensing Officials
(http://www.nbblo.org/)

National Conference of State Legislatures
(http://www.ncsl.org/)

National Congress of Community Economic Development
(http://www.ncced.org/)

National Council for Urban Economic Development
(http://www.cued.org/)

National Development Council
(http://nationaldevelopmentcouncil.org/)

National Law Center
(http://www.nationallawcenter.org/)

National League of Cities
(http://www.nlc.org/)

National Main Street Center
(http://www.mainst.org/)

National Obscenity Law Center
(http://www.moralityinmedia/nolc.org/)

Partners for Livable Communities
(http://www.livable.com/)

United States Conference of Mayors
(http://www.usmayors.org/)

Urban Institute
(http://www.urban.org/)

Urban Land Institute
(http://www.uli.org/)

F. U.S. Supreme Court Cases and Adult Businesses

Various U.S. Supreme Court cases have had a direct impact on government's ability to regulate adult businesses. Listed below are 25 such U.S. Supreme Court decisions since 1953. For ease of reference, they are shown in four categories related to adult businesses. The entire cases can be reviewed at the First Amendment Center website, which is listed in the *National Resource Directory*.

Pornography & Obscenity

Ashcroft v. Free Speech Coalition, 535 U.S. 234 (2002)

Ashcroft v. ACLU, 535 U.S. 564 (2002)

Osborne v. Ohio, 495 U.S. 103 (1990)

Sable Communications of California, Inc. v. FCC, 492 U.S. 115 (1989)

New York v. Ferber, 458 U.S. 747 (1982)

Jenkins v. Georgia, 418 U.S. 153 (1975)

Miller v. California, 413 U.S. 15 (1973)

Mishkin v. State of N.Y., 383 U.S. 502 (1966)

Jacobellis v. Ohio, 378 U.S. 184 (1964)

Adult Bookstores

Freedman v. Maryland, 380 U.S. 51 (1965)

FW/PBS v. City of Dallas, 493 U.S. 215 (1990)

City News & Novelty Inc. v. City of Waukesha, 531 U.S. 278 (2001)

City of Los Angeles v. Alameda Books, Inc., 535 U.S. 425 (2002)

Thomas v. Chicago Park District, 534 U.S. 316 (2002)

Nude Dancing

California v. LaRue, 409 U.S. 109 (1973)

Doran v. Salem Inn, 422 U.S. 922 (1975)

Schad v. Borough of Mount Ephraim, 452 U.S 61 (1981)

Barnes v. Glen Theatre, Inc., 501 U.S. 560 (1991)

U.S. v. Playboy Entertainment Group, 529 U.S. 803 (2000)

Secondary-effects Doctrine

City of Los Angeles v. Alameda Books, Inc., 535 U.S. 425 (2002)

City of Erie v. Pap's A.M., 120 S.Ct. 1382 (2000)

Barnes v. Glen Theatre, 501 U.S. 560 (1991)

Boos v. Berry, 485 U.S. 312 (1988)

Renton v. Playtime Theatres, 475 U.S. 41 (1986)

Young v. American Mini Theatres, 427 U.S. 50 (1976)

G. Secondary Effects Land-Use Studies of Adult Businesses in America

Many municipal regulations of adult businesses are based on "secondary effects" land-use studies. A listing of these studies done in communities in the United States is provided below, by state. The entire studies can be viewed at the Community Defense Counsel website, which is listed in the *National Resource Directory*.

Arizona

City of Phoenix (1979, 1984)

City of Tucson (1990)

California

City of Garden Grove (1991)

City of Los Angeles (1977, 1984)

City of Whittier (1978)

Colorado

Adams County (1990)

City of Denver (1998)

Connecticut

City of Milford (2004)

Florida

Manatee County (1987)

City of Daytona Beach (2004)

Ybor City (2003)

Georgia

City of St. Marys (1996)

City of Rome (1995)

Indiana

City of Indianapolis (1984)

Minnesota

City of Minneapolis (1980)

St. Paul (1983)

Missouri

Kansas City (1998–99)

North Carolina

New Hanover County (1989)

Nevada

City of Las Vegas (1978)

New York

Cattaraugus County (1998)

City of Ellicottville (1998)

City of New York (1994)

New York Times Square (1994)

Town of Islip (1980

Ohio

City of Cleveland (1977, 2002)

Oklahoma

Oklahoma City (1986, 1989, 1992)

Texas

City of Amarillo (1977)
City of Austin (1986)
City of Beaumont (1982)
City of Cleburne (1997)
City of Dallas (1997)
City of El Paso (1986)
City of Houston (1983, 1997)

Virginia
City of Newport News (1996)

Washington
City of Bellevue (1998)
City of Des Moines (1984)
City of Seattle (1989)

Wisconsin
St. Croix County (1993)

About the Editor and Contributors

Editor

Roger L. Kemp, Ph.D., has been a chief executive officer of cities on the West and East coasts for more than two decades and is presently a senior adjunct professor at Ageno School of Business, Golden Gate University, and a visiting scholar at the School of Business and Technology, Capella University, Minneapolis. He has also been an adjunct professor at leading universities on both coasts during his city management career and is a graduate of the Program for Senior Executives in State and Local Government from the John F. Kennedy School of Government at Harvard University. Kemp has written, edited or contributed to nearly 50 books.

Contributors

Affiliations are as of the times the materials contained in this volume were written.

Joe Albanese, Vice President of Operations, Shawmut Design and Construction, Boston, Massachusetts.

American City & County, Penton Media, Inc., Overland Park, Kansas.

Kelly Anders, Policy Specialist, Legislative Information Services Program, National Conference of State Legislatures, Denver, Colorado.

Jude Balsamo, Intern, Legislative Information Services Program, National Conference of State Legislatures, Denver, Colorado.

Alison A. Barratt-Green, City Attorney, City of Oakley, California.

Larry Bauman, Assistant City Manager, City of Shoreline, Washington.

Scott D. Bergthold, Owner, Law Office of Scott D. Bergthold, PLLC, Chattanooga, Tennessee.

Robert W. Bivens, career economic development professional and freelance writer, Glen Allen, Virginia.

J. Rolando Bono, City Manager, City of San Antonio, Texas.

Jeff Bowman, Business License Administrator, City of Greenville, South Carolina.

Ed Brock, Associate Editor, *American City & County*, Penton Media, Inc., Atlanta, Georgia.

James A. Brown, Community Development Director, Village of Lemont, Illinois.

Jason Burton, Chief Planner, Planning and Development Department, City of Orlando, Florida.

Jim Chappell, President, San Francisco Planning + Urban Research Association (SPUR), San Francisco, California.

Jim Constantine, Director of Planning and Research, Looney Ricks Kiss, Princeton, New Jersey.

Robert Deis, City Manager, City of Shoreline, Washington.

Steffanie Dorn, Finance Director, City of Greenwood, South Carolina.

Bill Dries, Senior Reporter, *The Daily News*, The Daily News Publishing Company, Inc., Memphis, Tennessee.

Mary M. Farmer, Town Clerk, Office of the Town Clerk, Town of Urbana, Hammondsport, New York.

Diane Filippi, Director, San Francisco Planning + Urban Research Association (SPUR), San Francisco, California.

Daniel J. Fluegel, City Attorney, City of Hastings, Minnesota.

George R. Frantz, Visiting Lecturer, Department of City and Regional Planning, Cornell University, Ithaca, New York.

Hunter Gee, Architect and Planner, Looney Ricks Kiss, Nashville, Tennessee.

Jeffrey Goldfarb, Partner, Rutan & Tucker, LLC, Costa Mesa, California. He also serves as the Assistant City Attorney for the cities of Irvine and San Clemente, California.

Jaclyn Hakes, Principal Planner, Planning Office, City of Saratoga Springs, New York.

Robert Henry, Lieutenant, Police Department, City of Toledo, Ohio.

David L. Hudson, Jr., First Amendment Scholar, First Amendment Center, Vanderbilt University, Nashville, Tennessee.

Roger Huebner, General Counsel, Illinois Municipal League, Springfield, Illinois.

D. Kay Johnson, Director, Department of Environmental Services, City of Wichita, Kansas.

Brad Kane, Correspondent, *The Boston Globe*, Globe Newspaper Company, Boston, Massachusetts.

Howard Kozloff, Candidate, Master of Science Degree in Real Estate Development, School of Architecture, Planning, and Preservation, Columbia University, New York City, New York.

John Laidler, Correspondent, *The Boston Globe*, Globe Newspaper Company, Boston, Massachusetts.

Deborah A. Lane, Clerk of the Council, Office of the City Clerk, City of Staunton, Virginia.

Philip C. Laurien, Executive Director, Delaware County Regional Planning Commission, Delaware, Ohio.

Neil J. Lehto, Attorney, O'Reilly, Rancilio, Nitz, Andrews, Turnbull & Scott, PC, Sterling Heights, Michigan.

Rebecca Lubin, Planner, Planning Department, Tompkins County, Ithaca, New York.

Lydia R. Marola, Attorney, Village of Scotia, New York.

Scott Martinelli, Project Manager, Shawmut Design and Construction, Boston, Massachusetts.

James Monge, Senior Land Use Attorney, League of Minnesota Cities, St. Paul, Minnesota.

Michael Morrison, Mayor, Office of the Mayor, City of Waco, Texas.

David W. Owens, Distinguished Professor of Government, Institute of Government, The University of North Carolina, Chapel Hill, North Carolina.

Ellen Perlman, Staff Writer, *Governing*, Congressional Quarterly Inc., Washington, D.C.

Emmett S. Pugh III, Mayor, City of Beckley, West Virginia.

Christopher Reinhart, Research Attorney, Office of Legislative Research, State of Connecticut, Hartford, Connecticut.

Robert D. Robbins, Chairman, Local Government Commission, Commonwealth of Pennsylvania, Harrisburg, Pennsylvania.

Bill Ryan, Community Business Development Specialist, Center for Community and Economic Development, University of Wisconsin, Madison, Wisconsin.

Mark G. Sellers, City Attorney, Office of the City Attorney, City of Thousand Oaks, California.

Kyle Shephard, Assistant City Attorney, Office of the City Attorney, City of Orlando, Florida.

Jim Siegel, Reporter, *The Columbus Dispatch*, Columbus, Ohio.

Ron Sims, County Executive, King County, Seattle, Washington.

Willis H. Stephens, Jr., Town Counsel, Town of Southeast, Brewster, New York.

Diane M. Sugimura, Director, Department of Planning and Development, City of Seattle, Washington.

Bella Travaglini, Correspondent, *The Boston Globe*, Globe Newspaper Company, Boston, Massachusetts.

Helena Varnavas, Student, College of Law, University of Illinois, Champaign, Illinois.

Susan L. Watson, General Counsel, Office of the General Counsel, Department of State, State of New York, Albany, New York.

Alan C. Weinstein, Professor, Colleges of Law and Urban Affairs, Cleveland State University, Cleveland, Ohio.

Rebecca Willis, Director of Community Development, City of Oakley, California.

Jerry Zarley, Paralegal, Illinois Municipal League, Springfield, Illinois.

Index

www.ingramcontent.com/pod-product-compliance
Lightning Source LLC
Chambersburg PA
CBHW080551270326
41929CB00019B/3262